Colombia's Political Economy at the Outset of the Twenty-First Century

SECURITY IN THE AMERICAS IN THE TWENTY-FIRST CENTURY

Series Editor: Jonathan D. Rosen

Countries throughout the Americas face many challenges in the twenty-first century such as drug trafficking, organized crime, environmental degradation, guerrilla movements, and terrorism, among many other major threats. In this series, titled Security in the Americas in the Twenty-First Century, we invite contributions on topics focusing on security issues in specific countries or regions within the Americas. We are interested in approaching this topic from a political science and international relations perspective. However, we invite manuscript submissions from other disciplines. The aim of this series is to highlight the major security challenges in the twenty-first century and contribute to the security studies literature. We invite both policy-oriented and theoretical submissions.

Recent Titles

Cooperation and Drug Policies in the Americas: Trends in the Twenty-First Century, edited by Roberto Zepeda and Jonathan D. Rosen

Reconceptualizing Security in the Americas in the Twenty-First Century, edited by Bruce M. Bagley, Jonathan D. Rosen, and Hanna S. Kassab

Prisons in the Americas in the 21st Century: Human Dumping Ground, edited by Jonathan D. Rosen and Marten W. Brienen

Colombia's Political Economy at the Outset of the 21st Century: From Uribe to Santos and Beyond, edited by Bruce M. Bagley and Jonathan D. Rosen

Decline of the United States Hegemony? A Challenge of ALBA and a New Latin American Integration of the Twenty-First Century, edited by Bruce M. Bagley and Magdalena Defort

Colombia's Political Economy at the Outset of the Twenty-First Century

From Uribe to Santos and Beyond

Edited by
Bruce M. Bagley and Jonathan D. Rosen

LEXINGTON BOOKS
Lanham • Boulder • New York • London

Published by Lexington Books
An imprint of The Rowman & Littlefield Publishing Group, Inc.
4501 Forbes Boulevard, Suite 200, Lanham, Maryland 20706
www.rowman.com

Unit A, Whitacre Mews, 26-34 Stannary Street, London SE11 4AB

British Library Cataloguing in Publication Information Available

Library of Congress Cataloging-in-Publication Data
The hardback edition of this book was previously catalogued by the Library of Congress as follows:

Colombia's political economy at the outset of the twenty-first century : from Uribe to Santos and beyond / edited by Bruce M. Bagley and Jonathan D. Rosen.
pages cm
Includes bibliographical references and index.
1. Colombia—Economic conditions—21st century. 2. Colombia—Social conditions—21st century. I. Bagley, Bruce Michael. II. Rosen, Jonathan D.
HC197.C638 2015
330.9861—dc23

2015015898

ISBN 978-0-7391-9292-4 (cloth)
ISBN 978-1-4985-0889-6 (pbk)
ISBN 978-0-7391-9293-1 (electronic)

Contents

Acknowledgments

Publishing an edited volume requires tremendous amounts of cooperation. We would like to thank all of the authors for their hard work and dedication and willingness to cooperate.

A special thanks to Justin Race of Lexington Books for this excellent opportunity. The staff at Lexington Books worked very hard, and we are very appreciative. Thanks to the editors and the production team for their attention to detail.

We also want to thank our respective institutions: the University of Miami and the Universidad del Mar, Campus Huatulco.

Finally, we would like to thank Vanessa Rayan and Christa Minardi for their editorial assistance and Nilda Garcia and Yulia Vorobyeva for their research assistance.

Introduction

Jonathan D. Rosen and Bruce M. Bagley

For decades, Colombia has been a major security concern not only for the United States but also for other countries in the region. During the 1970s, Colombia became and remains today deeply entrenched in coca cultivation,[1] the processing of narcotics, and drug trafficking. Colombia has been at the epicenter of the U.S. drug war for decades. Washington spent over 1 billion dollars during the 1990s alone combatting drug trafficking in Colombia. Despite such efforts, Colombia was the premier coca cultivator in the world from 2000 until 2013.[2] With the help of Washington, the Colombian government concentrated on killing the leaders of the major cartels, a tactic referred to as the kingpin strategy. Even after the death of Pablo Escobar in 1993 and the subsequent demise of the Medellín and Cali cartels, drug trafficking continued to flourish in the country as smaller cartels seized control of drug trafficking operations. The collapse of the two major cartels created a vacuum, and Colombia witnessed a fragmentation of the cartels into smaller organizations that battled for control of territory and trafficking routes.[3]

In addition to drug trafficking, Colombia has a long history of violence as it has had an internal armed conflict for decades. Russell Crandall argues, "To study the evolution of Colombia's current political dynamics is to study violence."[4] The first emergence of guerrilla organizations in Colombia can trace their origins back to a violent and bloody period in Colombian history known as *La Violencia*, which occurred from the mid-1940s to the mid-1950s. Guerrilla organizations began to form to protect against attacks from the Conservatives in power.[5] The Revolutionary Armed Forces of Colombia (*Fuerzas Armadas Revolucionarias de Colombia*-FARC) officially announced that they were a guerrilla movement during a conference in 1964. Crandall declares, "At that time, the FARC had much in its favor as it drew upon its organizational and logistical roots in the communist self-defense organizations active in the 1940s and 1950s. The FARC also maintained links with the Communist Party, although the ties between the two groups were never nearly as intimate as some in Colombia and the United States have suggested."[6] By the end of the 1990s, the Colombian government estimated that the FARC earned $400 million per year from drug-related activities. In addition, the FARC received approximately $500 million from other illegal endeavors, such as robbery, extortion, kidnapping, and taxing landowners.[7]

The internal armed conflict impacts regional security as Colombia occupies a key strategic position as it borders the Panama Canal, as well as Brazil, which is the emerging power in the region. The security dynamics in Colombia have become a major concern as the guerrilla organizations continue to attack infrastructure, particularly pipelines. Such attacks can impact the economic prosperity of the region. Colombia has witnessed a fivefold increase in the number of attacks by the guerrillas on oil pipelines since 2010, which has had major economic and environmental repercussions. As of November 2013, the FARC and the other major guerrilla organization, The National Liberation Army (*Ejercito Nacional de Liberación*-ELN), attacked oil pipelines 163 times. In 2012, 151 oil pipeline attacks occurred between the two groups, demonstrating that such incidents have continued to increase despite efforts by the Colombian government.[8]

COLOMBIA: A U.S. ALLY

Colombia is a key ally of the United States. Colombia is a democratic country and has a long history of democracy, and Washington has desired to support democracies, particularly after the turn to the left by many countries in the region. In the early 2000s, analysts began discussing the possibility that Colombia could become a failed state.[9] Washington provided billions of dollars in aid to Colombia, primarily through a counter-narcotics initiative known as Plan Colombia, to prevent the situation from spiraling out of control. At one point, Colombia received more aid than all other countries in the world except Egypt and Israel.[10] In sum, Washington has supported Bogotá because it did not want to see one of its crucial allies in the region become a failed state.

THE TRANSITION FROM URIBE TO SANTOS

This edited volume concentrates on the transition from President Álvaro Uribe (2002–2010) to President Juan Manuel Santos (2010–2018), focusing on Colombia's political economy at the outset of the twenty-first century. Álvaro Uribe came to power vowing to improve security and combat the guerrilla organizations in Colombia. Uribe refused to negotiate with the guerrillas after the failed negotiations of his predecessor, Andrés Pastrana (1998–2002). María Clemencia Ramírez Lemus, Kimberly Stanton, and John Walsh describe the situation, stating:

> Uribe was elected in May 2002 in reaction to the deep popular disillusionment that followed the collapse of Pastrana's negotiations with the FARC. Colombians who had voted for peace in 1998 opted in 2002 for a hard-line approach to dealing with the guerrillas. The FARC reacted to Uribe's inauguration on August 7, 2002, by launching gas cylinder bombs that missed the new president but killed several people in nearby neighborhoods.[11]

Uribe responded to the attacks by proclaiming a state of unrest and mobilizing the military to control various regions in Colombia. In 2002 and 2003, Uribe attempted to increase collaboration between the military and civilians by creating various programs. He also increased the number of Colombian combat troops in order to increase security and decrease internal unrest. In 2002 and 2003, he sought to reform the constitution with the aim of expanding the power of the military and decreasing judicial oversight over the institution.[12] In addition, Uribe increased aerial spraying campaigns to combat coca cultivation. In 2003, for example, Colombia sprayed the most acres of coca in the history of the country, ignoring the major environmental and health consequences of such programs.[13]

Uribe recognized that he had to alter the agenda of the Colombian government in order to comply with the shift in Washington's objectives after the Bush administration launched the global war on terrorism (GWOT) after September 11, 2001. President Uribe, in essence, changed the perceptions of the conflict in Colombia by arguing that Colombia did not have an internal armed conflict but rather a terrorist problem.[14] He declared that Colombia had narco-terrorists that needed to be defeated via conventional military tactics to prevent the situation in Colombia from worsening. The discourse regarding Colombia slowly began to change in Washington. During a conference about the major challenges in Colombia, the U.S. deputy Assistant Secretary of State for Western Hemisphere Affairs, Thomas Shannon, declared:

> U.S. recognition of such factors as the moribund nature of Colombia's peace process, the emergence of the Revolutionary Armed Forces of Colombia (FARC) as a narco-terrorist organization, the clear rejection of the FARC by the Colombian people, the increased involvement of the United Self-Defense Forces of Colombia (AUC) in drug trafficking, and that group's designation as a terrorist organization prompted "a fundamental shift" in U.S. policy toward Colombia.[15]

The Bush administration believed that Colombia presented a major security challenge for the region and vowed to support the Colombian government as Bush promised to assist countries combat terrorism as part of the GWOT. Uribe, therefore, became a close ally of former President Bush, who pledged to help Colombia defeat the narco-guerrillas and provided Uribe with the necessary assistance.

Plan Colombia was one of the main sources of funding for the Uribe administration. Over its lifespan, 2000 to 2012, the United States allocated $8 billion to this counter-narcotics program. President Clinton signed Plan Colombia into law in 2000.[16] However, the Clinton administration feared becoming involved in the internal armed conflict, and, therefore, focused on combatting drug trafficking. Uribe shifted the goals of Plan Colombia and drew the United States further into Colombia's internal conflict. Drugs remained an important part of Plan Colombia because drug trafficking increased insecurity in Colombia and acted as a source of revenue for the guerrillas. Some experts have argued that Plan Colombia began to resemble a nation-building exercise. Ted Galen Carpenter states, "The antinarcotics effort embodied in Plan Colombia is beginning to look a lot like the nation-building missions for which President Bush and his foreign policy advisers have expressed a wariness bordering on outright aversion."[17]

During his administration, Uribe's number one priority was increasing security in Colombia, and his policies clearly demonstrated that he was less concerned with underlying problems in Colombia, such as weak institutions, corruption, the environment, and human rights. Uribe continued to combat the FARC and other actors with military campaigns, seeking to increase security in Colombia by defeating the narco-terrorists. The Uribe administration dealt crushing blows to the FARC, and Uribe began to talk about a post-conflict stage. While Colombia had "partial victories"[18] as security increased as a result of Uribe's military campaigns against the various internal armed actors, some experts have questioned the security increases in Colombia as the country is still plagued by violence, drug trafficking, and organized crime. Adam Isacson argues, "Looked at more closely, though, **Colombia's security gains are partial, possibly reversible and weighed down by 'collateral damage.'** They have carried a great cost in lives and resources. Progress on security has been stagnating, and even reversing."[19]

As of 2014, Colombia still has an internal armed conflict and has witnessed the emergence of criminal bands referred to as the BACRIM as a result of the demobilization of the AUC paramilitaries. These former paramilitary members participate in drug trafficking and other illicit activities and represent a major security challenge for the Colombian government. María Victoria Llorente and Jeremy McDermott assert, "Indeed, with the removal of their ideological component, it might be argued that today's BACRIM now look a lot more like their Mexican counterparts."[20] In sum, Colombia still has an internal armed conflict and major problems with drug trafficking and organized crime.

President Santos, the former defense minister during the Uribe administration, came to power in 2010 and quickly sought to distance himself from his former boss. Santos, for example, declared that he wanted to solve the internal armed conflict and would negotiate with the most powerful guerrilla organization, the FARC, in order to bring peace[21] to Colombia as the costs of the internal armed conflict have been extremely high not only in terms of lives lost but also the impact on society. As of March 2013, approximately 4.7 million people have been displaced as a result of the conflict.[22] Santos's comments about being willing to negotiate with the guerrillas were more than just rhetoric as the Colombian government and the FARC have participated in several rounds of peace talks. In 2012, the FARC and the Colombian government began peace talks for the fourth time in Colombian history in an effort to put an end to the internal armed conflict.[23] Such strategies have irritated former President Uribe to no avail, and he has publicly criticized such decisions, even calling his former defense minister a traitor.[24] The former president has used social media to criticize Santos, arguing that the Colombian government should not negotiate with "'converted terrorists who were in the process of being defeated . . .'"[25]

The debates that have occurred in Cuba have focused on five major issues as well as one operational item: integral agricultural development policy, victims, a solution to the drug problem, the end of the internal armed conflict, political participation, and the implementation and ratification of the peace accords.[26] As of October 2014, the parties have agreed on three of the five points.[27] Colombia is closer than ever before in its history to achieving peace. Yet major challenges exist, particularly with regard to reintegrating former guerrillas into society as well as dealing with various transitional justice issues.

Santos also became a vocal critic of U.S. drug policies arguing that such policies have failed and that new strategies must be considered as many Colombians have suffered from the drug war. In a speech in September 2013 at the United Nations, Santos stated, "'Right here, in this same headquarters, 52 years ago, the convention that gave birth to the war on drugs was approved. Today, we must acknowledge, that war has not been won.'"[28] Santos has argued that he is willing to discuss alternative policies such as legalization as the war on drugs has been too costly for Colombia. Such statements represent a drastic contrast from Uribe who never discussed the failures of the war on drugs, but rather sought to destroy coca cultivation and drug trafficking as such activities help finance the guerrillas and have resulted in extreme levels of violence.

VOLUME ORGANIZATION

This book has contributions from leading scholars in the field and is organized into several major sections. The first section is titled "The Colombian Economy in Global Context: Economic Potential and Challenges." In his chapter, José Antonio Ocampo examines the Colombian economy and highlights the major opportunities as well as challenges that Colombia faces in the twenty-first century. Albert Berry's chapter concludes the section, analyzing agricultural development and land reform.

The next section examines Colombian politics, focusing on issues such as institutions and corruption. Fernando Cepeda Ulloa analyzes the role of governance and corruption in Colombia, while Juan Pablo Milanese examines the concept of executive and legislative power during the Uribe administration.

This section is followed by an analysis of the internal armed conflict in Colombia, highlighting the major challenges and opportunities for peace. Colombia has a better chance of obtaining peace in 2015 than ever before but major obstacles still exist. Malcolm Deas begins the section by providing an exhaustive history of Colombia's complicated internal armed conflict. Without the historical context, it is not possible to understand the situation in Colombia today. This chapter is followed by Angelika Rettberg's piece on the Colombian government's treatment of victims, focusing specifically on reparations. Rettberg addresses the policies of the Uribe and Santos administrations with regard to reparations for victims. This is a key topic as so many people have suffered as a result of the internal armed conflict. Marc Chernick concludes the section by analyzing the evolution of the peace negotiations with the FARC. Colombia's future rests on the peace negotiations and a resolution to the internal armed conflict.

The subsequent section focuses on Colombian foreign policy. Sandra Borda and Santiago Gómez begin the section analyzing the internationalization of the peace negotiations, focusing on the role of the international community in the peace talks. This chapter provides an exhaustive analysis of the differences between Uribe and Santos and analyzes the role that other actors have played in the peace negotiations. This piece is followed by an analysis of Colombia's relations with another key neighbor, Venezuela. Luz del Soccorro Ramírez highlights the often cantankerous bilateral relations between Colombia and Venezuela, focusing on the Uribe and Santos administrations as well as the administrations of Hugo Chávez and Nicolás Maduro. Arlene Tickner and Mateo Morales Callejas conclude the section with their chapter titled "Colombian Security Expertise and Foreign Policy." This work uses discourse analysis to analyze the concept of exporting security knowledge. Colombia has been perceived as a success story by many experts and politicians and the argument is that other countries can learn lessons from Colombia.

The concluding section of the book addresses various critical issues, specifically, human rights, drug trafficking, and the role of the military. Lisa Haugaard begins the section analyzing human rights abuses in Colombia and the responses of both Presidents Uribe and Santos. She highlights the differences in the strategies and the major challenges that still exist in the twenty-first century with regard to human rights. The chapter is followed by Adam Isacson's piece on the role of the U.S. military in Colombia and its consequences. The section concludes with an analysis by Coletta A. Youngers and Jonathan D. Rosen of drug policies in Colombia, questioning whether Colombia has experienced a paradigm shift. The chapter highlights the different strategies of the Uribe and Santos administrations with regard to drug trafficking.

CONCLUDING REMARKS

The goal of this volume is to examine Colombia at the outset of the twenty-first century, focusing on the policy differences between Uribe and Santos. In this work, we evaluate the performance of the economy, highlighting the promises of the Colombian economy as well as analyzing the major obstacles. Colombia has improved in many socioeconomic aspects but major challenges still exist. Much of the future of Colombia remains uncertain and will be determined by the negotiations with the FARC. Santos desires to bring peace to Colombia through dialogue, but he has made it clear that he is willing to become a war president if the negotiations fail. The emergence of other actors such as the BACRIM also present major challenges. The routes from drug trafficking are beginning to return to Colombia, and, despite the progress made, Colombia could experience a "back to the future" scenario where violence and drug trafficking increase.[29] In this volume, we emphasize the role of institutions and the political situation in Colombia. While Colombia has a long history of democracy, institutions are still weak and corruption and impunity are extremely high and have prohibited the strengthening of institutions.

Ultimately, only time will tell, but the experts in this volume shed light on the major challenges that Colombia faces in the twenty-first century.

NOTES

1. Coca leafs are processed into cocaine.

2. Bruce Bagley, *Drug Trafficking, Political Violence, and U.S. Policy in Colombia in the 1990s* (Miami: 2001), 1. See Bagley footnote 1–5; Today, Peru is the leading coca cultivator in the world. Natalie Southwick, "Peru Now World's Biggest Coca Cultivator: UN," *Insight Crime.* September 25, 2013.

3. Bruce Bagley, Drug *Trafficking and Organized Crime in the Americas: Major Trends in the Twenty-First Century* (Washington, D.C.: Woodrow Wilson International Center for Scholars, 2012).

4. Russell Crandall, *Driven by Drug: US Policy Toward Colombia* (Boulder, Colo.: Lynne Rienner Publishers, 2002), 53.

5. Russell Crandall, *Driven by Drug: US Policy Toward Colombia*, 58.

6. Russell Crandall, *Driven by Drugs: U.S. Policy Toward Colombia*, 61.

7. Bruce Bagley, *Drug Trafficking, Political Violence, and U.S. Policy in Colombia in the 1990s*, 10; Douglas Farah, "Drug Sales Change Colombia's Power Balance," *The Washington Post*, Nov. 4, 1999.

8. Charles Parkinson, "Guerrilla Oil Pipeline Attacks Surge Amid Colombia's Peace Talks," *InSight Crime*, December 12, 2013. http://www.insightcrime.org/news-briefs/guerrilla-oil-pipeline-attacks-surge-amid-colombias-slow-peace-talks, accessed October 2014.

9. For more, see *All Bush's Horses and All Bush's Men: How Far Should the U.S. Go to Help Put Colombia Back Together Again?* (Washington, D.C.: National Defense University and National War College, 2003); For more on the topic, see Phillip McLean, "Colombia: Failed, Failing, or Just Weak?" *The Washington Quarterly* 25.3 (2002): 123–134.

10. Russell Crandall, *Driven By Drugs: US Policy Toward Colombia.*

11. María Celmencia Ramírez Lemus, Kimberly Stanton, and John Walsh, "Colombia: A Vicious Circle of Drugs and War," in *Drugs and Democracy in Latin America: The Impact of U.S.* Policy, eds, Coletta Youngers and Eileen Rosin (Boulder, CO: Lynne Rienner Publishers, 2005), 111–112.

12. María Celmencia Ramírez Lemus, Kimberly Stanton, and Josh Walsh, "Colombia: A Vicious Circle of Drugs and War," 111–112.

13. María Celmencia Ramírez Lemus, Kimberly Stanton, and Josh Walsh, "Colombia: A Vicious Circle of Drugs and War," 112.

14. Marc Chernick, Interview, Bogotá, 2012 (approved by Institutional Review Board Approved, University of Miami). For more, see Jonathan D. Rosen, *The Losing War: Plan Colombia and Beyond* (Albany, N.Y.: SUNY, 2014).

15. Quoted in Brian Loveman, "U.S. Security Policies in Latin America and the Andean Region," in Brian Loveman, *Addicted to Failure: U.S. Security Policy in Latin America and the Andean Region* (Lanham, Md.: Rowman & Littlefield Publishers, 2006), 24–25.

16. Bruce Bagley, Drug *Trafficking and Organized Crime in the Americas: Major Trends in the Twenty-First Century*, 5.

17. Ted Galen Carpenter, *Bad Neighbor Policy: Washington's Futile War on Drugs in Latin America* (New York, N.Y.: Palgrave Macmillan, 2003), 86–87.

18. Bruce Bagley, Drug *Trafficking and Organized Crime in the Americas: Major Trends in the Twenty-First Century*, 5.

19. Adam Isacson, *Colombia: Don't Call It a Model On Plan Colombia 10th Anniversary, Claims of "Success" Don't Stand Up to Scrutiny*, (Washington, D.C.: WOLA, 2010), 1.

20. María Victoria Llorente and Jeremy McDermott, "Colombia's Lessons for Mexico," in Cynthia J. Arnson, Eric L. Olson with Christine Zaino, *One Goal, Two Struggles" Confronting Crime and Violence in Mexico and Colombia* (Washington, D.C.: Woodrow Wilson International Center for Scholars), 12.

21. For more on the peace process, see June S. Beittel, *Peace Talks in Colombia* (Washington, D.C., Congressional Research Service, 2013).

22. UNHRC, "2014 UNHCR country operations profile—Colombia," UNHRC: The UN Refugee Agency, http://www.unhcr.org/cgi-bin/texis/vtx/page?page=49e492ad6.

23. Adam Isacson, *Ending 50 years of Conflict: The Challenges Ahead and the U.S. Role in Colombia*, (Washington, D.C.: WOLA, 2014), 2.

24. Juan Forero and Marina Villeneuve, "Colombian ex-president sounds off on his successor's peace talks with FARC rebels," *Washington Post*, October 5, 2013, Section, the Americas.

25. Juan Forero and Marina Villeneuve, "Colombian ex-president sounds off on his successor's peace talks with FARC rebels."

26. Adam Isacson, *Ending 50 years of Conflict: The Challenges Ahead and the U.S. Role in Colombia*, 2.

27. Peter Murphy, "Colombia president says 'demented' FARC attacks could end peace talks," *Reuters*, July 30, 2014; Adam Isacson, *Ending 50 years of Conflict*, 2.

28. Daniel Trotta, "Colombian president tells U.N. the drug war has not been won," *Reuters,* Sept. 24, 2013.

29. Jonathan D. Rosen, *The Losing War: Plan Colombia and Beyond* (Albany, NY: SUNY Press, 2014).

Section One

THE COLOMBIAN ECONOMY IN GLOBAL CONTEXT

Economic Potential and Challenges

Chapter One

Performance and Challenges of the Colombian Economy

José Antonio Ocampo

The Colombian economy has experienced reasonable economic growth since the major reform efforts of the early 1990s. However, the growth witnessed during this period can best be characterized as slower and more volatile than growth prior to 1980. The Colombian economy also has experienced a significant restructuring, characterized by greater integration into the world economy, growing importance of oil and mining exports and of mining and services in GDP. In addition, Colombia has experienced larger private sector participation in economic activity but also larger state spending, particularly in social services. As of 2013, Colombia faces various challenges associated with managing an uncertain international economic environment and reversing adverse long-term trends, notably high domestic inequalities and the weakening of its manufacturing and agricultural sectors. Even more importantly, it must reform its economic and social policies to implement the outcome of the ongoing peace process.

This chapter analyzes how the interaction between domestic and external factors has affected the Colombian economy over the past decades and derives from that analysis the major challenges that the Colombian economy faces today. It is divided into five sections. The first briefly summarizes the major domestic and external factors affecting the economy. The second examines what I will refer to as the "dual-track" reform agenda that the country has followed since the early 1990s. The third and fourth analyze in detail the macroeconomic performance and the evolution of economic structure. Some social outcomes are discussed in the second and third sections, but this is not the central focus of this chapter, as this issue is considered in other chapters in this volume. The last section highlights the major challenges that Colombia faces. Several comparisons are made throughout the chapter with Latin America, mainly based on data from the United Nations Economic Commission for Latin America and the Caribbean (ECLAC), which is simply referred to as ECLAC data.[1]

FACTORS AFFECTING THE COLOMBIAN ECONOMY

The evolution of the Colombian economy has been affected over the past quarter century by two sets of factors. The first are the major reforms implemented in the early 1990s, which in fact responded, in a sort of dual track, to entirely different challenges that the country faced at the time. On the one hand, a series of market liberalization reforms were enacted, aimed at more fully integrating Colombia into the global economy and expanding private sector development. According to the authorities, these reforms were aimed at overcoming the inefficiencies that the inward-looking development model with heavy state interventions had generated, which were constraining productivity and therefore economic growth. On the other hand, the demands for a more equitable society, which were also seen as part of a peace-building effort,[2] led to the decision to convene a Constitutional Assembly in 1991 that changed the century-old 1886 Constitution. In economic and social terms, the 1991 Constitution placed economic and social rights as the center of public policies and created a more decentralized system of social service provisions, along with reforms that can be considered as part of the market liberalization agenda, notably the creation of an autonomous central bank (Banco de la República).

The second set of factors that have affected the performance of the Colombian economy have external origins. The most favorable were: the very high (super-cycle) of commodity prices, particularly of energy and mineral prices since 2004;[3] the boom of international trade that characterized the 1986–2007 period; the ample (though still somewhat unstable) access to financing from international capital markets at exceptional conditions in terms of costs and maturity since the mid-2000s, which included the return, in 2011, to the investment-grade status that the economy had lost in 1999; and the opportunities that the United States and Spain offered for (regular and irregular) migration up to 2007, which also led to a rapid growth of migrants' remittances. The most adverse external factors have been two major international crises: the succession of emerging-country financial crises that started in East Asia in 1997, and the global (or, better, North-Atlantic) financial crisis, which started with the collapse of subprime lending in the United States and the bankruptcy of some European banks during the summer of 2007, and was speeded up with the collapse of the investment bank Lehman Brothers in September 2008.

The September 2008 shock led to the most dramatic global financial meltdown since that of Wall Street in October 1929, to a deep global recession—now called the "Great Recession" by many analysts—and to a collapse of international trade that was initially steeper than during the Great Depression of the 1930s.[4] Although the global economy and global trade have experienced since the 2nd/3rd quarters of 2009 a "multi-speed" recovery, to use the International Monetary Fund's terminology, there are two effects that are more permanent: it has sharply slowed down the growth of international trade[5] and closed the opportunities for migrants. It may also be starting to affect a third: a weakening of commodity prices, leading perhaps to the end of the super-cycle of commodity prices that the world economy has experienced over the past decade. In this way, among the very favorable trends experienced until 2007–2008, only remains firmly in place: ample access to external financing, though at somewhat less exceptional conditions since mid-2013, due to the tendency of U.S. interest rates to normalize.

THE DUAL-TRACK REFORM AGENDA

The reform agenda that Colombia adopted in the early 1990s is clearly atypical by the standards of the market reforms that Latin American and other developing countries adopted during the last two decades of the twentieth century. Indeed, the mix of a market liberalization agenda with a more active state intervention to guarantee economic and social rights is peculiar by international standards. For this reason, it is hard to refer to these reforms as a "neo-liberal" agenda—although the first component did contain some neoliberal elements. Also, although some reforms were initiated in the mid-1980s under World Bank pressure as well as the weight of ideological trends and demonstration effects from other countries in the region, the reforms had a clearly *domestic* origin, as reflected not in the particular mix of policies but also the modalities that some of them adopted.

As already indicated, the first part of the agenda aimed at overcoming the inefficiencies and slow economic growth that, according to the authorities, had been the result of excessive protection and state intervention. In this view, market reforms would accelerate productivity and therefore GDP growth.[6] This was reflected, first of all, in the trade liberalization that was launched by the Barco administration in 1990 and was radicalized and accelerated by the Gaviria administration in 1990–1991. As a result, average tariffs fell in a short period of time—from an average of 44 percent prior to the 1990 reforms to 12 percent by March 1992—quantitative import restrictions were essentially eliminated—except during a transition for sensitive agricultural goods—, and export incentives were reduced to make them consistent with World Trade Organization (WTO) rules.

This was accompanied by the revitalization of the Andean Group (transformed into the Andean Community in 1997) starting with the presidential Summit in the Galápagos Islands in December 1989, which led to (mostly) full trade liberalization among its members, and the subscription of free trade agreements with several Latin American countries. Andean decisions led to a boom of trade in the 1990s, particularly with Venezuela and Ecuador, whereas the second increased trade with other Latin American countries. This would be joined by a broader set of free trade agreements with non-regional partners, particularly with Canada, the United States, and the European Union (in historical order of implementation), with that with Korea still subject to Congressional approval and others under negotiation.[7] However, political tensions among members of the Andean Community on the consistency of the integration arrangements with free trade agreements with extra-regional partners led to Venezuela's decision to withdraw from the Community in 2006. In turn, bilateral political tensions resulted in sharp reduction in exports to Venezuela between 2008 and 2010 (see below).

Trade liberalization was accompanied with liberalization of foreign direct investment (FDI), which implied the elimination of sectorial limitations (with very few exceptions[8]) and of the restrictions on profit remittances that the Andean Community had established in the 1970s. Colombian firms and investors also became increasingly active abroad, particularly in other Latin American countries. This was accompanied, furthermore, by the elimination of the exchange controls that the country had held, in one form or another, since 1931. This was reflected, in particular, in the liberalization of financial flows in 1993, though subject to a system of reserve requirements on capital inflows that forced investors to hold deposits in the central bank proportionally to the amount of funds they brought into the country or pay a tax equivalent to the opportunity costs of those deposits. These mechanisms were eliminated in 2000 but reestablished temporarily in 2007–2008. As a result of the liberalization of capital flows, Colombia would experience greater access to both FDI and financial flows, but also the volatility associated with the latter.

These reforms were accompanied by the privatization of a number of state-owned enterprises (SOEs), and the opening up of several public sector services to private investments, including a concession program for private investments in infrastructure. Given the nature of the SOEs inherited from the past, most of the privatization occurred in mining, public utilities, ports and the financial sector—including, in the latter case, some banks that had been nationalized during the domestic financial crisis of the early 1980s. However, the privatization process included different modalities (total private and mixed public-private ownership, as well as private administration of mixed or state-owned firms and assets) and left a significant number of SOEs, which in a sense were considered to be "strategic." This included the state oil company (Ecopetrol), national and local utility firms (e.g., Interconexión Eléctrica S.A., Isagen, Telecom, Empresa de Energía de Bogotá,[9] and Empresas Públicas de Medellín, among others), the network of five (now four) development banks[10] and a commercial bank (Banco Agrario, a transformation of the previously existing Caja Agraria). Since the mid-2000s, the government has opened up some of the SOEs (Ecopetrol and Interconexión Eléctrica S.A.) to partial private ownership through the issuance of shares, and has privatized two of them (Telecom in 2006 and Isagen, under privatization at the time of writing). One of the major implications of the privatization process, and more generally of the opening up of utilities to private investment, is that the regulation of utilities became a specialized function of three regulatory commissions—for energy, telecommunications, and water and sanitation—comprised of various ministers and independent experts.

The modalities of central bank independence defined by the 1991 Constitution were also peculiar by international standards. So, although it determined that inflation should be the main objective of Banco de la República, and it gave it autonomy to manage monetary and foreign exchange policy, it also required that it had to exercise its functions in "coordination with the general economic policy," which is the responsibility of the government. To guarantee this coordination, it determined that the minister of finance would chair the central bank board, although as the only government representative in the seven-member board. The Constitutional Court decreed in 1999 that the obligation of coordination implied that, although a stable purchasing power of the peso should be the major objective of monetary policy, such policy could not ignore other economic policy objectives, particularly employment generation and economic growth.[11]

The other track of the reform agenda was the expansion of the responsibilities to guarantee access to social services, which were decreed by the 1991 Constitutions as "social rights." The reform process also opened up opportunities for private agents (many of them nonprofit institutions) to participate in the provision of these services. Such participation followed different models. In the case of housing, public sector provision was replaced by direct subsidies to poor households (which includes, since 2012, a program with 100 percent subsidy). In pensions, a private capitalization system was put in place in competition with the old pay-as-go public-sector system. In health insurance (social security health), private agents were allowed to participate in competition with public sector institutions, both in the contributory and subsidized sub-systems.[12] In education, the attempt to gradually introduce a voucher system, particularly for secondary schooling, was soon suspended, but several municipalities introduced a mechanism by which private agents were allowed to manage public sector schools. Of course, fully private schools and non-social security health services were permitted, as in the past.

The decision to expand state responsibilities in the social area was accompanied with a significant decentralization, by which departments and municipalities were given greater participation in national rents[13] that they would then allocate to different social services according to the legal allocation rules; however, some flexibility was kept for the use of these resources. This system was more redistributive than the preexisting one, and it particularly increased the resources available to the poor by municipalities. Although there have been later attempts to strengthen controls by the central government, the decentralization process has been largely resilient to this centralization backlash. In practice, it means that the level of decentralization of public sector spending in Colombia is only somewhat lower than in two of the federal countries of the region, Argentina and Brazil, but larger than in the two remaining federations, Mexico and Venezuela.

There have been two major implications of this second track of the reform agenda: a significant increase in access to public sector services and an equally significant expansion in the size of public sector spending, which in turn resulted in various tax reforms to finance rising spending. Access to public sector services has indeed expanded and has improved living standards, particularly in rural areas. The most dramatic has been access to health social security, which increased from 24 percent in 1993 to 91 percent in 2012 (a bit over half of them in the subsidized sub-system). In turn, the coverage of secondary education increased from 43 percent to 72 percent over the same period.[14] If measured by the unsatisfied basic needs, poverty decreased from 45 percent in 1993 to 26 percent in 1998 and 18 percent in 2005, with a much larger absolute decline in rural areas (see Table 1.1). This also reflects the fact that access to clean water and electricity increased much more in rural than urban areas, where coverage was high in 1993. Measured by the new multidimensional index, which also measures access to basic public services as well as labor market conditions, poverty decreased from 60 percent in 1997 to 27 percent in 2012, again with stronger absolute gains in rural areas (see again Table 1.1). According to this index, the most important advances have occurred in access to health insurance, and the major remaining problems are labor market informality and low educational performance, with some improvements in the latter case but a very limited one in reducing the weight of informality.

Table 1.1. Poverty Indicators

Multidimensional Poverty Indicators			
	National	*Urban*	*Rural*
A. Unsatisfied Basic Needs (%)			
1985	45.0	32.3	71.8
1993	37.2	26.8	62.5
1997	25.9	17.8	46.5
2003	17.5	11.8	33.5
B. Multidimensional Poverty (%)			
1997	60.4	50.7	86.0
2003	49.2	39.8	76.8
2008	34.7	26.9	59.6
2012	27.0	20.6	48.3

Source: DANE. Data for 1985 and 1993 refers to population census. The rest to household surveys.

In any case, major gaps in access by different social groups remain in all social areas. This includes low access to some services, notably pensions, where it remains very low: 32 percent of the working population in 2012, according to the national household survey. There are also large differences in quality and strong segmentation in the provision of social services received by the rich vs. the poor. The administration of service provisions also remains a problem, notably in the case of social security health.

In turn, following a step-wise increase, consolidated primary public sector spending increased from 16–17 percent to 20 percent in the late 1970s and early 1980s and to 26–28 percent in the 1990s and early 2000s.[15] Whereas the first of these increases was concentrated in infrastructure spending, the spending of the 1990s focused on social spending and was associated with the implementation of the reforms introduced by the 1991 Constitution. This led to various major tax reforms allocated to public sector revenues to finance increases in spending. Eleven major tax reforms have been adopted since 1990,[16]—which is an average of almost one every two years. Most of these reforms have sought to increase public sector revenues. At the same time, a myriad of tax benefits were introduced during the Uribe administrations (2002–2010), eroding the effort to increase revenues and making the tax structure less horizontally equitable than was typical up to the early 2000s.

In sum, the two-track reform agenda can be understood as a competition between two paradigms on the role of the state in the economy, and has generated a continuous confrontation between the defenders of one or the other vision.[17] Whereas defenders of the concept of social rights have wanted to scrap the liberalization agenda, defenders of the latter have been extremely critical of the rising public sector spending that is essential to implement the social reform agenda. The two tracks have, in any case, continued to be in place.

MACROECONOMIC PERFORMANCE

The expectation of the supporters of the liberalization agenda that reforms would lead to rapid productivity and economic growth have not materialized. Table 1.2 presents the performance in terms of GDP growth and the volatility of this variable during the post-reform period (1990–2012) compared to the historical performance during the period of state-led industrialization (1950–1980).[18] The decrease in economic growth in Colombia, from an average of 5.1 to 3.7 percent is stronger than the unweighted average for Latin America, though more moderate than the slowdown of the region's weighted average, which is heavily influenced by the poor performance of the two largest economies (Brazil and Mexico) in recent decades. As a result, whereas Colombia's performance was somewhat better than the unweighted regional average in the earlier period, it has been somewhat worse since 1990. The slowdown in productivity growth is also a major feature of the post-reform period compared to state-led industrialization, again defeating the expectations of the supporters of the liberalization agenda; this is not inconsistent with the significant modernization of many firms and sectors, but rather shows the growing underutilization of resources, notably of labor, which has experienced increased informality.[19] What is equally important, the tradition of stable economic growth in the earlier historical period has given way to greater GDP volatility—though still somewhat lower than that typical in other Latin American countries.

Table 1.2. GDP Growth: Dynamics and Volatility

	Average Growth	*Standard Deviation*	*Coefficient of Variation*
Weighted Average			
1950–1980	5.5%	1.7%	31.3%
1990–2012	3.3%	2.3%	69.4%
Simple Average			
1950–1980	4.9%	3.7%	75.0%
1990–2012	3.9%	3.2%	80.8%
Colombia			
1950–1980	5.1%	1.6%	31.6%
1990–2012	3.7%	2.5%	68.7%

Source: Author's estimates based on GDP data from ECLAC. Data excludes Cuba and Haiti.

The economy has experienced three business cycles since 1990, with the third still ongoing (see Figure 1.1A). The first was particularly sharp, and indeed sharper than that of Latin America as a whole. It was characterized by an initial boom fueled by the expansionary fiscal and monetary policies that accompanied the launch of market reforms. After a domestically induced slowdown in 1995 (which thus had different origins to the regional one generated by the December 1994 Mexican crisis), the economy recovered but then was plunged in 1999 into the worst crisis of the twentieth century and the first recession in almost seven decades.

The recovery was somewhat faster than the average of the region and was followed by a boom in 2005–2007. Although some analysts would underscore the positive effects of the enhanced domestic security environment generated by the Uribe administrations,[20] the reasons for the boom were similar to that which the region as a whole experienced: the very favorable external conditions that characterized those years, including the beginning of upward phase of a super-cycle of commodity prices that would significantly benefit the energy and mineral exporters, Colombia among them (see a closer analysis of this issue in the next section). The 2008–2009 global crisis hit Colombia as Latin America and the whole world, but the country was able to perform in this occasion better than the regional average. The country then lagged in the strong regional post-crisis recovery, but then performed better during the 2011–2013 slowdown, which affected the region and the emerging world as a whole.

The poor performance of Colombia during the first cycle explains its somewhat poorer growth relative to the unweighted Latin American average: 2.7 percent between 1990 and 2003 compared to an unweighted regional average of 3.2 percent. Between 2003 and 2012 both Colombia's and the regional average are similar: 4.9 percent and much stronger in 2003–2007 than in 2007–2012. Improved performance since 2003 is associated, again, to exceptional terms of trade conditions and, during 2003–2007, to the broader set of favorable external conditions analyzed in a previous section. Also, thanks to slower population growth, performance in terms of GDP per capita reached one of the highest historical rates in 2003–2007 (4.3 percent a year) and slightly exceeded in 2007–2012 the 1950–1980 average (2.5 percent vs. 2.2 percent).[21]

The high level of GDP volatility reflects the weaker counter-cyclical tools that the country has used to manage external shocks relative to its own past. During the liberalization period, Colombia abandoned the use of trade and balance of payments instruments that were typical of past macroeconomic management, particularly the tendency to liberalize imports during booms and restrict them during crises, to increase nontraditional export incentives to manage decreases in coffee revenues, and to manage exchange controls in

Macroeconomic Performance, 1990–2012

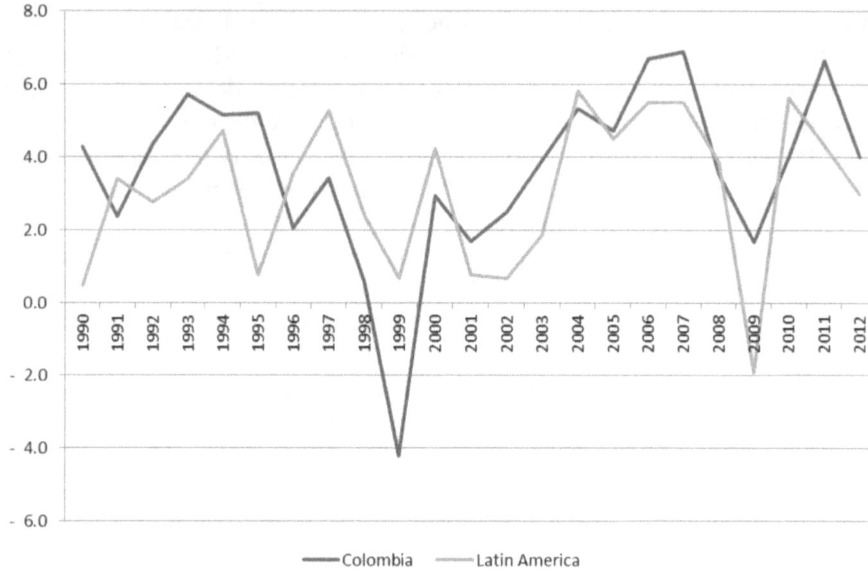

Figure 1.1A. GDP Growth
Source: ECLAC

Figure 1.1B. Fixed Captial Investment (% of GDP)
Source: ECLAC

an equally counter-cyclical fashion. The mild instruments of capital account management that were kept after the dismantling of exchange controls have been used rather sparingly and have been clearly insufficient to smooth out the sharp capital account fluctuations. Given the rising commitments in terms of social spending, fiscal policy has faced many difficulties in exercising a counter-cyclical role. In turn, monetary policy has been successful in keeping low levels of inflation over the past decade, but much less effective in smoothing aggregate demand and GDP cycles, and in avoiding significant level of real exchange appreciation during booms.

Two success stories of macroeconomic performance have been inflation and investment. In the first case, the moderate inflation that had characterized the Colombian economy since the mid-1970s ended during the strong recession at the turn of the century. This was associated much more with the strength of the recession than with monetary policy itself, but policy is, no doubt, behind the maintenance of low inflation. Fixed capital formation has exceeded the Latin American average, except during the late twentieth century recession (Figure 1.1B). However, since this has coincided with lower rates of growth relative to the historical average, this implies that the capital-output ratio has been significantly higher than in the past, reflecting the high capital intensity of the booming sectors, oil and mining.

In contrast to these success stories, fiscal policy has been overburdened by the additional responsibilities given to the state by the 1991 Constitution. Despite increasing revenues generated by the initial tax reforms, the budget deficit began to increase in the mid-1990s and reached its highest levels during the recession of the late 1990s (Figure 2.A). Since the central government had to assume most of the increased spending responsibilities, it was the source of the rising deficit. Indeed, the central government has run consistent deficits since then, which have been compensated partly (in some years fully) by surpluses in the rest of the public sector (particularly the social security administration). The large deficits at the end of the 1990s were, however, more the *result* of the strong recession and led to a massive increase in public sector indebtedness: from less than 20 percent prior to 1997 to slightly over 50 percent by 2002 (Figure 1.2B). With the fiscal adjustments implemented during the crisis, particularly to increase revenues, the additional income and transfers to the government generated in recent years by the state-oil company (Ecopetrol), the greater stability of central government spending and the additional fiscal surpluses in the rest of the public sector (which now include in a few years large surpluses from local governments), the fiscal situation improved significantly during the 2003–2007 expansion, and has remained strong since the mid-2000s, with just a temporary reversal during the 2009 growth slowdown. As a result of these improvements in the

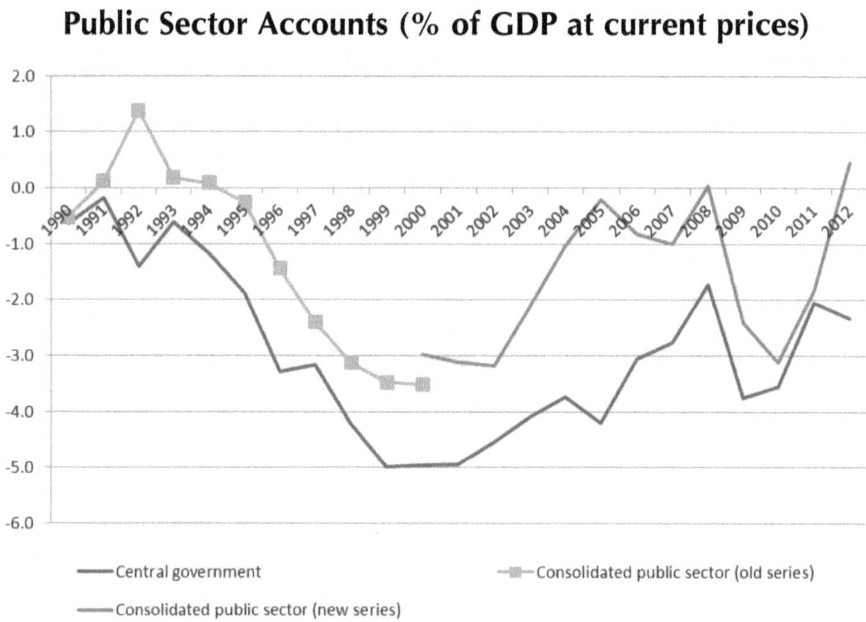

Figure 1.2A. Public Sector Deficit
Source: Ministry of Finance

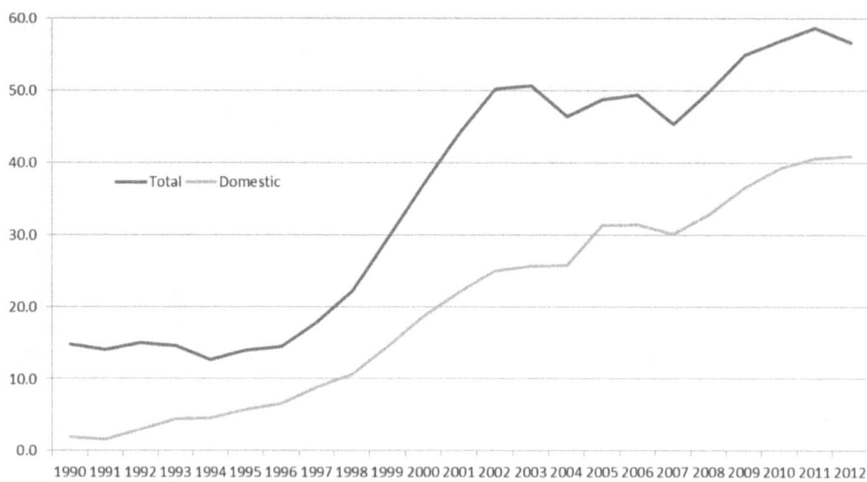

Figure 1.2B. Central Government Debt
Source: Banco de la República

fiscal accounts, the central government public sector debt stabilized, though it increased again during the Great Recession. In turn, the consolidated public sector debt started to decline, though at a much slower rate than the rest of Latin America, leading to a situation in which, in contrast to the past, the public sector debt now exceeds the Latin American average (39.1 percent of GDP in 2012 for the consolidated public sector vs. a regional average of 32.2 percent according to ECLAC).

The social effects of macroeconomic performance belong to the category of mixed performance, and remarkably so during the first cycle. This is particularly reflected in the evolution of the labor market indicators. Although the strong expansion of domestic demand and, therefore, of economic growth after the liberalization process facilitated a temporary improvement in employment conditions, a sharp deterioration started in the mid-1990s and peaked in 1999–2002 in terms of both open unemployment and informality (Figure 1.3A). Faster growth rates facilitated a significant recovery in labor markets, particularly during the 2003–2007 boom, when unemployment fell sharply and the quality of employment increased, as reflected, in particular, in the falling share of informality.

However, labor market conditions experienced a long-term deterioration, as evidenced by the facts that open unemployment remained above 10 percent and informality continued to be high. This is also reflected in the estimates of "modern employment" (defined as wage labor plus highly educated independent workers, which is the inverse of ECLAC's definition of "low productivity employment"), which reached 63 percent of employment in 2010 in the seven major cities compared to 69 percent in 1994.[22] In both dimensions, labor market conditions continued to be worse than Latin America's averages. It must be underscored, however, that labor market participation is much higher in Colombia than in the region, and for that reason Colombia actually has a *higher* employment rate (percentage of working age population employed, including in informal occupations) than the regional average: 57.9 percent in 2012 compared to a regional average of 55.8 percent according to ECLAC.

The evolution of poverty also shows the contrast between the first post-reform business cycle and performance since 2003.[23] After experiencing just a mild improvement during the expansion of the first half of the 1990s, poverty increased sharply during the crisis of the late twentieth century, peaking in the early 2000s. With faster growth, it fell sharply after 2003, by an accumulated 17 percentage points from 2002 to 2012 according to the national estimates reproduced in Figure 1.3B. These trends, though positive, imply a lag vis-à-vis the strong performance in the region as a whole, which was particularly true in 2003–2008.[24] The basic difference is the fact that Colombia does not

Labor Market Conditions and Poverty

Figure 1.3A. Labor Market Conditions

Source: Urban unemployment according to ECLAC (7 cities up to 2000, 13 cities since then). National unemployment and informality according to Departmento Nacional de Estadística (DANE)

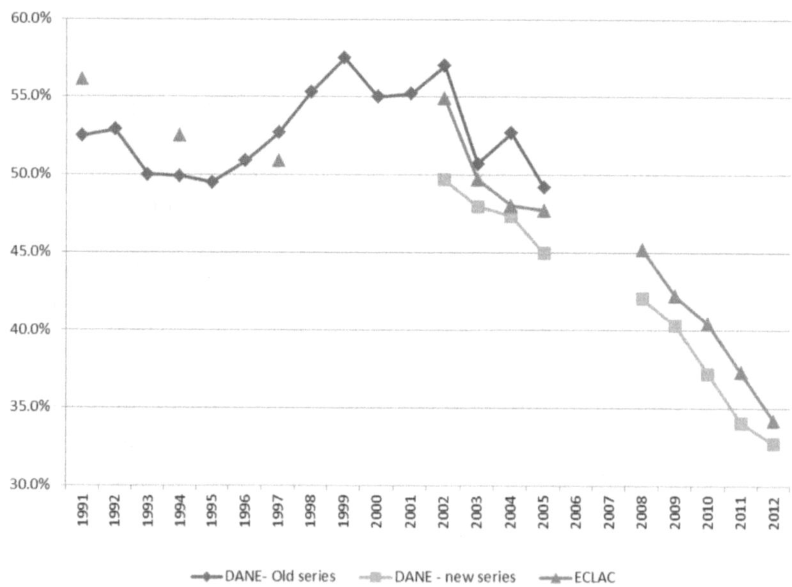

Figure 1.3B. Poverty (headcount ratio)

Source: ECLAC and DANE. Old series referes to MERDP; new series to MESEP

belong to the countries that have experienced significant improvements in income distribution over the past decade.[25] Domestic sources as well as international estimates do show some improvement in this regard, but they lag those in the region. For example, ECLAC data shows an improvement of one percentage point in the Gini coefficient between 2002 and 2010, but this lags the 3.5 points reduction in the unweighted average for Latin America. Recent estimates also show an extremely high concentration of income at the top one percent of earners (which concentrate around 20 percent of income since 1993), implying that the Gini coefficient adjusted upward when this factor is taken into account—from 0.554 to 0.587 in 2010, both of course among the highest in the world.[26]

Furthermore, in contrast to improvements in living conditions associated with the expansion of social services and public utilities, reduction in income poverty in urban areas has been stronger in relative terms than in rural areas (16.5 vs. 10.0 percentage points between 2003 and 2012), and the rural-urban gap has thus significantly increased. On a broader basis, the past decade shows a strong polarization between improvements in income poverty and distribution in the thirteen largest metropolitan areas and the rest of the country.[27] Regional studies also show that Bogotá has been the greatest winner of development patterns over the past decades, thanks to its role as the central provider of services in the country.[28] Indeed, the bias of economic restructuring toward services, which are heavily concentrated in larger cities, has been a source of both rising rural-urban gaps and of the strong demand for skilled labor, which has been the major factor leading to rising income inequality—though compensated by other, positive trends.

CHANGING STRUCTURAL PATTERNS

Economic structures have changed significantly as a result of the liberalization reforms but also of external shocks, particularly the commodity-price boom that took off in 2004. As a result, Colombia is more open to trade and foreign investment, some Colombian firms have expanded abroad, the private sector plays a growing role in activities that were previously reserved for the state, the share of mining and services in GDP has increased at the cost of agriculture and manufacturing, and oil and mining have come to dominate exports.

Rising trade coefficients (estimated at constant prices) are shown in Figure 1.4. Export coefficients have increased in a step-wise fashion, with two major jumps: the first one during the second half of the 1980s, and thus prior to the trade liberalization proper, and the second during the crisis

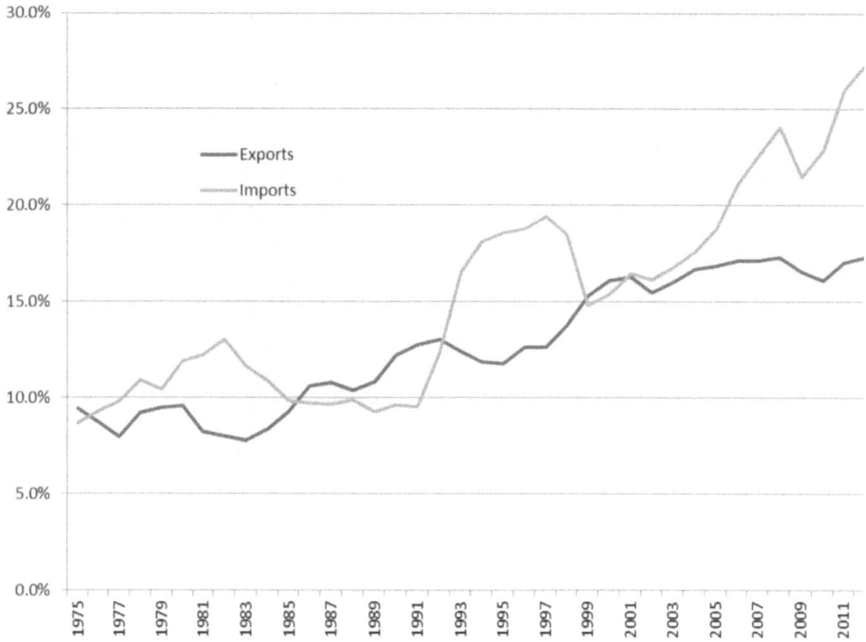

Figure 1.4. Exports and Imports as % of GDP (at 2005 prices)
Estimated based on DANE data

at the turn of the century. It is remarkable that exports in real terms have growth at a similar rate than overall GDP during the major periods of expansion (1991–1997 and since 2003), making it difficult to claim that trade liberalization has generated export-led growth. Import coefficients show a steeper but unstable rise, with sharp increases during periods of expansion that were not entirely reversed during the crisis of the late twentieth century. As we will see, the mix of these export and import patterns has been a sharp deterioration of external accounts during periods of economic growth. They have also affected changes in economic structure.

As a result of liberalization reforms, the role of foreign direct investment (FDI) has also increased. According to ECLAC data, FDI has represented, on average, 2.2 percent of GDP since 1994, the year when it showed the first significant jump vis-à-vis the fraction of one percentage point that it had represented until then. This is similar to the Latin American average (2.3 percent in 1994–2012 according to ECLAC data). FDI mainly focused on services in the second half of the 1990s and in oil and mining in the 2000s.[29] With a lag, Colombian firms have also expanded abroad, particularly in Latin America but also in the United States and some European countries, with a select group of Colombian firms—both private and public—joining the ranks of the "multilatinas" (Latin multinationals).[30]

The external factor that has had the strongest effects on the economic structure is the commodity price boom which took off in 2004, and which was particularly strong in the energy and mining sectors. To understand the strength of this boom, Figure 1.5 shows the terms of trade of Colombia since the early twentieth century. As it is clear, the still ongoing boom has been stronger than any the economy experienced in the twentieth century. This can be shown by how many years the terms of trade index has exceeded by 20 percent the value in the base year (1970 in the graph): *eight* years during the recent boom vs. five in 1976–1980, three in the period 1950–1954 and only two in the second half of the 1920s. Booming oil and mineral prices have, of course, fed into export as well as fiscal revenues, in the latter case through the rise in income taxes of mining companies in general and the profits of Ecopetrol transferred to the central government.

The mix of these trends has been a boom in oil and mining exports, which have come to dominate Colombia's export basket. Oil and mining exports had already experienced a strong expansion in the 1980s and represented

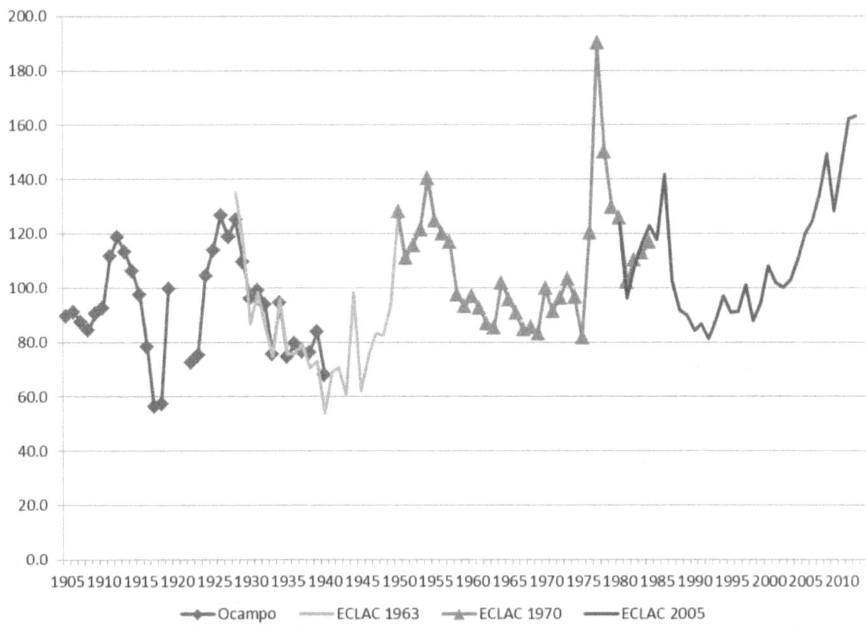

Figure 1.5. Terms of trade of Colombia, 1905–2012

Source: ECLAC and for the first series, José Antonio Ocampo y Santiago Montenegro, Crisis mundial, protección e industrialización: Ensayps de historia económica colombiana (Bogotá: CEREC, 1984), ch. 2

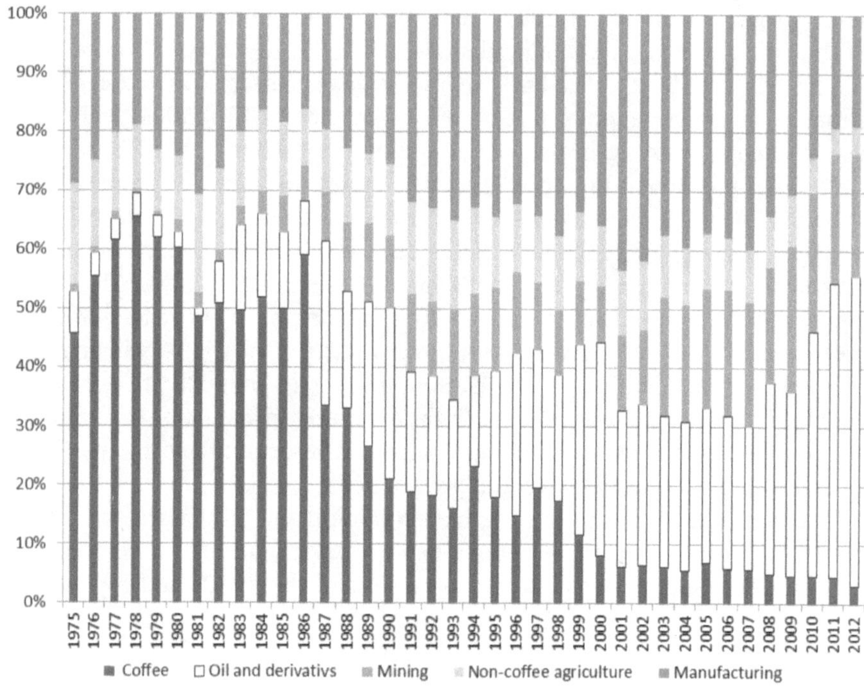

Figure 1.6. Export Composition (% of total exports)
Source: Banco de la República on the basis of information collected by DANE

over 30 percent of the country's exports since the later part of that decade (Figure 1.6). The major coal and nickel projects that the government had promoted since the 1970s had added these two commodities to the list of mining products in the 1980s to the renewed exports of oil and derivatives, and the ancestral though highly cyclical gold exports (which are not fully reflected in trade statistics). Oil itself benefited from the more private sector–friendly and, particularly, FDI-friendly contracts introduced in the mid-1970s. The Uribe Administrations placed the encouragement of FDI in mining at the center of its economic policy, to the point of approving (entirely unnecessary) tax incentives for investments in the sector, and the Santos administration used the term "mining locomotive" in its Development Plan to refer to the priority placed on this sector. The share of oil and mining exports continued to increase through the 1990s and then speeded up during the recent commodity boom to reach over 70 percent of Colombian exports in 2011–2012—enhanced, of course, by the high oil and mining prices in place. The great loser was the traditional staple of Colombia, coffee, which has come to represent in recent years almost a marginal share in the export basket.

"Nontraditional," and particularly manufacturing exports, are destined in a high proportion to other Latin American countries. They had been the great success story of the second half of the 1980s, and further increased in the 1990s thanks to the liberalization of Andean trade and the multiplication of trade agreements with other countries in the region. However, they have faced two adverse trends: periodic real exchange rate appreciations (see below) and the instability of sales to some countries, notably Venezuela. Thus, exports to this country boomed in 1990–1998 but then experienced a period of high instability, with sharp falls in some years (1999 and, particularly, 2003). They increased again from 2003 to 2008 but then became victim to the political tensions between the two countries and fell by 77 percent over the next two years; although they have recovered thereafter, they remained at 42 percent of their 2008 peak in 2012. Both the 2004–2008 export boom to Venezuela as well as the 2008–2010 contraction were major external shocks for Colombia.[31] Overall, the net result of trends in the share of nontraditional exports is that after peaking at over two-fifths of total exports, the share of manufacturing exports fell to less than one-fifth in recent years. Non-coffee exports peaked earlier, in 1991–1992, at over 15 percent of total exports but then fell in a steady manner to 4–5 percent.

The net effect of export and import trends has been a highly cyclical balance of payments: current account balances have tended to deteriorate massively during booms and adjust during crises. Since the current account of the balance of payments is the counterpart of changes in domestic production and aggregate demand, this highly cyclical behavior implies that aggregate demand has been more volatile than GDP, indicating again that attempts by natural authorities to smooth demand fluctuations—counter-cyclical macroeconomic policy—has not been particularly effective.

Figure 1.7A shows this cyclical behavior. It estimates the current account balance in two different ways: at current prices and adjusting exports of goods and services by the changes in the terms of trade vis-à-vis 2003, the year before commodity prices started to boom. The difference was not very important up to 2003 but then became quite significant. Looking at the first period of expansion, the economy went from a boom from a peak surplus of 4 percent of GDP in 1991 to a deficit which fluctuated around 4 percent in 1994–1998. This deficit was transformed into a small surplus in 1999–2000 and small deficits in the early 2000s. The boom that ensued thereafter generated again a deficit, but the two estimates now vary widely, reflecting the terms of trade boom that the economy experienced during this period. If adjusted by the terms of trade, the deficit reaches 10 percent of GDP in 2011–2012. Since at current prices the deficit was around 3 percent of GDP, this

Current Account and Trade Balances as % of GDP

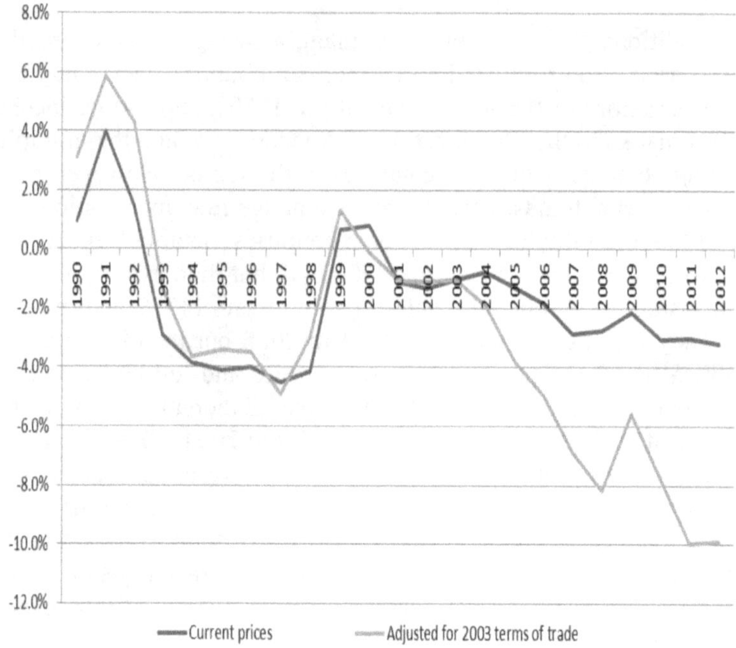

Figure 1.7A. Current account balances as % of GDP
Source: Estimates based on ECLAC data

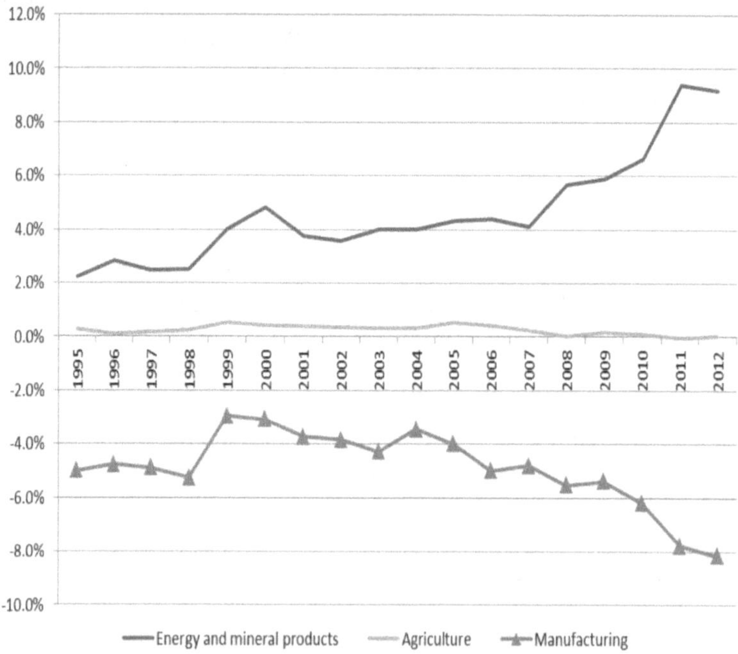

Figure 1.7B. Current sectoral balances as % of GDP
Source: Sectoral balances according to Fedesarrollo; GDP in dollars according to ECLAC

means that the terms of trade gains since 2004 have come to represent about 7 percent of GDP, which are likely to fall in the next few years as commodity prices come down. This also means that Colombia has been *over*-spending its terms of trade increase.

At the policy level, the major reflection of the strong cyclical performance of the balance of payments is the volatility of the real exchange rate. This is shown in Figure 1.8, which follows the Latin American tradition of estimating the real exchange rate in such a way that a rise means a depreciation and a fall an appreciation. As a comparison of Figures 1.7 and 1.8 indicates, the counterpart of the current account is the sharp fluctuations in the real exchange rate: almost persistent appreciation between 1991 and early 1997, a strong depreciation between then and 2003 and an equally strong apprecia-

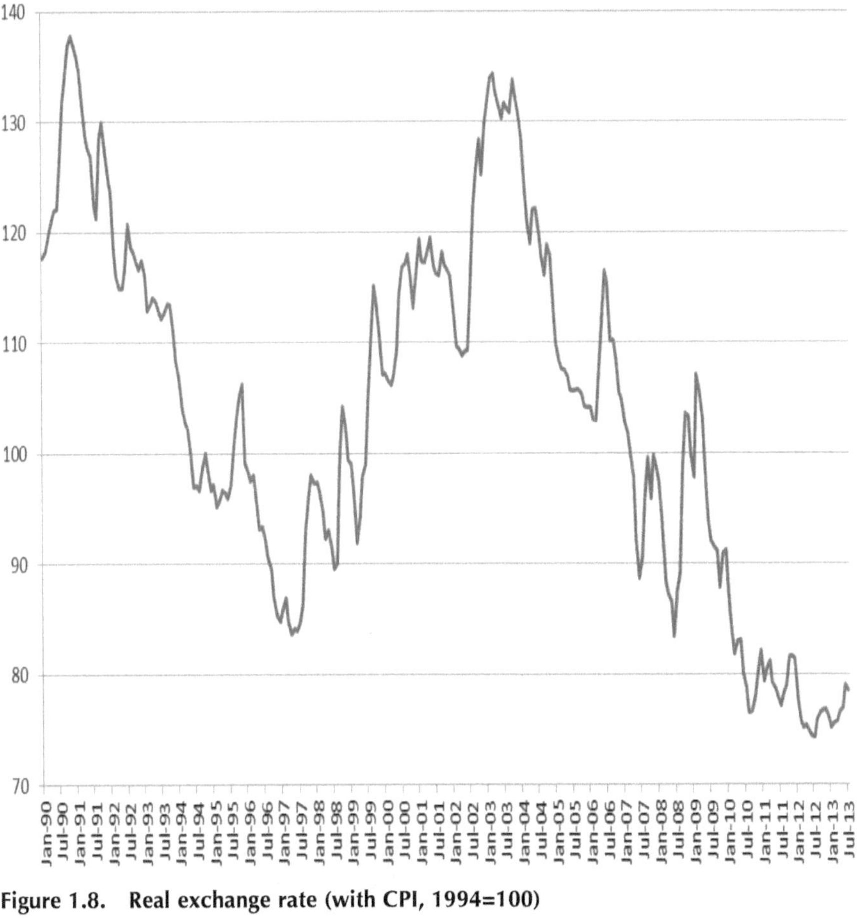

Figure 1.8. Real exchange rate (with CPI, 1994=100)

Source: Banco de la República

tion trend until mid-2013, which has been interrupted by a few conjunctures, particularly the global financial meltdown of September 2008.[32] What is also important, the most recent appreciation is the strongest of all. For example, if we define a strongly appreciated exchange rate—or, better, an undervalued exchange rate—as a real exchange rate that is more than 10 percent below the reference point for the graph (the year 2004), there were twelve months of strong appreciation between September 1996 and August 1997, one in 2007 (June), six in 2008 (March–August) but *thirty-one* during the most recent episode of overvaluation (January 2010–July 2012, the last month available when this chapter was written). What is equally important, the previous episodes led to strong regulations of capital flows aimed at reducing booming inflows; the most recent one did not. In all of them, there have also been central bank interventions to accumulate foreign exchange reserves, though generally weaker than similar efforts by other Latin American countries.

Since the overwhelming share of imports is comprised of manufactures, the net effect of trade trends during the recent boom has been a spectacular surplus of energy and mining exports accompanied by a massive increase in the manufacturing trade deficit, particularly in 2008–2012. The latter reached 8.2 percent of GDP in 2012 (Figure 1.7B). Agriculture has continued to enjoy a small trade surplus, which almost disappeared since 2008 and represents a fraction of that which the economy enjoyed during most of the twentieth century, when coffee was king.

Although the massive manufacturing deficit has been determined, in part, by booming investment in machinery and equipment, thus bringing into the economy manufactures that do not necessarily compete with domestic production, it has also been the determinant of the large-scale de-industrialization that the country has experienced. Although de-industrialization had started in the mid-1970s, it was mild up to the beginning of trade liberalization and had actually experienced a revival in the second half of the 1980s. After liberalization, de-industrialization was extremely sharp in 1991–1994, when its share in domestic value added decreased by more than three percentage points, but continued until the end of the decade at a slower pace; it was again very strong in 2007–2012 when its share in value added fell by more than two percentage points.

The two periods of intense de-industrialization have coincided with import booms, and the associated appreciation pressures and deterioration of the current account of the balance of payments. They also coincide with periods of GDP growth, when manufacturing demand picks up, and thus cannot be associated with weak demand, such as that typical of recessions. There is, however, one exception: the 2003–2007 expansion, when the share of manufacturing in value added actually increased. As Figure 1.7B indicates,

2003–2007 was also a period of more moderate manufacturing trade deficits than the period that followed. The increase in the share of manufacturing had actually started with the adjustment of the balance of payments at the turn of the century, and reflects also the more competitive real exchange rate that characterized most of this period. It was also facilitated by growing exports to Venezuela up to 2008.

The trends in the share of manufacturing are part of a broader and massive restructuring that the Colombian economy has experienced since the liberalization policies were adopted in the early 1990s, but which partly come from the mid-1970s. Figure 1.9 summarizes structural changes. The two sectors that have been most adversely affected are agriculture and manufacturing. In the case of agriculture, the falling trend is a long-term feature of structural change, but it was enhanced by the liberalization reforms, which had strong negative effects on some agricultural products (particularly cotton, cereals and oilseeds). Agriculture, notably coffee, has also been affected by low international prices up to the early 2000s and by the periodic exchange rate appreciations. Overall, agriculture's participation in domestic value added has fallen by slightly over four percentage points, close to four-fifths of its 1975 share. Manufacturing has seen its own share fall by almost seven per-

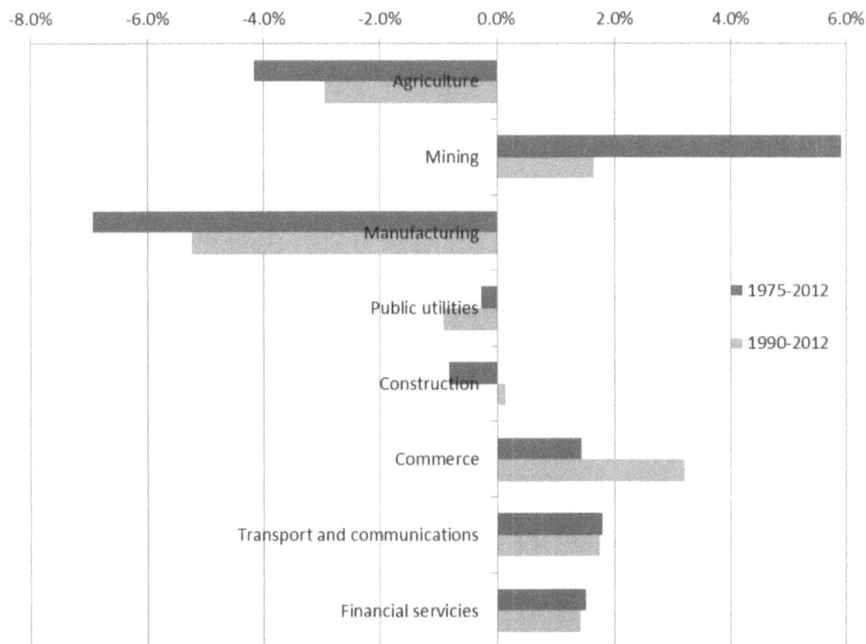

Figure 1.9. Changing shares in GDP (at 2005 prices)
Source: Departmento Nacional de Estadística (DANE)

centage points since the mid-1970s—over five since 1990. This has reduced manufacture's portion of domestic value added by over a third since 1975.[33]

The counterpart has been the rising share of mining (including, of course, oil mining), which had started to increase in the 1980s, as indicated also by its rising share in exports already analyzed. Overall, mining has more than tripled its share in domestic value added, increasing by six percentage points since 1975. The growing role of mining in both GDP and exports has been interpreted by some as the dominance of an "extractive" economic model.[34] All service sectors have also expanded, by a total of over six percentage points of GDP. In short, mining and services increased at the cost of agriculture and manufacturing.

While structural change in the 1990s was driven by trade liberalization, the most recent episode can be correctly interpreted as a case of "Dutch disease" associated with the oil and mining boom. In fact, a major difference between the 1990s and recent years has been the attitude toward mining activities. In the early 1990s, the expectation of expansion of oil exports, associated with the development of recently discovered Cusiana fields, was widely accompanied by a public debate, promoted by the Gaviria administration, on how to avoid the Dutch disease. No such debate took place in recent years. Indeed, as already indicated, both the Uribe and Santos administrations not only welcomed but actually encouraged the expansion of oil and mining.

In contrast, agriculture and manufacturing have been hurt not only by liberalization but also by the dismantling of the active production sector policies that the country developed for the promotion of both sectors during the age of state-led industrialization. There have been attempts to reconstruct policies for both sectors, but these efforts have been discontinuous and, particularly, have been relatively weak and thus unable to counteract the stronger negative shocks generated by trade liberalization (which now include a growing number of extra-regional free trade agreements) and recurrent exchange rate overvaluation.

Agricultural policies introduced in the 1990s some incentives for investment and additional sectorial funds for research, to which direct subsidies were added in the 2000s. This is also the only case in which directed credit was maintained after domestic financial liberalization. There were also attempts to reconstruct an industrial policy during the Samper (1994–1998) and Pastrana (1998–2002) administrations, but they were discontinued during the Uribe governments. At the end of the second Uribe administration, the seeds of new industrial policies were adopted, which were maintained by the Santos government.[35] A technology policy was also put in place by the Samper administration but discontinued during the Pastrana government, to revive also at the end of the second Uribe administration. During the Santos government, research and development was given a share in mining royalties, though on the basis of projects that must be negotiated at the regional level, with this model still in the process of implementation. All in all, these policies have thus an important element of discontinuity and have been weak relative to other factors that have adversely affected agriculture and manufacturing.

CHALLENGES

The analysis of this chapter indicates that the best results of the dual-track reform agenda that was put in place in the early 1990s has been improved access by the poor to social services, leading to rapidly falling poverty as measured by unsatisfied basic needs and multidimensional poverty. Significant challenges remain in this area, however, in terms of access in rural areas, quality of services, and organization of service provisions, particularly in health. The Colombian economy has experienced also reasonable economic growth since the early 1990s, but much weaker and more volatile than during state-led industrialization. Growth has been more dynamic since 2004, thanks to the most impressive terms of trade boom in over a century, and growth in per capita terms has been enhanced by falling population growth.

Overall, it can thus be argued that the 1991 Constitution has been more successful than economic liberalization in inducing positive trends. One deficiency of both has been, however, the incapacity to improve income distribution, and to reduce rural-urban gaps and labor market informality. It can be argued again that most of these negative trends are associated with the incapacity of the liberalization agenda to induce a growth pattern with favorable social trends.

The Colombian economy shows improvements in other areas: in reducing inflation, increasing investment, in attracting FDI and contributing to the growing family of "multilatinas" and, notably, in expanding its service economy and exploiting its mineral wealth, with the latter now dominating the country's export basket. At the same time, countercyclical macroeconomic policy has become less capable of smoothing out external shocks—though with a better performance in this regard during the recent global financial crisis than that which hit the developing world at the end of the twentieth century. Growing mining and service sectors have also come at the cost of a weakening of agriculture and manufacturing, which were in the past the pillars of the diversification of the Colombian economy, including its regional diversity—both, no doubt, significant past strengths of the country.

This indicates that the most important challenge for Colombia lies in improving equity, particularly improving its extremely high income distribution and reducing the large rural-urban gap. Both of these challenges are central to peace-building, either if the ongoing peace negotiations succeed but also if they fail. In economic terms, a stronger agricultural sector and a re-industrialization drive based on strong production and technology policies must also be at the center of economic policy. Given the contribution that exchange rate overvaluation has played in the adverse trends experienced by agriculture and manufacturing, it is important to design a macroeconomic policy in which the objective of a competitive exchange rate is placed at the center, indeed as part of a broader effort to rebuild a stronger counter-cyclical macroeconomic policy.

The dependence of recent growth on exceptional terms of trade also pose a major problem, given the expectation that the super-cycle of commodity prices that the world economy has experienced for over a decade may have come to the end. Depending on the strength of the fall in commodity prices, this could become a major challenge, given the fact that Colombia has overspent its commodity price boom. Macroeconomic adjustment thus faces the major challenges of reducing the current account deficit, and replacing the fiscal revenues associated with the commodity boom. In the context of the demands for public sector spending that the peace process will generate, the latter challenge implies that the country would have to continue to strengthen its tax base, largely by dismantling the massive benefits that the Uribe administrations granted to capital income.

There are also other challenges that have not been analyzed in this chapter. Notably among them are the major lags in infrastructure, particularly in transport infrastructure. According to existing studies, Colombia must at least double its past rates of investment in this area.[36] A major implication of this, together with high levels of inequality, rural-urban gaps and reversing the adverse trends in agriculture and manufacturing, is that the country may have to look more *inward* and at regional markets, where the most important opportunities for manufacturing exports lie, rather than follow the recent route of multiplying free trade agreements with extra-regional partners.

NOTES

1. The associated data is extracted from the ECLAC website or from the Statistical Appendix of the *Economic Survey of Latin America and the Caribbean 2013* (Santiago, Chile: ECLAC, 2013), and earlier editions.

2. Negotiations led to several successful peace agreements with M-19, EPL and Quintin Lame, but also to the failure of negotiations with the largest guerrilla group, the FARC.

3. Bilge Erten and José Antonio Ocampo, "Super Cycles of Commodity Prices since the Mid-Nineteenth Century," *World Development* 44, pp. 14–30, 2013.

4. See Barry Eichengreen and Kevin O'Rourke, "A Tale of Two Depressions," *Vox*, April 6, 2009, and "What Do the New Data Tell Us?," *Vox*, March 8, 2010. The two are available at http://www.voxeu.org/article/tale-two-depressions-what-do-new-data-tell-us-february-2010-update.

5. This issue is not widely recognized. Using United Nations and, for the most recent period, International Monetary Fund data, it can be estimated that global trade (as measured by exports) grew at an real annual rate of 7.3 percent in 1986–2007, only slightly lower than the rate of growth during the 1950–74 post-Second World War boom, but then slowed down to only 2.7 percent in 2007–12.

6. The most articulate version of this view was that of the Development Plan of the Gaviria administration (1990–1994). See Presidencia de la República, *La revolución pacífica: Plan de desarrollo económico social 1990–1994* (Bogotá: Departamento Nacional de Planeación, 1991).

7. Free-trade agreements are currently being negotiated with Israel, Japan and Turkey.

8. The exceptions are national defense and security, disposal of toxic wastes and a 40 percent limit on ownership of broadcasting services.

9. This is a holding company with investments in Colombia and several other Latin American countries. The energy operations of Bogotá are in the hands of the private group Endesa, which has a slight minority share but the right to manage energy generation and distribution under the operating firm, Emgesa.

10. This includes Banco de Comercio Exterior de Colombia, Bancoldex, which absorbed the previous industrial development bank, Instituto de Fomento Industrial, IFI; Fondo para el Financiamiento del Sector Agropecuario, Finagro; Financiera de Desarrollo Territorial, Findeter; and the Financiera Eléctrica Nacional being recently transformed into Financiera de Desarrollo Nacional with broader objectives associated with infrastructure financing.

11. See the Sentence 481/99 on Banco de la República at http://www.corteconstitucional.gov.co/relatoria/1999/C-481-99.htm.

12. Law 100 of 1993 created two sub-systems of social security health: one financed with contributions from firms and workers and another subsidized by the government.

13. Following national terminology, I refer here to "participation in national revenues" rather than "transfers," although economically speaking the latter term may be appropriate.

14. These are official estimates from the Ministries of Health and Education, respectively. In the latter case, it refers to net school attendance; the 1993 was calculated based on data from gross attendance and the difference between gross and net attendance in 1996.

15. See José Antonio Ocampo, "Un siglo de desarrollo pausado e inequitativo: La economía colombiana, 1910–2010," in *Colombia 1919–2010*, eds. María Teresa Calderón and Isabela Restrepo (Bogotá: Taurus, 2010), 119–196, Table 3.

16. Major tax reforms were adopted in 1990, 1992, 1995, 1998, 2000, 2002, 2003, 2006, 2009, 2010 and 2012.

17. See, in this regard, José Antonio Ocampo, "Reforma del Estado y el desarrollo económico y social en Colombia," *Análisis Político*, no. 17 (September–December 1992), which was reproduced in a shortened version in José Antonio Ocampo, *Entre las reformas y el conflicto: Economía y política en Colombia* (Bogotá: Grupo Editorial Norma, 2004), Essay 1.

18. I prefer this concept over "import-substitution industrialization" for the reasons that are explained at length in Luis Bértola and José Antonio Ocampo, *The Economic Development of Latin America since Independence* (Oxford: Oxford University Press, 2012).

19. See Ocampo, "Un siglo," Table 1.

20. In fact, it is hard to see any clear influence of political and security events on economic performance. Despite the recurrent estimates of the costs of the internal conflict, Colombian GDP trends and cycles mimic regional trends—particularly those of market reforms and external shocks, both positive and negative—, and should thus be better explained in terms of those factors.

21. Indeed, the country only requires now a 3.6 percent GDP growth to reach the per capita performance of 1950–1980, and 4.9 percent to reach the record of that period, reached in 1967–1974.

22. See Hugo López, "El Mercado laboral colombiano, tendencias de largo plazo," in *El Mercado de trabajo en Colombia: Hechos, tendencias e instituciones,* Luis Eduardo Arango and Franz Hamann, eds. (Bogotá: Banco de la República, 2012), ch. 2, who provides an excellent analysis of trends in the labor market since the mid-1980s.

23. For an analysis of these trends, see Hugo López and Jairo Núñez, *Pobreza y desigualdad en Colombia: diagnóstico y estrategias*, (Bogotá: DNP, 2007) and official estimates of poverty by Departamento Adminstrativo Nacional de Estadistica (DANE).

24. See ECLAC, "Statistical Appendix, Table 4," in *Social Panorama of Latin America 2012* (Santiago, Chile: United Nations Publication, 2013), which shows a weaker reduction of Colombia than the regional average in 2002–2008 but a stronger one in 2008–2011.

25. The best known study for Latin America is Luis Felipe López-Calva and Nora Lustig (eds.), *Declining Inequality in Latin America: A Decade of Progress.* Washington, D.C. and New York: Brookings Institution Press and UNDP, 2010.

26. Facundo Alvaredo and Juliana Londoño Vélez, "High Incomes and Personal Taxation in a Developing Economy: Colombia 1993–2010," Working Paper no. 12, Commitment to Equity Program of the Inter-American Dialogue, Center for Inter-American Policy and Research and Tulane University, March 2013, Table 4, http://www.commitmentoequity.org/publications_files/CEQWPNo12%20HighTaxationDevEconColombia1993-2010_19March2013.pdf.

27. See the Santos administration Development Plan: DNP, *Plan Nacional de Desarrollo 2010–2014 'Prosperidad para todos'* (Bogotá: DNP, 2010), ch. 4.

28. Jaime Bonet and Adolfo Meisel Roca, "Polarización del ingreso per cápita departamental en Colombia," *Ensayos sobre Política Económica* 25, no. 54 (2007).

29. See ECLAC, *La inversión extranjera directa en América Latina y el Caribe 2002* (Santiago, Chile: Naciones Unidas, 2003), ch. 2, and annual follow-ups of this report, and Miguel Posada Betancourt, "Inward FDI in Colombia and Its Policy Context," *Columbia FDI Profiles*, Vale Columbia Center on Sustainable International Investment, November 10, 2010, http://www.vcc.columbia.edu/files/vale/documents/Colombia_IFDI_updated_Nov_10_2010_final.pdf.

30. See Ana María Poveda Garcés, "Outward FDI from Colombia and Its Policy Context," *Columbia FDI Profiles*, Vale Columbia Center on Sustainable International Investment, September 1, 2011, http://www.vcc.columbia.edu/files/vale/documents/Colombia_OFDI_-_1_Sept_2011_-_FINAL_-_REV_2.pdf. The stock of outward investment grew from $3 billion in 2000 to $23 billion in 2010. It has involved both private companies, financial (Bancolombia, Colpatria and Grupo Aval, among others) as well as non-financial (Carvajal, Cementos Argos, Hoteles Decamerón, Nutresa and Repsol, among others; we should also add Avianca, although it is now controlled by a Brazilian investor), as well as public sector firms, both public (Ecopetrol, Interconexión Eléctrica S.A) and local (Empresas Públicas de Medellín and Empresa de Energía de Bogotá).

31. Thus, the 2004–2008 represented a positive shock of 1.8 percent of 2008 GDP in a four-year period; the 2008–2010 a negative shock of 1.6 percent of 2010 GDP, of course in a shorter period.

32. The best analysis of appreciation over the last decade is Mauricio Cabrera, *10 años de revaluación* (Bogotá: Oveja Negra, 2013).

33. Following international trends, this has been partly compensated by the tertiarization of some manufacturing activities.

34. Luis Jorge Garay Salamanca (director), *Minería en Colombia: Fundamentos para superar el modelo extractivista* (Bogotá: Contraloría General de la República, 2013).

35. See an analysis of these policies in Astrid Martínez and José Antonio Ocampo, *Hacia una política industrial de nueva generación para Colombia* (Bogotá: Coalición para la Promoción de la Industria Colombia, 2011). Jaime Acosta Puertas, "¿Es la política de competitividad y de innovación la nueva política industrial de Colombia?," Report presented to the Friedrich Ebert Foundation of Colombia, Bogotá, October 2012. Consejo Privado de Competitividad, *Informe Nacional de Competitividad 2012–2013: Ruta a la prosperidad colectiva* (Bogotá: Consejo Privado de Competitividad, 2012), ch. 15.

36. See two recent studies: Fedesarrollo, *Infraestructura de transporte en Colombia*, Report to Cámara de Comercio de Infraestructura (Bogotá: Fedesarrollo, 2012) and Cecilia López et al., *Infraestructura y equidad* (Bogotá: Centro Internacional de Pensamiento Social y Económico (CISOE), 2013).

Chapter Two

Agriculture, Rural Development, and Attempts at Land Reform in Colombia

Into the 21st Century

Albert Berry

Like any other agricultural sector, Colombia's has confronted two major economic challenges; to grow at an adequate rate, thereby supplying food and other products to the local and international markets, and to contribute to employment and equality, both in the sector and more generally. Growth figures point to a decent record both for Colombia's agricultural sector and its overall economy during the second half of the twentieth century, at rates of 3.3–3.5 and 4.3 percent, respectively. But by the 1990s, much was going awry both in agriculture and economy-wide and Colombia entered the twenty-first century with a heavy burden of conflict, violence, and death in its rural areas, an enormous number of displaced people, and a set of serious challenges in the realms of employment and equality, most obviously involving the displaced people but also economy-wide problems, as a consequence among other things of the premature and involuntary stream of rural to urban migrants that has contributed to continuing high levels of informality and inequality. All of these challenges bear the stamp of the increasing failure of rural development since the 1970s to bring a stable, peaceful, and reasonably equitable society. Contributing factors have included a long legacy of rural injustice and violence; the sometime inability and sometime lack of interest of the Colombian government to protect the rural citizenry and to implement a socially oriented rural development strategy; and the disruptive effects of the guerrilla groups, the drug industry and the various reactions to them, including Plan Colombia and the paramilitaries.

These background factors have led to bad outcomes primarily through two main channels—the extreme inequality of access to and control of land, and the failure of the public sector to provide adequate and steady support to the family (*campesino*) sector so that it could be the motor of equitable growth within the agricultural domain. That policy would often favor larger farmers against smaller ones is a predictable reflection of political power in an elite–dominated polity. That "vested interest" bias has unfortunately been complemented by a striking degree of ignorance on the part of many policy-makers as to the characteristics and potential of the family farming sector, particularly the myth that it is inherently inefficient (e.g., because economies of scale are important in agriculture), that it produces essentially for home consumption and that it cannot be dynamic. All of these views are demonstrably false in the case of Colombia,[1] but are also given the lie by the successful family farm histories of most now industrial countries and many developing ones.[2]

GENERAL BACKGROUND ON COLOMBIAN AGRICULTURE

As in virtually all developing countries, Colombia's agricultural sector was until fairly recently dominant in terms of output, employment and exports, with coffee facilitating the country's twentieth-century entry into the international economy on a large scale and effectively financing much of the industrial development that followed. Five features of the unfolding pattern of control over land and its use from the time of independence in Colombia are particularly worthy of note:

1. an extremely high level of concentration of ownership and/or control of the land;
2. frequent ambiguity as to who has rights to land;
3. the important role of the state, given that land was continuously shifting from the public domain to the private;
4. the inconsistency of state action, partly because different parties and factions have had different views on land questions, but also because local governments systematically favored the largeholders (or aspirants to that status) while the national governments might sometimes take a broader view;
5. control of land as part of the broader issue of who controls the factors of agricultural production. Many of the tensions over the years can be seen, not only as tugs-of-war pitting largeholders against smallholders (or aspirants to those two statuses) but also as disputes between labor and land/capital, where those who controlled the bulk of the land also needed access to labor.

During the first decades of the twentieth century, while coffee forged into a dominant position in Colombia's external trade, the rest of the sector consisted mainly of large-scale extensive cattle-raising and small-scale family farms producing food for home consumption and sale in the domestic market. In the standard process of land expansion, small squatters ("colonos") typically in search of a livelihood and economic independence, settled on public lands, and initiated production. But they could not usually acquire solid property rights to that land. Tension morphed into violence when the balance of power between contenders for land was less unequal than usual.

By midcentury large-scale agriculture was undergoing a major transition with the expansion of crops like rice, cotton, sugar and eventually African palm, often onto good land previously dedicated to extensive cattle-raising and sometimes onto land used or usable by small farmers. From the 1970s on a new element was added, the production of illicit drugs, first marijuana, later coca and poppies. Various forms of cooperation (and at times competition) occurred among the drug industry, the guerrillas, and the paramilitaries, who arose initially as a defense group to protect large farmers from kidnapping at the hands of the guerrillas and then morphed into an independent power group characterized by unusual brutality. The recent conflict-ridden decades fit into a pattern of striking historical continuity, though the modes of settler eviction have changed, the actors are somewhat different with the arrival of drug lords, paramilitaries, and guerrillas, and the last wave of violence has generated more displacement than any previous one. During the period beginning in the 1980s, however, land also became literally an instrument of war[3] and of political power in a war context, as well as a mechanism for the laundering of drug money. Control of local politics and the use of local political bases to increase influence at the national level have increasingly been achieved by the drug lords and paramilitaries,[4] as contrasted to the traditional local elites with their base mainly in agriculture.

This period of extreme conflict covering the last quarter of the twentieth century left as its legacy slowing agricultural growth (though recovering to 2.7 percent over 2000–2009;[5] rising concentration of landholding to reach one of the most extreme levels in the world,[6] with much of this process occurring illicitly through the displacement of the small farmers who formed the bulk of the millions of displaced people and the majority of the tens of thousands of deaths. The century ended with Colombia's largest economic downturn of the century, as GDP fell by 7 percent over 1997–99 and only recovered its 1997 level in 2004. Among its causes was the heavy spending mandated by the new Constitution of 1991 and the civil war,[7] together with an exchange rate appreciation fostered by large capital inflows, and an inadequately prepared and supervised financial system.

Most of the standard features of developing country agriculture which have made the family farm the most economically and socially attractive system around the world are shared by Colombia. As far back as data provide any hints, small farms have been relatively efficient in terms of the land productivity they achieve.[8] With its average land productivity typically higher (mainly because of greater dedication of its resources to high value products) and its total factor productivity (TFP) not too different from that of larger farms, family farming's employment, income distribution and food and economic security advantages (often there are environmental benefits as well) give an overall contribution to economic welfare that is normally significantly superior to that of larger farms. The last three decades of the twentieth century, however, saw the agrarian structure shift still farther away from this model. Factors at work included the increasing battle for land; limited and inadequate investment in agriculture, although with considerable variation across regions and products; and—most damaging to the chances, then or later, of developing a healthy family farm system—the declining public sector spending on research, development, and diffusion of new technologies to smaller farmers and other forms of support for those farms.

AGRARIAN STRUCTURE AND EFFORTS TO REFORM IT

Success or failure in the pursuit of the objectives of equality of opportunity can be substantially read from the trajectory of the pattern of land ownership and control. The most reliable recent measures[9] show for 2009 a Gini coefficient of 0.875 for the distribution of land among owners.[10] A breakdown of units by size in 2000 (Table 2.1) implies that the 78 percent of the owners with fewer than 10 hectares had just 5.6 percent of the total area while the 0.1 percent with 2000 hectares or more had 51.8 percent of it, for a ratio of nearly 12,000 times more land per owner in the latter group than in the former. The effects of rural conflict on who controls land are not hard to guess.

Table 2.1. Distribution of Land among Owners, by Area, 2000

Size of Unit (Hectares)	*Owners (thousands)*	*Owners (percent)*	*Land Area (thousands of hectares)*	*Land Area (percent)*
Micro (<3)	2,049.7	57.3	1,324.8	1.8
Very small (3–10)	751.0	21.0	2,834.1	3.8
Small (10–20)	287.8	8.0	2,797.3	3.7
Medium (20–200 has.)	442.6	12.4	16,947.9	22.5
Large (200–2000)	44.8	1.2.	12,459.3	16.5
Very large (>2000)	2.2	0.1	39,004.8	51.8
Total	3,578.2	100.0	75,368.2	100.0

Source: Salomon Kalmanovitz and Enrique López Enciso (2006) *La Agricultura Colombiana en el Siglo XX.* Bogota: Banco de la Republica and Fondo de Cultura Economica, 322, based on data from IGAC.

The extreme inequality in the distribution of access to agricultural land and the serious ambiguities around property rights have long been recognized as serious problems by independent observers, political parties, and some governments, leading on occasion to attempts to "reform" the agrarian structure.[11] Had any of the pre-1980s attempts been able to significantly improve the size distribution of landownership and clarify land rights, Colombia might have avoided much of the tragedy of recent decades.

The first window of opportunity came in the 1930s when a combination of circumstances led to serious rural unrest of direct concern to political leaders, both because of its destabilizing political impact and because of its possible damping effect on agricultural production, especially of food crops at a time when their supply appeared insecure. Important figures in the Liberal Party saw the dissatisfied squatters and smallholders as a political resource on which they might draw. By the time the famous Law 200 of 1936 was passed the balance of power had shifted back to the landlords and, in its application that law, commonly thought to favor the settlers,[12] reinforced the position of the large estate owners by making it easier for them to claim land. It also provided an incentive for aspirants to large holdings to evict small squatters in order to avoid future conflicts over claims, and was accompanied by a vagrancy law which facilitated the removal of expelled *colonos*.[13]

The next opportunity came in the 1960s, by which time Colombia had entered a period of relatively fast but very dualistic growth in agriculture, with the expanding power of modern commercial farmers now representing another obstacle to agrarian reform efforts.[14] Fajardo[15] and others describe massive expulsions of *campesinos* during this period, some through the displacement of former workers and tenants on the traditional haciendas as they converted to modern agriculture. Law 135 of 1961 which founded the *Instituto Colombiano para la Reforma Agraria* (INCORA) prioritized the colonization route, promising to touch private property only in special cases. As well as being too small to have a major impact on agrarian structure, the reform was inadequately designed and executed.[16] President Carlos Lleras Restrepo (1966–1970) took the agrarian issue seriously; the potentially most important step of his administration was to promote a *campesino* organization (the *Asociación Nacional de Usuarios Campesinos*-ANUC), designed as a sort of pseudo pressure group for the recipients of government services in rural areas, while still essentially under the control of the government. Lleras saw the need for *campesino* involvement to assure that agrarian reform would in fact help them, and realized they would not organize unless its potential was clear to them.[17] Eventually ANUC's heterogeneity (members ranging from small and medium-sized capitalist farmers to landless workers) made it vulnerable to division, and its internal differences were deftly exploited by the opponents of reform, especially under the next administration of Conservative Misael Pastrana (1970–74). The *Acuerdo de Chicoral* of 1972, at which that government confirmed its decision to abandon redistributive land reform and to shift to a policy of encouraging the rapid capitalization and commercialization of agriculture through tax and fiscal incentives[18] is often interpreted as signaling the end of any hopes for serious land reform at this time.

President Alfonso Lopez (1974–78), the former leader of the left-leaning dissident wing of the liberal party (MRL), campaigned on the promise to replace an agrarian reform that "had not worked" with a program of rural development that recognized farmers' need for more than land, in particular for managerial skills, technical assistance and training. Rural development was pursued in part through Integrated Rural Development (DRI), designed to raise efficiency and food production in *campesino* zones, and focusing on food production through increased use of fertilizers together with better strains. In fact, the small farmers needed both more land and more of the complementary inputs[19] and though this approach remained for some time a significant element of overall agricultural-rural policy, like other policies that have been incremental in character rather than transformative, DRI's positive contributions could be and were either reversed or eroded over time. Such general support for existing small farmers can indeed achieve much if carried out in an effective manner, and probably has made a significantly positive contribution in Colombia. But to achieve its potential this approach requires a substantial flow of resources, a good understanding of what is needed, and a good level of continuity. Given that the initial understanding of what will work best is usually not very good, a capacity to learn, modify and refine also becomes important. For Colombia it is arguable that, in the absence of a distribution of land that protected existing and new small farmers from future encroachment, nothing else could pay off much in the medium or long run.

By the early 1990s, rural violence was again very high, fueled by a deadly mix of strong guerrilla groups, the drug industry and the paramilitaries. This difficult setting provided the context for the recent "market-oriented" effort at land reform in Colombia, an approach reflecting the contemporary popularity of market mechanisms in the supporting IFIs like the World Bank. The immediate goal of "negotiated" land transfer to aspiring smallholders was to subsidize (by up to 70 percent of the negotiated price of the land) the purchase of 1 million has. to benefit 70,000 families between 1995 and 1998.[20] It is unclear what its potential might have been under more favorable circumstances, but operational difficulties quickly left it far short of its goals and the fiscal constraints of the 2000s decade then helped to put it on the back burner.

The political lessons from Colombia's experience, apart from the obvious fact that there will always be powerful *status quo* opposition to proposals for major reform, and the important corollary that the political conditions that might permit a serious reform will usually be transitory, include the following:

1. The failure to successfully confront rural poverty and dissatisfaction through astute agrarian policy provided a base of strength for the guerrilla groups, a fertile ground for the illicit drug industry,[21] and (indirectly) a razon d'etre for the paramilitary forces. It has thus arguably been the single main explanatory factor of Colombia's social, political, and economic crises and tragedies of the last half-century.
2. It is probably true, as Lleras Restrepo believed, that some form of empowerment of the rural poor is ultimately essential to the consolidation of a healthy agrarian structure if not to its establishment.
3. The many prevalent but mistaken views on the economics of Colombian agriculture have been damaging. These include the always widespread impression that small farmers are less efficient economically than large ones; a faulty understanding of the economic logic of such landlord-tenant arrangements as share-cropping, whose discouragement through legislation led landlords to displace tenants; and the tantalizing idea that cooperative farming has a lot to be said for it. Rigid Marxist views have guided some interpretations of the *campesino* world in Colombia while rigid conservative (status quo) and/or neo-liberal views have guided most policy makers. All three have tended to be seriously disconnected from the reality of agriculture.

AGRICULTURAL GROWTH SINCE THE 1960s: WHAT HAPPENED AND WHY?

What mainly matters about Colombia's agricultural growth performance are the aggregate growth rate of output and where and how the growth occurs, and in particular how important the family farm is in the process. Colombia's policy makers had import substitution as the direct objective of their support for most of the commercial crops that eventually became productive and competitive. Typically a private association of producers of a given item developed to complement public support and to undertake some tasks that it might do better than the state; eventually they also gained political clout and used it to defend themselves against reductions in the public support received; most of these *gremios* operated at a good level of professionalism and most involved crops produced mainly by large farmers. The Coffee Growers Federation was different; although large producers had much weight in its management, most of the coffee came from small and medium producers. Many other small farmers, however, were diversified (albeit decreasingly so with time) and focused mainly on food crops for home consumption and for the domestic market. Thus, the initial protection of commercial crops by state action and their later promotion and protection through the political muscle of the *gremios* that represented them had the potential to and did frequently act in ways prejudicial to the small farm sector, both by lowering the perceived need of the state to support that sub-sector and by raising the demand for land by the commercial sub-sector.

Success in some crops notwithstanding, the overall performance of Colombian agriculture has left a good deal to be desired over recent decades. Aggregate growth is mainly the result of increases in resources applied (land, capital, labor, water, etc.) together with technological advances (which raises the amount of output achievable from a given amount of inputs); the latter plays a pivotal role. At the global level the best-confirmed source of productivity increase is public spending on research and development of new technologies. The evidence for Colombia is consistent with the general findings; most single-crop estimates of rates of return to investment in such research have exceeded 40 percent.[22] These stellar rates have not, however, manifested themselves in high average adoption rates of so-called Green Revolution Modern Varieties (GRMVs). Instead, in a recent (2000) ranking, where the highest adopting countries exceeded 65 percent of land planted in such varieties (all ten of the countries in this range except for Argentina were Asian, including low income nations like India and Vietnam), Colombia fell in the 20–30 percent range, behind nearly all of the other large countries of Latin America (the exceptions being Venezuela and Ecuador) and ahead mainly of the low income African countries.[23] Still, it is likely that total factor productivity (TFP) growth was decent or better (between 1 and 2 percent per year) over 1950–80; after that it appears to have fallen and by some estimates became negative by the 1990s,[24] for an overall record at best mediocre. In spite of complaints about it, the basic problem has not been weak agronomic research but rather a level of spending that has been much too low. As of 1996, non-private research spending in Colombia was just 0.79 percent of agricultural GDP with the public component 0.53 percent.[25] All of the other large countries of Latin America exceeded these levels by at least 2:1. From this low base, Colombia's public R&D spending was then drastically cut from 2002 on, mainly in favor of direct support payments to producers. Private research investment has grown but has neither taken up the slack left by the low level of state spending nor provided many benefits for small farmers (except in those crops where smaller farms coexist with large ones), since it is carried out by the crop-specific *gremios*. Other forms of investment in agriculture have also been generally inadequate to allow the country to make the best use of its ample resources and given the political structure surrounding agricultural policy, much of it has been biased toward the large and powerful.

International trade policy may affect growth in agriculture as in other sectors of an economy. In this regard a significant change of setting was wrought by the opening ("*apertura*") of the early 1990s, though its application to agriculture was far from uniform, with some groups better able to soften its effects than others. Tovar and Uribe[26] contend that the sluggish performance of Colombian agriculture since this time is traceable at least in part to the freer trade. In contrast to manufacturing, which showed significant capacity to adapt to the new more globalized setting, agriculture did not react with comparable adjustments and productivity improvements. A Fedesarrollo publication[27] puts the case for including agriculture in a tariff reform undertaken in 2010 by the Santos government, emphasizing the growing world demand for agricultural products and the fact that Colombia was the only country of Latin America in which agriculture had over the 2000–2010 decade grown significantly less than the economy. Optimal trade policy for agriculture remains a matter of considerable dispute.

EVOLUTION OF FAMILY FARMING[28]

Between a setting of conflict, violence and displacement on the one hand and a lack of positive public sector support on the other, much of the family farm sector has for several decades been placed in a difficult situation. In spite of this, its performance has been creditable, albeit no doubt a good deal less impressive than it might have been. Where it competed on a reasonably even footing with larger-scale agriculture, the family sector did well, as in potatoes, coffee (where the recent price crash drove out larger farmers but not the smaller ones), vegetables and fruits, plantains, and a variety of other items. Family farming's share of domestically consumed foods remains significant (around 60 percent in 1999–2001, according to Forero et al.[29]) and its share of the traditional Colombian staples somewhat higher.

Given its very limited capacity to defend itself politically in the context of the trade opening, it would not be surprising if the small farm sector wound up as a significant loser. In the context of the U.S.-Colombia FTA Garay et al[30] estimated that 22 percent of total small farm income came from activities that would potentially compete with U.S. imports (4 percent came from crops with export potential); that with an average price and exchange rate scenario, aggregate small farm income would fall by about 10 percent; and that for the 14 percent of producers estimated to suffer maximum impact that fall would be 40 percent. Meanwhile, Forero et al.[31] have noted that in the wake of the 1990s opening the large-scale commercial sector suffered a greater hit in terms of area and output than did the *campesino* sector; whereas area under crops produced mainly by large-scale agriculture fell by 36 percent over 1990–2001, the area under those mainly in the hands of *campesinos* did not decline. This impressive robustness is interpreted by Forero et al. as due to relatively low monetary costs of production, a flexible combination of commercial activities such that the composition of products can be changed fairly readily, the importance of home-consumption (whose value to the family is independent of what happens in the market), and cooperative activities among the producers and with agricultural financiers who emerged mostly from among the *campesinos* to provide capital that helps keep resources in efficient use. This greater resilience of family farming (exemplified also by the story of coffee), suggests that in good times (high prices) these farmers are making greater economic profits per hectare over the opportunity costs of factors than are the large ones; this greater profit margin (not necessarily all in monetary form) allows them to remain in business in the face of substantial price decreases. But, although they may resist better in terms of area than does capitalist agriculture, their incomes may fall more in the process. Capitalist units are likely to be better able to shift their capital to other sectors or to other agricultural products in different regions.

RECENT INSTITUTIONAL AND POLICY TRENDS[32]

The rather erratic path of Colombia's agricultural institutions and policy over the last forty years reflects the lack of a solid and shared diagnosis, together with the normal differences of policy preference across governments and the changes of context like globalization. Most administrations have been unable to identify and enforce a reasonable balance of interests between the large-scale and the family sectors. In this vacuum, the former has elaborated and pushed for policies in its own interests; the family farm sector lacks the institutional capacity to do likewise, and the state has increasingly abdicated its natural responsibility as provider of public goods to this sector. Thus policy has fluctuated, according to the setting and the political currents of the day, between what is from a societal point of view clearly perverse and what is mildly beneficial but not implanted firmly enough to guarantee continuity. Over the past couple of decades the institutional development that had been evolving from the 1940s or so has been in important respects reversed. As of 2010 the institutional/policy structure had become notably precarious.[33]

The 1990s and the beginning of the 2000s saw the disappearance of many programs created in previous decades, including DRI, the *Plan Nacional de Rehabilitación* (PNR), agrarian reform (except for the modest market versions thereof), and the successful national program of technological transfer (PRONATA) in research. Institutions like the *Corporaciones Autónomas Regionales* (CAR) became weaker and more politicized. Meanwhile a plethora of small programs and projects were created, but lacked articulation with any development strategy or the technical capability to have much of an impact.

Among the notable changes of the last two decades, mostly during the first Uribe government (2000–2004), has been a shift away from a more diversified structure of public institutions (with the Ministry of Agriculture and Rural Development–MADR as coordinator and policy maker) toward one with fewer agencies and a greater centralization of budget and execution in the ministry itself and in INCODER. The concentration of power in the ministry, in a context of weak planning, evaluation and monitoring, increased the likelihood of capture by vested interests.The changes of institutional structure have been accompanied by equally striking shifts in the level and patterns of public spending in agriculture. After averaging nearly 0.7 percent of GDP over 1990–1996, that spending plummeted to under 0.3 percent over 2000–2009.[34] The big decline during the late 1990s was concentrated in investment. Worse, the science and technology (S&T) component of sectoral spending fell from 12 percent over 1995–98 to 8.6 percent in 2003 and to 3 percent in 2010;[35] its share of agricultural GDP (a common performance yardstick) hit 0.11 percent in 2010, which appears to be a historic low.

Meanwhile, subsidies in the form of the AIS (*agricultura, ingreso, seguro*) income security mechanism have become the major component of spending, since being seen as a political necessity if Colombia was to sign a free trade agreement (FTA) with the United States. The government first considered a Planning Commission (DNP) approach that would have directed assistance to those most affected, but the SAC (Colombian Agricultural Society) argued in favor of a focus on raising productivity (through special credit lines along with incentives to invest to access technical assistance) without distinguishing by sectors or by need. Their idea won the day; with a focus on inducing private investment at the farm level rather than on the provision of public goods, it favored groups with the resources and organization to take advantage of it. By the beginning of 2010, however, program difficulties and scandals related to the favoring of large farmers prompted the government to modify the rules of access and use. Although some benefits have reached the smaller producers,[36] they appear to have been modest.

WHAT IS NEEDED NOW

Given the powerful bias in favor of large farms that on average generate little employment, it may be presumed that the income distribution and welfare impacts of agriculture's evolution over the last several decades have remained far inferior to what a healthy family farm system would have generated, and have thereby contributed to the continuing economy-wide employment challenge and the high levels of inequality and urban informality. In addition the lack of support for small farming has left both economic and food insecurity higher for many families than they might have been. Finally, the rural conflict and the enormous number of displacements have led to many deaths and have had a traumatic effect on many families even where no one has been killed.[37] When these realities are factored into the picture it is evident that the perverse pattern of agricultural development has contributed importantly to the social ills from which Colombia has suffered over this period.

More than anything else, therefore, Colombia's agricultural policy needs a renewed emphasis on family farming and the associated inclusive form of rural development. The lessons learned and the changes of context in recent decades mean that support for small farming must take account of the environmental and economic dangers that accompany new and more productive varieties. The trade opening should be seen as an opportunity for a number of small farm products as well as a threat to others. The new setting, like previous ones, involves taking advantage of market processes and also of public sector involvement where appropriate.

The question of interest in Colombia today is not whether the country would have fared better with a much more equal distribution of land beginning at some point in the past, together with a government inclined to and competent enough to support such agriculture, but rather what is the optimal feasible path from today's socially dysfunctional structure toward the best attainable outcome for Colombia in the future.

Useful policy steps may be classified by their direct objectives as follows:

1. To discourage land accumulation for speculative purposes, like a land tax;
2. To recover land illegitimately obtained either from others with a better right to it or from the state—Colombia is in the unusual position of having a great amount of land in this category.
3. To protect the rights and potential of existing small farms. Here a major concern is that a formal structure of property rights, when instituted in a setting dominated by asymmetrical power, information and access to legal assistance and bureaucratic support may further exacerbate the injustices

and unfairness which it might be expected to help to counteract. Property rights must be designed to effectively protect the family farm against the incursion from other types of agriculture, but doing so will require more than formality and legal registration.

4. To improve the productivity and income generated in relatively small family farms; this calls for a rapid ramping up of S&T spending, and of the systems for diffusion of technology. The most obvious practical need here is to rebuild the lost capacity of the public sector to provide public goods for the family farm sector and to further enhance it. In the early stages of this rebuilding process it will be important to take full advantage of nongovernmental capacity, including NGOs which have often proven effective at transmitting new technologies, and those private companies that have developed expertise in the socially desirable aspects of agricultural technology.
5. To encourage the transfer of land from legitimate large producing units to smaller ones, such as progressive land taxes and market-based land reform.[38]
6. To encourage association and collective action by small farmers, possibly in pursuit of land rights, possibly to assist in government decision making on public investment in the sector (a la ANUC);
7. To take advantage of potential contributions that larger farms may make through their interface with small family farms. This area may provide the toughest challenges, since some of the natural behavior patterns of large farms are likely to bring net social loss, either through squeezing the land area available to small farms, reducing their own labor inputs, or competing too successfully for public sector resources. An important question is how to use in a socially productive manner the entrepreneurial skills currently found in large-scale commercial agriculture. Innovative projects to do this must be clearly designed to avoid ultimate takeover by large units.

NOTES

1. See, for example, Jaime Forero Álvarez, Ricardo Gómez Mora, Luís Jorge Garay Salamanca, Fernando Barberi Gómez and Clara Ramírez Gómez "La eficiencia económica de los grandes, medianos y pequeños productores agrícolas colombianos" draft (2013).
2. For an encyclopedic recent review, see Michael Lipton *Land Reform in Developing Countries; Property Rights and Property Wrongs* (London: Routledge, 2009).
3. Alejandro Reyes, *Guerreros y campesinos: El despojo de la tierra en Colombia* (Bogotá: FESCL, Grupo Editorial Norma, 2008).

4. For a detailed discussion of Colombia's "second government" see Edgar Reveiz *El Estado Lego y la Fractura Social* (Bogota: Academia Colombiana de Ciencias Económicas, y Centro Colombiano de Responsabilidad Empresarial (CCRE), 2007).

5. Programa de las Naciones Unidas para el Desarrollo *Informe Nacional de Desarrollo Colombia* (Bogotá: PNUD, 2011), 341.

6. Instituto Geográfico Agustín Codazzi (IGAC) and Centro de Estudios Sobre el Desarrollo (CEDE), Universidad de Los Andes, *Atlas de la Distribución de la Propiedad Rural en Colombia.* (Bogota: Instituto Geográfico Agustín Codazzi, 2012).

7. María Angélica Arbelaez, Juan José Echavarría and Alejandro Gaviria, "Colombian long run growth and the crisis of the 1990s" A report submitted to the Global Development Network/Interamerican Development Bank project, 2002.

8. As of 1960, there was a strongly negative relationship between farm size and land productivity, with estimates based on national figures for total value of output by farm size suggesting that such productivity was about 60–100 percent greater on units of under five hectares than on those with over fifty hectares (Albert Berry, "Farm Size Distribution, Income Distribution and the Efficiency of Agricultural Production: Colombia," *American Economic Review*, Vol. 62, 1972, 406). Recent studies suggest that such a relationship probably still exists, albeit less marked than before; see Jaime Forero Álvarez, Ricardo Gómez Mora, Luís Jorge Garay Salamanca, Fernando Barberi Gómez and Clara Ramírez Gómez "La eficiencia económica de los grandes, medianos y pequeños productores agrícolas colombianos."

9. IGAC-CEDE, 71.

10. Programa de las Naciones Unidas para el Desarrollo *Informe Nacional de Desarrollo Colombia,* 197.

11. This section draws on Albert Berry "Has Colombia Finally Found an Agrarian Reform that Works?" in James K. Boyce, Stephen Cullenberg, Prasanta K. Pattanaik and Robert Pollin (editors) *Human Development in the Era of Globalization: Essays in Honor of Keith B. Griffin* (Cheltenham, U.K. and Northhampton, MA, USA: Edward Elgar, 2006).

12. See Albert O. Hirschman "Land Use and Land Reform in Colombia" in his *Journeys Towards Progress* (New York: Twentieth Century Fund, 1963)

13. Frank Safford "Agrarian Systems and the State: The Case of Colombia" in Evelyne Huber and Frank Safford (editors) *Agrarian Structure and Political Power: Landlord and Peasant in the Making of the State* (Pittsburgh and London: University of Pittsburgh Press, 1995), 141.

14. Alain de Janvry and Elisabeth Sadoulet, "Path-Dependent Policy Reforms: From Land Reform to Rural Development in Colombia,' in Karla Hoff, Avishay Braverman and Joseph E. Stiglitz *The Economics of Rural Organization: Theory, Practice and Policy* (New York: Oxford University Press, 1993).

15. Darío Fajardo M., *Haciendas, Campesinos y Politicas Agrarias en Colombia, 1920–1980* (Bogotá: Universidad Nacional de Colombia, Centro de Investigaciones Para el Desarrollo, 1986), 93.

16. See, for example, Santiago Perry, *La Crisis Agraria en Colombia: 1950–1980* (Bogotá: El Ancora Editores. Segunda Edición, 1985).

17. Darío Fajardo M., *Haciendas, Campesinos y Politicas Agrarias en Colombia, 1920–1980*, 111.

18. Bruce Michael Bagley, "Political Power, Public Policy and the State in Colombia: Case Studies of the Urban and Agrarian Reforms During the National Front, 1958–1974." Unpublished Ph.D. Thesis, Department of Political Science, University of California at Los Angeles, 1979.

19. Cristobal Kay, "Rural poverty and development strategies in Latin America" *Journal of Agrarian Change*, Vol. 6, No. 4. 2006.

20. Carlos Felipe Jaramillo, *Liberalization, Crisis and Change in Colombian Agriculture* (Boulder, Colorado: Westview Press, 1998), 93.

21. Jackeline Barragán and Ricardo Vargas, "Economía y violencia del narcotráfico en Colombia: 1981–1991," in Fernán González et al (editors) *Violencia en la región Andina. El Caso Colombia* (Bogota: CINEP-APEP, second edition, 1994).

22. For a list, see Antonio Flavio Dias Avila, Luis Romano and Fernando Garagorry, "Agricultural Productivity in Latin America and the Caribbean and Sources of Growth," in Prabhu Pingali and Robert Evenson (editors) *Handbook of Agricultural Economics, Volume 4*, 2010).

23. Robert E. Evenson, "The Green Revolution" in Amitava Krishna Dutt and Jaime Ros (editors) *International Handbook of Development Economics, Volume 1.* (Cheltenham, UK and Northampton, US: Edward Elgar, 2008).

24. Albert Berry "Agriculture, Rural Development and the 20th century Attempts at Land Reform in Colombia: Prelude to the 21st Century." Unpublished manuscript.

25. See Antonio Flavio Dias Avila, Luis Romano and Fernando Garagorry, "Agricultural Productivity in Latin America and the Caribbean and Sources of Growth," 3738.

26. Tovar, Jorge and Eduardo Uribe "Reflexiones sobre el crecimiento de largo plazo del sector agrícola en Colombia." Bogota; Universidad de los Andes, Documentos CEDE, ISSN 1657–5334, 2008.

27. Gómez, Hernando José et al "La Política Comercial del Sector Agrícola en Colombia" (Bogotá: Fedesarrollo, *Cuadernos Fedesarrollo* 38, 2011).

28. For a more detailed discussion, see Albert Berry "Has Colombia Finally Found an Agrarian Reform that Works?"

29. Forero Álvarez, Jaime, with Juan Andrés Galarza, Luz Elba Torres and José Luis Forero "La Economía Campesina Colombiana 1990–2001." *Cuadernos Tierra y Justicia*, No.2, 2002, 23.

30. Luis Jorge Garay Salamanca, Fernando Barberi Gomez, and Ivan Cardona Laninez "Impact of the US-Colombia FTA on the Small Farm Economy in Colombia" (Bogota, 2009), 21–22.

31. Forero Álvarez, Jaime, with Juan Andrés Galarza, Luz Elba Torres and José Luis Forero "La Economía Campesina Colombiana 1990–2001," 27–29.

32. This section draws heavily on PNUD,

33. Juan José Perfetti and Mauricio Olivera (2010) "La política agropecuaria y el desarrollo del sector." Documento de trabajo elaborado para el INDH, (Bogotá, 2010).

34. PNUD, 315.
35. Ibid, 317.
36. Ibid, 321–322.
37. Ana María Ibáñez and Carlos Eduardo Vélez "Civil Conflict and Forced Migration: The Micro Determinants and Welfare Losses of Displacement in Colombia," *World Development* Vol. 36, No.4, 2008.
38. Lipton, Michael ("Market, redistributive and proto-reform: can liberalizatin help the poor?" *Asian Development Review*, Vol. 13, 1995) makes the case that new style market-based reform has potential, probably when combined with old-style ceilings. Threats of expropriation can be complementary with the market approach by making largeholders more willing to sell part of their land.

Section Two

COLOMBIAN POLITICS AND INSTITUTIONS

Chapter Three

Corruption in Colombia[1]

Fernando Cepeda Ulloa

Colombia has been undergoing dramatic transformations for decades. Until the 1970s, Colombia was considered an honest country with small cases of petty corruption. However, the panorama drastically worsened overtime. Larceny, for instance, occurred in official financial institutions (1980–1992) such as the Central Mortgage Bank or *Banco Central Hipotecario*, the State Bank or *Banco del Estado* and the Agrarian Bank or *Caja Agraria*. The privatization of Colpuertos (the main Port Authority in 1991) led to the creation (1992) of a special Fund (*Foncolpuertos*) for the payment of pensions. The historical records were falsified in order to inflate enormously the value of many individual pensions. It was a multibillion peso corruption scandal. Many lawyers and former workers have been sentenced. In addition, the illicit drugs[2] phenomenon corrupted many public and private institutions and have become an important source of financing for illegal armed groups.[3]

The above-mentioned factors fomented the emergence of criminal networks, particularly political mafia organizations that, through the use of violence, have been able to infiltrate elements of the Colombian state within its various municipalities and states, producing perverse effects at the national, municipal, and regional level. This explanation, however, contrasts with the opinion offered by Professor Robert Dix on his classic book, which features a debate between Malcolm Deas of Oxford University. Deas states:

> For many years, Colombia has been a country with strong political competition, a poor government and a formidable severe criticism of it. This pattern did not allow exaggerated "serruchos"—popular Spanish expression to refer to briberies—. The small proportion of rich Colombians made visible any economic ascent. Politicians controlled themselves not because of virtue but due to political

> hate or jealousy. Presidents and politicians did not become rich during or after being in power nor bureaucrats.[4]

He continues:

"In the last three decades, this panorama has changed (. . .). New temptations and opportunities have appeared in the environment (. . .). I think this is a more corrupt country than before."[5]

COLOMBIA'S INCREASING WEALTH

Colombia has experienced high economic growth and a rising middle class, dramatically altering expectations. A newly developed ambition to get rich easily and suddenly has also arisen as a result. Colombia has been affected by the booms of an illegal economy in which contraband, illegal transaction of emeralds, money laundering, and so forth, creates conditions which stimulate corrupt behaviors and practices.

CRISIS OF THE TRADITIONAL VALUE SYSTEM

Colombia has been characterized by its austerity and the high value its citizens give to honesty, but this panorama has transformed these identifying qualities radically. It has been argued that the diminished influence of the Roman Catholic Church in the school system has eroded the traditional values in Colombian society. In addition, the mass media in Colombia has made certain criminals who obtained their wealth through various illegal activities into celebrities, which, in turn, has contributed to the model of corruption in Colombia. Some of these celebrity criminals have become cultural icons, while noncriminal Colombians remain unnoticed. In sum, the glorification of the ostentatious criminal lifestyle contributes to the culture of crime and corruption.

THE DIVISION AND WEAKENING OF POLITICAL PARTIES

Colombia has had a two party system for over two centuries. Despite its factionalism, one could argue that this strong system defends a value system against corruption. The necessary alliance between the two political parties (liberal and conservative) to end intraparty violence led to a constitutional system of shared power that existed for sixteen years (1958–1974). This agreement was later extended until 1991 (with one interruption from

1986–1990 when the government-opposition model was introduced). Intraparty violent conflict successfully ended in the national, state, and municipal (executive, legislative, and judiciary) levels.[6]

This scheme, however, was easily corruptible, as demonstrated by various scandals in the 1970s. The Constitution of 1991 that replaced the 1886 Constitution fostered a multiparty system that had over sixty political parties and created political chaos. However, recent electoral reforms which occurred in 2003 have reduced the number of parties to ten. In reality, four parties have a significant representation: the Party of Social Unity or *Partido Social de la Unidad Nacional*, the Liberal Party, and the Conservative Party, and the leftist party, *Polo Democrático Alternativo*. Party fragmentation has caused Colombia to experience what Italians refer to as "personal parties," which are prone to corrupt political exchanges due to campaign finance regulations. Furthermore, the various organized criminal networks have been able to penetrate the state apparatus. The profits from illegal drugs and other illicit activities have eroded institutions and fomented corruption within Colombia.

To some extent, political parties were substituted by "personal parties" that quickly became electoral small businesses. These parties raise funds for their political campaigns, and afterward, reward donors with jobs, contracts and favors. In some cases, political parties even began buying votes outright. These corrupt activities contributed to the deterioration of the electoral and political decision-making process within democratic Colombia. The corruption scandal in the capital city known as "the contracting carrousel of Bogotá" (*carrusel de la contratación en Bogotá*), began with dubious agreements during the electoral campaign that translated into profitable contracts. Journalists have been investigating the case for more than two years. Civil servants, contractors, and even the mayor of Bogotá are being prosecuted; some of them have been incarcerated.

Nonetheless, we have the appearance of a city with an organized and vigilant civil society, a robust network of mass media and numerous enterprises interested in obtaining contracts with the city government. If a larceny of such dimensions occurred in a city like Bogotá, it is easy to imagine what can happen in other cities or even in small and remote municipalities in Colombia that are rich in resources.

Prior to the corruption scandal, Bogotá had been governed by honest mayors and praised as a model of progress and effective management. However, it is surprising that such things happen when the mayor and the civil servants involved belonged to the left wing party *Polo Democrático Alternativo*. The absence of strong, organized, and centralized parties with efficient mechanisms of internal ethical control has contributed to corruption. The various forms of corruption in capital cities as well as lesser municipalities resemble the behavior of organized criminals.

INEFFICACY OF THE JUDICIAL POWER

Colombia has experienced the paradox of having a state governed by the rule of law (high courts, tribunals, proliferation of law schools of varying degrees of quality, an exaggerated attachment to "legal fetishism,") with simultaneous long periods of violence and, situations of impunity and illegality. Madeleine Albright, as United States Secretary of State, wrote an article titled "Colombia's struggles How we can help?"[7] Secretary Albright described Colombia's judicial system in the following terms: "(. . .) *and Colombia's judicial system is plagued by corruption, inadequate resources and a backlog of 3.5 million cases. Success will not come quickly but progress is possible if the Government has international support.*" Despite its harsh tone, Albright's statement was not debated in Colombia. Other criticisms of corruption were made by the Colombian president Alfonso López Michelsen (1974–78). Professor Gutiérrez Anzola, a reputed professor of criminal law, wrote in 1962 in his book *Violence and Justice* that Colombia had 15 million inhabitants. From this, he[8] establishes that the number of judges did not correspond to the number of cases resulting from such a population. This had ended in an accumulation of cases that the judicial system was unable to solve. Based on a report of the Criminal Procurator of the special District of Bogotá, Professor Gutiérrez quoted the following conclusion: ". . . the Special District of Bogotá was under the tyranny of impunity. . . . Only a small number of processes ended in a resolution or sentence of condemnation (3.89 percent). The rest, approximately 90.67 percent of the complaints exceeded the statute of limitations.[9] Gutiérrez Anzola states: "The judge that is able to affirm that his office is capable of dealing with 3.000 records is incompetent and cannot be considered serious."[10] The report quoted by Gutiérrez, issued by the Ministry of Justice and titled "Five years of apparent criminality," asserts: "We are in the brink of a catastrophic national collapse (. . .) It is a crazy race that leads to a total demoralization. In Antioquia, in 1959, there was a crime occurrence of 58.4% more than in 1955; in Cundinamarca, 57.1%; in Norte de Santander, 49.3%; in Caldas, 45.8%."[11] The same report identified two critical problems that, for our analysis, are useful to remember:

1. The refusal of society and the ruling class to deal with the problem. As stated by the Ministry of Justice, "a society that is responsible for the emergence of crimes, as the Colombian one, has a ruling class that is

deaf to the claims of the judicial system and that does not demand more resources for combatting crime."[12]

2. The absence of a criminal policy or examples of an erroneous criminal policy.[13]
3. Professor Gutiérrez adds: "For many years, an absurd criminal policy has been established in the country via laws and decrees. There is a general ignorance of the problem."[14] This diagnosis does not differ from the opinion of Justice Secretaries, high civil servants and professors. It is alarming the lack of statistics that makes the construction of a public policy for justice administration even more difficult. Below is a summary of a report written by two researchers of the Center for the Study of Economic Development of Los Andes University, which openly differ from the statistics that have been published for decades.[15]

The authors of this study do not have any reserve in concluding: "Until today, we cannot measure criminal impunity because there is not an official record of the real entries or crimes that reach the criminal system. It is because of that, figures like the one of 99% impunity is only a dangerous myth. We do not know, with certainty, the true figures of crimes, complaints or entries to the criminal system."[16] The researchers argued, "One of the most important questions that we can ask ourselves after the analysis is if the mediocrity and lack of criminal statistics is the result of a general disorder (incompetence-inefficiency) or if a judicial sector has been decidedly obstructing data recollection . . ." The absence of a reliable system of judicial statistics, historical and current, compounds the problem.[17]

The inefficacy of this judicial system invites corruption. In addition, the 99 percent rate of impunity only exaggerates the problems of the Colombian judicial system and helps foster corruption. We must, however, also recognize the significant efforts some members of Congress, governors, mayors, judges of the Supreme Court of Justice, the Attorney General, and municipal Judges have made to overcome this situation with courage and diligence.

THE IMPACT OF THE ILLICIT DRUG TRADE

In his August 2, 2000, visit, President Clinton stated that the illicit drug trade phenomenon had exacerbated all the problems of the country, which obviously includes issues of corruption. The combination of the above-mentioned factor continues to foster corruption within the state apparatus and, in essence, the illegal armed groups can only be compared with organized crime. Guerrillas, self-defense forces (often referred to as paramilitary groups) and

Table 3.1. Studies of Impunity in Colombia

Methodology	%	*Source*
1. Unreported crimes: 720.000 crimes reported—3.5 million criminal cases occurred	74%	DANE, household survey 1955
2. Impunity rate based on unreported crimes:		
Case evaluation / reports of personal injury	94.8%	Giraldo, Reyes, Avevedo, 1987
Citations to appear before the court / reported crimes	91.7%	
Sentences / reported crimes	98.6%	
Number of trials / (reported, settled, dismissed cases)	90.5%	Commission of Rationalization for Public Finances and Spending (Comisión de Racionalización del Gasto y las Finanzas Públicas), 1997
Number of sentences / (reported, dismissed cases)	99.9%	
		Armando Montenegro, "Justicia y desarrollo económico," 1994
The probability of a criminal to be sentenced:	97%	
3. Judgment based on the case summary:		Social indicators in *Coyuntura social*, No. 1, 1989
1987: Judgments of cessation of the procedure (60% due to a lapse of legal time) and closure of the case:	80%	
4. Impunity rate associated with the Attorney General's office:		
—cases that exceed the normative time period / total open cases (682,983)	55.4%	FGN management report 1997
—cases at the preliminary investigation stage	41.2%	2001 (2001), based on the study by Cider
—cases at the preparation stage	14.2%	

Methodology	%	*Source*
5. Probabilistic model to quantify, impunity applied to Bogotá (3.192 households surveyed and 34 government attorney's offices)		
—Probability of non-reporting a crime by an affected household (1.030 affected households)	63.7%	The Higher Council of the Judiciary, "Modelo Probabilístico para cuantificar la impunidad" via Matematics and Statistics Department, January 2000
—Procedural impunity at the preliminary investigation stage	12.1%	
Prob. Expired Criminal proceeding + prob. criminal proceeding suspended for not identifying the responsible, circuit and municipal court jurisdiction	41.7%	
Prob. Criminal proceeding finished based on limitation of criminal liability + prob. criminal proceeding finished based on expiration of terms, circuit and municipal court jurisdiction	1.1%	
6. According to termination of criminal proceeding		
—preliminary investigation: percentage of suspended and reallocated cases within the totality of terminations of cases	39.3%	As of 2000, Excellence in Justice Corporation, "Informe de coyuntura de la justicia," labor de la Fiscalía General de la Nación," June 2001
—preparation: change of jurisdiction within and outside of the Attorney General's office, termination based on death, challenges, impediments and partial closure		
7. Attorney General's office indicators		
—Exact impunity rate = (crimes reported—significant judicial decisions) / crimes reported	32%	Attorney General's office performance indicators 2000-2003, Fiscalía General de la Nación, December 30, 2003

Source: This table was created by Elvira María Restrepo. See Elvira María Restrepo, "La Justicia como instrumento de Paz," *Debates de Coyuntura Social Fedesarrollo,* No. 15, June 2003; see aslo Elvira María Restrepo and Mariana Martínez Cuellar, "Impunidad penal: mitos y realidades, CEDE, Junio de 2004; ISSN 1657–7191. Data from Colombian Attorney General's office.

now criminal groups such as the BACRIM gathered strength and presence in different regions and municipalities of the country.[18] As a result of this, these organizations could determine, in some cases, the electoral results through various means of coercion. They developed the capability to appoint members of these groups to key government position, in various agencies, such as the departments of health, education, and infrastructure. In this vein, these groups were able to capture large amounts of public resources.

The aforementioned organized crime groups evolved into criminal networks that had links with various national institutions like the Colombian Congress. This was evident during the demobilization of the "paramilitaries" and the confessions of some of the chiefs of these organizations as well as the information found in their computers.[19]

UNCHECKED DECENTRALIZATION

The Constitution of 1991 established an ambitious decentralization scheme both in political terms as well as in administrative and budgetary ones. Mayors since 1988 and governors since 1991 started to assume office via universal suffrage. In addition, more than 50 percent of the total budget is sent to departments and municipalities. Furthermore, the royalties paid by the gas and mining industry (carbon, gold, nickel, and coltan) were directly paid to some municipalities and departments.

In a context of judicial inefficacy, illegal armed groups (guerrilla and "paramilitaries"), personal political parties, wasted taxes and royalties at the national and municipal level. This situation encouraged the government to submit to Congress a proposal to modify the distribution of royalties. The Legislative Act 5 of 2011, constituted a Unique System of Royalties and modified articles 360 and 261 of the Colombian Constitution. This reform recentralizes the management of royalties to avoid corruption and mismanagement.

As of 2013, the political discourse of "recentralization" has begun to appear again. The Legislative Act 5 of 2011, however, was the only way to temporally control the resources and combat corruption. Decentralization has been seen as an anticorruption tool, however, the sociopolitical and judicial context in Colombia and the absence of efficient checks have made it a somewhat perverse strategy.

In the regions, municipalities, and cities, instances of corruption have evolved as a result of organized crime or criminal networks.[20] More than 100 congressmen have been investigated by the Supreme Court,[21] or the General Prosecutor Office. Fifty members of Congress (Senators and Representatives) have been convicted, demonstrating the power of organized criminal groups and various actors to penetrate the Colombian system, eroding the institutional capacity and integrity of various state apparatuses. As of today the International Criminal Court produced the following incomplete list of the proceedings against congressmen:[22]

Table 3.2. Proceeding Against Congressman in Parapolitics Cases

The following congressmen have been convicted by the Supreme Court of Justice for the crime of promoting illegal armed groups pursuant to an agreement (*concierto para delinquir agravado para promover grupos armados ilegales*):

Name	*Conviction*	*Sentence*
Congressmen convicted for promoting Salvatore Mancuso and other paramilitary leaders (*Estado Mayor*)		
Juan Manuel López Cabrales	Convicted in November 2008 for promoting illegal armed groups pursuant to an agreement (*Pacto Santa Fe de Ralito*).	74 months of imprisonment
Jose Maria Imbeth Bermudez	Convicted in January 2012 for promoting illegal armed groups pursuant to the agreement (*Pacto Santa Fe de Ralito*).	90 months of imprisonment
Luis Feris Chadid	Convicted in January 2012 for promoting illegal armed groups pursuant to the agreement (*Pacto Santa Fe de Ralito*).	90 months of imprisonment
William Alfonso Montes Medina	Convicted in January 2012 for promoting illegal armed groups pursuant to the agreement (*Pacto Santa Fe de Ralito*).	90 months of imprisonment
Miguel Alfonso De la Espriella Burgos	Convicted in February 2008 for promoting illegal armed groups pursuant to the agreement (*Pacto Santa Fe de Ralito*).	43 months and 15 days
Eleonora Pineda	Convicted for promoting illegal armed groups pursuant to the agreement (*Pacto Santa Fe de Ralito*).	45 months of imprisonment.
Congressmen convicted for promoting the Bloc *Norte* of the AUC		
Mauricio Pimiento Barrera	Convicted in May 2008 for promoting illegal armed groups pursuant to an agreement (*Acuerdo de Magdalena*) and electoral crimes.	7 years of imprisonment
Luis Eduardo Vives Lacouture	Convicted in August 2008 for promoting illegal armed groups pursuant to an agreement.	84 months of imprisonment
Karelly Patricia Lara Vence	Convicted in August 2009 for promoting illegal armed groups pursuant to an agreement (*Pacto de Chibolo*).	72 months of imprisonment

(continued)

Table 3.2. *Continued.*

Name	*Conviction*	*Sentence*
Alvaro Araujo Castro	Convicted in March 2010 for promoting illegal armed groups pursuant to an agreement and electoral crimes.	112 months of imprisonment
Jorge de Jesus Castro Pacheco	Convicted in May 2010 for promoting illegal armed groups pursuant to an agreement.	90 months of imprisonment
Hernando Cesar Molina Araujo	Convicted in May 2010 for promoting illegal armed groups pursuant to an agreement.	90 months of imprisonment
Miguel Pinedo Vidal	Convicted in February 2012 for promoting illegal armed groups pursuant to an agreement.	108 months of imprisonment
Muriel de Jesús Benito Rebollo	Convicted in February 2008 for promoting illegal armed groups pursuant to an agreement.	47 months of imprisonment
Jorge Luís Ramírez Urbina	Convicted in January 2009 for promoting illegal armed groups pursuant to an agreement.	36 months of imprisonment
Jorge Luís Caballero Caballero	Convicted in June 2012 for promoting illegal armed groups pursuant to an agreement.	5 years and 5 months of imprisonment
Congressmen convicted for promoting the Bloc *Héroes de los Montes de María*		
Jorge Eliecer Anaya Hernandez	Convicted in February 2010 for promoting illegal armed groups pursuant to an agreement and for murder committed on 19 November 1997.	480 months of imprisnment
Javier Caceres Leal	Convicted in April 2012 for promoting illegal armed groups pursuant to an agreement.	108 months of imprisonment
Jairo Merlano	Convicted in July 2011 for promoting illegal armed groups pursuant to an agreement and electoral crimes.	100 months of imprisonment
Jose Maria Conde Romero	Convicted in March 2011 for promoting illegal armed groups pursuant to an agreement.	60 months of imprisonment
Congressmen convicted for promoting the Bloc *Central Bolivar*		
Vicente Bled Saad	Convicted in January 2010 for promoting illegal armed groups pursuant to an agreement.	90 months of imprisonment
Miguel Angel Rangel Sossa	Convicted in September 2010 for promoting illegal armed groups pursuant to an agreement	90 months of imprisonment

Name	*Conviction*	*Sentence*
Ciro Ramirez Pinzon	Convicted in March 2011 for promoting illegal armed groups pursuant to an agreement.	90 months of imprisonment
Luis Alberto Gil	Convicted in January 2012 for promoting illegal armed groups pursuant to an agreement.	90 months of imprisonment
Alfonso Riaño Castillo	Convicted in January 2012 for promoting illegal armed groups pursuant to an agreement.	90 months of imprisonment
Oscar Josue Reyes	Convicted in January 2012 for promoting illegal armed groups pursuant to an agreement.	90 months of imprisonment
Carlos Arturo Clavijo Vargas	Convicted in September 2008 for promoting illegal armed groups pursuant to an agreement.	45 months of imprisonment
Congressmen convicted for promoting the Bloc *Central Bolivar* and Front *Cacique Pipinta*		
Enrique Emilio Ángel Barco	Convicted in August 2008 for promoting illegal armed groups pursuant to an agreement.	45 months of imprisonment
Congressmen convicted for promoting the Front *Cacique Pipinta*		
Dixon Ferney Tapasco Triviño	Convicted in February 2010 for promoting illegal armed groups pursuant to an agreement.	90 months of imprisonment
Congressmen convicted for promoting the Bloc *Central Bolivar* and Bloc *Mineros*		
Rocio Arias Hoyos	Convicted in July 2008 for promoting illegal armed groups pursuant to an agreement.	45 months of imprisonment
Congressmen convicted for promoting the Bloc *Elmer Cardenas*		
Odin Sanchez Montes de Oca	Convicted in July 2011 for promoting illegal armed groups pursuant to an agreement.	108 months of imprisonment
Edgar Eulises Torres Murillo	Convicted in July 2011 for promoting illegal armed groups pursuant to an agreement.	108 months of imprisonment
Mario Salomon Nader Muskus	Convicted in May 2012 for promoting illegal armed groups pursuant to an agreement.	90 months of imprisonment

(*continued*)

Table 3.2. *Continued.*

Name	*Conviction*	*Sentence*
Congressmen convicted for promoting the Bloc *Elmer Cardenas* and Bloc *Bananero*		
Humberto de Jesus Builes Correa	Convicted in August 2010 for promoting illegal armed groups pursuant to an agreement.	90 months of imprisonment
Ruben Dario Quintero Villada	Convicted in September 2010 for promoting illegal armed groups pursuant to an agreement.	90 months of imprisonment
Congressmen convicted for promoting the Bloc *Elmer Cardenas,* Bloc *Bananero* and Bloc *Arles Hurtado*		
Manuel Dario Ávila Peralta	Convicted in August 2011 for promoting illegal armed groups pursuant to an agreement.	55 months of imprisonment
Jesús Enrique Doval Urango	Convicted in August 2011 for promoting illegal armed groups pursuant to an agreement.	55 months of imprisonment
César Augusto Andrade Moreno	Convicted in August 2011 for promoting illegal armed groups pursuant to an agreement.	55 months of imprisonment
Congressmen convicted for promoting the Bloc *Tolima*		
Gonzalo Garcia Angarita	Convicted in December 2009 for promoting illegal armed groups pursuant to an agreement.	90 months of imprisonment
Luis Humberto Gomez Gallo	Convicted in May 2011 for promoting illegal armed groups pursuant to an agreement.	108 months of imprisonment
Congressmen convicted for promoting the Bloc *Resistencia Tayrona*		
Jose Domingo Davila Armenta	Convicted in February 2011 for promoting illegal armed groups pursuant to an agreement.	90 months of imprisonment
Enrique Rafael Caballero Aduen	Convicted in March 2011 for promoting illegal armed groups pursuant to an agreement.	67 months and 15 days of imprisonment
Congressmen convicted for promoting the Bloc *Catatumbo*		
Ricardo Ariel Elcure Chacon	Convicted in September 2009 for promoting illegal armed groups pursuant to an agreement.	72 months of imprisonment

Name	*Conviction*	*Sentence*
Congressmen convicted for promoting the Bloc *Calima*		
Juan Carlos Martinez Siniestra	Convicted for promoting illegal armed groups pursuant to an agreement.	90 months of imprisonment
Congressmen convicted for promoting the Bloc *Centauro*		
Edilberto Castro Rincon	Convicted in November 2007 for promoting illegal armed groups pursuant to an agreement and murder committed on 13 September 2004.	40 years of imprisonment
Ruben Dario Quintero Villada	Convicted in September 2010 for promoting illegal armed groups pursuant to an agreement.	90 months of imprisonment
Congressmen convicted for promoting the Bloc *Cordoba*		
Mario de Jesus Uribe Escobar	Convicted in February 2011 for promoting illegal armed groups pursuant to an agreement.	90 months of imprisonment
Congressmen convicted for promoting *Autodefensas Campesinas del Casanare*		
Oscar Leonidas Wilches Carreño	Convicted in April 2011 for promoting illegal armed groups pursuant to an agreement.	90 months of imprisonment
Congressmen convicted for promoting the Bloc *Heroes del Guaviare*		
Oscar de Jesús López Cadavid	Convicted in January 2011 for promoting illegal armed groups pursuant to an agreement.	90 months of imprisonment
Congressmen convicted for promoting the other armed groups		
Erik Julio Morris Taboada	Convicted in December 2007 for promoting illegal armed groups pursuant to an agreement with paramilitary groups operating in Sucre.	6 years of imprisonment
Reginaldo Enrique Montes Alvarez	Convicted in November 2008 for promoting illegal armed groups pursuant to an agreement with AUC.	72 months of imprisonment
Yidis Medina	Convicted in August 2012 for promoting illegal armed groups pursuant to an agreement with the ELN and kidnapping two men in 2000.	32 years of imprisonment

(*continued*)

Investigations of Congressmen for Crimes committed by Paramilitary Groups

The Supreme Court ordered investigations into the level of participation and responsibility of the following congressmen in the crimes committed by specific paramilitary groups, including crimes against humanity.

Name	*Investigation*
Jorge de Jesus Castro Pacheco	In May 2010, the Supreme Court ordered investigation into the level of participation in crimes attributed to the *Bloque Norte* of the AUC, including crimes against humanity after finding that he was effectively part of the same criminal hierarchy and organizational structure.
Dieb Nicolas Maloof	In May 2010, the Supreme Court ordered investigation into the level of participation in crimes attributed to the *Bloque Norte* of the AUC, including crimes against humanity
Jose Gamarra Sierra	In May 2010, the Supreme Court ordered investigation into the level of participation in crimes attributed to the *Bloque Norte* of the AUC, including crimes against humanity
Luis Eduardo Vives	In May 2010, the Supreme Court ordered investigation into the level of participation in crimes attributed to the *Bloque Norte* of the AUC, including crimes against humanity.
Alfonso Campo Escobar	In May 2010, the Supreme Court ordered investigation into the level of participation in crimes attributed to the *Bloque Norte* of the AUC, including crimes against humanity.
Salomón Saade Abdala	In May 2010, the Supreme Court ordered investigation into the level of participation in crimes attributed to the *Bloque Norte* of the AUC, including crimes against humanity.
Jorge Luis Caballero	In May 2010, the Supreme Court ordered investigation into the level of participation in crimes attributed to the *Bloque Norte* of the AUC, including crimes against humanity.
Mauricio Pimiento	In May 2010, the Supreme Court ordered investigation into the level of participation in crimes attributed to the *Bloque Norte* of the AUC, including crimes against humanity.
Álvaro Araújo Castro	In March 2010, the Supreme Court ordered investigation into the level of participation in crimes attributed to the *Bloque Norte* of the AUC, including crimes against humanity.
Jose Domingo Davila Armenta	In February 2011, the Supreme Court ordered investigation into the level of participation in crimes attributed to the *Bloque Norte* of the AUC, including crimes against humanity.
Gonzalo Angarita Garcia	In December 2009, the Supreme Court ordered investigation into the level of participation in a massacre known as "*Masacre del Neme*" committed in April 2001, attributed to the *Bloque Tolima* of the AUC.
Humberto de Jesus Builes Correa	In August 2010, the Supreme Court ordered investigation into the level of participation in crimes attributed to the *Bloque Elmer Cardenas, Bloque Bananero* and *Bloque Arles Hurtado*, including crimes against humanity.

1. Article 340 of the Colombian Penal Code.

Source: Information from International Criminal Courts

Overall, there has been an association to commit crimes between some congressmen and criminal organizations like the "paramilitaries." Judicial cases proved a relation with the illegal armed group FARC-EP (*Fuerzas Armadas Revolucionarias de Colombia—Ejército del Pueblo*) and ELN (*Ejército de Liberación Nacional*) have not been successful.

Luis Jorge Garay and Eduardo Salcedo-Albarán, well-known researchers in Colombia, investigated the social, political and economic influence of criminal networks in Colombia. They conclude:

> Social Network Analysis (SNA) and Social Network Analysis for Institutional Diagnosis (SNAID) allow us to understand and demonstrate the institutional impacts of the symbiosis between (i) political agents and public officers, (ii) unlawful armed groups and (iii) other criminal networks like those focused on drug trafficking. Furthermore, SNA and SNAID allow us to see how that symbiosis undermines processes of democracy consolidation and peace building. Both processes are affected when formal democratic institutions and even national administrations are at risk of being manipulated by the action of lawful and/or unlawful agents carrying out processes of Co-opted State Reconfiguration CStR.[23]

This analysis demonstrates that corruption has evolved. Garay illustrates such arguments using three cases and affirms, "There are serious situations in which political leaders, candidates and civil servants have taken advantage of the coercive capacity of criminal groups to perpetuate their political and electoral power."[24] When referring to illegal armed groups, he discusses the municipality of Soledad in Atlántico, a state in the Caribbean coast. "The interaction of some civil servants of the municipal executive branch with 'paramilitaries' or members of the AUC (*Autodefensas Unidas de Colombia*) was essential to manipulate administrative and contractual processes and favour (sic) the perverse interests of criminals."[25] Garay argues that Soledad, Atlántico is characterized by "serious faults in the provision of health and education services and important mistakes during contracting processes, among others."[26]

The authors examine the state of Arauca and the influence of the guerrilla armed group ELN and prove that there is a criminal network that started operating with the support and participation of civil society organizations in the 1980s. The guerrilla group was able to "decide over the administrative procedures, especially the contractual ones."[27] "In this sense, important resources of the national budget aimed to improve education, sanitation and infrastructure ended up in hands of contractors that were allied to the ELN and did not meet the requisites and qualifications for handling complex contracts."[28]

FINANCING POLITICS

Several factors have increased the costs of political campaigns in Colombia:

- The decay of political parties
- The emergence of "personal" parties
- With the Constitution of 1991, the enactment of a national electoral constituency meaning that senators need to campaign in various states or departments
- An increase in the cost of media and new modern electoral technology

State campaign financing is not enough to be elected.[29] The sheer cost of running for office leads to the temptation of making pacts with armed illegal groups, drug traffickers, organized criminal networks, investors, contractors, and various other criminal activities.

THE WEAKNESS OF THE OPPOSITION

Historically, Colombia has experienced party hegemonies and coalition governments. From 1958 on, the only exception has been the 1986–1990 government of President Virgilio Barco. Two-party coalitions were constitutionally ordered from 1958 until 1974. Since then, "adequate and fair participation" was constitutionally ordered. In 1986, the Conservative party decided not to participate in the Cabinet as it believed that the number of Secretaries (3 out of 13) granted by President Barco was insufficient. From 1991 onward, government coalitions have not been constitutionally enacted but have been necessary in order to obtain democratic governability.[30] The weakness of the Opposition (that today does not represent more than 10 percent of the total votes in Congress) facilitates corruption at the national level. State Assemblies and Municipal Councils lack attentive and watchful servants.

GOVERNMENT WEAKNESS AND TOOLS TO COMBAT CORRUPTION

Traditionally, Colombia has had weak governments. Even the dictatorship spanning from 1953 to 1957 was called a "*dictablanda*" or "weak dictatorship." President Álvaro Uribe (2002–2010) fortified the Armed Forces as well as the state apparatus. However, the efficiency of public institutions leaves a lot to be desired. Weak governments facilitate corruption.

Colombia, however, has valuable experience in fighting some aspects of corruption and can offer its experience to other countries. Its efforts have been significant, but not sufficient to deal with the enormous challenges it faces daily such as the power of the various criminal networks. Recently, the Attorney General announced a reorientation of the Colombian General Prosecutor Office's strategy to combat organized crime. Colombia has created several useful tools to fight corruption:

1. In 1991, Colombia ruled out parliamentary immunity. A special privilege administered by the Supreme Court of Justice appeared in its place. It is an exemplary measure as the Court has been quite efficient in prosecuting and condemning Congressmen.
2. The Colombian Constitution introduced the figure of *pérdida de investidura* (political death). It is a measure aimed to sanction elected Congressmen, Representatives, Councilmen and Councilors that violate the Conflict of Interest Statute or other legal norms. More than fifty congressmen and more than 150 elected Councilmen and Deputies have been sanctioned by the State Council[31] (*Consejo de Estado*).
3. Under the Decree 1895 of 1989, illicit enrichment was criminalized. High public servants and Congressmen were called to Court in the famous "8.000 process" that investigated the events surrounding the illegal funding of the 1994 presidential campaign.
4. The General Comptroller (article 168 of the Constitution) and the General Procurator of the nation (article 278 of the Constitution) have the power to dismiss public servants via a simplified procedure. The Procurator has used this tool more times than the Comptroller and has affected members of the National Congress, Ministers, Governors, and Mayors.
5. President Santos introduced a similar strategy to the one he used when he acted as Secretary of Defense during the Uribe administration. He identified high-level objectives that are monitored by elite groups (Comptroller, Procurator, Attorney General, National Intelligence service, etc.). Thanks to this strategy, the government was able to identify three critical cases: 1) Corruption within the National Tax Agency (fictitious exportations); 2) An investigation of one of the most prestigious health providers of the country, "Saludcoop," for fictitious payments, double payments, inflated invoices, etc.; 3) The existence of "phantom" students and schools. In all three cases, the government was able to act rapidly and dismantle criminal networks. The capture and initial prosecution of the chiefs and implied servants was showed almost immediately on television.

Colombia has been successful in applying conventional methods to combat "petty corruption." The efficacy of international treaties and conventions against corruption and the recommendations of multilateral organisms have been precarious. The same can be said of the Anti-Corruption Statutes or the Office of the Anti-corruption Czar. Recently, Colombia adhered to the OECD Convention on Combatting Bribery that is very well monitored and has had results in many countries. A March 2013 survey showed that 62 percent of investors and CEOs in Colombia consider that without the payment of bribes no contract or transaction is made. The average of bribe payments is of 14.8 percent of the contract value.[32] At the same time, scandals in the private sector complicate the corruption picture. INTERBOLSA, the main actor in the Colombian Bourse, is under investigation both by the pertinent agency and the Prosecutor Office.[33]

CONCLUSION

Colombia should be admired as its judges prefer death to bribes. We can say the same about most of the citizens that have maintained honesty and have rejected different forms of corruption. The illicit drugs criminal phenomenon that has stricken the country since the 1970s was instrumental to promote corrupt behaviors that ended up in criminal networks. This tendency weakened the state and Colombia´s law enforcement institutions.

The state and society have combatted corruption heroically. Presidential candidates, Congressmen, Supreme judges, judges, members of the Armed Forces, governors, mayors, ministers, members of political or business families, witnesses, and so forth, have been brutally killed or have suffered the effects of extortion and kidnapping. There is a portion of the population, nevertheless, that betrayed trust and honesty.

Colombia´s weak democracy was able to stand against the terrible menace of illegal drugs, corruption, and organized crime. The task, however, is incomplete as today, there are criminal and organized criminal networks that are more dangerous and powerful than the illegal groups of the past. The Supreme Court of Justice, the State Council, the Constitutional Court, the Prosecutor Office, the Procurator, and the Comptroller have made extraordinary achievements and their work is recognized as courageous and valuable. Of course, there have been notable exceptions. We should analyze the behavior of honest citizens. Despite many complex and difficult situations like the ones Colombia has suffered, honesty is more present than corruption, a fact that we cannot forget.

NOTES

1. Thanks to Nicolás Ávila for translating this work from Spanish to English.
2. For more on drug trafficking and violence in Colombia, see Jennifer S. Holmes, Sheila Amin Gutiéreez de Piñeres, and Kevin M. Curtin, *Guns, Drugs & Development in Colombia* (Austin, TX: University of Texas Press, 2008).

3. María Alejandra Velez, *FARC-ELN evolución y expansión territroial. Documente 2000–2008* (Bogotá: CECE, Universidad de los Andes, 2000); Pulido Villamarín and Luis Alberto, *El cartel de las FARC* (Bogotá: Ediciones El Faraón, 1996).
4. Malcolm Deas, Siete especulaciones sobre la corrupción en Colombia. *Política colombiana.* 1993: vol. 3, no. 3.
5. Ibid.
6. For more on the formation of modern Colombia, see David Bushnell, *The Making of Modern Colombia: A Nation in Spite of Itself* (Berkeley and Los Angeles: University of California Press, 1993); the more complete work on political parties is Felipe Botero, comp., Partidos y elecciones en Colombia (Bogotá, Ediciones Uniandes, 2010).
7. Madeline K. Albright, "Colombia's Struggles, and How We Can Help," *The New York Times*, August 10, 1999.
8. JE Gutiérrez Anzola,. *Violencia y Justicia* (Bogotá: Tercer Mundo, 1962), 12.
9. The data is based on the report written by the government official for criminal issues in Bogotá, Hugo Humberto Rodríguez in 1961.
10. Ibid, 105.
11. Ibid, 117.
12. Ibid, 117.
13. Ibid, 111, 117, and 119.
14. Idem, 121.
15. Elvira María Restrepo Mariana Martinez Cuéllar, *Impunidad penal: mitos y realidades* (Bogotá: CEDE Document 2004-24).
16. Ibid, 34
17. Ibid., 34–36.
18. For more on the BACRIM, see Bruce Bagley, *Drug Trafficking and Organized Crime in the Americas: Major Trends in the Twenty-First Century* (Washington, D.C.: Woodrow Wilson International Center for Scholars, 2012), 7–9. See also Bilal Y. Saab, Alexandra W. Taylor, Criminality and Armed Groups: A comparative study of FARC and Paramilitary Groups in Colombia. (Studies in conflict and Terrorism, 32:455–475, 2009. See also Mónica Serrano and María Celia Toro, "From Drug Trafficking to Transnational Organized Crime in Latin America," in Mats Berdal and Mónica Serrano, eds., Transnational Organized Crime and International Security (Boulder, Lynne Rienner Publishers, 2002). Mauricio Romero, "Changing identities and Contested Settings: Regionall Elites and Paramilitaries in Colombia," *International Journal of Politics*, Culture and Society 14(1) (2000).
19. L.J. Garay, and E. Salcedo *Redes ilícitas y reconfiguración del Estado: el caso Colombia.* (Bogotá: Fundación Vortex, 2012).
20. Ibid.
21. Corte Suprema de Justicia, Procesos contra aforados constitucionales (parapolítica). Compilación de Autos y Sentencias (Dic. 2007–Sept. 2010).
22. International Criminal Court. Situation in Colombia: Interim Report, Nov. 2012.
23. "Institutional impact of criminal networks in Colombia and Mexico," Luis Jorge Garay-Salamanca y Eduardo Salcedo-Albarán, Published online: 25 November 2011. # Springer Science+Business Media B.V. 2011.

24. L.J Garay, and E. Salcedo, *Redes ilícitas y reconfiguración del Estado: el caso Colombia* (Bogotá: Fundación Vortex, 2012), 14–15.

25. Ibid, 15.

26. Ibid, 15.

27. Ibid., 15.

28. Ibid, 17.

29. Fernadno Cepeda Ulloa, *Narcotráfico, financiación política y corrupción.* (Bogotá: ECOE, 2011).

30. Fernando Cepeda Ulloa, *La mesa de Unidad Nacional.* (Bogotá: ECOE, 2011).

31. Fernando Cepeda Ulloa *Pérdida de investidura 1991–2011: una herramienta eficaz contra la corrupción de los congresistas, diputados y concejales.* (Bogotá: ECOE, 2011).

32. Survey prepared by International Transparency and the Universidad Externado de Colombia, issued March 12, 2013.

33. Alberto Donadio. "El cartel de Interbolsa. Crónica de una estafa financiera." Editorial Sílaba, 2013.

Chapter Four

The Relationships Between the Executive and Legislative Branches of Power

During the First Term of Álvaro Uribe Velez (2002–2006)

Juan Pablo Milanese

This chapter describes the relationships between the executive and the legislative branches during the first term of Álvaro Uribe Velez (2002–2006), using two classic variables: presidential party power and constitutional power,[1] and tries to show how this relationship tends to be more complex than previously thought.

Before the 1990s, a number of seminal papers like those of Archer, Archer and Shugart, and Hartlyn[2] were published, and the links between the two branches were thoroughly analyzed. However, beyond these authors' work, there were many common unsubstantiated presumptions regarding the interactions between the two branches, as well as the relationship between the two branches, which tends to be much more complex than is usually presumed. Subsequently, however, academic research on the nature of this relationship declined significantly as scholars assumed uncompromising positions regarding the dominance of one branch of power over another.[3] The dissatisfaction with the existing literature has led researchers to search for alternative explanations closer to those proposed by the aforementioned authors.

It is important to clarify before proceeding that this work does not constitute an attempt to evaluate neither the quality of the Colombian democracy nor the quality of the overall political system. Instead, it will analyze the interactions between the various institutional powers during the entire first term of the Uribe administration. This work, however, does not extensively explore the changes that could have possibly occurred during this period.[4] The goal of this chapter is to provide a better understanding of the inter-institutional relationship and is organized into three sections. The first section reviews the legislation of each branch and analyzes their efficiency and effectiveness. The second section examines the presidency and the constitutional powers of the president. The third section discusses the notion of party powers, and analyzes whether the powers in question have provided the executive with a privileged position in the legislative process.

LEGISLATION EFFICIENCY, EFFECTIVENESS, AND VOLUME: AN INITIAL APPROACH TO THE INTER-INSTITUTIONAL RELATIONSHIP

When studying institutional relationships, it is important to conduct an empirical analysis of the conventional legislative production, focusing particularly on the law.[5] Let us begin by assessing the effectiveness of each of the branches of power involved in conducting and evaluating the *success rate*; the success rate represents the relationship between the number of bills passed, which is calculated according to the type of initiative (i.e., executive or legislative), followed by an examination of the total number of bills submitted by each branch. This will allow us to observe the capability of the branches of power to promote their own bills: the higher the rate, the higher the capacity to achieve such goals.

As Table 4.1 shows, during the first four years of the Uribe administration, there was a wide gap between the success rate of the executive and legislative powers, evidently in favor of the former. This means that the government was able to pass an extraordinarily higher proportion of bills when compared to the ones that were submitted by the legislators. As will be discussed in more detail below, this is rather a common situation that can be explained by the shortage of the number of instruments that congressmen have to discipline the other members of the Congress. As a result, lower expectations exist that bills drafted by a member of the Congress can be approved and become law.

In a scenario in which the costs of introduction and failure of the bills are extraordinarily low, the submission of a large number of bills may represent an important asset regardless of whether the bills are passed.[6] The direct result of this type of behavior of congressmen is the increase in legislative initiatives that overload the Congress's agenda. If the initiatives have a low success rate, then the initiatives of the legislative body as a whole can be considered as unsuccessful. On the contrary, if the government-initiated bills do not pass, this could represent a significant defeat.[7] Furthermore, the ability of the government—from an institutional perspective—to acquire great political resources will increase its capability of disciplining the legislators and will result in a scenario that is the opposite of that produced by the congressmen.

Table 4.1. Effectiveness and Efficiency of the Executive Branch in the Legislative Process

Kind of Initiative	*Passing Rate*	*Success Rate*	*μ days in the Congress (legislative transit)*
Executive	42.5%	66.0%	308
Legislative	54.0%	11.0%	477
Executive (without international treaties)	N/A	N/A	260
Total	96.5%*	N/A	407

Note: the sum is not equal to 100% since third party proposals are not included.

Source: Secretaría General Honorable Cámara de Representantes y Secretaría General del Senado de la República.

The above scenario demonstrates the extraordinary gap between the success rates of the executive and the legislative branches. For the aforementioned reasons, the key indicator that has been taken into consideration is of intrinsic fragility and tends to overestimate the weight of the government and underestimate the weight of the legislatures. This indicator also helps highlight the fact that the executive branch was notably more effective than the legislative branch as a promoter of its own bills.[8]

The notion of effectiveness of each of the branches can be calculated not only with the success rate but also taking into consideration the *passing rate*. Effectiveness, therefore, represents the correlation between passed bills, according to the initiative, over the total amount of bills, and shows the weight that each branch has over the legislative production. Here, in contrast to what happens with the success rate, the opposite trend can be observed. It is an important fact to be taken into consideration, because it implies a less reactive Congress than usually tends to be expected.

In other words, legislators during this period did not limit themselves to endorsing, amending or rejecting governmental bills. On the contrary, they played a key role in the legislative production. As a result, we can conclude that the information above implies presidential predominance and causes experts to question not only the perception of the irrelevance of the legislative branch, but also the passivity of the institution. In fact, the data reveals that its power was not strictly limited to exercising its veto power.[9]

As previously mentioned, the aforementioned information leads one to question the relevance of the legislative branch. However, it only partially impacts the predominance of the executive branch. Therefore, the impact of each power should not be assessed only in terms of legislative volume, but scholars must also examine the potential and effective reach of the institution. In this regard, a thorough observation of the bills that were passed according

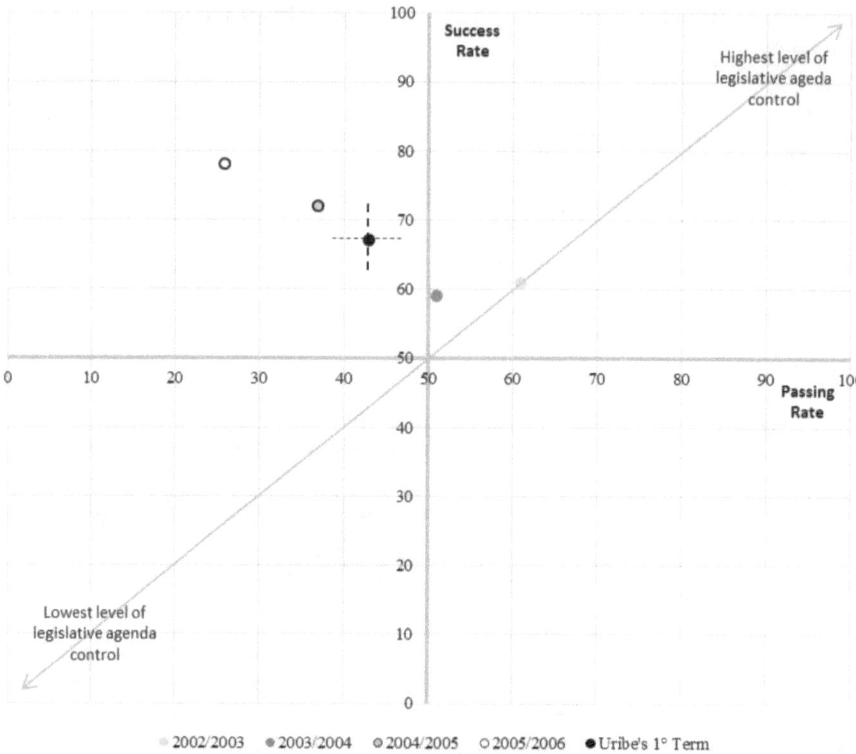

Figure 4.1. Level of Executive Branch Legislative Agenda Control (Uribe's first term)
Source: Juan Pablo Milanese, "Participación, éxito y prioridad. Un análisis macro de los equilibrios en las relaciones entre poderes ejecutivo y legislative en Colombia, 2002–2006," Revista CS en Ciencias Sociales no 8 (julio–diciembre 2011): 119.

to the type of initiative demonstrates the greater importance of those submitted by the government.

Table 4.2 indicates a clear specialization of the executive branch regarding the national coverage bills (excluding the international treaties). Yet in the case of the legislature, the distribution is more even. This trend is quite normal, considering that legislators represent sectorial and/or regional interests, while the executive branch has the government responsibility to exercise.

National bills are those that cover the entire national territory and are not directed toward a specific social group. In addition, these bills have resulted in a greater impact on the political processes as a consequence of their universal nature. On the contrary, bills of a particular nature that have a national geographic reach but are focused on a specific social group—or the regional ones—have an impact on a limited sub-national geographic space.

Before delving deeper, it is important to recognize that we do not deny the relevance of the regional and/or particular bills, but rather identify them as

Table 4.2. Kind of Bills Submitted during the Term and Eventually Sanctioned, According to the Initiative

	Kind of Initiative	
Kind of Bill	*Executive*	*Legislative*
National	71.6%	24.8%
Regional	0.0%	46.1%
Particular	28.4%	29.1%

Note: the sum is not equal to 100% since third party proposals are not included.

Source: Secretaría General Honorable Cámara de Representantes y Secretaría General del Senado de la República.

less important in terms of the national dimension of politics. As a matter of fact, their presence is a sign of how the separation of powers works; in addition, it is a sign of the function of the Congress and its desire to represent a diversity of interests. In this respect, dividing the work resulting from such agendas helps avoid delays and potential deadlock. However, returning to the original matter, it is important to mention that the proportion of national bills and legislative initiatives passed with respect to the total number of bills—bills of this nature—is actually quite significant.

Finally, it is important to analyze another key element, or indicator, which facilitates the observation of the stakeholders regarding the legislative agenda: the average time from the time of bill submission to the passage of the bills into law. This is an indicator that provides relevant information regarding the priority of particular bills, and it allows us to define a key element that highlights the predominance of the executive branch in this process.

As with any indicator discussed in this chapter, the efficiency indicator still has weaknesses if it is used in an isolated or de-contextualized way. It is nec-

Table 4.3. Share of Bills Submitted during the Term and Eventually Sanctioned, According to the Initiative

	Kind of Initiative	
Kind of Bill	*Executive*	*Legislative*
National	53.3%	45.3%
Regional	0.0%	100%
Particular	27.9%	70.6%

Note: the sum is not equal to 100% since third party proposals are not included.

Source: Secretaría General Honorable Cámara de Representantes y Secretaría General del Senado de la República.

essary to clarify this because, usually, the time periods of the governmental initiatives in the Congress tend to be shorter. This occurs due to the unequal priorities of the branches. Any behavior based on the electoral schedule is the priority for legislators (bills are an instrument of the elections for being shown to the voters in order to maximize the flow of the votes); this behavior also is based on the low expectations of the bills being passed. It is important to remember that the government's actions are contingent upon this decision-making process and the solving of critical junctures should be included without ignoring the influence of the election schedules.[10]

According to this framework and regardless of its limitations, the proposed indicator was considered a reliable measure to assess the efficiency of each branch in the legislative process. With this fact as a starting point, it is now time to analyze what kind of initiative has preference. We understand preference as a period of time shorter than the average time lapse of all the bills submitted from 2002–2006; it is important to note that these bills also eventually passed.

A general approximation allows us to state that executive initiative bills have a clear preference. Additionally, the trend becomes more well-defined if we split them into smaller sub-sets (except for the international treaties), focusing on those that normally represent the majority of the main political initiatives of the government. In short, if we observe the data contained in Table 4.3, we can highlight that the governmental as its bills receive priority treatment.

This prioritization occurs as a result of a constitutional instrument of the president, which enables him to use the message of urgency. This guarantees that the treatment of his bills in the legislative agenda takes precedence. In fact, approximately 40 percent of these bills, with the exception of matters pertaining to international treaties that reached this level, contained such messages. Nevertheless, this option does not guarantee that the bills will be passed, meaning that the sole presence of this attribute without reasonable party powers is not enough to guarantee efficiency.

Finally, it is also important to highlight that 71.2 percent of the executive initiative bills (again excluding the ratification of treaties) had to pass through a conciliation commission before being passed. However, this does not necessarily mean that the bills were subject to considerable modifications. Instead, it implies that there were discrepancies between the houses and, therefore, the majority in one of them did not agree with the original submission.

FIRST PARTIAL ASSESSMENT

A first assessment of the information presented so far enables analysts to identify a political system characterized—*de facto*—by asymmetrical decision-making processes that favor the executive branch. The executive branch has been more effective and efficient than the congressmen. Nonetheless, it can be interpreted as a form of limited centralism.[11] Thus, when we start to observe inequalities in the relationship, we also see horizontal relations. In fact, a higher approval rating of the legislative initiative bills proves that the legislature had a greater impact on the legislation. Therefore, the legislators did not ignore their own initiatives even when they prioritized governmental initiatives. In sum, the previous information reveals that the president is the main legislator within the political system, but that does not imply the presence of passive attitudes from the congressmen and, even less, the irrelevance of this body as a stakeholder.

THE PRESIDENT'S CONSTITUTIONAL POWERS AS AN INTERVENING VARIABLE

After analyzing the inter-institutional relationship, this section of the chapter examines the president's constitutional powers. The goal is to understand the powers as a tool of the executive branch that can be used to impact the relationship between both branches and improve his legislative performance. The president's constitutional powers could be seen as an indicator of tensions and conflicts, or of the agreements between both branches.[12]

DECREES AND THEIR IMPACT ON THE LEGISLATIVE PRODUCTION

The first of the constitutional powers is the legislative decree power. This mechanism is the executive branch's most powerful legislative instrument. It provides the president an evident proactive profile that enables the president to alter the *status quo* automatically, bestowing it a great strategic advantage in the inter-institutional relationship, which increases its predominance potential. However, the impact decreases as a consequence of the temporal restrictions suffered by the power of decree due to the requirement that a state of exception must be declared.[13]

After reviewing the data, we can state that the execution of the different types of decrees increased the production volume of the executive branch, reducing also the time of the legislative process. In fact, with its incorporation, governmental production increased by 35.8 percent, matching that of the congressmen. This fact reinforces the idea of a scenario defined by an executive branch advantage and helps demonstrate the role of delegating mechanisms.

In fact, in 52 percent of the cases, the type of decree that was used implied an explicit delegation—Article 150,—while in 39.6 percent of the cases, we assumed an implicit delegation because they were carried out under a state of exception and the Senate approved extensions (even though the extension was declared unenforceable by the Constitutional Court). Additionally, in the last case, the lack of reaction of the legislators should also be considered, as they could have surpassed the executive branch with a majority. This, in turn, helps contribute to the notion of presidential predominance, a situation that has only been moderately observed thus far.

THE PRESIDENTIAL CAPABILITY TO OBJECT BILLS AND ITS IMPACT ON THE LEGISLATIVE PROCESS

Now, we shall consider another indicator: the presidential objections, which despite the visible technical differences in their mechanics, we will understand as the functional equivalent to a veto. It can be observed that, in an overwhelming majority of the cases (almost 90 percent), this instrument was used against the bill initiative by legislators. This fact also exhibits the shortage of discrepancies linked to the bills submitted by the cabinet, which provides evidence of an important acceptance of the presidential directives from the pro-government congressmen. As a matter of fact, the existence of tensions between powers was much more intensively linked to bills submitted by congressmen, and the objections were fundamentally related to the financing of policies with regional or particular coverage.

Such tensions can be observed more clearly if the congressional overrides made to the objected bills are included in the analysis. It is important to note that if the veto is the result of a relative degree of autonomy of the legislators, the overrides represent the main formal mechanism to explicitly defy the president.[14] In addition, it is important to emphasize that the intensity of the defiance depends on the type of bill. To override an executive bill represents a greater defiance than if the insistence is focused on a legislative bill, especially if the latter is a bill with regional or particular coverage.

In the case that concerns us, almost 47 percent of the objected bills initiated by congressmen were subject to partial insistences, highlighting the fact that the actors defended their interests but were not defiant against the executive branch (only one in five vetoed executive bills was subject to override, representing only 5 percent of the total insistences). This fact drives us to state that the overrides did not represent or produce scenarios characterized by high intensity conflicts between both branches. That is, the acts of insistence did not have a traumatic effect on the inter-institutional relationship because the presidential leadership was not questioned.

Analysis of the aforementioned scenario concludes that the legislators did not make significant changes to the bills which the president submitted, and subsequently he did not use his veto power as a strategy to preserve such initiatives. Nevertheless, his lack of power from this viewpoint forced him to be tolerant of the preferences of the legislators. As a result, modifications were more easily accepted to the presidential initiatives. These tendencies can be observed in several of the executive initiatives.

In fact, the limited veto power acts as a mechanism to halt progress for the insistences. This could be to execute penalties related to their party powers, and according to the limitations observed with regard to these powers, the cost for the legislators for trying to overcome the presidential veto is relatively low. This situation caused the president to accept the fact that he would prioritize parts of each bill differently from others, necessarily forcing him to act as a negotiator and try to ensure that his bills did not stray away from his own priorities as a result of the political actions of the legislators.

The procedure of the veto system also impacted the situation. In order to become valid, the veto must be approved by a majority of both chambers, which gives the last word to the Congress, or else to the Constitutional Court, but never to the president (also, in the case the observations made by him to a bill that was passed by both chambers are not ratified or subject to insistence by the legislators, such observations will be filed away, maintaining the *status quo*, which is a situation that reduces the "correction" power of the head of the executive branch). Essentially, the president was often forced to make changes that would enable him to preserve the bills as a result of the aforementioned factors. Said differently, the veto—albeit a weak veto—acted as a shock absorber of the president's power and limited his capabilities.

THE PRESIDENT'S PARTY POWER AS AN INTERVENING VARIABLE

We understand party powers as the presidential capability to control a legislative contingent whether it is due to breadth of vision or discipline, and his ability to make decisions that he deems to be fundamental. Nonetheless, it is important to mention that this control does not necessarily imply subordinate behavior from the legislature. As a matter of fact, it normally can only be achieved through different types of interactions characterized by exchanges with varying difficulty levels or, in other words, the introduction of transactional components to the system. These components constitute the factor that provides temporal consistency to the government coalitions or majorities.[15]

As Mustpic points out, the presence of similar majorities is not enough, but rather, governments must continually work on the production and reproduction of discipline because both the number of legislators and the intensity with which they support the president are not static factors. In this regard, the heterogeneous nature of the legislative majorities, reinforced by the type of incentives the presidential systems produce regarding the parties,[16] facilitated the presence of limited discipline scenarios. These scenarios were also promoted by characteristics of the Colombian party system, such as its high level of fragmentation and low degree of structure.[17]

Uribe managed to establish a bipolar system—the *uribism/anti-uribism* logic—that led to positive legislative results described in the first part of the chapter.[18] Uribe was able to achieve such goals as a result of the political fragmentation from the 1991 constitutional reform to 2002. Such a period can best be characterized by a progressive decomposition of the traditional party system. In fact, the 2002 elections were significant because they highlighted the extraordinary degree of fragmentation that the political system experienced at both the inter-party and intra-party levels.[19]

This scenario resulted from the limited barriers to entry to electoral politics—or the "electoral game"—, generating what Carroll and Shugart called a *hyper-personalistic* system.[20] This system was defined by the fact that the party lists only represented a vehicle for the individual candidacy, favoring the clientelism-oriented strategies and not the representative ones.

As a result of the scenarios, some experts began to describe the Colombian political system as one of the most personalistic systems in the world. In other words, the Colombian system can best be characterized by a competition focused on the parties.[21] In summary, we can observe a system that

Table 4.4. Government's Legislative Support Coalition, 2002–2006

Faction	*House of Representatives*	*Senate*	
***Uribistas* (liberal provenance)**	36.14%	29.41%	
Partido Conservador	28.92%	29.41%	**Uribe's legislative support coalition**
***Uribistas* (independent provenance)**	0.00%	2.94%	
Partido Liberal	28.92%	19.61%	
Other parties	6.02%	18.63%	

Source: based on the data from Mauricio Cárdenas, Roberto Junguito and Mónica Pachón, "Political Institutions and Policy Outcomes in Colombia: The Effects of the 1991 Constitution," Banco Interamericano de Desarrollo, research network working paper # R-505, 2006.

favors the option of the search for personal reputation above a party reputation, encouraging the candidates to differentiate themselves from their peers of the same party.[22]

In this context, the 2002 elections were defined as a strong setback for the majority parties, demonstrating the breakdown of bipartisanship. Thus, the two traditional forces, which until 2002 managed to be indispensable electoral "brands" for any presidential candidate, started experiencing difficulties maintaining the presidency within a political system that—as a consequence of their negative image—perceived them as incapable of securing electoral-related agreements.[23]

This situation contributed to the decreasing incentives to discipline the Congress, due to the inability to punish the congressmen for such behavior. Beginning at the premise that the more personalistic the vote, the more individualistic the behaviors of the legislators,[24] one could argue that high levels of personalization led to the establishment of weak legislative parties, which tended to increase the transaction costs of modifying the *status quo*.

It would be expected that this situation would intensify, especially when we consider that despite President Uribe's liberal past, he was elected without being a member of any of the parties with significant legislative representation. In fact, he ran for president through the *Primero Colombia* movement, which was for the sole purpose of his candidacy and remained inactive until the 2006 elections. As a result, this situation led some observers to describe the government (most particularly the cabinet) as nonpartisan.[25]

Nonetheless, the president had consistent support from the legislators, that is, even with the difficulties explained above, he managed to establish discipline. This phenomenon occurred, to a large extent, due to the already mentioned polarization scenario that he produced himself, and through which he managed to organize a support base formed by dissident groups from the various parties who were able to achieve and ally themselves with the majorities in both Chambers of the Congress as demonstrated in Table 4. Thus, Uribe managed to achieve high governability levels despite fragmentation and weak party loyalties.

As a matter of fact, and as it was demonstrated by Rodríguez Raga and Botero,[26] the candidates with the highest potential for success in the 2006 legislative elections were congressmen who had endorsed the president. Uribe's support provided these congressmen with a considerable advantage as a consequence of the power generated by his popularity, which was supplemented with the rise in the public exposure level and the increasing state resource management. However, it implied the need to sustain the executive branch initiatives in the Congress as well; in other words, they had to behave in a reasonably disciplined way.

Moreover, under the previously described conditions, which are defined by a poorly structured party system, congressmen are considerably more vulnerable in terms of access to government resources. Therefore, in a low intensity scenario in which party loyalties serve as a vote-guarantor instrument, many political leaders resort to exchanges with the executive branch to obtain the necessary resources. In spite of this situation, it is important to highlight that a partial rearrangement of the party system began to occur from the 2003 political reform,[27] and other initiatives.[28] These initiatives resulted in the rearrangement of political party affiliations. In addition, the legislative act enabled the presidential reelection to be declared enforceable by the Constitutional Court.[29]

In this respect, the government managed to establish a convincing support basis from both the legislative and the electoral sectors. The government avoided traditional party labels, while still supporting Congress. In addition, there were processes that produced discipline and were related to the same internal operational regulations of the Congress. These processes were based on the capability of the authorities from the chambers and the commissions, which have more resources than the rest of the legislators, to obtain support and control the legislative agenda. In this vein, they established a hierarchical logic within the legislative branch that increased the discipline levels, although always according to a logic defined by the presence of a strong transactional component.

It is important to emphasize that the basis of the organization inside the Congress is not established in the party blocks, but through the commissions that are established as formal and informal structures of hierarchies under a reasonable level of structuring and internal institutionalization.[30] Thus, a structuring dynamic was established based on the selection by the congressional authorities (Directors Boards of the Chambers and Presidencies of the Commissions) and by the sponsors of executive initiative bills. These stakeholders, in accordance to the effectiveness of their work, received larger amounts of political resources as pork barrel, patronage, or other types of funds not necessarily characterized by a high degree of transparency.[31]

Therefore, the Commissions evolved into distribution agents in a process that began with the Directors Boards and ended with the bill sponsors, allowing the establishment of procedural coalitions that managed to simplify the path of the bills and only allowed few possibilities of amendments.[32] Such events enabled the establishment of a post-electoral re-centralization in which the government managed to overcome its great weakness from the viewpoint of the parties and form a coalition that at one time represented more than 60 percent of the support (although in an oscillating manner). This coalition was not only maintained over time, guaranteeing an important support over the entire term but was also essential for passing the legislative act that contributed to Uribe's reelection.

However, the use of this strategy had high transaction costs; the government had to constantly use selective incentives and compensation mechanisms that would maintain this support. The individualized negotiation mechanisms were a constant and significant strategy in terms of their intensity, but they increased the decision-making costs of distributing resources. In this regard, it is important to note that even if the presence of an oversized coalition reduces the risks of inaction, it concurrently reduces the costs of the penalties for the legislators that behave in such an undisciplined manner. And, even if they do not act in such a way, the congressmen who are aware of such situations use this information to support their positions during the transactional processes.

CONCLUSION

The inter-institutional relationships between the executive and legislative branches tend to be more complex than thought. Even during a critical circumstance, legislators never stopped playing a key role in the decision-making process. Thus, contrary to what many scholars have shown, the executive branch is far from being established as a hegemonic actor of the legislative process. Therefore, in spite of its superior position, the use of transactions with the legislators was always indispensable for the president. This situation highlights the notion of hierarchies in reciprocal interactions and the concept of inter-institutional relationships.

Furthermore, although we can observe the presence of a president that established himself as a strong legislator (thanks to the asymmetric impact that favored him in the decision-making processes and enabled him to achieve an important part of his agenda), the limitations experienced in everything related to the party powers, forced him to assume a more flexible posture with regard to his bills. But, especially, those limitations forced him to agree to a constant and complex mechanism of selective particularistic transaction and incentive application.

At the same time, it is important to emphasize that this situation should not be confused with an interest-clash scenario among the studied stakeholders. On the contrary, we make reference to a scenario defined by arrangements that, even if they are not exempt from conflicts, are inevitably linked to the differentiated agendas of every power with regard to its preferences, urgencies, and priorities.

NOTES

1. See Matthew Soberg Shugart and Scott Mainwaring, "Presidentialism and Democracy in Latin America: Rethinking the Terms of the Debate," in *Presidentialism and Democracy in Latin America*, eds. Scott Mainwaring and Matthew Soberg Shugart (New York: Cambridge University Press, 1997).

2. Ronald Archer, "Fuerza y debilidad partidaria en la asediada democracia colombiana," in *La Construcción de Instituciones Democráticas*, eds. Scott Mainwaring and Timoyhy Scully (Santiago, CIEPLAN, 1997). Ronald Archer and Matthew Shugart, "The Urealized Potential of Presidential Dominance in Colombia" (New York: Cambridge University Press, 1997). Jonathan Hartlyn, "El Presidencialismo y la Política Colombiana," in *La Crisis del Presidencialismo*, eds. Juan Linz and Arturo Valenzuela (Madrid, Alianza Editorial, Vol. 2. 1998).

3. I.E., Medellín perceives the existence of a "besieged president" by the legislators. On the contrary, Vargas argues that the Colombian political regime is moving toward an "imperial presidency" characterized by a weak legislative branch. More balanced positions can be found in Pachón (2003; 2004), Cárdenas, Junguito y Pachón (2006) or Milanese (2011). Alejo Vargas, "Paz y nación en la perspectiva histórica colombiana," *Convergencia*, no. 30 (Septiembre–Diciembre 2002): 209–239. Mónica Pachón, "Congreso y partidos políticos en Colombia: una mirada a las instituciones," in *Fortalezas de Colombia*, ed. Fernando Cepeda (Washington: Banco Interamericano de Desarrollo, Ariel, 2004). Mónica Pachón, "Explaining the Performance of the Colombian Congress: Electoral and Legislature Rules, and Interactions with the Executive," presented at the *Asociación de Estudios Latinoamericanos* conference, Dallas, March 27–29, 2003. Mauricio Cárdenas, Roberto Junguito and Mónica Pachón, "Political Institutions and Policy Outcomes in Colombia: The Effects of the 1991 Constitution," Banco Interamericano de Desarrollo, research network working paper # R-505, 2006. Juan Pablo Milanese, "Participación, éxito y prioridad. Un análisis macro de los equilibrios en las relaciones entre poderes ejecutivo y legislative en Colombia, 2002–2006," *Revista CS en Ciencias Sociales* no 8 (julio-diciembre 2011): 111–146.

4. A dynamic analysis could be found in Juan Pablo Milanese, "Dinámicas cambiantes de la relación interinstitucional entre poder ejecutivo y legislativo en Colombia (2002/2006)," *Desafíos* 24, no. 1 (2012): 231–271.

5. Other kinds of legislative production as *actos legislativos*—constitutional reform bills—are excluded from the analysis.

6. It produces a legislative inflation. That is, legislators tend to introduce a broad amount of regional or particular bills in order to preserve or increase the number of voters. Many of these bills are usually not significant, and most of the time, they never are discussed. In addition, the introduction of such bills is merely symbolic.

Analyzing the behavior of the government legislators, the introduction of this amount of bills could be read as a way to decompress the tension produced by the potentially opposite expectation of the government and their own electorate.

7. Gianfranco Pasquino e Riccardo Pelizzo, *Parlamenti democratici* (Bologna: Il Mulino, 2006).

8. This situation is in line with most Latin American cases. In fact, from a comparative point of view, these "success rates" are not particularly high. This means although the government is a strong player promoting its bills, it was far from being infallible.

9. It is worth mentioning that usually, the legislatures are not, in fact, qualified organizations to produce certain kinds of technical legislation. Despite the fact that they have juridical attributions to do so, they usually do not have enough expertise.

10. Within this context, the expectations of the congressmen are to achieve the sanction of their bills at the end of each legislative period, while the government expects that they get approved as soon as possible.

11. Ana María Mustapic "Oficialistas y diputados": las relaciones Ejecutivo-Legislativo en la Argentina," *Desarrollo Económico* 39, no. 156 (Enero—Marzo 2000): 571–595.

12. For example, if the legislators override a project vetoed by the government is a clear sign of challenges. On the contrary, if the legislators delegate decree powers, this is not only a sign of agreement but of subordination.

13. The president is only able to produce legislative decrees under state of siege, and he is forced to send them to the Constitutional Court making them a legislative veto player.

14. Ibid.

15. Ibid.

16. David Samuels and Matthew Shugart, *Presidents, Parties, and Prime Ministers How the Separation of Powers Affects Party Organization and Behavior* (Boston: Cambridge University Press, 2010).

17. Giovanni Sartori, *Parties and Party Systems: A Framework for Analysis* (Cambridge, U.K.: University Press, 1976).

18. In fact, Uribe did not try to build a party, but a political movement formed by parties, factions and individuals (the Uribismo). Its main catalyst was Uribe, who had charisma, popularity, and the capacity to read effectively the social preferences under a critical juncture polarized the political system.

19. Francisco Gutierrez Sanín "Estrenando sistema de partidos," *Análisis Político* 19, no. 57 (2006): 106–125. Francisco Gutierrez Sanín "Fragmentación electoral y política tradicional en Colombia: piezas para un rompecabezas en muchas dimensiones," *Perfiles latinoamericanos,* no. 20 (2002): 53–77. Eduardo Pizarro, "La atomización partidista en Colombia: el fenómeno de las microempresas electorales," in *Degradación o cambio: evolución del sistema político colombiano*, ed. Francisco Gutiérrez Sanín (Bogotá: Norma, 2002). Matthew Shugart, Erika Moreno and Luis Fajardo, "Deepening Democracy through Renovating Political Practices: The Struggle for Electoral Reform in Colombia," in *Peace, Democracy, and Human Rights in Colombia,* ed. Christopher Welna and Gustavo Gallon (Notre Dame: Notre Dame University Press, 2007). Mónica Pachón and Matthew Shugart "Party System Rationalization and the Mirror Image of Interparty and Intraparty Competition: The Adoption of Party Lists in Colombia," in *Primer Congreso de la Asociación Colombiana de Ciencia Política*, Bogotá, September 30–October 4, 2008. Juan Carlos Rodríguez Raga and Felipe Botero, "Ordenando el caos. Elecciones legislativas y reforma

electoral en Colombia," *Revista de Ciencia Política* 26, no. 1 (2006): 138–151. Brian Crisp and Rachel Ingall, "Institutional Engineering and the Nature of Representation: Mapping the Effects of Electoral Reform in Colombia," *American Journal of Political Science* 46, no. 4 (2002): 733–748.

20. Roice Carroll and Matthew Shugart "Neo-Madisonian Theory and Latin American Institutions," in *Regimes and Democracy in Latin America. Theories and Methods*, ed. Gerardo Munck (Oxford: Oxford University, 2007).

21. Matthew Shugart y John Carey, *Presidenti de assemblee: disegno costituzionale e dinamiche elettorali* (Bologna, Il Mulino, 1995). Shugart, Moreno and Fajardo, "Deepening Democracy."

22. Crisp and Ingall, "Institutional Engineering and the Nature of Representation." Felipe Botero y Lucio Rennó, "Career choice and legislative reelection: evidence from Brazil and Colombia," *Brazilian Political Science Review* 1, no. 1 (2007): 102–124. Maria Escobar-Lemmon and Erika Moreno, "Mejor solos que mal acompañados: Political Entrepreneurs in Colombia," paper presented at the Latin American Studies Association, Las Vegas, October 7–9, 2003.

23. Francisco Gutiérrez Sanín, Tatiana Acevedo y Juan Manuel Viatela, "¿Olivos y Aceitunos? Los partidos políticos colombianos y sus bases sociales en la primera mitad del siglo XX," *Análisis Político* 21, no. 62 (2008): 3–24. Francisco Gutiérrez Sanín y Luisa Ramírez, "Familias, Redes y Facciones," *Revista de Estudios Sociales*, no. 11 (February 2002).

24. Octavio Amorim Neto y Fabiano Santos, "The Executive Connection: Presidentially Defined Factions and Party Discipline in Brazil," *Dados* 44, no. 2 (2001).

25. A nonpartisan cabinet is one in which the portfolios are not delivered considering a partisan criteria, i.e., what Amorim Neto calls coalescent cabinet. In this way, this kind of cabinet is formed by nonpartisan technocrats, cronies, or interest group representatives, etc. Octavio Amorim Neto, "The Presidential Calculus: Executive Policy Making and Cabinet Formation in the Americas." *Comparative Political Studies* 39, no. 4 (2006): 415–440.

26. Raga and Botero, "Ordenando el caos."

27. In 2003, a congressional initiative resulted in a complete overhaul of the electoral system and other rules. Firstly, the Hare quota was changed for the D'Hondt electoral formula. Secondly, an electoral threshold was introduced which requires parties to obtain at least 2 percent of valid votes in the elections for the Senate or a percentage of the simple quota in House elections to participate in the distribution of seats (although reaching this threshold does not guarantee obtaining a seat). Thirdly, single-party lists were introduced. Fourthly, parties were given the possibility to choose between closed or open lists. Furthermore, parties are now required to obtain at least 2 percent of votes in the Senate election (or 2 percent of votes casted in House elections nationwide) in order to maintain legal recognition as a party. Requirements to register independent candidates and the magnitudes of electoral districts remained unchanged.

28. An example is the Bench Law.

29. Raga and Botero, "Ordenando el caos." Juan Gómez Albarello and Juan Carlos Rodríguez Raga, "Competencia electoral en grandes circunscripciones. El caso

del Senado colombiano," in *Entre la persistencia y el cambio. Reconfiguración del escenario partidista en Colombia*, ed. Diana Hoyos Gómez (Bogotá: Universidad del Rosario, 2007). Frenando Giraldo and José Daniel López, "El comportamiento electoral y de partidos en los comicios para Cámara de Representantes de 2002 y 2006: un estudio comparado desde la Reforma Política," *Colombia Internacional*, no. 64 (July/Dec. 2007).

30. Pachón, "Explaining the Performance of the Colombian Congress."

31. Elections for the House of Representatives (lower house) were held in thirty-three districts whose magnitude varied from two (in the smallest *departamentos*) to eighteen (in Bogotá). In 1991, the Constitutional Assembly introduced a nationwide electoral district to elect the members of the upper house (Senate).

32. Pachón, "Explaining the Performance of the Colombian Congress. Cárdenas, Junguito and Pachón, "Political Institutions and Policy Outcomes."

Section Three

INTERNAL ARMED CONFLICT IN HISTORICAL PERSPECTIVE

Chapter Five

The Colombian Conflict

A Historical Perspective

Malcolm Deas

It is common for writers on long-lasting conflicts to say that they are complicated. This usually attracts criticism from those who favor one explanation rather than another, or a single one over many, that the writer is trying to excuse or minimize some element in obedience to his or her political bias. Nonetheless it is well to insist that the Colombian conflict of the last five decades, which this chapter seeks to examine in a long perspective of the republic's history, is certainly complicated. Chains of historical causation are of course present, but they are multiple, and they are not simple.[1] They are there linking one era with another, even though the two may seem to show little in common. They can certainly contribute to an understanding, and a careful historical analysis can perhaps help to assess their importance, as well as to determine what in the more recent conflict has been new and unprecedented. To understand the complexities of the Colombian conflict, it is necessary to begin to follow the threads of causation in what may seem a distant past.

Let us start with the most frequently made argument: Colombia is seen as having had since independence a uniquely violent past, one of incessant civil wars in the nineteenth century and of violent political conflict ever since. At the time of writing, one of the FARC negotiators in Havana has reiterated this assertion.

Yet the mere number of nineteenth-century wars is not obviously pertinent. It is not clear that Colombia suffered more wars than other republics of Spanish America, which have not experienced high levels of political violence in the last century or in this. Most of Colombia's wars were small and short. Though the last formal civil war, the War of a Thousand Days, 1899–1902, was certainly the longest and most lethal, the intensity of violence was clearly less than that reached in *La Violencia*, 1946–c.1960, and in the last three decades.[2] They had other characteristics that separate them from the political violence of the twentieth century.

The social structure was on the whole unscathed. Though one can find episodes in them of what can be seen as class war—for example, in the Cauca Valley at mid-century—they were struggles for power that resist that sort of analysis. The leadership remained in the hands of men who were essentially politicians, and many of them from the upper classes, both Liberals and Conservatives.

There were guerrillas in all these wars, but they were not guerrilla wars. Armies moved around in what they saw as strategies, they fought battles, some of them decisive. Though it threatened to become so toward the end of the last war, the guerrilla mode was not the predominant one.[3] The wars had clear beginnings and also clear ends: peace treaties and amnesties. Atrocities such as massacres were relatively few, and the wars do not appear to have left behind them long sequels of less formal violence.[4]

Although there are some correlations with the ups and downs of the national economy—depressions made conflict more likely and prolonged, making governments more unpopular and vulnerable, and increasing the numbers of those disposed to join a rebellion—the wars were not fought around economic issues. To a degree property rights were respected, particularly real property rights.[5]

The wars were of very little interest to the rest of the world, apart from some sporadic concern to Colombia's immediate neighbors.[6] They were likewise little influenced by events outside Colombia, or by any outside intervention. The one exception to this was the destiny of Panama, resolved on November 3, 1903, with the assistance of the United States.

Finally, the last war was followed by some forty years of peace, not wholly uninterrupted, but broken only by episodes that are insignificant when compared with what had passed and what was to come. There was what seemed to be a break in the chain.

However, there are aspects of this past which are part of an explanation of twentieth-century violence, even that of the last few decades.

THE NATURE OF THE WARS

One is the nature, not the number, of the wars. Fought to the end between Liberals and Conservatives, they left a legacy of intense partisan loyalties right through the social scale, and throughout the country. This was not the case elsewhere in Spanish America to the same degree. Liberal versus Conservative rivalries were common enough in the region after independence, but nowhere else so constant and so overtly persistent—for example, in Mexico the French intervention and the brief empire of Maximilian was fatal for self-proclaimed Conservatives, and in Venezuela they disappear with the midcentury Monagas regime and the Federal War. Colombia was also from the earliest days a republic where there were no ethnic bars to political participation: at least one foreign observer discerned politics to be in the hands of "the mestizos," the majority of the population, and found political conversation remarkably frequent among the common people. Landowners often lacked both the ability and the motive to control local politics.[7] Nor were indigenous communities or blacks excluded: their participation is clear in many contemporary accounts. This wide and deep involvement was channeled and articulated by the two "traditional" parties. There were no good reasons for changing sides.

The forty years of peace between them after the end of the War of a Thousand Days has no doubt more than a single explanation. The loss of Panama in the immediate wake of the war was traumatic and humiliating, and the destruction caused by the war palpable.[8] It was thought that modern arms and superior government resources increasingly lessened the chances of successful revolution.[9] The administration of President Rafael Reyes introduced guarantees for minority representation: a system of "incomplete voting" gave the Liberals something like a third share of the spoils. One critic of the centralist Constitution of 1886, which despite its promise of "scientific peace" had failed to prevent the wars of 1895 and 1899–1902, had rightly questioned its diagnosis that conflict was a product of the excessive decentralization embodied in the previous federalist document of 1863. It was caused by exclusive and arbitrary government, which could flourish under both centralist and federalist arrangements: minority rights alone could bring peace.[10]

Certain other features visible in the nineteenth century also persisted, and continue to persist to this day. One such feature is the geopolitics of the country.

Bogotá, the capital, occupied a strong defensive position. If one excludes the removal of the brief and illegitimate military government of General Melo in 1854, not a typical affair, the city fell to an insurgent army only once, when in 1860 the exceptionally energetic, ambitious, and militarily competent Tomás Cipriano de Mosquera overthrew the lethargic and militarily inept civilian President Mariano Ospina Rodríguez. It was difficult for rebel forces raised in the provinces to combine against the capital, which had the further advantage of being in the center of the largest and most easily recruited population, the upland peasantry of Cundinamarca and Boyacá.

Some even see this pattern in Colombia's pre-conquest past, where the comparatively peaceful and settled Chibchas inhabited the highland plateau lands, and by controlling the passes kept out the more warlike Pijaos and others down below.[11] That may be stretching the *longue durée* a bit far, but the observation is still pertinent for the twentieth and twenty-first centuries. The seat of the national government has been little affected by distant provincial conflicts, and the national government has constantly taken little interest in resolving them.

THE COLOMBIAN MILITARY IN HISTORICAL CONTEXT

Apparent also in the era of civil wars was the historic weakness and lack of capacity of the Colombian state; it was poor. The nature and size of the economy made it difficult to raise revenue. The population was scant, scattered and heavily rural, much of it living at a bare subsistence level. The foreign trade sector, the most easily taxed, was proportionately one of the smallest in Latin America.[12] The result was inevitably a skeletal administration and a small army. No government in its senses wanted to keep under arms soldiers it could not pay. The practice was to retain only a minimal force, enough to look after the small arsenals and perform a few other peacetime tasks, and when the need arose to expand its numbers by forceful recruiting. When civil war ended, the ranks would be reduced as rapidly as possible. The soldiers in the standing force were few, and in the 1850s their number dropped as low as 500. It increased toward the end of the century, but 6,000 men were considered by contemporary critics to be an intolerable burden on the national budget.

Colombia now has the largest and most experienced army in Latin America, but this unmilitary tradition is still relevant to understanding the course of twentieth-century history and that of recent decades. As an institution the army was too small and too subordinated to have any autonomous political role, military government was unrealizable, practically inconceivable. Colombia produced no military caste, those who commanded in the civil wars could only rarely be considered professional soldiers, and the few who made the army a career were not from, and did not enter into, the upper ranks of society. The army remained an unattractive career for well-born Colombians after a degree of professionalism was achieved in the first decade of the twentieth century, with the aid of a Chilean military mission contracted by President Reyes. It carried little weight in national politics, and received only a meager share of the budget.[13]

This seemingly ancient history certainly has meaning for the twentieth century. Formal civil war was not now an accepted course of action, though there were occasions when some Liberals advocated it, and the specter still lingered as late as the 1940s. Despite the fact that among the party leaders there were many veterans of the last war, the predominant mood of the minority party remained pacifist, as can be seen in the record of the convention that met in Ibagué in 1922.[14]

The sectarian loyalties that were a legacy of the nineteenth century nonetheless persisted. Those who question the profundity of the four decades or so of comparative peace that followed the treaties of 1902 point to the tensions and sporadic violence surrounding the election of 1930, where the Liberal Enrique Olaya Herrera, running as a candidate of "National Concentration," won the presidency with a minority vote against a divided Conservative party. Olaya insisted on presenting his candidature in the way he did so that the Conservatives would not instinctively close ranks when faced with a Liberal, and in order to mute the inevitable sectarian reaction. Nonetheless, the consequences were not entirely peaceful, and there was fighting between Liberals and Conservatives not only in Boyacá, Santander and Norte de Santander, departments seen as particularly prone to such conflict, but in several other parts of the country as well.[15]

Colombia was still governed under the centralist Constitution of 1886, under which the president appointed the governors of the departments and the governors appointed the municipal *alcaldes*, the mayors. Olaya certainly attempted to manage the transfer of power from one party to the other with tact and prudence, but in the face of fierce local feelings and ambitions this was not everywhere possible. Violence was not a matter of oligarchic provocation—if there was such a thing at this juncture as an effective Colombian oligarchy represented in the upper reaches of national politics, which one may very well doubt, it sought to avoid violence. Its sources were provincial, local, and even popular.[16]

Nineteen hundred thirty was not so many years distant from the last war, a mere twenty-eight, much less than the time elapsed between today and the *Frente Nacional* agreement made to bury sectarian enmities in 1957. Though he had not played any conspicuous part in it, Olaya Herrera was himself a veteran of that war.

These episodes, though fewer in number and far less lethal than what was to come to pass after 1946, are still significant, as they formed part of an argument employed by some Conservatives who saw their actions after their 1946 victory over the divided Liberals as a justified revenge. They are also significant in the way that they show the persistent weakness of the government's instruments for controlling provincial violence. The army was no longer the nakedly partisan affair it had always been in the nineteenth century. Though most of its officers were still from Conservative families, it was at least seen as the least partisan of the country's institutions, its relative neutrality deriving in part from the fact that, unlike the police, it did not receive orders directly from local politicians—the police were mainly local forces, and easily politicized. Though it had managed to remain at a distance from the 1930 elections—the best officers resented being employed for political ends, and the army was soon to renounce the vote—it was still far too small and ill-equipped to keep the peace everywhere in their aftermath.[17]

After 1930 the scheme of minority representation established by Reyes was abandoned in favor of what was seen as a more sophisticated and just form of proportional representation, instead of the "incomplete vote" that had guaranteed the Liberals their smaller proportion of the spoils.[18] However, the new system failed. Though in retrospect one can see that social change, particularly urbanization and a larger urban working class, might be on the side of the Liberals—even that being less obvious than simple versions of the coming of "modernity" suggest—it was certainly far from clear to all in the 1930s and 1940s which party had the majority. The Conservatives were naturally convinced that it was theirs, given the voting figures of 1930, where the combined total of their candidates' tallies easily outnumbered the votes for Olaya Herrera.

Memories of the dire consequences of intense competition had faded somewhat since 1902. The new legislation posed difficulties for what was still a thin and feeble national administration, and in the subsequent elections in which the Liberals sought to change their minority victory of 1930 into a government based on a majority the Conservatives were quick to denounce illegitimate pressures and Liberal fraud, with some justification—there was large-scale Liberal fraud in the election of 1934. They were of course well acquainted with fraudulent practices themselves. An essential element of the system was the *cédula*, a national identity card, with a photograph, for every citizen. It was no easy task to issue these to the scattered peasant population, and the Conservatives cast doubt on the process: "one million eight hundred thousand false cédulas" was the curiously precise claim of the Conservative leader Laureano Gómez, no doubt exaggerated, but not without some plausibility.

Between 1930 and 1946 changes occurred that help to explain the much more intense violence that followed the loss of power by the divided Liberals in that last year, and the election of the Conservative Mariano Ospina Pérez on a minority vote—a reversal of the experience of 1930.

First, the breakdown of minority representation, with Conservative abstention and the attempt of President Alfonso Lopez Pumarejo to institute a scheme of government and opposition, in which his Liberal modernizers would be faced by a "loyal" Conservative antagonist. This did not succeed. The opposition was anything but loyal, and under the leadership of Gómez would go to extreme lengths to discredit and harass the government. The Conservatives were aided and abetted, as in the nineteenth century, by the Church.

Secondly, the intense mobilization on the left of the Liberal party led by Jorge Eliécer Gaitán, whose appeal to the masses was unprecedented and has not since been equaled. In 1946, he split the Liberal vote, which ended a decade and a half of Liberal rule, but Gaitán captured the leadership of the party and remained its unchallenged leader until his assassination on April 9, 1948. The political temperature had risen high: both Gaitán and Gómez were formidable orators, and both were demagogues who could now reach their followers directly through the radio, without the mediation of local politicians. Gaitán had had from his earliest ventures in politics an unusual degree of cross-party appeal, but circumstances and the underlying realities of Colombian political loyalties meant that he chose to end his career as leader of the Liberals, and his superior popular following should not lead one to underestimate Gómez's relentless capacity as an opponent, and his ascendancy over the Conservative rank and file, particularly in the rural parts of a still very rural country. Sectarian strife, present even before the elections of 1946 and spreading thereafter, reached new heights after Gaitán's death. It culminated under Gómez's brief presidency from 1950–1953, diminished a bit under the military government of General Gustavo Rojas Pinilla, 1953–1957, and was effectively ended by the National Front power-sharing agreement between the leaders of the two parties of 1957. The conventional figure for lives lost in this period of "the Classic Violence," sanctified by much repetition, is 200,000.[19]

This violence was predominantly sectarian, and its scene the small towns and the countryside. From that background emerged the Liberal guerrillas—perhaps 10,000 in all, in the Llanos, Tolima, Huila, Cundinamarca, Boyacá, the Santanders, Antioquia, Caldas—and their leaders, and the Conservative counter-guerrillas.[20] The party leaders did not join the fight. With the exception of the *Bogotazo*, the rioting and destruction in the capital that followed Gaitán's assassination, the larger towns and cities were relatively unaffected, as were certain regions of the country, particularly the departments of the Caribbean coast.

Foreigners, and a number of later academics, have found this emphasis on the sectarian nature of the conflict hard to believe, and have sought underlying causes such as a struggle for land, or have tried to place it into the frame of a more general class struggle. Such elements were undoubtedly present, and that is important for understanding the next stage of this history, but they were not predominant. An indication of this is that most guerrillas accepted the amnesties that were offered first by Rojas Pinilla in 1953 and later by the incipient National Front in 1957 and after. They laid down their arms because the government had changed, on the first occasion because Gómez was ousted and exiled and on the second because the Liberal-Conservative rivalry was formally ended.

A consequence of the sectarian essence of the conflict was the nature of the National Front agreement, whose alleged exclusiveness was also to be seen by many later as one of the causes of continuing violence. It was a fifty-fifty split of offices, and of the spoils, the loaves and the fishes, between the Liberals and the Conservatives. It is hard to see that it could have been anything else. The issue of the representation of other minority parties was briefly aired at the time, but it was not judged feasible: the Communist Party, small and pacific, which had suffered a ban under Rojas Pinilla, was seen by the Conservatives as being apart from anything else a subservient ally of the Liberals; its inclusion would upset the balance, and was bound to be unacceptable to the Conservatives.

Critics have also argued that the National Front arrangements failed to confront the reality of what had happened, and that this failure to apportion blame and register memory was another reason why violence persisted. Again, one must ask whether such criticism is realistic. In the Colombia of 1957 the idea of a truth commission was not entirely absent, and it did produce the pioneering and quasi-official work of Mons Germán Guzmán, Eduardo Umaña Luna and Orlando Fals Borda, *La violencia en Colombia*.[21] The book was greeted with a storm of criticism that for a time inhibited further inquiry. Transitional justice and the therapeutic cultivation of memory were notions entirely absent at that time, not only in Colombia but elsewhere.[22] In Colombia there was a broad consensus on ending the fighting, as was shown by the approval by referendum of the National Front agreement; there was no consensus on enquiring into its causes, let alone on who should do the inquiring. There was much fear that any such attempt would only cause further violence.

THE BEGINNING OF A HALF-CENTURY OF CONFLICT

This next section of this chapter seeks to answer the question why was peace not achieved by the National Front? Some general contributory reasons: the assassination of Gaitán and *La Violencia* left a legacy of bitterness and frustration, a sense of betrayal and a rejection of the status quo in the minds of many, which inevitably sought expression.

For some it would be opposition politics, still quite possible under the Front, through party factions, openly dissident parties and organizations and the trade unions, more powerful then than now. The National Front looked exclusive, was easily and frequently pictured as an agreement among oligarchs to monopolize politics, but the reality was different.[23] The early

Liberal dissidence, the *Movimiento Revolucionario Liberal*, MRL, participated in elections and paved the way for the eventual presidency of its leader Alfonso López Michelsen. The populist ANAPO, the party of Rojas Pinilla, likewise fielded candidates and may well have been denied victory by fraud in the presidential election of 1970—a frustration that eventually produced the guerrilla M-19, the 19 being the date, April 19, of that election.

For some it would be a descent into banditry: Chispas, Sangre Negra, Desquite, Efraín González, figures emerging from the Violencia who would have their final flings in the early 1960s. For others it would be the path of the revolutionary guerrillas, principally the FARC and the ELN. Here one touches on the question of the origins of the guerrilla. Though too many think that explaining origins explains persistence, this in itself is interesting. The FARC leadership is exceptionally insistent on the details of their history, to the degree that one is tempted to define them as an *historic* guerrilla, rather than use any other adjective. They insistently promulgate their version of their origins and progress, a version few have bothered to question.[24] At times it reads as if the essential justification for their existence is this history of survival and expansion, that nothing more is needed, and one concludes that the fight will continue until this history receives some sort of official recognition. That may well be the case, though the details of such a possible recognition are still hard to define.

There are other aspects of these origins that contribute to an understanding not only of origins but of persistence.[25] One is their relation to the land, to agrarian conflicts. Some of these were quite extensive in the 1920s and 1930s, particularly, or at least most visibly, in Cundinamarca and Tolima. Some were settled by government intervention, others lingered, and the Communist Party established a significant presence in the region. A number of the guerrillas that appeared in the 1950s were under the party's umbrella. Among these *autodefensas campesinas* was the nucleus which would in 1964 call itself the FARC, and set out on the long revolutionary road.[26]

However, the FARC cannot be simply categorized as an agrarian insurgency. It was and is largely peasant, *campesino*, in leadership and in composition, and it is rural: it is in rural Colombia that it has operated and grown. Nonetheless, at the time of its emergence it was not the largest or most effective peasant movement in the country—the prize for that would go to the Sumapaz peasantry in Cundinamarca and Tolima under the leadership of Juan de la Cruz Varela, which intent on specific regional demands did not aim at any national revolution.[27] The conflicts from which the FARC emerged were of peasants against peasants, between rival *autodefensas compesinas*, Liberals and Communists, and of these against the police and army: landowners do not figure prominently. Landowners, particularly cattlemen, have been in the first line as targets for extortion by this guerrilla organization, but that is more because they are vulnerable and proximate sources of cash than because they are *latifundistas*.[28] The FARC have always had in their successive programs a demand for agrarian reform, but it has usually been somewhat muted.[29] There was little articulate pressure for agrarian reform from below in the traumatized countryside at the end of *La Violencia*. The main impulse came in the early 1960s from above, as part of the terms of the Alliance for Progress, and this had faded into insignificance a decade later. The more the FARC has concentrated on achieving military success, as was the case in the 1980s and 1990s, the less has it emphasized agrarian questions. It protested hardly at all against the vast seizure of lands by the *narcos* and paramilitaries that occurred during this period.[30]

Conditions in much of rural Colombia are certainly part of any explanation of the guerrilla's birth and survival. Insofar as one can generalize about the rank and file, it is made up of rural and small-town youth with little education and no prospects. The FARC have also been successful in organizing by force or persuasion the *colonos* of the many internal frontiers of the country, particularly those engaged in the growing and processing of coca.

Nonetheless, though the FARC are now insisting once again in the Havana talks that the land question is at the center of the conflict, the historical record does not show so clearly that this has been the case.[31] These are internal complications. It is also necessary to look at the evolving international context, something that most Colombian commentators are reluctant to do, as they wish to emphasize the autonomous and the national, though some make passing references to imperialism.

As was stated above, the nineteenth-century civil wars were of little or no interest to the rest of the world, and of not much concern even to Colombia's immediate neighbors. As previously mentioned, the shock of the separation of Panama contributed to the desire to avoid civil war in the subsequent decades, and a brief war with Peru in 1932 had the beneficial effect of muting party strife at the time, leading one to reflect that one contributory reason for the persistent lack of solidarity among Colombians has been the country's lack of any external enemy. Nonetheless it is only after World War II that significant international influences appear.

Colombia's entry into the Cold War can be dated to the *Bogotazo*, April 9, 1948. Many sought to blame the riot on the communists, and the anticommunist strain in the thinking of soldiers was strengthened by Gómez's decision to send a battalion to fight in Korea.[32] However, there was never any evidence that the Colombian communist party was significantly involved in the events of the *9 de abril*, and though important for the army, involvement in the Korean War did not have a profound impact on local opinion.

The Colombian communist party was small, mostly urban and moderate, and frequently in subordinate alliance with the Liberal party.

THE CUBAN REVOLUTION AND ITS IMPACT ON COLOMBIA

The formation of the National Front was achieved shortly before the Cuban revolution: Fidel Castro took power on January 1, 1959. This brought an international dimension of far greater importance to Colombia's conflicts than any previous event. First, apprehension—or excitement—at the prospect of the revolution spreading, of the Andes becoming "the *sierra maestra* of South America." Second, the diplomatic consequences of the deterioration of Cuba's relations with the United Sates and entry into the Soviet camp. The Colombian government was soon more closely aligned with the United States, and Castro responded with support for the Colombian government's enemies.[33]

The most notorious example of Cuban inspiration was the founding of the ELN, the *Ejército de Liberación Nacional*, the guerrilla second to the FARC in seniority, size and longevity, but the influence was more pervasive.[34] Colombian versions of the conflict of recent decades have tended, as already noted, to regard the guerrillas as particularly autonomous, national, native, and have largely ignored the international context. Would there have been persistent armed subversion in Colombia after the formation of the National Front had there been no Cuban Revolution? The question, a valid one, has rarely been raised.

For the Colombian communist party, the Cuban revolution was a challenge: for a party to claim to be the vanguard of the left, a guerrilla had now become a necessary attribute. The Colombian comrades could point to the *autodefensas campesinas* of Cundinamarca, Tolima and Huila, which the right now pictured as subversive *repúblicas independientes*, the "independent republics" of Marquetalia and El Pato, and to their doctrine of "the combination of all forms of struggle": while continuing with the more mundane tasks of elections and trades unions, the Party would defend these armed rural outposts, proof of its vanguard status, and the army obligingly confirmed the claim by attacking them. However, relations between the Colombian party and Cuba were never easy, as the party refused to subordinate its other activities, the *trabajo de masas*, to the support of the FARC. It is nonetheless to the old Moscow-line party that the FARC owes its vertical structure of authority and its discipline, which have been essential to its survival. The Party could point to before the *autodefensas campesinas* of Cundinamarca.

The international context evolved, and the Colombian guerrillas, though never dependent on outside aid, received from abroad successive stimuli. Ideological influences multiplied with the sino-soviet split, and as well as those aligned with Cuba or Moscow, Colombia had guerrillas who took their inspiration from China and even Albania, Mao and Enver Hoxha. The M-19 at first emulated the Uruguayan Tupamaros, with their emphasis on urban publicity. The victory of the Sandinistas in Nicaragua and the wars in El Salvador and Guatemala provided further inspiration in the 1980s. The collapse of the Soviet Union had little effect, further evidence of the FARC's autonomy; the leadership dismissed Gorbachev as a CIA agent, and now asserted the guerrilla's primacy over the dwindling remnants of the civilian party. At the end of the 1990s the election of Hugo Chávez as president of Venezuela promised further opportunities.[35]

To return to the military aspect of the conflicts of the last half-century, one can begin by noting that the army's record in the years 1946–c1960 was not impressive. Its experience in the brief war with Peru, though a creditable effort for a most unmilitary country, left it with preoccupations and doctrines that were of no relevance to the tasks it was faced with after 1946. The army was still very small, both in officers and in troops—less than 10,000 in 1946, and wretchedly equipped. In maintaining internal order it showed little understanding or competence, and committed some spectacular abuses, as in the *Guerra de Villarica* in 1955.[36] Though its record was better than that of the police, politicized first by the Liberals and then by the Conservatives, it was not an effective neutral force.[37]

With some small amounts of U.S. assistance, it improved in the early 1960s and revised its thinking, to the degree that later in the decade U.S. observers were confident that it could be left to deal with the country's problems while U.S. experts and forces acquired their own in Vietnam.[38] Che Guevara and Camilo Torres were both now dead. The guerrillas were contained in remote parts, and offered no significant threat, and this should be born in mind in the face of much current rhetoric about "fifty years of civil war." The impetus of military improvement was now lost.

It was not fully regained until the end of the century, despite the palpable expansion of guerrilla numbers and capacity that began in the 1980s and continued even beyond the end of the century. President Belisario Betancur had poor relations with the army, who regarded his peacemaking efforts with skepticism. Virgilio Barco was primarily concerned with combating the threat of the *narcos*, Pablo Escobar and the Medellín cartel. A beginning was made in making security a matter of high priority and of civilian as well as military concern under César Gaviria, who among other initiatives took the essential step of appointing a civilian Minister of Defense.[39] However, the momentum was lost again in the following administration of Ernesto Samper. Recovery began with additional resources for the armed forces under Andrés Pastrana, but a coherent policy had to wait until the election of Álvaro Uribe Vélez in 2002.

Given that any successful counterinsurgency has to have a political drive, the costs of this long neglect have been high. There is surely a rough correlation between the absence in any administration of a credible security policy and the rise of paramilitarism, with its successive waves under Presidents Betancur, Samper and Pastrana.

CONCLUSION

Some aspects of Colombia's recent conflicts are better understood when viewed in the long perspective of the 200 years of the republic's history. Others have no clear precedent: ideologies, international influences, drugs, the arms trade, kidnapping and extortion on such large scales, a new geography of violence, the displacement of millions of people, the involvement of numerous NGOs, and the elaboration of new doctrines of international law.

Many of what have been seen by some as the "objective causes" of violence—in themselves part of a new debate—are present in many other relatively peaceful countries. What is unique to Colombia is, in the local phrase, the "*combinación de males*," the combination of ills. In sum, this chapter has attempted to show how the history of the country can help to explain how that combination has come about. Other chapters in the book will illuminate in detail what has happened in recent decades.

NOTES

1. A stimulating model of possible analysis of Colombia is provided by a work on another much-studied complex conflict with deep historical roots, the late John Whyte's indispensable *Interpreting Northern Ireland* (Oxford: Oxford University Press, 1990). He classified explanations according to type—historical, geographical, religious, sociological, Marxist, etcetera—and set out what each can contribute to an overall analysis, and how each falls short of being entirely satisfactory. He doubted that the entirely satisfactory explanation could ever be reached. It is certainly way beyond the capacity of a single historian in a short chapter, touching on themes where there is much argument. Those who find themselves inclined to disagree with this author's speculations can find many alternative views in the sources cited. John Whyte was also careful not to exaggerate the role of academic studies and experts in conflict resolution and peacemaking: peace had been made before in Ulster without such as-

sistance. For successful peacemaking in Colombia's past, see Medófilo Medina and Efraín Sánchez, eds., *Tiempos de Paz: acuerdos en Colombia, 1902–1994*, (Bogotá: Alcaldía Mayor de Bogotá, Instituto Distrital de Cultura, 2003).

2. The nineteenth-century statistics both for the number of wars, if one includes local conflicts, and for the number of dead are naturally precarious. The accepted number of wars considered national, leaving aside the birth-pangs of the emerging republic, is eight; for local conflicts, Gustavo Arboleda, *Las revoluciones locales en Colombia* (Popayán, 1907.) counts 50, For estimates of dead see Fernando Gaitán Daza, 'Una indagación sobre las causas de la violencia en Colombia,' 200 et seq., in Malcolm Deas, Fernado Gaitán Daza, *Dos ensayos especulativos sobre la violencia en Colombia*, (Bogotá, Fonade, Departamento de Planneación Nacional, 1995). The figure he gives for the dead of the last civil war far excedes that for all the others put together, but seems to me on the high side. For recent decades, see the references below: Stephen Pinker's thesis of diminishing violence—in *The Better Angels of Our Nature*, (New York and London: Allen Lane, 2011)—, may be sustainable about humanity in general, but the beating of those angels' wings has not been heard recently in Colombia.

3. See Carlos Eduardo Jaramillo, *Los guerrilleros del novecientos*, (Bogotá: CEREC, 1991); Gonzalo Sánchez and Mario Aguilera, eds. *Memoria de un país en guerra: los mil días, 1899–1902*, (Bogotá: Planeta, 2001).

4. There is some contemporary support for these conclusions: see Medardo Rivas, *Errores de la justicia y víctimas humanas en Colombia* (Bogotá: Imprenta de Medardo Rivas, 1894), 27: "The people do not make revolutions: they hate war and want peace, but it is with the people that revolutions are made, the people pays the price of war, and one should observe their behaviour in the war . . . Those who are not involved in arms stay quiet in the presence of property they could devour, keep watch on the riches of the peaceful, do not engage in disorder or devastation, never call for blood, do not commit murder or violation." There are no San Bartolomés or Sicilian Vespers. "The revolution passes, leaving the fields strewn with the bodies of their sons: one party has won and the other lost, the armies are disbanded anywhere they stand, and the soldier who yesterday was a lion in the fight has to walk a hundred leagues back to the humble dwelling of his family, holding out his hand even to the defeated for alms to help him on his way." (My translation.) A romanticized version, no doubt, but not one to be entirely rejected. See also the observations in the chapter by David Bushnell, ' Política y partidos en el siglo XIX. Algunos antecedents históricos,' in Gonzalo Sánchez and Ricardo Peñaranda, eds., *Pasado y presente de la violencia en Colombia* (Medellín: La Carreta Histórica, 2007).

5. For correlations with depressions in the economy see my 'Pobreza, Guerra civil y política: Ricardo Gaitán Obeso y su campaña en el río Magdalena en Colombia, 1885.,' in Malcolm Deas, *Del poder y la gramática* (3rd ed., Bogotá: Taurus, 2006). For insecurity in general in the nineteenth century see my article 'Insecurity and economic development in Colombia in the first century of Independence,' in *Revista de Historia Económica—Journal of Iberian and Latin American Economic History*, 2011, vol 29, no 2.

6. The last war brought complications with Venezuela, the two governments each backing the rebels on the other side—see the classic memoir of Nemecio Parada,

Visperas y conmienzos de la revolución de Cipriano Castro;el Táchira de mi infancia y juventud, (Caracas: Monte Avila, 1968).

7. The Swedish naval officer Carl August Gosselman, who traveled throughout South America and whose observations have a rare comparative value. See his *Viaje por Colombia, 1825 y 1826* (Bogotá: Banco de la República, 1981); *Informes sobre los estados suramericanos en los años de 1837 y 1838* (ed. Magnus Morner, Stockholm: F.Amengot, 1962). On the limited power of landowners, see the 1880s testimony of Rufino Gutiérrez, quoted in my "Algunas notas sobre la historia del caciquismo en Colombia,' in *Del poder y la gramática*"' cited above in n. 5.

8. The best account of the wrecked state of the country at the end of the war is in Baldomero Sanín Cano, *Administración Reyes* (Lausanne: Jorge Bridel, 1909).

9. A widely-read contemporary survey which conveys the belief that the era of civil wars in the region was now firmly in the past is Francisco García Calderón, *Latin America. Its Rise and Progress*, (London: J. Fisher Unwin, 1908).

10. Rafael Rocha Gutierrez, *La verdadera y la falsa democracia* (Paris, 1886; 2cd ed. Bogotá: Banco Popular, 1974).

11. I owe this observation to the ecologist Julio Carrisoza.

12. See my article 'The Fiscal Problems of Nineteenth Century Colombia' in *Journal of Latin American Studies*, vol. 14, part 2, November 1982.

13. See the description of the Guardia Colombiana, the national forces, in the early 1880s in the dispatches of J.A. Soffia, the Chilean Minister in Bogotá, in Ricardo Donoso, *José Antonio Soffia en Bogotá*, (Bogotá: Instituto Caro y Cuervo, 1976); for the army and the Chilean mission, the series of contemporary articles by Tomás Rueda Vargas reprinted in *El ejército nacional*, (Bogotá: Librería Colombiana, 1944); Adolfo León Atehortúa Cruz, *Construccción del Ejército Nacional en Colombia, 1907–1930: Reforma Militar y Misiones Extranjeros* (Medellín: La Carreta Histórica, 2009).

14. When violence broke out after 1946 some Liberals believed that their party had set up a formal military *Estado Mayor* in the eastern plains, and some guerrilla groups sought out veterans of the War of the Thousand Days to give them training—see Eduardo Franco Isaza, *Las guerrillas del Llano: testimonio de una lucha de cuatro años por la libertad*, (Caracas: Editorial Universo, 1955), and Alfredo Molano, *Los años de tropel: crónicas de violencia* (Bogotá: El Ancora, 1985). For the Ibagué Convention, Felipe Santiago Paz and Armando Solano, *Convención de Ibagué, 1922* (Bogotá: Editorial Cromos, 1922). Many of the veterans present now held pacifist convictions, including the party leader General Benjamín Herrera.

15. For details see Javier Guerrero, *Los años del olvido*, (Bogotá: Tercer Mundo / IEPRI, 1991); Blas N. Muñoz, *Crónicas de Guaca. La ruina de un pueblo*, (Cúcuta: Tip. El Granito de Arena, 1937); Alejandro Galvis Galvis, *Memorias de un político centenarista*, (2 vols, [no publisher], Bucaramanga, 1975). Both Boyacá and Santander were departments where it appeared that force could swing the majority from one party to the other. It is probably also relevant that the Santanders were the scene of much of the fighting in the War of a Thousand Days.

16. It is worth stressing this point as Colombian politics are so frequently seen inside and outside academia as being particularly "oligarchic," and this item of local

political rhetoric is so often taken as fact. It is the case that Colombia has experienced neither social revolution nor populist government, and that certain families have shown durable political prominence, a phenomenon common in many democracies. Nonetheless political competition has always been intense, and there was always a marked "circulation of elites": politics has been a career open to talent.

17. See *Crónicas de Guaca*, cited in my previous note; Ricardo Bayona Posada, *Memorias de un ochentón*, (Bogotá: Editorial Kelly, 1984), for the experience of a young army officer attempting to keep the peace in Santander. For the history of the army's role in elections, see Patricia Pinzón de Lewin, *El ejército y las elecciones* (Bogotá: Cerec,1994).

18. For details see James A. Robinson and Sebastián L. Mazzuca, 'Political Conflict and Power Sharing in the Origins of Modern Colombia,' *Hispanic American Historical Review*, 89, no. 2, 2009.

19. A short selection from a large bibliography: James D. Henderson, *Modernization in Colombia. The Laureano Gómez Years, 1889–1965*, (Gainsville: University Press of Florida, 2001); W. John Green, *Gaitanismo, Left Liberalism and Popular Mobilization in Colombia*, (Gainesville: University Press of Florida, 2003); Herbert Braun, *The Assassination of Gaitán: Public Life and Urban Violence in Colombia*, (Madison: University of Wisconsin Press, 1985); Paul Oquist, *Violence, Conflict and Politics in Colombia* (New York: Academic Press, 1980); Carlos Miguel Ortíz, *Estado y subversiuón en Colombia, La Violencia en el Quindío*, (Bogotá: CEREC, 1985). Adolfo León Atehortua Cruz, *El poder y la sangre: las historias de Trujillo, (Valle)*, (Bogotá: Cinep and Universidad Javeriana, seccional Cali, 1995); Mary Roldan, *Blood and Fire: La Violencia en Antioquia, Colombia, 1946–1953*, (Durham and London: Duke University Press, 2002); Gonzalo Sanchez and Donny Meertens, *Bandoleros, gamonales y campesinos: El caso de la Violencia en Colombia*, (Bogotá: El Ancora, 1983). There are many valuable studies besides those in this short list, but it is worth mentioning that most of the Colombian literature has been written by Liberals, or authors avowedly on the left: Conservatives write much less, probably because from 1946 to 1953 they were in power.

For samples of contemporary evidence of sectarian division and violence in the 1940s and 1950s see Eduardo Caballero Calderón, "La Chiquinquira de hoy" in *Cartas colombianas*, in vol. 2 of his *Obras Completas* (3 vols, Medellín: Bedout, 1963), which describes in memorable detail the physical frontiers between the two parties in the town, and José I.González E., *Concordia, años de frenesí y de guerra*, (Medellín: Secretaria de Educación y Cultura de Antioquia, 1988), for the fighting in Antioquia.

20. The Conservative counter-guerrillas and the semi-irregular Conservative police recruited after the 9 de abril, the *chulavitas* (the name comes from a Conservative region of peasant Boyacá) to some degree prefigure the paramilitaries of recent decades, for example, in their practice of arriving in a Liberal district "*lista en mano*," with a list in hand of those to be killed. The same list-carrying is told of the paras.

21. Germán Guzmán Campos, Eduardo Umaña Luna, Orlando Fals Borda, *La Violencia en Colombia: Estudio de un proceso social*, (2 vols, Bogotá: Tercer Mundo, 1962, 1964).

22. For the wider historical context see Jon Elster, *Closing the Books*, (Cambridge: Cambridge University Press, 2004); In 1960, Juan de la Cruz was elected to the *Cámera de Representantes* of Congress as suplente to the leader of the MRL, the future President Alfonso López Michelsen.

23. When considering the exclusive nature of the National Front arrangements as part of an explanation of continuing violence, it should be remembered that they were for a fixed term, four four-year presidencies, and that they were wound up in the 1970s. Likewise, the centralist Constitution of 1886, another alleged culprit, was abrogated by the new Constitution of 1991, the product of a constitutional convention with the prominent participation of the M-19 guerrilla.

24. Manuel Marulanda's famous account, in the speech read for him at the start of the Caguán peace talks with the Pastrana administration, of the government's attack on the peasant self-defense community—*autodefensa campesina*—of Marquetalia in 1964, has been questioned by General Alvaro Valencia Tovar, but receives wide uncritical acceptance.

25. Another exploration of this question is that of Daniel Pecaut, "Las FARC: Fuentes de su longevidad y de la conservación de su cohesión," in his *La experiencia de la violencia: Los desafíos del relato y la memoria*, (Medellín: La Carreta Histórica, 2013).

26. For the FARC's own account of these early stages see Manuel Marulanda, *Cuadernos de campaña*, (Bogotá: various editions); Eduardo Pizarro Leongomez, *Las FARC: de la autodefensa a la combinación de todas las formas de lucha*, (Bogotá: Tercer Mundo, 1992); Carlos Medina Gallego, *FARC-EP 1958–2008. Notas para una Historia Política*, (Bogotá: Universidad Nacional, 2009), Medofilo Medina, "La resistencia campesina en el sur del Tolima" in Sánchez and Peñaranda, op. cit.

27. For Juan de la Cruz Varela and the history of rural conflict and peasant organization in Cundinamarca see Rocío Londoño Botero, *Juan de la Cruz Varela, Sociedad y política en la región de Sumapaz*, (Bogotá: Universidad Nacional, 2011). Colombian peasant movements have varied between the legalistic and the less legalistic: in the 1970s the *Asociación de Usuarios Campesinos*, ANUC, the peasant association originally set up by President Carlos Lleras Restrepo to support his attempts at agrarian reform, itself divided into a hard and soft line on this issue of tactics.

28. For cattlemen victims of assassination or kidnapping by the FARC and the ELN, see the appendix in Adeleida Sourdis Nájera, *Ganadería en Colombia, Cinco Siglos Construyendo País*, (Bogotá: Fedegan, 2008). As simple versions of *latifundismo* and cattle-raising often figure among the causes of violence, see also Alberto G. Flórez—Malagón, ed., *El poder de la carne: Historias de ganaderías en la primera mitad del siglo XX en Colombia* (Bogotá: Universidad Javeriana, 2008) and Gloria Isabel Ocampo, *La instauración de la ganadería en el valle del Sinú: la hacienda Marta Magdalena, 1881–1956*, (Medellín: Universidad de Antioquia, Instituto Colombiano de Antropología e Historia, 2007).

29. The FARC leadership has tended to avoid controversy about their ends with the argument that their business is to take power, and that policies will then be decided by the people, *el pueblo*. The absence of a detailed program is rational: it makes the guerrilla less vulnerable to outside criticism and avoids any internal dissension.

30. Land changed hands in previous conflicts—for details of the changes in one region during the *Violencia* see Carlos Miguel Ortiz, op.cit. That does not mean that land disputes were at the root of *La Violencia*.

31. See the two chapters by Pierre Gilhodes, "La cuestión agraria en Colombia, 1900–1946" and "La cuestión agraria en Colombia 1958–1985" in vol. 3 of Alvaro Tirado Mejía, ed., *Nueva historia de Colombia*, (6 vols., Bogotá: Planeta, 1989), and his "Movimientos sociales en los años ochenta y noventa," in the subsequent vol. 8, (Bogotá: Planeta, 1998).

32. For anti-communism, see Rocío Londoño Botero, "El anticomunismo en Colombia," in Rubén Sierra, Mejía, ed., *La restauración consevadora, 1946–1957*, (Bogotá: Universidad Nacional, 2012).

33. For Colombian relations with the United States at this time, Bradley Lynn Coleman, *Colombia and the United States. The Making of an Inter-American Alliance, 1939–1960*, (Kent, Ohio: Kent State University Press, 2008).

34. For the origins of the ELN, Jaime Arenas, *La guerrilla por dentro:Análisis del ELN colombiano*, (Bogotá: Tercer Mundo, 1971); for evidence of early Cuban contacts with subversives, Alonso Moncada Abello, *Un aspecto de la violencia*, (Bogotá: Promotora Colombiana de Ediciones, 1963); Fidel Castro has published his own account, with surprisingly little impact for something coming from such a well-known author: *La paz en Colombia*, (Havana:, Editora Política, 2008); Carlos Medina Gallego, *Elementos para una historia de las ideas políticas del Ejército de Liberación Nacional: la historia de los primeros tiempos* (1958–1978), (vol. 1, Bogotá: Rodríguez Quito Editores, 2001).

35. For the subsequent course of the FARC's relations with Venezuela, see International Institute of Strategic Studies (IISS), *The FARC Files:Venezuela, Ecuador and the Secret Archive of "Raúl Reyes,"* (London: IISS, 2011). Sanctuary in Venezuela has been of great advantage to the FARC.

36. Jacques Aprile-Gniset, *La crónica de Villarica*, (Bogotá: Ediciones Antropos, 1991).

37. The best source, frequently critical, is still the memoirs of General Alvaro Valencia Tovar, *Testimonio de una epoca*, (Bogotá: Editorial Planeta, 1992).

38. On U.S. military aid to Colombia in the wake of the Cuban Revolution, Dennis M. Rempe, *The Past as Prologue? A History of U.S. Counterinsurgency Policy in Colombia, 1958–1966*, (Carlisle, Pa: Strategic Studies Institute Monograph Series, 2002). On Colombian military thought, Pierre Gilhodes, "El Ejército colombiano analiza la violencia," in Sánchez and Peñaranda, op. cit.; two samples: General Juan Salcedo Lora, "Respuestas personalísimas de un General de la república sobre cosas que casi todo el mundo sabe," in Malcolm Deas, María Victoria Llorente, eds, *Reconocer la Guerra para Construir la Paz*, (Bogotá: Uniandes, Cerec, Norma, 1999); "Los militares—Documento confidencial del Estado Mayor Conjunto de las Fuerzas Militares—junio de 1982," in Olga Behar, *Las guerras de la paz*, (Bogotá: Planeta, 1985). There is little evidence that "National Security Doctrine" had any significant influence in Colombia. It is also a myth that in his speech to the officers in the Teatro Patria, May 9, 1958, President Alberto Lleras Camargo promised the army autonomy in dealing with public order: what he promised was that civilian politicians would not

interfere in the strictly professional concerns of the military, such as promotions. The two main strands in military thinking have been the anticommunist, which should come as no surprise in the context of the conflict, and the constitutional.

39. Rafael Pardo Rueda was the first civilian to hold the post for thirty-seven years. Though some of his successors have been more effective than others, the change has been of fundamental importance. Given the internal structures, loyalties and jealousies of any army, it is very hard for a military minister of defense to make necessary changes, and the army becomes fossilized. It is hard too, in a country such as Colombia where soldiers are effectively banned from entering public debate, for a minister who is also a serving soldier to present the armed forces' views and arguments on matters of legitimate concern: such a soldier is immediately accused of entering public debate, of *deliberando*, and in doing so of violating the constitution. A civilian minister is also an essential fuse in preventing civil-military disagreements from becoming unmanageable, as has sometimes threatened in the years since Pardo's appointment: a signal case was the resignation of the minister Rodrigo Lloreda in May 1999, which prevented the resignation of over a dozen generals in protest against Pastrana's conduct of the peace negotiations in the Caguán, a step that would have caused more than mild consternation: Lloreda persuaded them to stay.

Chapter Six

Victims of the Colombian Armed Conflict

The Birth of a Political Actor[1]

Angelika Rettberg

A significant addition to the Colombian political landscape over the past ten years is the participation of victims in the debate over the country's model of transitional justice. Ever since discussions began in 2003 about the *Proyecto de Ley de Alternatividad Penal*, which became the seed of the Colombian transitional justice institutional framework,[2] the over six million victims of forced displacement, homicides, massacres, kidnappings, and other forms of violence[3] have become crucial interlocutors and points of reference. In less than a decade, the reparation and the memory of victims has become part of political debates and of contentious aspirations of actors at the national and sub-national levels. The budget allocated to the development of the institutional framework designed to provide material and symbolic reparations to the victims of the Colombian armed conflict amounts to over USD 29 billion (*54.9 billones de pesos*),[4] including the development of individual and collective reparation schemes as well as initiatives to celebrate the memory of the dead, wounded, and disappeared. In the ongoing peace talks between the Colombian government and the *Fuerzas Armadas Revolucionarias de Colombia* (FARC), the treatment of victims is part of the formal negotiation agenda.[5] The final report of the Colombian Center for Historical Memory, entitled *Basta ya!* (*Enough now!*), was dedicated foremost to the memory of victims.[6] For at least ten more years, victims and their reparations, will play a crucial role in the Colombian state's expenditures as well as in the definition of the mechanisms of transitional justice.

This stands in stark contrast with previous periods in Colombian history, when victims—despite their already growing numbers[7]—were largely invisible in not only more than twenty successful and unsuccessful peace negotiations that have taken place in the country,[8] but also in the overall political debate.[9] What explains this shift in public attention to the plight of millions of Colombians? How does the average Colombian population evaluate the cause and preferential treatment of the Colombian victims? In what way do these opinions reflect tensions between the overall goal of repairing victims and other goals of the Colombian peace building and development agenda? What implications does this have for efforts to build sustainable peace in Colombia?

In brief, this chapter argues that international and domestic factors combined to make visible the plight and number of victims in the country. These factors developed a vast and ambitious transitional justice institutional framework, which will set the tone of transformations for years to come. Similar to other policies, this has not occurred in a political vacuum: victims as well as other actors concerned with the shape and scope of transitional justice in Colombia have become mobilized in the pursuit of their interests, endowed with political preferences and a more or less effective repertoire of political strategies. As a result, the discussion about the role of victims and the state and society's responses to their needs is likely to become a central issue of public debate in the near future.

However, the debate has occurred predominantly among a small group of experts, ignoring and perhaps underestimating some of the prevailing opinions and attitudes about transitional justice held by the general Colombian population. This may prove problematic as several features of the trade-offs and bargains involved in transitional justice mechanisms will impact large parts of the population via elections, taxes, and processes of community integration of victims and perpetrators, all of which are challenges to the ultimate viability and success of transitional justice mechanisms.

For these reasons, this chapter argues that it is important to complement the normative statements of policy makers, activists, and organizations with data on the overall victims' population and on the opinions and attitudes of the average Colombian. In order to do so, it employs data from the *Registro Único de Víctimas* (RUV)—the first attempt to unify information on all types of victimization in the country conducted by the Colombian state—and data from a 2012 survey conducted by a consortium of public and private entities. The RUV data serves to underscore the extent of the suffering. The survey results illustrate some of the structural impediments faced by Colombian victims (such as poverty and little education). In addition, the survey shows that almost a decade of transitional justice pedagogy has paid off in the country: In general, the Colombian population is more aware and understands the magnitude of people impacted by the armed conflict as well as the plight of victims. As a result, a majority of Colombians sympathize with the atrocity of the victims' experiences and endorse the need for reparations.

At the same time, the long duration and the complex nature of the Colombian armed conflict—especially the simultaneous presence of multiple illegal armed actors who have fought over territories for many years, and the similar socioeconomic and often geographic origin of victims and combatants (referred to here as social proximity)—have had an impact on people's opinions and attitudes. Important fractions of the Colombian population, including victims, are fearful of opportunism in accessing state-provided privileges associated with the status of victims and are reticent to accept privileges for victimized populations to the detriment of larger development goals benefiting all Colombians, illustrating the classic peace building versus development dilemma that has historically haunted the peace-building community.[10]

The chapter also explores the organizational dimension of the victims' population: according to available data, 7 percent of the more than six million victims are organized in more than 3,000 organizations, seeking to represent their diverse interests and needs.[11] This level of dispersion is a result both of heterogeneous experiences of victimization and, so far, of a severe incapability of producing collective action. The small percentage of organized victims raises questions about representation in the political debate.

The findings presented here aim to contribute to the developing academic and empirical literature on transitional justice[12] that is still incipient in Colombia, and provide elements for testing some of the prevailing opinions and attitudes about victims in Colombia. It also aims to provide useful insights for practitioners in the global field of transitional justice, as many of the findings about the Colombian case are relevant to other transitional contexts around the world.

The following section will provide a general background of the development of the Colombian transitional justice institutional framework. The third section presents a socio-demographic overview of Colombian victims, based on official and survey sources,[13] in order to help understand who they are, when, and by whom they were victimized. The fourth section will present some general insights about victims, their needs, and proper policy responses, based on public opinion surveys. The fifth section discusses the findings. The conclusions provide a summary and hint at future research directions.

BACKGROUND: THE DEVELOPMENT OF AN INSTITUTIONAL FRAMEWORK

Peace processes in Colombia during the 1980s and 1990s recurrently led to amnesties and pardons of demobilized combatants.[14] Although these are standard mechanisms of the transitional justice repertoire, none of these previous negotiations took into consideration the interests of civil society actors. In-depth discussions about the way Colombia as a whole should cope with its vast record of human rights violations formally began only over the past decade (see table 1 for a list of laws and project laws associated with the development of the Colombian transitional justice framework). In Latin America, Argentina, Chile, Guatemala, and Peru, which had had recent experiences with truth- and justice-seeking, leading to international judicial processes (Chile and Argentina) as well as to domestic truth-seeking reports and commissions (Guatemala's *Comisión de Esclarecimiento Histórico* and Peru's truth commission) all preceded Colombia in the recognition and acknowledgment of its human rights victims.

In 2002, in the aftermath of the failed peace negotiations with the Leftist *Fuerzas Armadas Revolucionarias* (FARC) guerrilla group, the *Autodefensas Unidas de Colombia*—an alliance of several illegal extreme right armed groups also known as paramilitaries—announced a unilateral cease-fire as well as their willingness to begin peace talks leading to their demobilization.[15] This domestic background combined with increased international attention to the development of extensive and comprehensive mechanisms to identify and punish perpetrators, define and register victims, design mechanisms to bring truth and preserve the memory of the dead and wounded, and develop adequate institutional frameworks in so-called transitional countries (i.e., countries emerging from an authoritarian or violent past). The peace process with the AUC thus formally marked the beginning of Colombia's development of a transitional justice framework, defined as a "set of judicial and non-judicial measures (. . .) to redress the legacies of massive human rights abuses."[16]

The development of such a framework has been progressive and began during the government of Álvaro Uribe (2002–2006; 2006–2010). In August

Table 6.1. Milestones in the Development of the Colombian Transitional Justice Framework

Milestone	*Date*
Declaration for the Peace of Colombia "Declaración por la Paz de Colombia"), announcing AUC's ceasefire and willingness to initiate formal peace talks	November 29, 2002
Ley de Alternatividad Penal submitted to Congress	August 21, 2003
Ley de Justicia y Paz submitted to Congress	September 2, 2005
Ley de Justicia y Paz (Ley 975) approved	August 25, 2005
Ley de Víctimas y Restitución de Tierras submitted to Congress	September 27, 2010
Ley de Víctimas y Restitución de Tierras (Ley 1448) approved	June 6, 2011
Marco Jurídico para la Paz submitted to Congress	September 12, 2012
Marco Jurídico para la Paz approved	July 31, 2012

Source: *Congreso Visible* and the author's own elaboration (http://congresovisible.org).

2003, the *Proyecto de Ley de Alternatividad Penal* (or Project Law for Alternative Criminal Procedures) was presented to Congress and inaugurated the debate on these topics in Colombia.[17] However, objections regarding its form and content led to its defeat. A new attempt, the Law for Justice and Peace (*Ley de Justicia y Paz, Ley 975*) was passed by Congress in August 2005, laying the basis of the current, mostly state-funded transitional justice framework. The law created the *Unidad de Justicia y Paz* (Justice and Peace Unity) as part of the Attorney General's Office (*Fiscalía General de la Nación*). In this instance, demobilized combatants could tell their versions of their involvement and responsibility in different crimes in so-called *versiones libres* (or free—as unverified—versions of events).[18] In addition, mechanisms have been developed for the prosecution of crimes, with up to eight years of imprisonment. However, only fourteen cases have been decided[19] and thousands are likely to remain unprosecuted and unpunished. In addition, the Justice and Peace Law created an instance for the reparation of victims (the *Comisión Nacional de Reparación y Reconciliación*), designed several reparation schemes and managed related funds.[20] The CNRR also supervised the work of the Group for Historical Memory, which was in charge of researching and producing reports about so-called emblematic cases of human rights violations in different regions of the country.[21]

In order to complement and strengthen the attention of victims, the government of Juan Manuel Santos supported the development of a Victims' Law and for the Restitution of Land (*Ley 1448 de 2011*). Its author, Senator Juan Fernando Cristo,[22] himself a victim (the *Ejército de Liberación Nacional*—ELN killed his father in 1997), argued that while the Law for Justice and Peace had been tailored to the needs of the perpetrators, this law was designed for the purpose of protecting victims. Adding to previous efforts, the Victims' Law contemplates the creation of the *Unidad de Víctimas*, an organization endowed with a generous budget designed to register and provide reparations over six million people.[23]

The definition of victims in this law has guided policy formulation ever since. It states that "to the effects of this law, victims are people who individually or collectively have suffered harm since January 1, 1985, as a result of violations of International Humanitarian Law or other grave violations of International Human Rights norms,"[24] as well as their partners (including same-sex partners), siblings, and children. Third parties who were harmed when intervening to prevent victimization are also considered victims, as well as members of the Public Forces. Members of the illegal armed groups shall not be considered victims except if they qualified as minors at the moment of their demobilization.[25]

While the Law for Justice and Peace was designed against the background of the demobilization of the paramilitaries and the Victims' Law was directed specifically at victims, the last addition to the Colombian transitional justice framework—the project law for a Judicial Framework for Peace (*Acto Legislativo para un Marco Jurídico para la Paz*)—is aimed at providing a platform for the expected demobilization of the FARC and, most likely, the ELN.[26] It has both palliative and prescriptive elements, integrating lessons from previous experience—mostly problems—with the Justice and Peace Law while designing new approaches to allow for a swift demobilization of over 8,000 FARC fighters expected to hand in their weapons.

As in the case of its predecessors, justice and politics are intertwined in this law. Involved actors struggle to balance maximum justice with stable peace. Actors on the Right are aligned with actors on the Left in defense of minimum impunity. The FARC, the projected law's main target, has also opposed the law arguing it has not been discussed on the negotiation table and assumes military surrender.[27] In addition, the FARC has only grudgingly admitted its part in the violation of human rights in Colombia, claiming that the FARC is an organization of victims who have suffered from state repression and abandonment.[28] Others have highlighted the need to provide a peace agreement with stability, which will be imperiled should demobilized combatants face lengthy jail sentences, leading them to abandon the process. In addition, policy makers and scholars have pointed to the limited capacity of the Colombian judicial system in terms of prosecution and imprisonment, with an impunity rate of around 90 percent.[29] In response, the Colombian government supports the introduction of priority and selection criteria in order to limit judicial sentences to those with the most responsibility in the case of the worst crimes, as well as the protection of victims' rights in terms of truth and reparation. The proposed framework was backed by the Constitutional Court.

Public discussion of transitional justice mechanisms has had the unexpected effect of adding a new perspective for evaluating the background and motivations of those currently involved in the Colombian armed conflict. Alias *Pablo Catatumbo*, one of the FARC's negotiators involved in the Havana (Cuba) peace talks, has said that he too has been a victim of torture and kidnapping.[30] People as diverse as Carlos Castaño, the now deceased former leader of the paramilitary forces, Juan Fernando Cristo, the senator behind the Victims' Law, and former President Álvaro Uribe had their fathers killed by different guerrilla groups, illustrating the impact that widespread victimization has had on Colombian politics.

In addition, demobilized combatants in the Justice and Peace process have recurrently emphasized their own victimization previous to taking up arms. In what has been referred to as a tension between "*verdad judicial o verdad histórica* (judicial truth or historical truth),"[31] this strategic use of the victim status likely will have implications on future debates on the extent and conditions of transitional justice mechanisms.

More importantly, the development of this framework has had the effect of raising awareness about the plight of victims as well as what society owes them. In this sense, the changes that have occurred over the past years in the institutional framework have increased the legitimacy of victims when speaking out and demanding their rights. As a result, their rights and needs have not only been acknowledged by a vast set of rules, institutions, and organizations, but have also become substantially enmeshed in the Colombian state's concerns and policy priorities. At the same time, the institutional incentives as well as the material and intangible resources at stake have provided a platform for the development of political preferences and strategies by all actors involved. In this context, victims as political actors have shown a growing interest in making their voices heard in congressional and other debates, often times in alliance with Colombian and foreign NGOs.

VICTIMS IN COLOMBIA: A DESCRIPTION

This section will present a general overview of the Colombian victim population.[32] It will present official data from the *Registro Único de Víctimas* (*RUV*), the first attempt to centralize information from different sources on victimization in Colombia. The RUV draws from information collected mainly by the *Unidad de Víctimas*, but adds several previously developed sources, including Acción Social on forced displacement, *Programa de Acción Integral contra Minas Antipersonal* (PAICMA) on land mines, FONDELIBERTAD on kidnappings, and *Instituto Colombiano de Bienestar* Familiar (ICBF) on minors. The development of the RUV was mandated by the Victims' Law (1448 of 2011) and is being led by the *Unidad de Víctimas*. In addition, the section draws from a representative survey of the Colombian population conducted in 2012.[33]

Table 6.2 begins with a distinction by types of victimization registered since 1987. Some figures, such as those for forced displacement, have been periodically reviewed and monitored by state and nongovernmental organizations. As can be seen, forced displacement is by far the most frequent form of victimization in Colombia. It is also one on which foreign and domestic organizations have most energetically worked on and dedicated resources to since the 1990s, at the onset of the most acute wave of the humanitarian crisis, well in advance of any discussion on transitional justice mechanisms in the country.[34] Other forms of victimization include homicides and massacres, kidnappings, and forced disappearances. The recruitment of minors by illegal

Table 6.2. Types and Frequency of Victimization (1987–2012)

Type of Victimization	*Male*	*Female*	*LGBTI*	*Does Not Report*	*Under Review*	*Sub-total*
Crimes against sexual freedom and integrity due to armed conflict	445	2.637	4	30	154	3.270
Massive events	3.982	4.032	2	21	90	8.127
Recruitment of minors to armed groups	5.626	3.017	0	123	557	9.323
Torture	5.158	4.314	2	96	289	9.859
Land mines, unexploded ordnance and improvised explosive devices	11.686	1.072	1	11	986	13.756
Others	7.095	4.665	0	333	9.419	21.512
Kidnapping	31.827	10.998	0	237	666	43.728
Terrorist acts, attacks, combats, confrontations and other forms of harassment	26.398	16.902	7	3.686	1.389	48.382
Threats	33.432	35.488	39	380	324	69.663
Forced disappearance	49.156	47.502	4	1.226	2.397	100.285
Land abandonment and forced dispossession	59.389	53.548	2	37.758	2.832	153.529
Homicides	367.066	349.332	35	9.448	14.680	740.561
Forced displacement	2.549.358	2.662.856	219	1.788	16.784	5.231.005
Total number of different types of victimization reported	3.150.618	3.196.363	315	55.137	50.567	6.453.000

Baseline: 6.453.000 reported types of victimization. Cutoff date: April 30, 2012.
Note: Individuals may report more than one type of victimization.

Source: Unidad para la Atención y Reparación Integral de las Víctimas—Registro Único de Víctimas (RUV).

armed groups is a widespread phenomenon among illegal actors. Estimates, however, suggest that the FARC and ELN recruit more minors that other internal armed actors in Colombia (up to half of FARC fighters are presumed to have been recruited when they were minors).[35]

According to RUV, as of April 2012, 5,565,609 people had been formally registered as victims in Colombia (some of whom reported more than one form of victimization). According to Figure 6.1, they are almost evenly split according to gender. According to Figure 6.2, most registered victims are young adults, with over 40 percent under the age of nineteen. In addition, the average age of the whole population of victims is twenty-eight. Figure 6.3 illustrates the ethnicity of the victims. Afro-Colombian and indigenous communities are represented in lower proportions than among the general

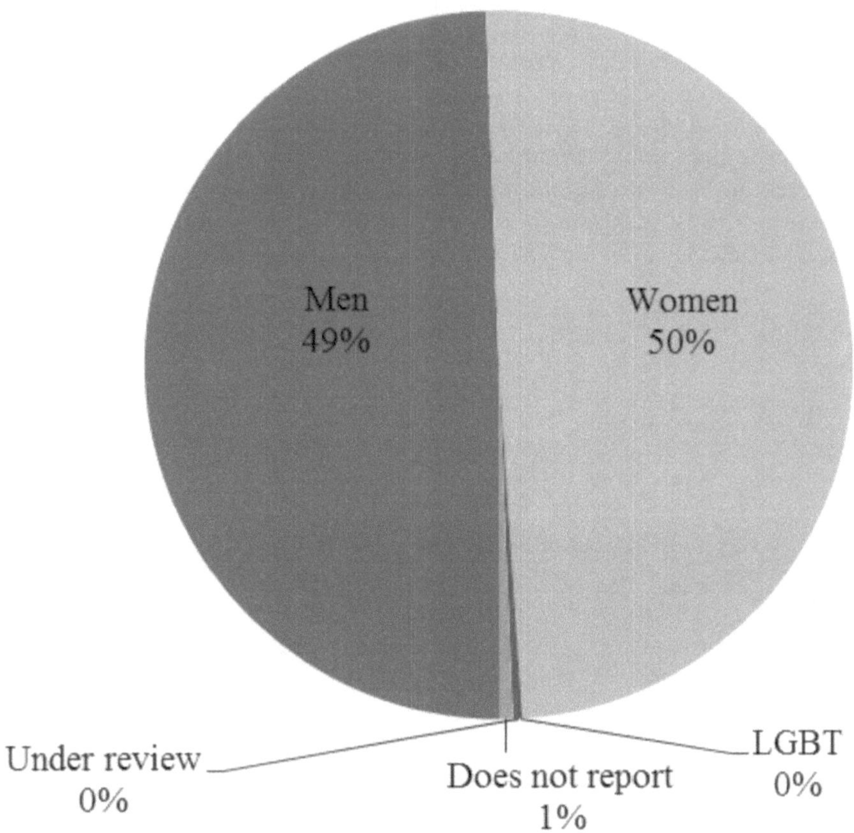

Figure 6.1. Victims' Distribution by Gender

Source: Unidad para la Atención y Reparación Integral de las Víctimas—Registro Único de Víctimas. Baseline: 5.565.609 registered victims. Cutoff date: April 30, 2012. Note: The data base includes self-identifications as LGBT (Lesbian, Gay, Bi- or Transexual Gender) since 1984.

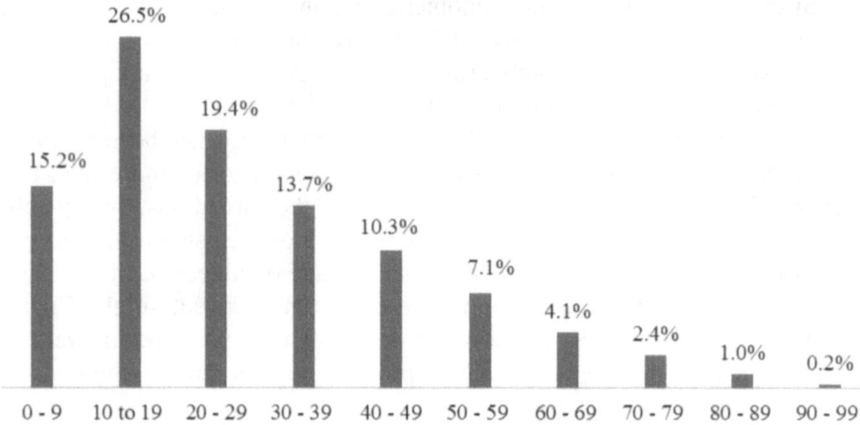

Figure 6.2. Victims' Distribution by Age

Source: Unidad para la Atención y Reparación Integral de las Víctimas—Registro Único de Víctimas. Baseline: 4.902.961 registered victims who declared their age. Cutoff date: April 30, 2012.

Colombian population. Very few victims are registered as disabled. Figure 6.4 shows that victims are not evenly spread across Colombia: The Caribbean region in the North and the Central region have been hit the hardest. Figure 6.5 illustrates one of the most daunting tasks for policy makers: Poverty is widespread among Colombian conflict victims, with most be-

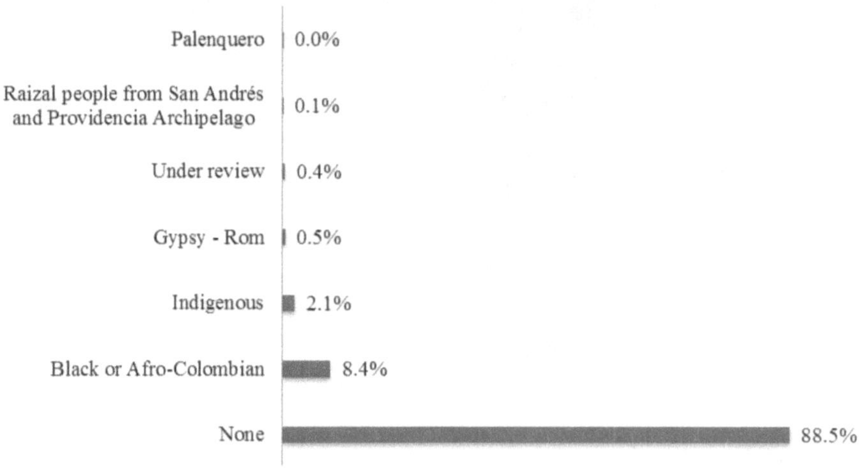

Figure 6.3. Victims' Ethnicity

Source: Unidad para la Atención y Reparación Integral de las Víctimas—Registro Único de Víctimas. Baseline: 5.565.609 registered victims. Cutoff date: April 30, 2012. Note: The options offered to respondents regarding their ethnicity followed the structure of the National Census of 2005: indigenous population, Rom, raizal of the San Andrés and Providencia Archipelago, palenquero, black or Afrocolombian, and "none of the above." No distinction was made between mestizos and Caucasian origins, as if ethnicity was limited to non-whites. "Raizal" and "palenquero" are categories contemplated to account for different historical trajectories: "Palenqueros" are descendants of runaway slaves living along the Caribbean Coast. "Raizales" are also descendants of slaves, but of English-speaking communities in the United States who migrated to several Caribbean islands.

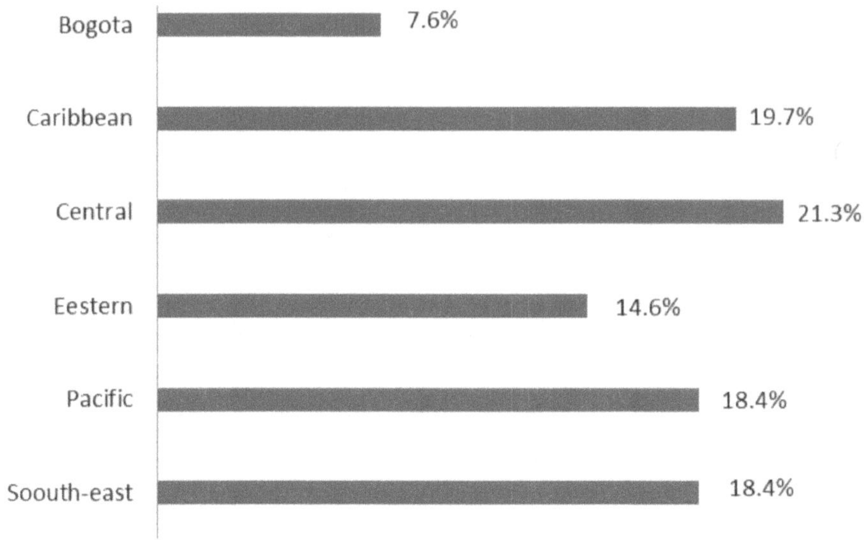

Figure 6.4. Victims' Distribution by Region

Source: Centro de Memoria Histórica (CMH), International Organization for Migrations (IOM), Fundación Social (FS), and Universidad de los Andes, Encuesta nacional: ¿Qué piensan los colombianos después de siete años de justicia y paz? (Bogota: CMH, IOM, Universidad de los Andes, 2012) The regions are made up as follows: East (Boyacá, Cundinamarca, Santander, Norte de Santander), South-East (Huila, Meta, Tolima), Caribbean (Atlántico, Bolívar, Cesar, Córdoba, La Guajira, Sucre), Central (Antioquia, Caldas, Quindío), Pacific Coast (Nariño, Valle), and Bogotá. Baseline: 315 surveys to victims.

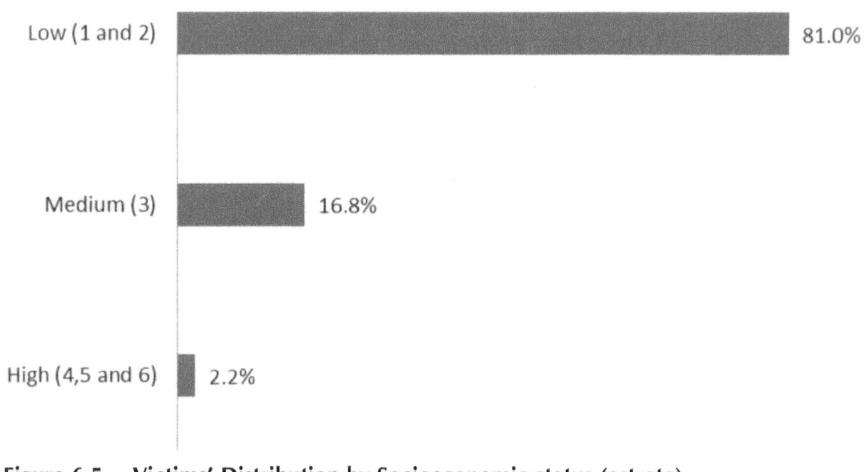

Figure 6.5. Victims' Distribution by Socioeconomic status (estrato)

Source: Centro de Memoria Histórica (CMH), International Organization for Migrations (IOM), Fundación Social (FS), and Universidad de los Andes, Encuesta nacional: ¿Qué piensan los colombianos después de siete años de justicia y paz? (Bogota: CMH, IOM, Universidad de los Andes, 2012) Note: Estratos are socioeconomic categories defined not by family income but by home characteristics and access to public services and utilities (DANE 2013). Baseline: 315 surveys to victims.

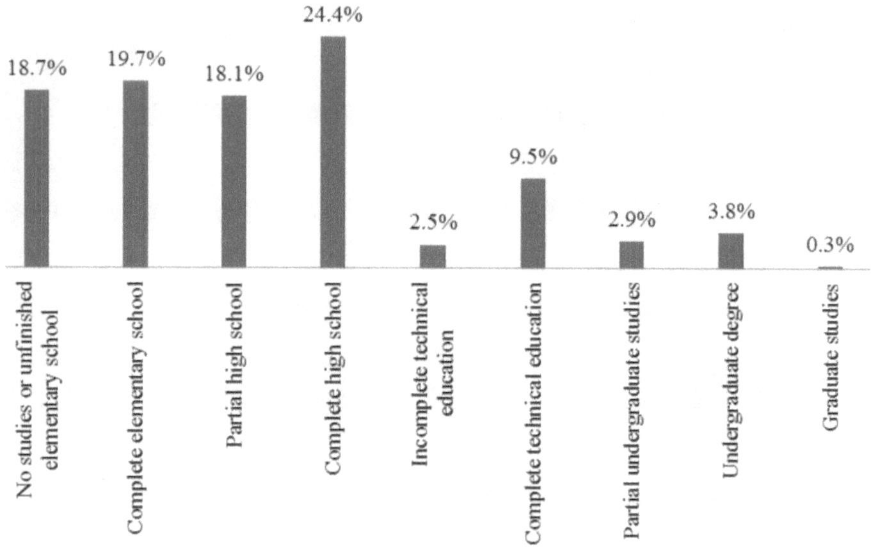

Figure 6.6. Victims' Distribution by Education

Source: Centro de Memoria Histórica (CMH), International Organization for Migrations (IOM), Fundación Social (FS), and Universidad de los Andes, Encuesta nacional: ¿Qué piensan los colombianos después de siete años de justicia y paz? (Bogota: CMH, IOM, Universidad de los Andes, 2012) Baseline: 315 surveys to victims.

longing to low *estratos* (*estratos* are socioeconomic categories defined not by family income but by home characteristics and access to public services and utilities).[36] Figure 6.6 shows the implications of widespread poverty: almost a fifth of the victims' population has received no formal education, over half have less than a high school degree. Only one-quarter of the population finished high school.

Figures 6.7 and 6.8 highlight the alleged identities of the perpetrators and the varying intensity of the waves of violence in Colombia. With 38.7 percent, guerrilla groups lead the alleged perpetrators according to the National Registry of Victims (Figure 6.7), whereas paramilitary groups appear to be responsible for 18.6 percent of crimes. "Others" or "unidentified" perpetrators make up more than 40 percent of those alleged to be responsible. Criminal bands and the Armed Forces are represented only by small fractions. While these are unverified data and originate in the statements of victims at the time of their registration reports, the numbers confirm that the guerrillas and the paramilitary groups have been, and continue to be, responsible for widespread suffering and destruction. In addition, the large number of "others" or "unidentified" groups included in the registry suggests that people may be fearful when reporting their victimization, leading them to withhold infor-

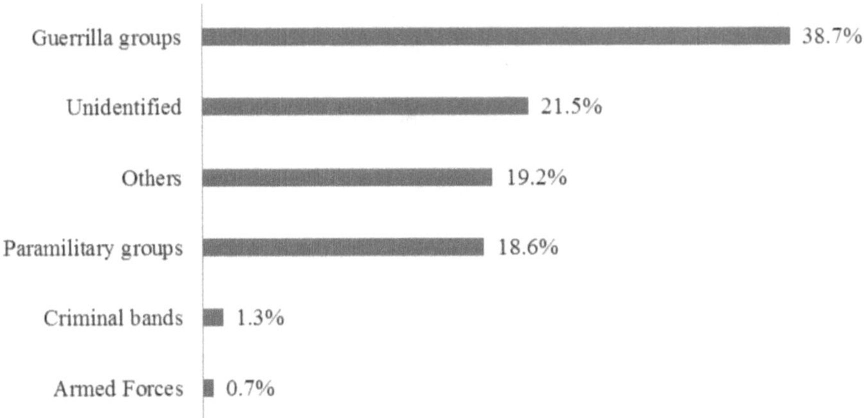

Figure 6.7. Alleged Perpetrators

Source: Unidad para la Atención y Reparación Integral de las Víctimas—Registro Único de Víctimas (RUV). Baseline: 5.573.111 reported crimes. Cutoff date: April 30, 2012.

mation, or that people actually ignore who and what caused their problems, bringing home the often confusing nature of the local contexts of violence.

Figure 6.8 presents information about Colombia's recent waves of violence. While unverified and based on date of register and not on when events actually occurred (some facts may therefore be reported much later than they occurred), the figure is consistent with data on conflict intensity: The humanitarian crisis of the mid to end 1990s—which saw a surge in forced displacement[37]—is well captured by this data,[38] as well as the steady decline in levels

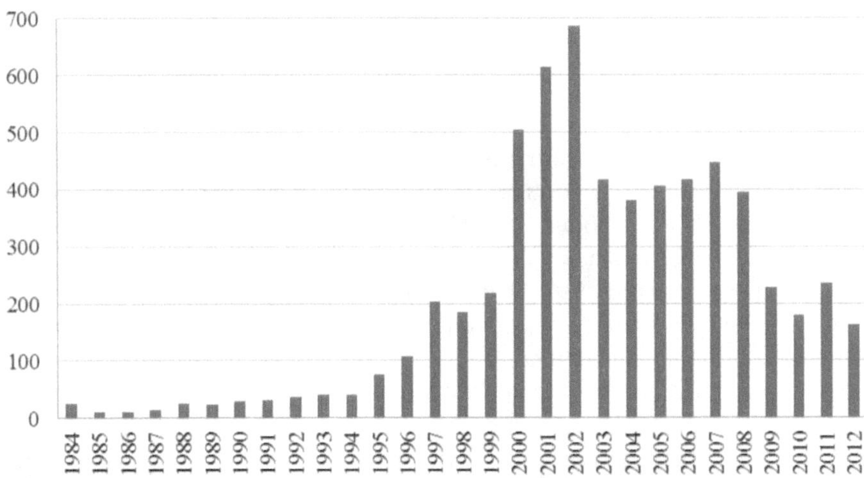

Figure 6.8. Year in Which Victimization Was Reported

Source: Unidad para la Atención y Reparación Integral de las Víctimas—Registro Único de Víctimas (RUV). Baseline: 5.471.216 reported crimes. Cutoff date: April 30, 2012.

of violence that the country has been experiencing since 2002. However, victimization is ongoing, illustrating the challenges faced by the Colombian state both in terms of registering victims and designing reparation programs. The figure also suggests that victims responding to the institutional incentives today are likely to have been recently victimized.[39]

The previous paragraphs provide a somber picture of the state and challenges faced by victims in Colombia. The country leads other conflict countries in terms of the sheer size of the affected population. Despite recent trends regarding diminishing intensity of violence and growing state presence, rural areas especially continue to be threatened by a diverse set of criminal actors. Along with pressure by armed actors, Colombian victims face different structural disadvantages, such as poverty and little education. Taken together, these factors underscore the daunting task faced by policy makers in terms of identifying and addressing victims' needs and best reparations' programs in the context of a larger set of transitional justice measures. The development of a transitional justice institutional framework, described in the previous section, reflects some of the state's responses. Additionally, victims need to be understood as political actors within a larger context of public opinion and deep-seated population attitudes that, in addition to good policy, will be likely to define the prospects and success of transitional justice mechanisms in Colombia. The following section addresses some of these issues.

VICTIMS IN CONTEXT: GENERAL PERCEPTIONS AND COLLECTIVE ACTION

The design of transitional justice mechanisms in countries experiencing transitions tends to occur among small circles of experts and advocates. Larger debates about fundamental questions such as how much impunity a society is willing or capable of bearing in the long or the short run in exchange for silencing the guns are not routinely conducted in open forums.[40] However, the general population's opinions and attitudes can affect the success of transitional justice mechanisms in at least three ways.

First, in democratic systems elections and other forms of popular participation (such as referenda) operate both as a risk and as an opportunity for peace building, in general, and transitional justice, in particular. The population can directly vote on transitional justice dispositions or peace agreements, or can indirectly punish or support transitional justice mechanisms by electing like-minded politicians. The significance of popular participation for transitional justice was made clear in Guatemala in 1998, when constitutional reforms needed to implement the 1996 peace agreement were not only rejected but faced large levels of voting absenteeism.[41] In Colombia, institutions such as the presidency and Congress—both of electoral origins—have had leading roles (in addition to the courts) in developing transitional justice policy. At the beginning of his term, the government of Juan Manuel Santos was careful to consolidate a congressional coalition—the National Unity, *Unidad Nacional*—in order to promote a legislative agenda that included both the Victims' Law as well as the possibility of holding talks with the guerrillas.[42] Concerns about reelection and the electoral business cycle may thus operate as incentives or constraints in terms of content and timing of transitional justice mechanisms, in general, and in terms of attention paid to victims' needs, in particular.

However, the tensions between democracy and transitional justice are not limited to the consequences of popular participation. In addition, the majority principle may also potentially pose problems for transitional justice,[43] which is concerned mainly with the rights and needs of minorities. Majorities may be less willing to support measures aimed at truth-seeking or punishment of perpetrators for fear this might open wounds or destabilize political agreements. Another factor is that majorities may be reluctant to support reparations of victims for fear that this may distract valuable resources from other policy needs, including those of non-victims. When Carlos Castaño, the leader of the Colombian paramilitary groups, demobilized in 2003 prior to the publication of the Justice and Peace Law, many within the Colombian population were condescending and willing to forgive his confessed crimes. A survey commissioned by *Semana* magazine in 2007 showed that a third of the Colombian population—particularly more men and low-income individuals—agreed with the statement that "paramilitary groups were necessary in the country in order to stop the guerrillas."[44] While these are no majorities, the example helps to make a point regarding the potential tension between the public will and what is desirable for minorities, such as victims.

A related consideration is taxes. Against a background of diminishing international cooperation,[45] it is likely that the bulk of the burden to fund transitional justice, DDR, and other peace-building activities will fall on the general Colombian population's shoulder. In this context, it is important to learn whether the country's general population is willing to bear the costs implied by transitional justice and peace building, in general, and, specifically, by victims' reparations and other efforts to protect the memory of victimized populations. Tax evasion is still high in Latin America, and Colombia is no exception.[46] As elsewhere on the sub-continent, the majority of the country's population believes that paying taxes equals playing into the hands of corrupt state officials or fellow citizens and opportunists. If the population is reluctant to support the costs of transitional justice and given that tax evasion is an option, public officials and practitioners are better off knowing what type of measures the population is less likely to resist.

Finally, beyond democracy and taxes, there is the question of *community integration*, or the extent to which communities throughout Colombia will accept the social and symbolic costs of policies such as the reparation of victims and the reintegration of former fighters, can also have an impact on the effectiveness of transitional justice. According to Rettberg and Rettberg and Prieto,[47] social proximity among Colombian victims and demobilized combatants is quite high. Prieto[48] explored the implications of social proximity in several Colombian communities, and found that contrary to common expectations regarding deep-seated divisions and hatreds, victims and former combatants are and have been peacefully sharing work spaces, schools, and have even engaged in sentimental relations. In some communities this reflects a continued status of superior hierarchy by demobilized combatants. In others it may result from war fatigue, apathy, or a willingness to leave the past behind. Rettberg[49] shows that, on average, the Colombian population appears to be less vengeful and more prone to reconcile than the accumulation of atrocities throughout five decades of armed conflict as well as the dominant public discourse of victims' organizations would suggest.

PUBLIC OPINION ON VICTIMS IN COLOMBIA

The previous factors explain why it is important to learn about the Colombian population's opinions and attitudes faced with transitional justice mechanisms and trade-offs, as well as, specifically, with the fate and reparation of victims. The following paragraphs will explore some of these factors based on a national survey of the Colombian population.[50]

Figure 6.9 answers the question: who is responsible for the violence that occurred in the country? In general, people perceive the guerrillas as responsible, while "all of us Colombians" ranks second, suggesting a sense of shared responsibility for what has happened in the country and, likely, for what will happen in the future. This perception of collective responsibility is an important asset for politicians and practitioners seeking support for transitional justice measures, including victims' reparations.

Figure 6.10 addresses a crucial question regarding whether and how society values the experience of victims. The balance is positive: almost 70 percent of the general population, and 76 percent of victims included in the survey, agrees with the statement according to which "generally speaking, (victims) were innocent people who were unjustly affected." To be noted, and a cause for further investigation, is the fifth of the general population who

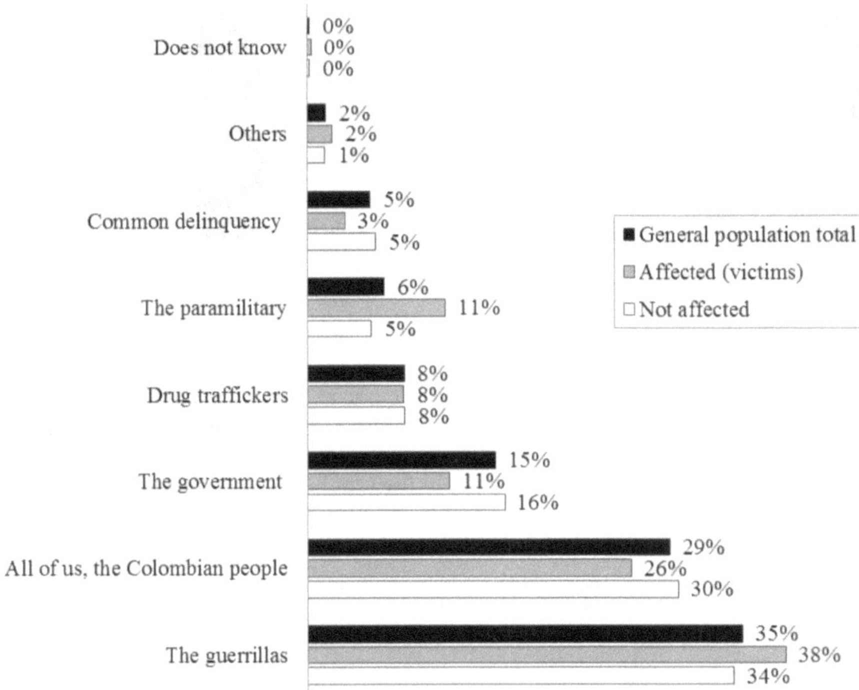

Figure 6.9. Who Is Responsible for Violence in Colombia?

Source: Centro de Memoria Histórica (CMH), International Organization for Migrations (IOM), Fundación Social (FS), and Universidad de los Andes, Encuesta nacional: ¿Qué piensan los colombianos después de siete años de justicia y paz? (Bogota: CMH, IOM, Universidad de los Andes, 2012) Baseline: 315 surveys to affected people; 1528 surveys to non-affected people.

agreed with the statement according to which "generally speaking, (victims) were people linked to illegal armed groups or who performed illegal activities and therefore were affected." Figure 6.11 presents responses to the following question: "Some people have told us their opinion about the reparations that victims are receiving. Which better reflects yours?" A decisive majority of the general population and of victims (over 70 percent) supported the statement that "although other people in the country face needs, in order for justice to occur it is important for victims to be repaired." Only a small percentage supported the view that "it is unfair for victims to receive reparations while other people in the country are in need."

In contrast with this extensive support for the victims' cause, figure 6.12 presents responses to the question of whether people who will benefit from the Victims' Law are "a) people who pose as victims to receive benefits or b) really are victims who deserve those benefits." Half of the general population supported each of the statements. Notably, victims were most critical of

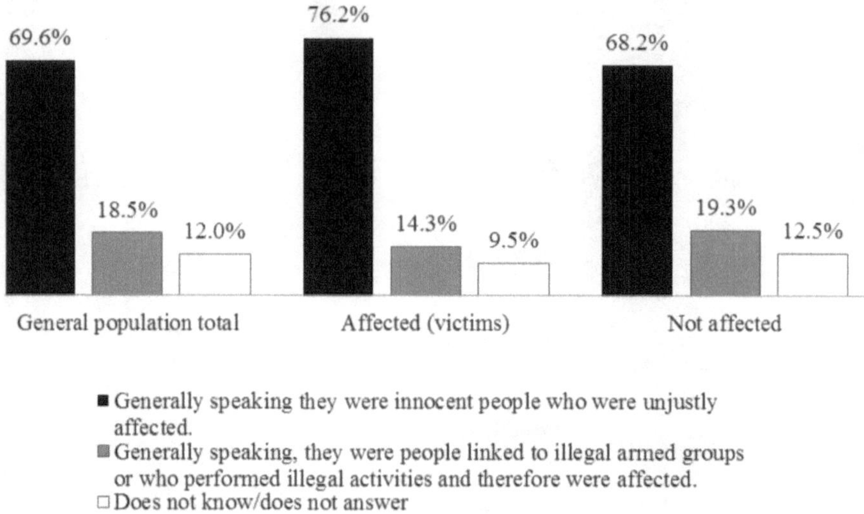

Figure 6.10. Thinking About the Victims of the Conflict, with Which of the Following Statements Do You Agree Most?

Source: Centro de Memoria Histórica (CMH), International Organization for Migrations (IOM), Fundación Social (FS), and Universidad de los Andes, Encuesta nacional: ¿Qué piensan los colombianos después de siete años de justicia y paz? (Bogota: CMH, IOM, Universidad de los Andes, 2012) Baseline: 315 surveys to affected people; 1528 surveys to non-affected people.

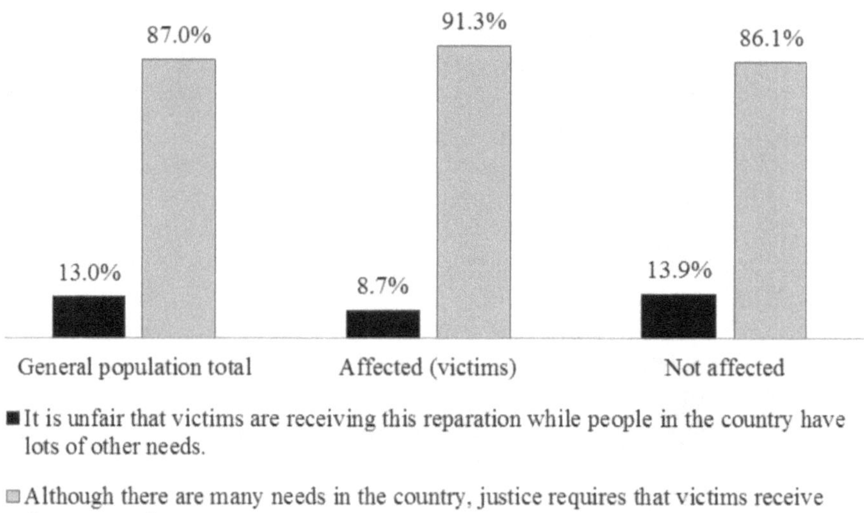

Figure 6.11. "Some people have told us their opinion about the reparations that victims are receiving. Which best reflects yours?"

Source: Centro de Memoria Histórica (CMH), International Organization for Migrations (IOM), Fundación Social (FS), and Universidad de los Andes, Encuesta nacional: ¿Qué piensan los colombianos después de siete años de justicia y paz? (Bogota: CMH, IOM, Universidad de los Andes, 2012) Baseline: 315 surveys to affected people; 1528 surveys to non-affected people.

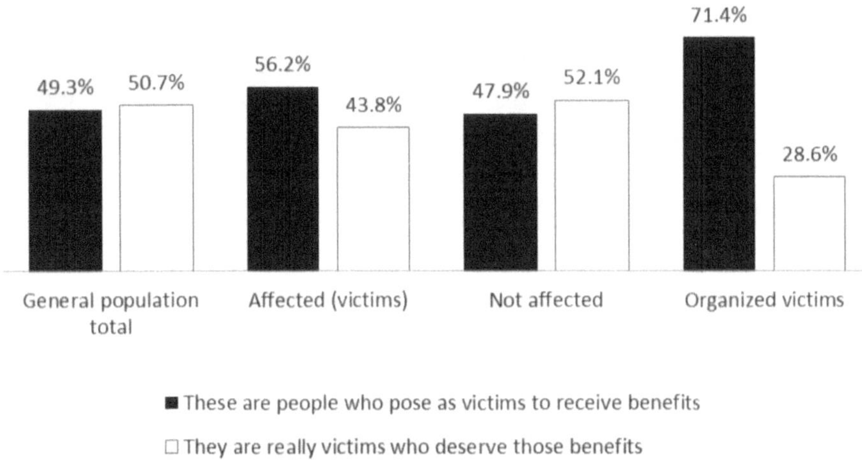

Figure 6.12. "Do you believe that most people who will benefit from the Law of Victims . . ."

Source: Centro de Memoria Histórica (CMH), International Organization for Migrations (IOM), Fundación Social (FS), and Universidad de los Andes, Encuesta nacional: ¿Qué piensan los colombianos después de siete años de justicia y paz? (Bogota: CMH, IOM, Universidad de los Andes, 2012) Baseline: 315 surveys to affected people; 1528 surveys to not affected people; 304 surveys to organized victims.

potential opportunists seeking to benefit from the law. Figure 6.13 produced similar results. When asked which statement reflected their own opinion better, 65 percent of the general population and 71 percent of the victims supported the opinion that "victims should receive the same attention by the state as those not affected by conflict" while 22 percent of both segments supported the view that "victims receive too many privileges by the state." Figure 6.14 engages the critical question of taxes: the majority of the three segments supported the view that, despite limited resources, the state must comply with all its obligations, including poverty reduction and victims' reparations, even if this means raising taxes. However, a quarter of the general population felt that sacrificing resources for reparations was justified in order to comply with obligations such as poverty reduction and development for all.

Finally, a few thoughts on the effects of victim organizations on opinions toward transitional justice will be discussed below. According to the *Unidad de Víctimas*, there are currently more than 3,000 victims' organizations in Colombia, competing for limited resources, legitimacy, and public attention. However, only approximately 7 percent of victims report to be linked to organizations.[51] No encompassing organization has emerged so far, in part because the experience of victimization differs widely for different groups, with class, region, and ideology associated with differing preferences (upper income segments of the population are most affected by kidnappings,

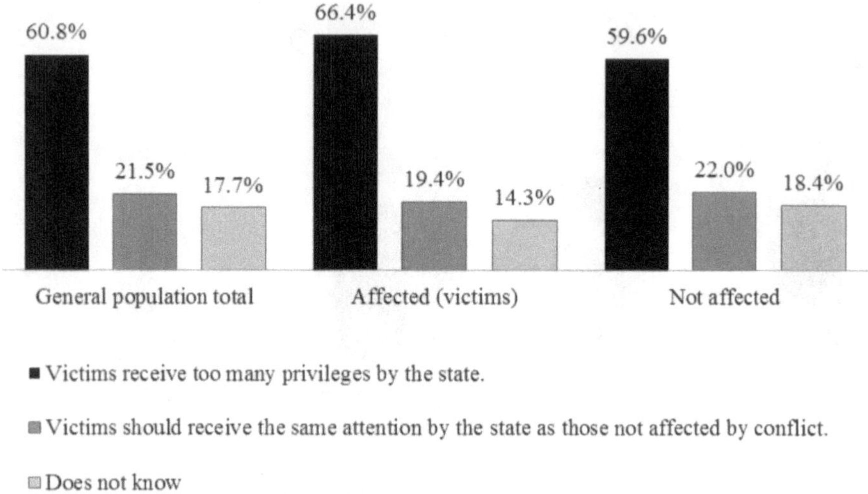

Figure 6.13. Which of these statements reflects your opinion better?

Source: Centro de Memoria Histórica (CMH), International Organization for Migrations (IOM), Fundación Social (FS), and Universidad de los Andes, Encuesta nacional: ¿Qué piensan los colombianos después de siete años de justicia y paz? (Bogota: CMH, IOM, Universidad de los Andes, 2012) Baseline: 315 surveys to affected people; 1528 surveys to not affected people.

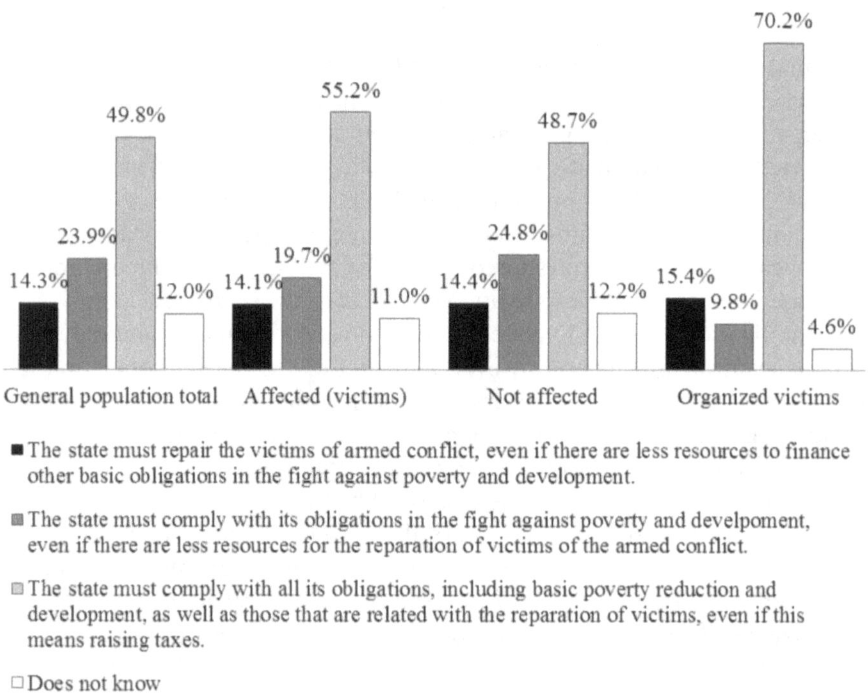

Figure 6.14. The Colombian state has limited resources. With this in mind, with which of the following statements do you agree with most?

Source: Centro de Memoria Histórica (CMH), International Organization for Migrations (IOM), Fundación Social (FS), and Universidad de los Andes, Encuesta nacional: ¿Qué piensan los colombianos después de siete años de justicia y paz? (Bogota: CMH, IOM, Universidad de los Andes, 2012) Baseline: 315 surveys to affected people; 1528 surveys to not affected people; 304 surveys to organized victims.

gender-related violence and massacres were more common in the north of the country, and forced disappearances are mainly linked to leftist activism).

The heterogeneous composition of the population of victims in Colombia has implications for victims' opinions on matters related to transitional justice. For example, organized victims more vehemently (71 percent) supported the view that people who will benefit from the Victims' Law "really are victims who deserve those benefits" (in contrast with 49.3 percent of the general population and 56.2 percent of victims, compare Figure 6.12). As shown in Figure 6.14, organizations also weigh heavier on the opinion that the state should fulfill all its obligations with victims in terms of reparations, even if this implies a tax raise (70 percent of organized victims share this opinion in contrast with 47 percent of the general population and 52 percent of unorganized victims).[52]

PERSPECTIVES ON VICTIMS OF ARMED CONFLICT IN COLOMBIA

The data presented in the previous sections depicts the diversity of Colombian victims, as well as several illuminating opinions by the Colombian population. As a whole, they offer insights that may be useful for scholars and practitioners alike.

United for Victims' Rights

Perhaps the most important finding regarding the role of victims in contemporary Colombian society is that almost ten years of transitional justice pedagogy seems to have paid off: Colombians seem to understand the challenges and dilemmas involved in defining the mechanisms that will allow the country to leave behind its violent past. Particularly victims benefit from this apparent policy consensus. While minority groups on the left and right question the implications of transitional justice mechanisms for obtaining justice, and other sectors fear the fiscal consequences of massive economic commitments to peace-building objectives, no systematic criticism has been levied against the cause of victims and their reparations, even if this is to imply that the Colombian population will absorb the associated costs. Overall, mainstream Colombians seem to have become growingly aware of the scope, intensity, and wrongfulness of the human rights violations. As illustrated by Figure 6.9, this collective sense of shared responsibility will be a critical asset for politicians and practitioners seeking to build a political support base for upcoming transitional justice measures and for sustaining efforts to repair victims throughout the years. It may also explain the vigorous support both of views about the general innocence of victims (Figure 6.10) as well as their reparations (Figure 6.11). Of course, social desirability, or the tendency for people to answer what they think a researcher would like to hear or what is politically correct, may tilt the balance in favor of the perceived benefits of transitional justice. Still, the size of the majorities of all segments that supported the relevant views lends credibility to the assertion that Colombians are generally supportive of victims of the armed conflict.

Fears of Cheating

At the same time, the data presented here highlights several challenges, which will have to be addressed. As in the case of any policy, the structure of incentives provided by the growingly complex Colombian transitional justice framework has activated a group of political actors, including victims, who compete over domestic and international resources and public attention. In doing so, the strategic value of depicting oneself as a victim has increased in contrast with previous periods in Colombian history. As mentioned above, former fighters tend to underscore their own previous victimization as a justification or a palliative of their actions.[53] In addition, so-called false victims have occasionally hired lawyers to reap the benefits of reparations, as was uncovered in relation to the massacre of Mapiripán.[54] While this is by no means a general practice, it does feed into people's fear of others cheating the system and potential resource squandering, as shown by Figures 6.12 and 6.14.

Social Proximity as an Opportunity?

In addition, the objective reality in many Colombian regions has been that many victims and combatants emerge from the same or similar communities. Recruitment practices by all illegal groups have been linked to the splitting up of families and communities. Also, the vagaries of war throughout decades of confrontation have led communities to change patrons frequently. Many fled from the consequences of changing allegiances or power shifts, as demonstrated by the high rates of forced displacement throughout the country. However, many did not, leading to what Orozco[55] has referred to as "shades of grey" in the distinction between victims and perpetrators. In contexts of high social proximity and weak state presence, to date the guerrilla commander or to cook for the passing troops may not only have been a result of coercion, but of simple convenience and lack of other options. Therefore, results in Figure 6.10, showing that an important percentage of all segments, including victims, distinguishing between "innocent" victims and "people linked to illegal armed groups," should not be surprising. Orozco[56] has provided a solution to this dilemma by stating that what really matters to qualify as a victim is not the degree to which someone was linked to previous acts of violence but the sheer state of vulnerability of the victim at the time of his/her victimization.

The Organized Voices of Victims

An additional challenge that can be deduced from the structure of incentives is reflected both in the number of victims' organizations as well as in the heterogeneous composition of the population of Colombian victims, resulting in a lack of capacity to produce joint policy positions and collective action. As expressed by Figure 6.14, organized victims—who participate in the political process—tend to hold opinions that may differ from those of non-organized victims. This has implications regarding who speaks for the victims in the political debate and how reparation policy is designed. A key challenge for the government is to collect needs and demands from all sectors and regions and combine them into an integral nationwide reparations policy.

Peace Versus Development?

A final challenge arises from questions regarding the need to distinguish between reparations—a specific peace-building purpose—and development, a more general aspiration shared by many non-transitional countries in the world. The discussion is not new but has not been solved. As addressed in Figures 6.11, 6.13, and 6.14, tensions may arise between non-victimized poor communities and communities including victims and demobilized fighters, who are benefiting from specific peace-building policies. Policy makers have been pressed to explain the peace-building components of projects such as building roads, bridges, and housing for victimized communities, while many victims themselves may prefer material forms of reparations (such as a home or a pension for old age) over intangible goods such as preserving the memory of the dead with a costly monument.[57] In part, the difficulty arises from the obvious connections between the peace-building and development agendas, especially in contexts such as the Colombian, in which so many development goals are still pending. In part, the dangers may also be associated with one-dimensional understandings of how people overcome loss and of the complex dynamics by which victimized communities resume collective life.

CONCLUSIONS

This chapter has addressed a factor of great relevance in contemporary Colombia, which will have a large impact on the country's imminent future: the victims of the armed conflict. Not only their presence on the current peace negotiation agenda between the government and the FARC, but also the development of a vast and ambitious institutional framework speak to the importance Colombian policy makers and society have assigned to this critical actor, in contrast with previous moments in national history. In this way, while they were largely absent from both sides' agendas during the last time the government and the FARC attempted peace talks in the region of Caguán (1999–2002), the benchmark of success for peace talks in Cuba in 2013 will likely be (in addition to the disarmament of the FARC) the degree to which victims are acknowledged and compensated. This reflects both the newly acquired legitimacy of their cause among the general population as well as the medium- to long-term commitments in terms of reparation assumed by the Colombian state.

NOTES

1. I want to thank Daniel Quiroga for his research assistance. Many data included in this chapter were obtained from a national survey conducted by an alliance of Centro de Memoria Histórica, Fundación Social, and Universidad de los Andes with the financial support of IOM. I also thank Paula Gaviria and Jaime González, of the *Unidad de Víctimas*, Departamento de Prosperidad Social, for making available the database of Colombian victims (*Registro Único de Víctimas—RUV*). Also, a special thanks to my brilliant colleague Iván Orozco, with whom I have had extensive and interesting conversations on many of these subjects. The completion of this chapter was made possible by a Humboldt Foundation Georg Forster fellowship for experienced researchers and by a research visit at the German Institute for Global and Regional Affairs (GIGA) in Hamburg (Germany).

2. Angelika Rettberg, ed., *Entre el perdón y el paredón: preguntas y dilemas de la justicia transicional* (Bogotá: International Development Research Centre (IDRC), Ediciones Uniandes, 2005).

3. Centro de Memoria Histórica (CMH), *Justicia y paz ¿Verdad judicial o verdad histórica?* (Bogotá: Centro de Memoria Histórica, 2012); Departamento Nacional de Planeación (DNP), *Plan de financiación para la sostenibilidad de la Ley 1448 de 2011,* Documento Conpes No. 3712 (Bogotá: Departamento Nacional de Planeación, 2011).

4. DNP, *Plan de financiación.*

5. Item 5 on the negotiation agenda (*Acuerdo General para la Terminación del Conflicto y la Construcción de una Paz Estable y Duradera*) mentions the need to retribute victims as a central purpose of the talks, including the procurement of human rights and truth.

6. Centro de Memoria Histórica (CMH), *Basta ya! Colombia: Memorias de Guerra y Dignidad* (Bogotá: Centro de Memoria Histórica, 2013).

7. According to a report by the Internal Displacement Monitoring Centre, Colombia (with 3,8 million) and Sudan (with 5 million) topped the list of countries with forced dis-

placement in the world (http://www.internal-displacement.org/8025708F004BE3B1/(httpInfoFiles)/9251510E3E5B6FC3C12572BF0029C267/$file/Global_Overview_2006.pdf). According to a UNODC report, Colombia's homicide rate dropped from 70 per 100.000 inhabitants in the 1990s (one of the highest in the world) to around 33/100.000 inhabitants in 2010 (http://www.unodc.org/documents/data-and-analysis/statistics/Homicide/Global_study_on_homicide_2011_embargoed.pdf).

8. Álvaro Villarraga, *El proceso de paz en Colombia, 1982–2002*, Vol. 5 (Bogotá: Fundación Cultura Democrática, 2013).

9. Eduardo Pizarro, "Bases para una política de reparación en Colombia viable, justa y sostenible," in *Construcción de paz en Colombia*, ed. Angelika Rettberg (Bogotá: Ediciones Uniandes, 2012), 141–167.

10. Roland Paris, "Peacebuilding and the Limits of International Liberalism," *International Security* 22, no. 2 (1997): 54–89; Timothy Shaw, "Beyond Post-Conflict Peacebuilding: What Links to Sustainable Development and Human Security?" *International Peacekeeping* 3, no. 2 (1996): 36–48; Peter Uvin, "The Development/Peacebuilding Nexus: A Typology and History of Changing Paradigms," *Journal of Peacebuilding & Development* 1, no. 1 (2002): 5–24.

11. Centro de Memoria Histórica (CMH), International Organization for Migrations (IOM), Fundación Social (FS), and Universidad de los Andes, *Encuesta nacional: ¿Qué piensan los colombianos después de siete años de justicia y paz?* (Bogota: CMH, IOM, Universidad de los Andes, 2012); Unidad de Víctimas, Personal communication (Bogotá, 2013).

12. See Paloma Aguilar, Laia Balcells, and Héctor Cebolla-Boado, "Determinants of Attitudes toward Transitional Justice: An Empirical Analysis of the Spanish Case," *Comparative Political Studies* 44, no. 10 (2011): 1397–1430; Tricia Olsen, Leigh Payne, and Andrew Reiter, "Transitional Justice in the World, 1970–2007: Insights from a New Dataset," *Journal of Peace Research* 47, no. 6 (2010): 803–809; Oskar Thoms, James Ron, and Roland Paris, "State-Level Effects of Transitional Justice: What Do We Know?" *International Journal of Transitional Justice* 4, no. 3 (2010): 329–354; Hugo Van der Merwe, Victoria Baxter, and Audrey Chapman, *Transitional Justice: Challenges for Empirical Research* (Washington, D.C.: United States Institute of Peace, 2009).

13. Registro Único de Víctimas (RUV); CMH, IOM, FS, and Universidad de los Andes, *Encuesta nacional.*

14. Marc Chernick, "Colombia. Does Injustice Cause Violence?" in *What Justice? Whose Justice? Fighting for Fairness in Latin America*, ed. Susan E. Eckstein and Timothy Wickham-Crowley (Berkeley: University of California Press, 2003), 185–214.

15. For a detailed description of the process, see Elvira María Restrepo and Bruce Bagley, eds., *La desmovilización de los paramilitares en Colombia: entre el escepticismo y la esperanza* (Bogotá: Ediciones Uniandes, University of Miami—Department of International Studies, 2011). For a discussion of fighter backgrounds and motivations, see Enzo Nussio, *La vida después de la desmovilización: Percepciones, emociones y estrategias de exparamilitares en Colombia* (Bogotá: Ediciones Uniandes, 2012).

16. International Center for Transitional Justice, http://ictj.org/about/transitional-justice; Also, see Javier Ciurlizza, "Justicia transicional en Colombia: un modelo para desarmar," in *Construcción de paz en Colombia*, ed. Angelika Rettberg (Bogotá: Ediciones Uniandes, 2012), 89–115; Pizarro, "Bases para una política de reparación"; Rettberg, *Entre el perdón y el paredón.*

17. See Rettberg, *Entre el perdón y el paredón.*

18. The *versiones libres* have not been properly analyzed in terms of their efficacy in providing justice. Anecdotal evidence suggests that they may be better at obtaining truth and healing, which may explain why attendance to these hearings is popular with victims. A study led by Iván Orozco (CMH, 2012) depicts the *versiones libres* performances in which former fighters make strategic use of their opportunity to provide self-justifications of their actions.

19. Fiscalía General de la Nación, Unidad de Justicia y Paz, *Estadísticas Unidad Nacional de Fiscalías para la Justicia y Paz,* http://www.fiscalia.gov.co/jyp/unidad-de-justicia-y-paz/.

20. Attention to victims of forced displacement—albeit not termed specifically as reparation—had been ongoing since the 1990s under the leadership of *Acción Social*, a public institution later merged into the *Departamento de Prosperidad Social.*

21. So far, GMH has produced twenty-six reports on cases related to gender-related violence, violence against the judicial system, indigenous and other minority populations, different massacres, kidnappings, forced displacement, land rights and disputes and historical memory (http://www.centrodememoriahistorica.gov.co/).

22. Juan Fernando Cristo, *La guerra por las víctimas: lo que nunca se supo de la ley* (Bogotá: Ediciones B Colombia, 2012).

23. CMH, *Justicia y paz ¿Verdad judicial o verdad histórica?*; Departamento Nacional de Planeación (DNP), *Plan de financiación.*

24. The decision to limit the period of application of the law was contentious, as there is general consensus that the armed conflict began in 1964 with the creation of FARC and ELN as insurgent peasant movements. Factors included in the discussion referred to fiscal constraints as well as difficulties to collect data.

25. The complete text of the law can be found here: http://www.leydevictimas.gov.co/

26. While no formal announcement has been made, the *Ejército de Liberación Nacional (ELN)*, founded in 1964 as well as the FARC, has also repeatedly expressed its interest to engage in peace negotiations with the Colombian government, which has shown its willingness to do so.

27. FARC-EP, "Sobre un Marco Jurídico fuera de contexto," August 6, 2013, http://www.pazfarc-ep.org/index.php/noticias-comunicados-documentos-farc-ep/delegacion-de-paz-farc-ep/item/1388-sobre-un-marco-juridico-fuera-de-contexto.html; "El no de las Farc al Marco Jurídico para la Paz," *El Espectador*, August 6, 2013, http://www.elespectador.com/noticias/politica/el-no-de-farc-al-marco-juridico-paz-articulo-438497.

28. "Farc abren puerta a la reparación de sus víctimas, " *El Tiempo*, August 20, 2013, http://www.eltiempo.com/politica/farc-admiten-que-generaron-victimas_13004098-4.

29. Libardo Ariza and Manuel Iturralde, *Los muros de la infamia: Prisiones en Colombia y en América Latina* (Bogotá: Ediciones Uniandes -Colección Estudios CIJUS, 2011).

30. "Pablo Catatumbo: 'También soy víctima, fui torturado y secuestrado,'" *Voz*, June 15, 2013, http://www.semanariovoz.com/2013/06/13/pablo-catatumbo-tambien-soy-victima-fui-torturado-y-secuestrado/.

31. CMH, *Justicia y paz ¿Verdad judicial o verdad histórica?*

32. A note of caution regarding numbers: while the Colombian state, nongovernmental and academic organizations have made stringent efforts to improve recording and classification of data regarding criminal activity related to armed conflict, data are often still an approximation and should be taken as general trends.

33. CMH, IOM, FS, and Universidad de los Andes, *Encuesta nacional.* The survey was commissioned in the context of Agreement DDR-360-1, "El saldo pedagógico de la Ley de Justicia y Paz," a part of Cooperation Agreement 245 (DDR-360), and was signed by the Departamento Administrativo de la Prosperidad Social (DPS), the Unidad Administrativa Especial de Atención y Reparación Integral and the International Organization for Migrations (IOM). The survey was carried out by Ipsos—Napoleón Franco and funded by Acción Social (now transformed into Departamento de Prosperidad Social), the Comisión Nacional de Reconciliación y Reparación (CNRR) (which ceased operating in 2011 and whose functions were transferred to the Unidad para la Atención y Reparación Integral a las Víctimas del Departamento de Prosperidad Social), and USAID, with the technical assistance of IOM. Instrument design and data analysis were carried out by a consortium of researchers at the Centro de Memoria Histórica, Universidad de los Andes, and Fundación Social (CMH, U Andes, Fundación Social and IOM, 2012). The survey was applied to a representative sample of Colombian residents (n=1,843) in six regions of the country, between January and February of 2012. The margin of error is 2.3 percent. The sample was divided between those "affected" (victims) and "not affected" by human rights violations in terms of the law.

34. Angelika Rettberg, "Construcción de paz en Colombia: contexto y balance," in *Construcción de paz en Colombia,* ed. Angelika Rettberg (Bogotá: Ediciones Uniandes, 2012), 3–49.

35. Human Rights Watch, *Aprenderás a no llorar: Niños combatientes en Colombia* (Bogotá: Editorial Gente Nueva, 2004); Natalia Springer, *Como corderos entre lobos: del uso y reclutamiento de niñas, niños y adolescentes en el marco del conflicto armado y la criminalidad en Colombia* (Bogotá: Springer Consulting Services, Taller Digital Image Printing, 2012).

36. A complete explanation of this system can be found here: http://www.dane.gov.co/index.php/component/content/article/126-geoestadistica/estratificacion/3039-estratificacion-socioeconomica

37. Marcela Ceballos, "Desplazamiento forzado en Colombia: retos para una transición," in *Construcción de paz en Colombia,* ed. Angelika Rettberg (Bogotá: Ediciones Uniandes, 2012), 203–237.

38. Rettberg, "Construcción de paz en Colombia."

39. Rettberg provides a discussion of the motivations of victims to report themselves as such and of the implications for the current political debate. See Angelika Rettberg, *Reparación en Colombia: ¿Qué quieren las víctimas?*, 1st edition (Bogotá: Gesellschaft für Technische Zusammenarbeit (GTZ), ConPaz—Universidad de los Andes, 2008).

40. Olsen, Payne, and Reiter, "Transitional Justice in the World."

41. Susanne Jonas, *Of Centaurs and Doves: Guatemala's Peace Process* (Boulder, Colorado: Westview Press, 2000); Carlo Nasi, *Cuando callan los fusiles: impacto de la paz negociada en Colombia y Centroamérica* (Bogotá: Grupo Editorial Norma, Universidad de los Andes, 2008).

42. Presidencia de la República, "Discurso del Presidente Juan Manuel Santos Calderón," August 7, 2010, http://wsp.presidencia.gov.co/Prensa/2010/Agosto/Paginas/20100807_15.aspx; "Así será la nueva relación entre el gobierno y el Congreso," *Semana*, July 29, 2010, http://www.semana.com/politica/articulo/asi-sera-nueva-relacion-entre-gobierno-congreso/119880-3.

43. Angelika Rettberg, "Reflexiones introductorias sobre la relación entre construcción de paz y justicia transicional," in *Entre el perdón y el paredón: preguntas y dilemas de la justicia transicional*, ed. Angelika Rettberg (Bogotá: International Development Research Centre—Ediciones Uniandes, 2005), 1–17.

44. "Estudio de opinión sobre el paramilitarismo y la "para-política" en Colombia," *Semana*, May 3, 2007, http://www.semana.com/documents/Doc-1439_200755.pdf. In Spanish, the question was: "Algunas personas creen que el paramilitarismo fue necesario en Colombia para acabar con la guerrilla. ¿Ud. personalmente está de acuerdo o en desacuerdo con esto?"

45. Rettberg, "Construcción de paz en Colombia."

46. Juan Carlos Gómez and Juan Pablo Jiménez, T*ax Structure and Tax Evasion in Latin America*, Serie Macroeconomía del Desarrollo, no. 118 (Santiago: CEPAL, 2012).

47. Rettberg, *Reparación en Colombia*; Angelika Rettberg and Juan Diego Prieto, "Víctimas, victimarios y vecinos: Proximidad social y actitudes de las víctimas frente a la reparación, la justicia y la paz," in *Reparación en Colombia: ¿Qué quieren las víctimas? Retos, desafíos y alternativas para garantizar la integralidad*, eds. Ernesto Kiza and Angelika Rettberg (Bogotá: ProFis—Gesellschaft für Technische Zusammenarbeit, 2010), 87–208.

48. Juan Diego Prieto, "Coexistencia local entre víctimas, excombatientes y comunidades en Colombia: implicaciones para la construcción de paz," in *Construcción de paz en Colombia*, ed. Angelika Rettberg (Bogotá: Ediciones Uniandes, 2012), 169–201; Juan Diego Prieto, *Guerras, paces y vidas entrelazadas: coexistencia y relaciones locales entre víctimas, excombatientes y comunidades en Colombia* (Bogotá: Ediciones Uniandes, 2012).

49. Angelika Rettberg, "Encuentro con los otros: Perspectivas para la reconciliación en Colombia," in *Costos del conflicto colombiano*, ed. Ana María Ibañez and Daniel Mejía (Bogotá: Ediciones Uniandes, forthcoming).

50. CMH, IOM, FS, and Universidad de los Andes, *Encuesta nacional.*

51. Ibid.

52. Ibid.

53. The discussion of whether having been victimized prior to committing acts of violence against others is an important one that will have to be dealt with in Colombia, especially when deciding about the judicial fate of demobilized fighters. However, the discussion exceeds the scope of this chapter.

54. "Las falsas víctimas de masacre de Mapiripán sí podrían ir a la cárcel," *El Tiempo,* November 24, 2011. http://www.eltiempo.com/justicia/ARTICULO-WEB-NEW_NOTA_INTERIOR-10826925.html.

55. Iván Orozco, "La posguerra colombiana: divagaciones sobre la venganza, la justicia y la reconciliación," *Análisis Político,* no. 46 (2002): 78–99.

56. Ibid.

57. Rettberg, *Reparación en Colombia.*

Chapter Seven

Santos, the FARC, and the Evolution of Peace Negotiations in Colombia

Marc Chernick

Colombia's internal war has endured, in one form or another, for almost seventy years—from the *Violencia* of the 1940s and 50s, through the low-intensity conflict of the 1960s and 1970s, through the explosion of violence fueled by the rise of the drug trade and paramilitarism beginning in the 1980s. Some have viewed each of these phases separately. Yet there is as much continuity as there is difference among these periods of violence. Many of the same regions and municipalities have been immersed in violent armed conflict without cease, while there has been a remarkable continuity of state and non-state armed actors, from the FARC (*Fuerzas Armadas Revolucionarias de Colombia,* The Revolutionary Armed Forces of Colombia) and the ELN (*Ejército de Liberación Nacional,* The National Liberation Army) to state and paramilitary forces, as one phase generated and shaped the next. As President Juan Manuel Santos stated when he announced in September 2012 that his government had been engaged in secret talks with the FARC, his generation, and all Colombians born since 1946, have never known a day of peace.

This chapter will review the evolution of peace negotiations in Colombia analyzing how political negotiations with the FARC returned to the center of the political agenda under President Santos and the likely impact that a final accord will have in ending Colombia's decadeslong armed conflict.

In addition to its history of protracted warfare, Colombia has a long tradition of peacemaking beginning with the foundational arrangement of the National Front in 1958 when the then warring Liberal and Conservative Parties negotiated an amendment to the national constitution mandating the obligatory sharing and alternating of power between the two historic parties.[1] The agreement brought an end to the partisan violence, yet it also was based on the exclusion of third parties. Further, it failed to address the demands of the more Andean and *campesino* faction of the Liberal guerillas that were calling for greater inclusion and state investments in rural development and land reform; this faction soon joined with existing rural communist self-defense groups to found the FARC. In the years that followed, several new guerrilla organizations emerged in the wake of the 1959 Cuban Revolution, many of these also with roots in the earlier period of partisan violence. The ELN, in 2015 the country's second largest guerrilla movement, dates to this period.[2]

The idea of a political settlement to the armed conflict returned to the national agenda in the 1980s. Since 1982, each Colombian president has attempted in one form or another to negotiate peace with the country's major guerrilla insurgencies. Most of these efforts failed and had the perverse effect of accelerating the formation and consolidation of paramilitary forces working with local and national state and societal actors to defeat the insurgencies. Failed peace making also stimulated efforts to revamp counterinsurgency strategy. Presidents Virgilio Barco (1986–1990), César Gaviria (1990–1994) and Andrés Pastrana (1998–2002) all launched new military initiatives following the breakdown of talks. The first two then watched their successors move to revive peace talks. Pastrana, for his part, pursued both approaches simultaneously. His Plan Colombia led to a major increase in outside military resources initially limited to anti-narcotics functions (though the line was quite blurred in relation to confronting the FARC),[3] even as he spent the first three years of his presidency also pursuing peace negotiations.

There were some successes over the last twenty-five years with the demobilization of a few of the smaller groups, including the M-19 (April 19th Movement), the Quintín Lame Revolutionary Movement (an indigenous armed movement in the Department of Cauca), and the EPL (*Ejercito Popular de Liberación,* Popular Liberation Army).[4] However despite multiple rounds of negotiations with both the FARC and the ELN, peace with these groups remained elusive.

Upon reaching office in 2002 following the collapse of peace talks under Pastrana, Álvaro Uribe radically departed from the approaches of his immediate predecessors. He emphasized a military solution to the country's internal armed conflict, and, in the post-September 11, 2001 world, allied the country closely with the United States Global War on Terrorism (GWOT). The United States Congress responded by lifting the prohibition against using U.S. assistance for counterinsurgency or counterterror activities found in the initial legislation supporting Plan Colombia and thus broadly reshaped the U.S. military role within Colombia's internal armed conflict.

The U.S. GWOT had no more success in Colombia than it did in other parts of the world. Introducing the concept of "terrorism" in Colombia led to an escalation of hostilities and combat operations and deferred and undermined the process of ending Colombia's protracted armed conflict through political negotiations. For the United States, Colombia was transformed into the principal non-Islamic site in the war on terrorism. For Colombia, the long armed conflict was now reduced to a problem of terrorism. The consequences of these changes were to erase and obfuscate the deep social, economic, political and historical roots of this long conflict. In one stroke, it led Colombians to believe that the problem was one of a few extremist terrorists—from the government's perspective particularly the FARC—and not one of a long history of exclusion, inequality and the violent pursuit and defense of political, social, and economic power.

To be clear, terrorism is a tactic of war that violates international humanitarian law. Targeting civilian populations is a war crime and a crime against humanity. Those that commit such crimes will need to be brought to justice, an issue discussed below. However Colombia was ill-served by erasing its own history of violence and reducing its protracted conflict to a set of illegal violent tactics that have been used by all sides.

Yet despite the escalation in military strategy, the residue of previous peace negotiations still endured. President Uribe opened up ultimately unsuccessful peace negotiations with the ELN in Cuba in the run-up up to his reelection campaign in 2006.[5] He also allowed intermediaries for several years to explore a prisoner exchange, known as a humanitarian accord with the FARC. Most visibly, Uribe negotiated the demobilization of the paramilitary AUC (*Autodefensa Unidad de Colombia,* United Self-Defense Group of Colombia).[6] In so doing, he redefined peace talks to include negotiations with a pro-state armed actor as opposed to the standard approach to peace negotiations which defines peace processes as negotiations with an armed *opposition.* That is to say, the literature on peacemaking focuses on negotiating with enemies that have taken up arms against the state, not negotiations with allies or strategic partners, even if the relationship with the latter is ambiguous and at times adversarial. The demobilization process with paramilitary groups from 2003–2006 did not represent a peace process. It represented an attempt, largely failed, by the state to reassert its monopoly on legitimate state violence.

Ultimately, Uribe's military and counterterror strategies were no more successful than the earlier political and military strategies. His Democratic Security policies together with the U.S.-backed *Plan Patrióta* and *Plan Consolidación* helped to rearrange the battlefield, weaken the guerrillas, transform the paramilitaries, strengthen the armed forces, and change the dynamics and tactics of each of the armed actors. They also aggravated the human rights and humanitarian crisis in the country. The Colombian government did not win the war. It did largely succeed in pushing the guerrilla groups out of the main urban areas and surrounding countryside. However, the FARC in particular responded to the escalated military force by receding into the mountains and jungles and toward the country's border regions, and by returning to more traditional guerrilla tactics involving small cells and units. However, they were not defeated. And despite the paramilitary demobilization, the political grip of paramilitary actors on large areas of rural Colombia was ultimately strengthened. Uribe did not achieve anything close to the kind of decisive military victory that Fujimori did in defeating *Sendero Luminoso* in Peru, or more recently, as President Mahinda Rajapaksa did over the Tamil Tigers in Sri Lanka.

At the end of his second term of office (2006–2010), Uribe nonetheless remained popular but the Constitutional Court blocked his efforts to again reform the constitution and permit a second reelection. His most enduring legacy, one that came to haunt his successor, was that he succeeded in imposing his vision of the country's protracted armed conflict as a "war on terrorism" against terrorists and narco-terrorists unconnected to the social, political and economic cleavages of the country. He argued that one must defeat militarily such groups, not negotiate substantive issues. This legacy has constantly weakened his successor's hand as he has tried to once again search for a negotiated settlement to the armed conflict.

RETURNING TO THE NEGOTIATING TABLE WITH THE FARC

Uribe's designated successor and former Minister of Defense, Juan Manuel Santos, recognized the limits of the military strategy that he inherited and which he had vigorously enacted in the previous government. He concluded that the existing strategy would only lead to continued, interminable, increasingly degraded warfare and that it was time to once again look for a political and negotiated settlement. The military strategy needed to give way to a political strategy despite the fact that he insisted that even as he pursued negotiations he would not pull back on the government's military campaign. This time he proposed that the government should study and learn from the mistakes of the country's earlier peace processes as well as from the experiences of other countries, such as El Salvador, Guatemala, and Northern Ireland in the U.K.[7]

In his inaugural address on August 7, 2010, President Santos surprised the nation by declaring that he had the key to peace in his pocket and that he would use it when the time was right. He repeated this idea regularly over the next two years. On September 4, 2012, he announced that his government had been engaged in secret talks with the FARC, facilitated by Norway, Cuba, and Venezuela, and that an agenda had been reached to begin formal talks. In the intervening years, he gradually changed the country's expectations and outlook by making the centerpiece of his legislative agenda a "Victims and Land Restitution Law," that would provide reparations to the country's more than six million victims since 1985 including those who were internally displaced, killed, tortured, massacred, disappeared or otherwise victimized by state or non-state actors, including guerrillas, paramilitaries, and the Armed Forces.[8] The Colombian Congress also passed, at Santos's behest, a constitutional reform that provides a "Juridical Framework for Peace" outlining the ways in which justice could be enacted for war crimes and crimes against humanity while still opening up the prospect of transforming insurgent groups into political parties through negotiations leading to disarmament, demobilization, and reintegration.[9]

Santos appears to want to be a historic president, not one that simply managed Colombia's violence for a period of four or eight years. His announcement brought about a wave of cautious optimism and clear support from many, though not all, sectors of society as well as resounding endorsement from the international community, including the Pope and the United States State Department.

How did this dramatic shift in strategy and public sentiment occur? Given the level of public support for a military strategy as well as the vocal opposition of the former president and his supporters toward "negotiating with terrorists," President Santos's move to open up talks with the FARC was quite audacious. One analysis that gained currency in certain policy circles in Bogotá and in Washington was that the movement toward formal talks reflected the success of the military strategy initiated under President Uribe, supported by the United States, and continued under President Santos even as he pursued talks and preempted the political debate. This analysis is not only simplistic; it is fundamentally flawed. It misjudges multiple factors including: 1) the battlefield capabilities of the FARC, and 2) the declared "successes" of Uribe's military strategy which were more vulnerable, reversible, and indeed more limited than what was declared in official statements and the press. A third element that led to a revised strategy and which will be discussed later in the chapter relates to the groundswell of activity from civil society and victims groups that had begun to mobilize to end the war.

First, the best evidence reveals that the FARC was able to reorganize its military capabilities and tactics during the Uribe years and by the outset of the Santos administration was able to respond to increased military pressure as well as to increasingly go on the offensive.[10] The FARC was no longer able to act as "an army of the people" as they had long proclaimed and could not amass hundreds and sometimes thousands of fighters to overtake military bases, medium-size towns or provincial capitals as they were able to do in the mid-1990s. However, the FARC was able to adjust its tactics and its collective leadership and absorbed the killings of several key individual leaders. By the end of Uribe's second administration, the FARC had been notably weakened in the cities and the countryside surrounding Bogotá, but they nevertheless were able to regroup in several rural areas where they had traditionally operated and turned the country's multiple border regions into conflict zones.

Moreover, some of the indicators of success of the military campaign turned out to be questionable. Following a major military operation known as *Plan Patriota* that took the offensive to the major strongholds of the FARC in southern Colombia and led to some of the most intensive combat operations in decades, the Colombian and U.S. governments then set up a strategy of consolidation zones throughout the country, a strategy which echoed the United States "clear, hold and build" strategy" in Iraq and Afghanistan.[11] As in those conflicts, Colombian forces were unable to advance past the "clear and hold" part. There was a clear lack of coordination from the Ministry of Defense and the other agencies of the state. Moreover occupying military units were unable to distinguish friends from enemies among the civilian population in the efforts to clear areas from subversion and to then hold the territory. Peasants were viewed as subversives and paramilitaries were seen as allies. Despite the great optimism at the launch of Operation Consolidation and the development of the consolidation zones, many of its key architects in the Ministry of Defense came to the realization that peace was not going to be built from militarized control and development of consolidation zones.[12]

If Santos surprised the country with his gestures for peace, the FARC too began to gradually change its approach to peace talks. A few weeks before Santos gave his inaugural address and spoke of the key to peace, the FARC's maximum leader, Alfonso Cano, released a video analyzing the previous forty-six years of war and the repeated failures to negotiate peace. He too extended his hand out to President Santos and forthrightly asserted the FARC's desire to negotiate. He outlined an agenda centered on addressing the issues of: 1) land and the plight of Colombian *campesinos*, 2) human rights and justice, 3) guarantees for political participation, and 4) economic opportunities. These were not new issues for the FARC.[13] Instead, it was a reiteration of the issues they have brought to the negotiating table for the last thirty years. The agenda was somewhat pared down compared to the past. Cano spoke in the video without rancor and without making demands. It was probably the clearest explanation that the FARC has ever made directly to the Colombian people about their view of the conflict and of their thoughts on peace.

Gone was the earlier insistence on a demilitarized or *despeje* zone as the site of potential peace talks. No longer did they insist on a "humanitarian accord" to exchange Colombian soldiers and police held by the FARC for FARC prisoners in Colombian prisons. Cano asked for no preconditions, which differed from their position during the prelude to all the other periods of talks.

In February 2012, the FARC announced that it would renounce the practice of kidnapping and that they would release the last of the soldiers and police that they still held captive.[14] The Brazilian government assisted with the logistics, as they had done on three earlier occasions, sending helicopters and working with the International Committee for the Red Cross. On April 2, four soldiers and six police were freed. President Santos responded cautiously, though much of the press remained skeptical.

Even as Santos quietly pursued secret talks, the Colombian Armed Forces continued to escalate the military pressure. The FARC, too, throughout 2010 and 2011 demonstrated an ability to orchestrate multiple attacks using traditional guerrilla tactics.[15] One month into Santos's presidency, in September 2010, the Armed Forces staged a major bombing campaign that killed the FARC's principal military leader, Jorge Briceño ("Mono Jojoy"). In November of 2011, the Colombian Air Force carpet-bombed Alfonso Cano's encampment in the mountains of Cauca, killing the FARC's maximum leader.

The killing of Cano represented a major setback for the FARC and potentially for the possibility of peace. He was the primary architect of the FARC's peace strategy, though the FARC's collective leadership was fully and directly involved at all levels of decision making. Killing Cano might have derailed the peace initiative even more than the high-profile killings of other FARC leaders since 2008. Yet the FARC continued to engage in secret talks with the government in Havana and elsewhere. This, perhaps more than any other indicator, could be seen as a demonstration of both their political will and interest to enter into formal negotiations.

Alfonso Cano had been part of a second generation of leadership within the FARC, following the deaths by natural causes of the early founders, Manuel Marulanda, Jacobo Arenas, and Ciro Trujillo. The founding generation were, with the exception of Arenas, mostly *campesinos*. Cano and the generation that came of age in the student movements of the 1960s and 1970s represent a different type of FARC leader, mostly urban and university educated. Cano was an anthropologist trained at the Universidad Nacional in Bogotá. The completion of this generational change has occurred since the breakdown of the talks in Caguán. The new FARC maximum leader, Timoleón Jimenez ("Timochenko"), quickly signaled his commitment to continue with the peace strategy laid out by Alfonso Cano.

Similarly, as the Santos government took up the Victim's Law and re-centered government efforts to deal with the plight of victims, the FARC had also begun to respond to the great clamor for peace that has arisen from civil society. Over the last decade, new social movements have emerged centered on victims, human rights, and peace. The war has threatened the very existence of indigenous and afro-descendant communities and has displaced millions of *campesinos*. These movements do not feel represented by the FARC: some are openly hostile to the FARC, and yet practically all have been victimized by the war.[16]

Timing is everything in peace negotiations, and this time, both the FARC and the government seemed ready to negotiate and committed to studying and learning from past mistakes. Both sides agreed to a timetable, to secrecy, and to international accompaniment. Perhaps most importantly, both sides agreed that the end of the process must be the termination of the conflict. The agenda calls for an end to hostilities and the "Abandoning of arms" ("*Dejación de las armas*") and the "Reincorporation of the FARC-EP into civilian life."[17] For some this language did not go far enough. The FARC did not agree to hand in or surrender arms, only to stop using them. However for the FARC, this language is unprecedented; the differences may be more semantic and procedural rather than substantive.

In many respects, the Havana agenda follows much of the agenda proposed by Alfonso Cano in his July 2010 video. It begins by addressing *integral agrarian development*, the FARC's primary issue since its founding by *campesinos* a half century ago. Other issues are: *political participation*, another long held grievance by the FARC particularly following the assassination of candidates and officials of the Patriotic Union party; *ending the conflict*, including disarmament and a parallel effort by the government to dismantle the remaining structures of paramlitarism; *illegal drugs,* an issue that harks back to the call for a Marshall Plan for the coca growing regions that was first proposed by President Pastrana but never implemented; and *victims,* calling for truth and justice for victims of the armed conflict. A sixth issue on how to ratify the amendment will also be discussed when all other issues are signed. The rules of the Havana talks are that no preliminary agreement is valid until all agreements are signed. There is also a commitment to not walk away from the table no matter the provocation.

The agenda, however, does not address all the major issues related to the conflict and does not open up to negotiation issues that have often been staples of other peace processes in other countries, such as the reorganization of the security forces of the state, the exploitation of natural resources, or the model of economic development. Notably, all of these issues were on the agenda the last time the FARC and the government met at the negotiating table in

Caguán from 1998 to 2002. The Caguán agenda had twelve major negotiating points and forty-seven sub-points. In four years, the two sides did not advance beyond the first issue and did not reach an agreement. In contrast, the Havana agenda is realistic, focused, and difficult; it is also achievable.[18]

Negotiations began in Havana, Cuba, in November 2012. By early 2015, three agreements had been reached: on rural development, political participation, and drug trafficking. In many ways, the first two are issues that have fueled the conflict for over half a century and have been closely linked to the FARC's long insurgency. Addressing these broad structural issues is necessary for an enduring peace and will help facilitate the final complicated issues relating to cease-fire; disarmament, demobilization, and reintegration (DDR); and transitional justice. Said another way, the first three issues on the agenda relate to what was once referred to as structural violence. To use the language of the Norwegian conflict resolution theorist Johan Galtung, these are issues that, if implemented, would address some of the root causes of the conflict. Galtung calls this "positive peace." The next set of issues on the Havana agenda have to do with the complicated process of ending the armed conflict and silencing the arms. This is a necessary but not sufficient condition for an enduring peace and is what Galtung calls "negative peace."[19]

The first preliminary agreements were eventually made public, following much speculation as to what they contained. The language in each is quite technical, free from polemics and sweeping affirmations. The technical nature of the language in many ways obscures the far-sweeping nature of each.

Land

The first agreement on land, if implemented, would amount to a major transformation in the Colombian countryside and would achieve what Colombian reformers have attempted since at least the 1930s: a major equitable rural development policy. Comprehensive agrarian reforms were attempted by the Liberal Party in the 1930s, the 1960s and the1990s.[20] Each of these reforms had only minimal impact. The FARC's origins lie with the radical Liberal Party *campesinos* and guerrillas of the 1940s and 1950s.

The first sub-agreement with the FARC would in many ways achieve a historic victory for land reform in Colombia. It would undo a process of increasingly concentrated land and unproductive agricultural production. At .88, Colombia has one of the worst land gini co-efficient in the world.[21] Over the past thirty years, land concentration has worsened as farmers have been evicted from their lands, sometimes violently, and small and medium size estates have been absorbed into mostly unproductive larger estates. This process has been called counter-agrarian reform. The accord calls for a major land census and would designate major areas of the country, particularly in the colonization zones, to be restricted to only small and medium size farms and would prohibit the further concentration of land. These provisions build on a part of the 1994 agrarian development law that called for Peasant Enterprise Zones, or *Zonas de Reservas Campesina.* The agreement also provides for adequate access to state resources, infrastructure and technological assistance to rural producers and designates certain areas of the country where large-scale agribusiness would be permitted.

The agreement would also empower the state to repossess illegally acquired state lands or lands that had been accumulated through illicit wealth or illegal means. Together, such lands could amount to several million hectares which then could be redistributed to landless peasants, internally displaced individuals, and ex-combatants.

Political Participation

The draft agreement guarantees the security of minority parties and would create temporary jurisdictions in conflict-affected regions where a demobilized FARC and other political parties would temporarily be given assistance for a limited number of election cycles to help consolidate their electoral presence to build an effective political party. The essence of a peace process is the transformation of an armed movement into a political party. This agreement would help facilitate that transition in key regions of the country and would provide guarantees to protect vulnerable parties and social movements.

Drugs

The agreement incorporates the coca growing regions into the areas identified in the first sub-agreement. The FARC promises to work with the state to provide assistance to coca growers and provide alternative development assistance to them within the context of the broader rural development program. The agreement proposes to de-militarize the fight against coca farmers and to re-orient the effort to combat illicit narcotics into fighting criminal and distribution networks. Aerial fumigation, an issue which has long been contentious in Colombia, will only be used as a last resort where efforts to peacefully promote alternative development fail.

As can be seen from this last provision, in many respects this agreement is quite conservative and does not fundamentally alter the prohibitionist strategy of the drug war. Through this agreement, the government promises to work with the FARC and vice versa in promoting alternative development in the coca growing zones. Alternative development was severely constrained when it was forced to rely on forced manual eradication or fumigation because of the FARC's control in these areas. However, the agreement does not contain the type of proposals found in Bolivia and among progressive advocates to legalize coca *production,* to create new markets for coca products or to fundamentally rethink the war on drugs. Nevertheless, with the FARC's co-operation and with renewed attention placed on dismantling criminal production and distribution networks, Colombia's role in the drug trade should be substantially transformed.

COMPREHENSIVE PEACE

As the peace process advances with the FARC, and as the ELN also moves to negotiate a parallel agreement, attention needs to be placed on other violent and nonviolent actors, from the post-AUC paramilitary groups, misleadingly named Bacrim, to the continued ties between state and paramilitary (Bacrim) power. There is also an overlay of organized crime among all actors, as well as a large, organized, and heterogeneous civil society groups that neither recognize the guerrillas nor the government as their representatives.

Any lasting peace will need to directly address all the factors of violence. A partial peace will not bring peace. Negotiations with the guerrillas, without addressing the extraordinary power of the Bacrim and the paramilitarization of power at local, regional, and national levels, will only ensure more violence, dirty war, and the consolidation of some of the most reactionary elements in society and the political arena. This paramilitary structure must be directly addressed and dismantled. It is this structure, which has fully penetrated elements of the state and which dominates entire regions, which represents the greatest threat to peace in Colombia and has, one way or another, played the role of spoiler in every previous peace process. This issue is already on the agenda, in the section entitled: End of Conflict. The key section reads "In parallel fashion, the national government will intensify the fight against criminal organizations and their support networks, including the fight against corruption and impunity, and in particular against those organizations responsible for homicides and massacres or who target human rights defenders, social movements and political movements"[22] (translation by author).

In reality, this is not an issue that can or should wait for the final phase of the peace process nor is it one which needs to be negotiated. Rather, it should be seen as a prerequisite for any durable peace. It will necessitate a major, parallel effort by the state. Until the state makes a concerted effort to regain the monopoly on the legitimate use of violence as a key element of a broad and comprehensive peace process, then negotiations with the guerrillas will not be successful and will not lead to peace.

Dismantling paramilitary power will not be easy. It will take a combination of judicial coercion and incentives, as well as the official and legitimate use of state law enforcement and security power. It must be relentless and comprehensive. It must pursue corruption and criminal networks even as they reach into the upper levels of state and social power. This dimension of the peace process will not involve negotiations over structural reforms. Instead, it will be dedicated exclusively to the dismantling of para-state power, both the paramilitary and the state sides of the equation.

Having said this, the centerpiece of the peace process is the negotiations and agreements with the FARC and ELN. Without a broad peace accord that eventually covers both groups, there will be no realistic possibility of dismantling the broad paramilitary structure and its tentacles into state and social power. The war with the guerrillas makes possible the tolerance of paramilitary groups, notwithstanding the many examples of the arrest and deportation of individual paramilitary leaders and of appointed and elected officials who have already been removed from office or convicted. A comprehensive peace necessarily must begin with the successful negotiations in Havana with the FARC.

TRUTH, JUSTICE AND NATIONAL RECONCILIATION

Ending the armed conflict is, in fact, more than just the construction of a "negative peace." Truth, justice, and national reconciliation are major elements of "positive peace" as well.

Truth

Following the end of an internal armed conflict, it is increasingly customary for states to establish a Truth and Reconciliation Commission.[23] In El Salvador and Guatemala, this was done under the auspices of the United Nations. In other situations, such as in Peru, the Truth and Reconciliation Commission was established by an interim president almost a decade after the capture of Abimael Guzmán and the collapse of *Sendero Luminoso*,[24] and was done in a period when most of the principal protagonists in the war were in prison or out of power. In South Africa, the Truth Commission was given the judicial authority to grant individual amnesties to perpetrators in exchange for truthful, complete and verifiable testimony. Absent the testimony of perpetrators, which is rarely provided without the type of judicial authority granted the South African Truth and Reconciliation Commission, testimony has primarily come from victims. In most cases, in most post-conflict situations, the Armed Forces have rarely cooperated. In some cases, such as in Guatemala, the Truth Commission was allowed to investigate events but was not permitted to name names.

Yet all of these commissions have produced reports which have helped nations come to terms with their historical past, which is an important step on the path to reconciliation. Truth Commissions can provide some solace to victims through the simple act of official acknowledgment of the crimes and injustices that have been committed.

In Colombia, the conflict has not yet ended and such commissions are normally established in a post-conflict period. Yet Colombia has been challenging the notion that the construction of historical memory must wait until the end of the conflict. The 2005 Justice and Peace Law, which regulated the collective demobilization of the paramilitary groups as well as individual demobilizations from all the illegal armed actors, established an Historical Memory Group as part of a larger known as the *Comisión Nacional de Reparación y Reconciliación* (CNRR). The Victims and Land Restitution Law of 2011 converted the Historical Memory Group into the Center of Historical memory. Since its founding, the Historical Memory Group, led by the respected historian Gonzalo Sánchez and supported by some of the leading social scientists in the country, has focused on investigating specific occurrences in the war. Its first report investigated the repeated massacres over multiple years between 1988 and 1994, in Trujillo (Valle de Cauca).[25] The Group has done pioneering work investigating sexual violence used as a tactic of war[26] and has produced reports on regional conflicts in Casanare, Comuna 13 de Medellín, and other conflict-affected areas.[27] From the beginning, the Historical Memory Group (GMH) and now the Center has insisted that historical memory is a form of reparation, is a means to empower victims whose voices are generally lost in the official characterization of events, and thus is essential to achieving goals of social integration and democracy. In other words, historical memory is a major building block for peace.

In Colombia, there will still be a need for a Truth Commission and a broad Truth Commission report similar to the ones produced in other conflict settings—*after the conflict has ended.* The scope of such a commission's work must be national, as well as regional and sectorial. It must provide a detailed investigation and a coherent and multilayered account of the long years of conflict. In Peru, for example, the *Comisión de Verdad y Reconciliación*, a work that spans ten volumes, has sections organized chronologically, as well as specific chapters on the evolution and territorial expansion of the *Partido Comunista del Peru—Sendero Luminoso, the Movimiento Revolucionario*

Túpac Amaru, the Armed Forces, the Police, the Self-Defense Groups, as well as sections dedicated to women, drug trafficking, civil society, the indigenous population, the judicial issues, the changes of government counterinsurgency strategies, the evolution of the conflict in distinct regions of the country, violations of human rights and international humanitarian law, and many other issues.[28] The report covers the conflict years from 1980 to 2000.

Over the long years of the Colombian war, the government has commissioned official studies of violence. The years of the *Violencia* of the 1940s and 1950s were the subject of one of the first such volumes ever produced anywhere on the dynamics and victims of an internal armed conflict. This was *La Violencia en Colombia*, written by Orlando Fals Borda, Monseñor Germán Guzmán, and Eduardo Umaña Luna, largely based on victim's testimony and social science analysis.[29]

The Barco administration in the 1980s commissioned a group of academic experts at the *Instituto de Estudios Políticos y Relaciones Internacionales* of the Universidad Nacional (IEPRI)—a group that many began to refer to as "*los violentólogos*"—to examine the Colombian violence in the period following the breakdown of the first peace process under Betancur. The result was: *Colombia: Violencia y Democracia, Informe presentado al Ministerio de Gobierno por la Comisión de Estudios sobre la Violencia.*[30] A decade later following the partial, but successful peace processes with the M-19 and EPL, Quintin Lame, and *Corriente Renovacion Socialista* (a faction of the ELN), the government again turned to academic experts at IEPRI to analyze the conflict from the perspective of the peace processes of the early 1990s. They produced: *Armar la Paz es Desarmar la Guerra.*[31]

These official studies, spanning six decades, together with the more detailed and focused work of the Historical Memory Group since 2005 provide a strong foundation for an eventual truth commission. Ideally a Truth Commission Report in Colombia should cover the entire conflict, from 1946 until the date establishing the Commission. The starting point of the conflict is a contested issue around which there is no consensus. Nevertheless, the conflict must be understood in its entirety, beginning with the elections of 1946 and the violence of the 1940s and 1950s. A truth commission, then, must integrate an analysis of the earlier years of the *Violencia* and its resolution into a study of the conflict that emerged in the country after the inauguration of the National Front and the founding of the major guerrilla groups, the FARC, ELN, and EPL in the 1960s. There must be an examination of the "second generation" groups in the 1970s such as the M-19 and Quintin Lame, and the report will need to analyze in detail the rise and evolution of the paramilitaries in the 1980s and 1990s, and the Bacrim in the 2000s. It would also be advisable to include an analysis of the impact of failed and partial peace processes on the subsequent evolution of violence. Like the Peruvian report, it should cover the regional and sectorial dimensions of violence examining changes over the time period under study.

The scope and methodologies of a report to be produced by a hypothetical Colombian Truth and Reconciliation Commission, of course, should be decided by a representative commission that is agreed to at a negotiating table. Equally important, once the Commission's work is done, if there is to be a genuine construction of a national historical memory as part of a durable peace process, there must be a national commitment to fully disseminate and promote the findings of such a commission. This has not happened sufficiently in many post-conflict countries. Colombia needs to learn from these experiences in El Salvador, Guatemala, Peru, South Africa, and elsewhere. Once a report—and an accessible abbreviated version—is completed, it must be widely integrated into the educational system and the popular cultural life of the country. In Argentina, where one of the very first truth commissions was established after the democratic transition in 1982, the report *Nunca Más* became a national bestseller and is still widely available in bookstores today.[32]

Such a mandate to recover national and regional memory over such a long period of Colombian history is beyond what is possible at present. The *Grupo de Memoria Histórica* has shown remarkable independence and a commitment to uncover the truth. It has produced studies, collected data, and assembled specialized, organized databases on types of violence, regions and victims, and perpetrators through the testimonies of demobilized combatants. It has initiated multiyear investigations using some of the best tools from the social sciences and from participatory research methods that allow the voices of the victims and the protagonists to be heard. No other truth commission in any other context has had access to such a rich trove of testimonies and analysis at the outset of their work. Yet if the work of the GMH is to have lasting impact, it will need to be integrated into a *post-conflict* peace-building project. Undertaking this work amid the conflict, as Colombia has done, is innovative. In the absence of peace, its reach will likely be limited. In the context of peace, it will likely prove to be precedent-setting.

Justice, Peacemaking, and National Reconciliation

Truth commissions are not substitutes for justice and today the issue of justice needs to be on the agenda of any peace process. Throughout the long history of Colombian violence and peacemaking, amnesties have been the norm. The guiding sentiment has been: *borrón y cuenta nueva* (Erase and start over!). Today, International Humanitarian Law has progressed to the point where amnesties for crimes that rise to the level of war crimes, genocide or crimes against humanity are no longer valid. In a pathbreaking ruling, the Inter-American Court of Human Rights overturned an amnesty granted to the Armed Forces by Alberto Fujimori in the Barrios Altos case of 2001.[33] The Rome Statute of 1998 creating the International Criminal Court extended the reach of international law to individuals accused of war crimes and crimes against humanity. Under the Statute, the ICC can assert its jurisdiction when states are unwilling or unable to act. Colombia signed the Rome treaty in July 2001 but President Pastrana also invoked Article 124 which permits states to defer ICC jurisdiction over war crimes committed in their national territory for up to seven years. Pastrana sought to leave some room for future negotiations with the guerrillas, even as the Caguán process collapsed. The seven year deadline expired in 2009, an occurrence that was hardly noticed in Colombia. Yet Colombia still left some room for future talks even beyond the seven year period. It attached a reservation to its signature explaining its understanding of the treaty: "None of the provisions of the Rome Statute concerning the exercise of jurisdiction by the International Criminal Court prevent the Colombian State from granting amnesties, reprieves or judicial pardons for political crimes, provided that they are granted in conformity with the Constitution and with the principles and norms of international law accepted by Colombia."[34]

This reservation opened up the possibility for President Santos and the Colombian Congress to amend the constitution and establish a *Marco Jurídico para la Paz* in 2012. The specific provisions will still need to be defined in implementing legislation. It might be questioned whether it is appropriate to address such issues through a constitutional reform. But the reform attempts to create a blueprint that allows Colombia to honor its international treaty commitments and also navigate the tensions between seeking justice and negotiating peace. Some human rights groups, most notably Human Rights Watch, have denounced the constitutional reform as a violation of international law declaring that the law is, essentially, a disguised amnesty, and that it will simply provide impunity to guerrillas, paramilitaries, and state security forces that have committed heinous crimes.[35]

These are issues that will need to be addressed directly at the negotiating table, as well as by Colombian courts and the International Criminal Court. In peacemaking, this tension between justice and peace represents a formidable challenge. A peace process seeks to transform armed competition into democratic competition, whereby all actors agree to respect the rules of a more open, legitimate and inclusive political system. Negotiations must open the way to broader political participation by all representative groups in civil society, including the armed actors that have entered the peace process. In El

Salvador, both the death squad right, ARENA, and the FMLN leftist guerrilla insurgents were able to transform themselves into the two dominant political parties during and after the peace process. Both groups made the transition from armed actor to a viable political party able to compete in elections at the local and national levels. A peace process must assist the transition from arms to politics. It should not shut the door to this process before arriving at the negotiating table. This is the tension between justice and peacemaking. A way needs to be found to alleviate this tension without promoting impunity.

NOTES

1. Jonathan Hartlyn, *The Politics of Coalition Rule in Colombia* (Cambridge University Press, 1988).

2. Carlos Medina Gallego, ELN Ejército de Liberación Nacional. Cincuenta años de lucha armadas (Bogotá: Universidad Nacional de Colombia 2014).

3. Jonathan D. Rosen, *The Losing War: Plan Colombia and Beyond* (Albany: SUNY Press, 2014).

4. See Marc Chernick, *Acuerdo posible: Solucion negociada al conflicto armado colombiano* (Bogotá: Ediciones Aurora, 4th ed. 2015; Carlo Nasi, *Cuando callan los fusiles: Impacto de la paz negociada en Colombia y Centroamerica* (Bogotá: Editorial Norma, 2007).

5. International Crisis Group, "Colombia: Moving Forward with the ELN." October 11, 2007.

6. See Elvira Maria Restrepo and Bruce Bagley, compiladores. *La desmobilizacion de los paramilitares en Colombia Entre el escepticismo y la esperanza* (Bogotá: Universidad de los Andes, 2011).

7. Enrique Santos Calderon, *Así empezó todo. El primer cara a cara secreto entre el gobiero y las FARC en La Habana.*

8. Ministerio de Interior y Justicia, *Ley de Víctimas. Por la cual se dictan medidas de atención,asistencia y reparación integral a las víctimas del conflicto armado interno y se dictanotras disposiciones.*

9. Acto Legislativó-No: 01 July 21, 2012 *Por Medio Del Cual Se Establecen Instrumentos Jurídicos De Justicia Transicional En El Marco Del Artículo 22 De LaConstitución Política Y Se Dictan Otras Disposiciones.*"

10. See León Valencia y Ariel Avila, "*La Nueva Realidad de las FARC* (Bogotá: Corporación Nuevo Arcoiris, Observatorio del Conflicto Armado, 2011) http://www.rebelion.org/docs/132833.pdf [viewed September 20, 2012].

11. General Accounting Office, GAO-09-71, "Plan Colombia: Drug Reduction Goals Were Not Fully Met, but Security Has Improved; U.S. Agencies Need More Detailed Plans for Reducing Assistance' which was released on November 5, 2009.

12. WOLA et al., *Waiting for Consolidation: Monitoring Colombia's U.S.-aided counterinsurgency and development program*. February 2012.

13. Marc Chernick "The FARC at the Negotiating Table," in Virginia M. Bouver, ed., *Colombia: Building Peace in a Time of War* (United States Institute of Peace Press, 2009), pp. 64–94.

14. El Espectador 17 OCT 2012—"Negociaciones de paz entre el Gobierno y las Farc."

15. See León Valencia y Ariel Avila, "*La Nueva Realidad de las FARC*. . . .

16. See Mauricio Garcia, *Movimiento por la paz en Colombia 1978–2003* (Bogotá, CINEP 2006).

17. Acuerdo general para la terminación del conflicto y la construcción de una paz estable y duradera https://www.mesadeconversaciones.com.co/sites/default/files/AcuerdoGeneralTerminacionConflicto.pdf.

18. Marc Chernick, "The FARC at the Negotiating Table."

19. Johan Galtung, "Violence, Peace, and Peace Research" *Journal of Peace Research*. Vol. 6, No. 3 (1969), pp. 167–.

20. Marco Palacios, *De quien es la tierra?* Fondo de Cultura Econimica y Universidad de los Andes, 2011.

21. Programa de las Naciones Unidas para el Desarrollo—PNUD, Informe Nacional de Desarrollo Humano 2011 *Colombia Rural. Razones por la Esperanza* (Bogota, 2011).

22. Acuerdo general para la terminación del conflicto.

23. Priscilla B. Hayner, 2nd Edition: *Unspeakable Truths: Transitional Justice and the Challenge of Truth Commissions* (Routledge, 2011).

24. Marc Chernick "The Defeat of Sendero Luminoso in Peru" in Marianne Heiberg, Brendan O'Leary, and John Tirman, eds. *Terror, Insurgencies, and States: Breaking the Cycles of Protracted Violence*. (Philadelphia: University of Pennsylvania, 2007).

25. *Trujillo: Una Tragedia que no cesa*. Primer Informe de Memoria Histórica de la Comisión Nacional de Reparación y Reconciliación (Bogotá: Editorial Planeta Colombiana, 2008).

26. *Mujeres y guerra: Víctimas y resistentes en el Caribe colombiano*. Informe del grupo de memoria histórica de la Comisión Nacional de Reparación y Reconciliación (Bogotá: Ediciones Semana, 2011).

27. Centro de Memoria Histórica, http://www.centrodememoriahistorica.gov.co/.

28. Comisión de Verdad y Reconciliación, http://www.cverdad.org.pe/ifinal/index.php.

29. Germán Guzman Campos, Orlando Fals Borda and Eduardo Umaña Luna, *La Violencia en Colombia Tomo I and II* (Bogotá, Editora Aguilar, ALtea, Taurus Alfagara, 2010).

30. *Colombia: Violencia y Democracia*, Informe presentado al Ministerio de Gobierno por la Comisión de Estudios sobre la Violencia (Bogotá: Centro Editorial Universidad Nacional, Bogotá, 1987).

31. *Armar la Paz es Desarmar la Guerra*. Compiladores: Álvaro Camacho Guizado, Francisco Leal Buitrago (Bogotá: IEPRI, DNP, Alto Comisionado para la Paz, 2000).

32. La Comisión Nacional sobre la Desaparición de Personas (CONADEP), *Nunca Más* (1984) http://www.derechoshumanos.net/lesahumanidad/informes/argentina/informe-de-la-CONADEP-Nunca-mas.htm.

33. Corte Interamericana de Derechos Humanos, Caso Barrios Altos Vs. Perú Sentencia de 14 de marzo de 2001 http://www.corteidh.or.cr/docs/casos/articulos/Seriec_75_esp.pdf.

34. Rome Statute of the International Criminal Court, 17 July 1998. Colombia Signature 10.12.1998. Ratfication/ Accession 05.08.2002. Reservations/ Declaration 05.08.2002. http://www.icrc.org/ihl.nsf/NORM/909EEAAE157FBD43412566E100542BDE?OpenDocument.

35. Human Rights Watch, "Colombia debe reformar el 'Marco Juridico para la Paz'" (May 31, 2012) http://www.hrw.org/es/news/2012/05/31/colombia-debe-reformar-el-marco-jur-dico-para-la-paz.

Section Four

COLOMBIAN FOREIGN POLICY

Chapter Eight

The Internationalization of Colombia's Current Peace Process

From Isolation to Containment[1]

Sandra Borda and Santiago Gómez

This chapter analyzes the internationalization of the peace process advanced in Colombia during Juan Manuel Santos administration. Our analysis is based on the theoretical premise that the internationalization is an explicit decision-making process designed and implemented by the various actors involved in the negotiations.[2] According to this definition, internationalizing is a verb, a policy directed toward certain international actors in search for military cooperation, legitimacy, or both. This chapter explores how the Colombian government and the *Fuerzas Armadas Revolucionarias de Colombia* (FARC) decided to internationalize Colombia's current peace process and explains the type of internationalization method they decided to implement. We argue that it is a contained form of internationalization.

There has been little effort to analyze how the Colombian state or the insurgent groups voluntarily internationalized their peace talks. The fundamental assumption of this chapter is that the Colombian state and the FARC have had room for autonomous decision making in front of the international actors. This space is undeniably limited and conditioned by multiple factors. While we focus specifically on Colombia in this case, key lessons can be learned for all countries that suffer from internal conflicts. This analysis intends to observe how the Colombian state and the guerrillas interact and maneuver and how, under strong restrictions, they develop international strategies to deal with the domestic conflict and advance the peace process. In sum, this chapter will analyze the active role of both parties to the Colombian conflict in the internationalization of its struggle and peace negotiation.

In this chapter, internalization does not refer to contagion effects or spill-over, and it does not refer to collateral damage or externalities produced by domestic conflicts either.[3] Our argument is based on the assumption that parties to the conflict are crucial actors to the extent that they make the decision to exclude or invite external actors to participate in internal conflicts or negotiations. The internationalization mechanism does not mean that parties to the conflict exercising such policy options are weak; nor do such activities necessarily diminish the sovereignty of the state or the strength of the insurgency. Secondly, internationalization is not unnoticed or involuntary and that is why the metaphors of spillover, contagion, and collateral damage are inappropriate. Internationalization is, in contrast, a conscious and explicit political decision that results from rational decision making. It is defined here as a deliberate and calculated process.[4]

This chapter utilizes the concept of internationalization to discuss the role of international actors in the current Colombian peace process. More generally, we analyze how the international system has facilitated the efforts by the Colombian state and the FARC to internationalize their peace process. In order to understand the internationalization strategy, we must analyze both opportunities and constraints. Although international forces form, transform, and to a certain extent limit the negotiators' choices, such forces have the capacity and ability to decide whether to facilitate or obstruct the participation of various actors in the dialogue.

This chapter begins by describing the main tendencies of the internationalization of the current peace process. Next, we will examine the internationalization process advanced toward key countries and international organizations. This section includes the most relevant actors for the current peace talks: the United States, Latin America, Europe—particularly Norway—, the United Nations (UN), the Union of South American Nations (UNASUR), and the Organization of American States (OAS). The work concludes with a comparison of the ongoing internationalization of the peace process and its relation to previous internationalization strategies implemented during previous negotiations.

TENDENCIES OF THE PEACE PROCESS: INTERNATIONALIZATION IN HAVANA, CUBA

In August 2012, the Santos administration announced the beginning of peace talks between the Colombian government and the insurgent organization the FARC. The last time negotiations between these two parties to the Colombian conflict occurred, was between 1998 and 2001 during the presidency of Andrés Pastrana (1998–2002). Between 2001 and the ongoing dialogues in 2014, the Álvaro Uribe administration (2002–2010) implemented a hardline approach—*mano dura*—in order to defeat the FARC

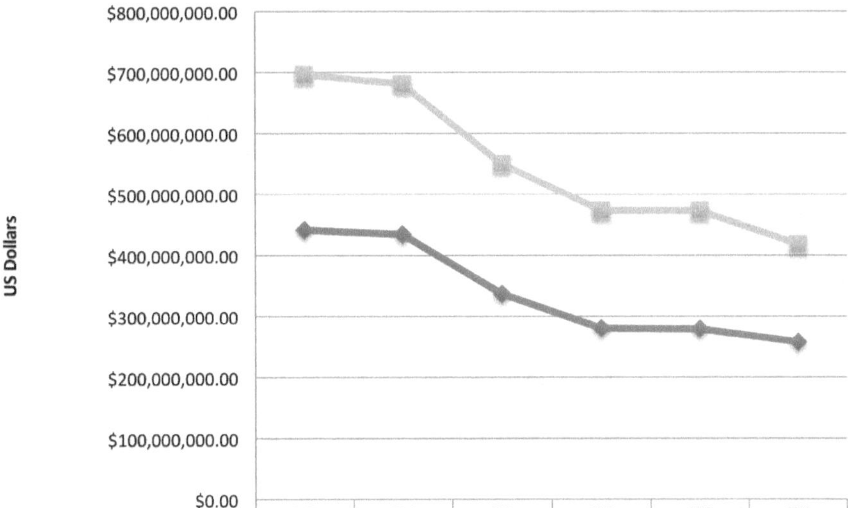

	2009	2010	2011	2012	2013	2014
Total Economic and Social Aid to Colombia	$254,699,183.00	$246,568,999.00	$213,176,000.00	$192,500,000.00	$193,488,732.00	$159,936,620.00
Total Military Assistance	$441,505,261.00	$434,177,248.00	$336,830,537.00	$280,454,537.00	$279,465,805.00	$257,678,917.00

Figure 8.1. US Assistance to Colombia

Source: Data from the Colombian Police and population estimates from the DANE. Elaborated by Javier Moreno.

using military action. However, the Uribe administration did not have clear successes after eight years of military offensives as the FARC still exists and Colombia still has an internal armed conflict. It is important to note though that in spite of the fact that his government did not defeat insurgent organizations, Uribe's Democratic Security policy was implemented with a high degree of success to the extent it ostensibly reduced Colombia's homicide rate, as Figure 8.1 demonstrates.

During both junctures, peace talks in the midst of war (1998–2001) and only war (2001–2012), different (but somehow compatible) internationalization strategies were implemented. Even though the Pastrana and the Uribe administrations represent very different moments of the Colombian conflict—Pastrana initiated peace talks while Uribe intensified the state war against guerrilla groups—their strategies have common elements. This might be explained by the fact that the war and military offensives did not stop even when parties to the conflict were at the negotiating table. For both administrations, the construction of international alliances eventually contributed to strengthening the Colombian state's military capacities. While President Pastrana thought a strong army would serve to push insurgent groups toward the negotiation table, Uribe was more ambivalent about the possibilities of negotiation and at times, his government only contemplated a military victory over the guerrillas. Pastrana invited international actors to the negotiation table under the premise "the more, the merrier" (the more actors, the more pressure over the FARC to remain at the negotiation table). Pastrana also sought to obtain legitimacy and continuity for talks in times when reelection was forbidden by the Constitution. On the other hand, Uribe preferred to consolidate (almost exclusively) military alliances with powerful international actors.

Consequently, while Pastrana used internationalization in both scenarios of war and peace, Uribe emphasized military internationalization and systematically abandoned or rejected forms of internationalization that could have been more conducive to a negotiated solution to the conflict. As a consequence, a strategy of military internationalization directed to the United States was almost a perfect complement to a strategy of political de-internationalization directed toward the United Nations and the international human rights community, particularly the NGO community. These organizations undermined governmental legitimacy and were not welcome to participate in the conflict and were constantly attacked and vilified by the Uribe administration.

The Santos administration has learned important lessons from both Pastrana and Uribe and, as a result, it has implemented a policy of what we refer to as contained internationalization. Santos began his presidency by describing Colombia's conflict and peace process as a purely Colombian process and for Colombians only. Gradually, the Santos administration invited certain international actors—very few—to participate in talks under strict confidentiality and under the premise that invitations resulted from a previous agreement with the FARC.

Interestingly, both the presidential campaigns of Pastrana and Uribe concentrated on Colombia's conflict. One of the strategies that allowed Pastrana to become president was the use of a photo his campaign made public in which he appeared next to the FARC's General Secretariat (as its highest command is known in Colombia). It was clear for the electorate that his main proposal was to advance peace talks with insurgents and the picture showed that he had access to this insurgent organization and the possibility of succeeding. His mandate was a mandate for peace. By February 2002, Pastrana's round of peace talks had ended and presidential elections were rapidly approaching. After numerous failed attempts to find a peaceful resolution to the conflict, Colombians decided to elect (on the first round in a two rounds system and with 53 percent of popular vote) the candidate, Álvaro Uribe, who offered a hardline approach for dealing with guerrilla groups.

Uribe, a member of the Liberal Party who ran for office on an independent platform, personified the frustration most Colombians felt with what appeared to be the insurgency's lack of commitment to peace. Hence, his political campaign highlighted the inadequacy of a political resolution to the conflict. Uribe's argument was simple and clear: these groups did not have a political agenda and threatened democratic institutions. Uribe argued that insurgencies were a terrorist threat and the only way to defeat them was through a military victory. As opposed to Pastrana's mandate, Uribe's mandate was a mandate for war.

By the end of his second term, Uribe remained popular among Colombians and the government was contemplating a third reelection. However, the Constitutional Court ruled that a third term was unconstitutional and Uribe was forced to nominate a successor. Juan Manuel Santos, Uribe's trusted Minister of Defense, appeared to be the right person since he was closely involved in the implementation of the Democratic Security policy and would likely continue with Uribe's hardline approach to the insurgency problem. According to Uribe's plans, having Santos in power would result in the defeat—through military means—of the FARC and other insurgent organizations.

However, soon after Santos took power in August 2010, the differences between both political leaders began to surface and rumors about a secret peace process began to circulate in Colombia. President Santos continued talking about war and the continuation and intensification of military offensives, and he repeated that he only sought to continue implementing Uribe's security strategy. He reminded Colombians that only he had the key that would open the door to peace and would only use it if the FARC demonstrated they had honest intentions to negotiate and be part of the political process as a legitimate force and not as an illegally armed organization. But rumors continued spreading until in August 2012 Santos finally admitted that his government was holding secret preliminary conversations with the FARC. By November 2012, peace talks officially began between a governmental team and the guerrillas. Even though Santos inherited a mandate for war, he began political negotiations with the FARC to achieve peace against the will of his own political patron.

Even though the dialogues have remained secret and public information has been scarce, it is still possible to establish clear differences between this peace process and the one held by President Pastrana.

First, Santos does not have a mandate for peace. He was elected as Uribe's successor and by Uribe's followers. According to his initial electoral base (today his most radical opposition) he was supposed to continue to confront guerrillas through military means and under no circumstances to hold peace talks. Support for negotiations is a highly divisive issue in Colombia and most of his main political opponents are precisely the ones that helped him win the election. Colombia's public opinion dwells between two extremes: on one hand, Colombians are tired of a long-lasting conflict that could not be ended by military means during Uribe's tenure in office; and on the other, public opinion does not trust the FARC's political intentions. The insurgency has previously used peace processes to strengthen its military apparatus and there is no reason to think they would not do the same thing again. Colombia's public opinion is polarized and support for negotiations continues to be volatile, weak, and unstable.

Second, Santos, as opposed to Pastrana, is limiting the participation of external actors in the current peace process. The contrast between Santos and Pastrana is evident. Pastrana acted under the premise that the process had to face Colombia's public opinion and civil society organizations and believe that it should incorporate as many international actors as possible. Additionally, national media broadcasted every detail of progress—or lack thereof—in the peace process. Santos's negotiation team has implemented a very different strategy: very few members of Colombia's political landscape have traveled to Havana (a very small group of congressmen and no civil society organizations) and the formal participation of international actors only includes Norway, Cuba, Venezuela, and Chile. These countries act only as key supporting actors and there is no international mediation in these negotiations. However, both the government and the guerrillas have left open the possibility for other international actors to participate in other capacities.[5]

Negotiations have taken place both in Oslo, Norway, and Havana, Cuba, and these two countries have served a crucial purpose: they both have conditions that make media access difficult. The Norwegian government, as well as Switzerland, has acted as an important facilitator of peace talks in the past. However, the latter was not contemplated as a facilitator during current talks due to a previous incident involving a Swiss citizen making a financial transaction with the FARC.[6] Cuba also has a substantial level of control over media access that no other country in Latin America could offer. As opposed to what some pundits have suggested, Cuba is not part of the process due to its political influence over the FARC. In fact, Cuba's participation during the peace talks in El Caguán—advanced by the Pastrana administration—demonstrated that the country had no power to change the insurgency's behavior.[7] Additionally, Cuban governmental declarations have been less than kind to FARC members and have been very critical of this organization's strong link to the production and trafficking of illegal drugs.

Venezuela and the Chávez regime proved to be politically and ideologically aligned with the FARC. Since the reconstruction of bilateral relations between Colombia and Venezuela at the beginning of the Santos administration, Caracas could serve as a legal and legitimate channel of communication between the government and the insurgency in the midst of negotiations. Chile also has provided ideological and political equilibrium but has not been a salient actor during the peace talks.

Third, the U.S. government is noticeably absent in these talks. Even though the Obama administration has declared support for President Santos's peace efforts, Washington is not playing the crucial role it played during the peace talks in El Caguán and in other initiatives such as the U.S.-financed counter-narcotic strategy referred to as Plan Colombia. This is mainly explained by two different but complementary factors: first, due to the financial crisis, the United States does not have the necessary resources to support Colombia's military efforts. In fact, military support has been constantly decreasing since the last year of United States president George W. Bush's second term in office. Consequently, the United States capacity to shape or influence negotiations has been severely undermined.

Second, Bogotá has not been able to frame the Colombian conflict in a manner that has interested Washington and has been unable to convince the United States of the need for military cooperation. The Obama administration has a more focused version of its combat against terrorism than that of Bush, which hinders Colombia's attempt to frame the internal armed conflict as part of the global terrorist network in order to obtain military and economic resources as it did before. Such strategies worked for Presidents Pastrana and Uribe but it will not work for President Santos and his administration is aware of it.

Finally, foreign policy has been used as a tool for negotiation in a very skillful and strategic manner. This might constitute a form of internationalization that does not relate to specific actors but to the international community as a whole. Even before the dialogues were announced publicly, the government was already changing Colombia's international positions on two key issues that later proved to be crucial for the negotiation table: the war against drugs and the country's human rights situation. So far, it seems that the FARC may be pushing the government toward a more progressive position in these two topics, and this might constitute good news for Colombia and the region.

HUMAN RIGHTS AND THE WAR ON DRUGS: CHANGING COLOMBIA'S INTERNATIONAL IDENTITY

Before the dialogues were made public, Santos started an international campaign to discuss the current terms of the global war on drugs. This campaign began with a speech before the UN General Assembly in September 2010 when the president spoke, for the first time, about the need to revise and restate the terms of the war on drugs. In November 2011, Santos gave interviews to various media outlets in the UK and spoke again about his idea of leading a global discussion about what he called a failed global strategy against illegal narcotics. In April 2013, these declarations were followed by a proposal at the Summit of the Americas to form an OAS special committee to analyze the hemispheric war against drugs and to propose policy alternatives.[8] Eventually, Colombia, Mexico, and Guatemala proposed a joint UN declaration requesting that governments start a discussion about this very same issue. These governments did not mention legalization as an option (and neither has the Colombian government) but they are insisting on the need to start a broad discussion that would eventually lead to the reform of the anti-narcotics regime. The FARC seems to have a position relatively compatible with the Colombian government's effort to reform the global regime against illegal drugs. In February 2013, the FARC proposed legalizing coca, marijuana, and poppy crops. If the peace process succeeds, Colombia's international position and leadership on this issue could be crucial for a change in this global policy.

Colombia's human rights foreign policy has historically been defensive and based on the constant denial of the country's human rights situation. This policy has started to change recently, although slowly and with some ambiguities. The Santos administration has decided to openly and explicitly acknowledge that human rights are systematically and constantly violated in Colombia. It also has implemented a human rights national policy and established a *Sistema Nacional de Derechos Humanos* for the first time in the history of Colombia that attempts to coordinate efforts among all national governmental and nongovernmental agencies and organizations related to and interested in the advancement of Colombia's human rights situation. The insurgency has insisted that state crimes against civilians must stop, and by using its foreign and domestic policy, the government has tried to meet the FARC's demands.

These two changes have been part of a particular evaluation of the national situation, which led the Colombian government to attempt to drastically change the international identity of the country. The goal of this project is to reject the traditional international identity of a "troubled country" or the almost classic "eye of the hurricane." These metaphors defined Colombia as a place where many of the most pressing problems of the international system are intertwined: drug trafficking, terrorism, organized crime, and violence. The objective was to generate solidarity through self-stigmatization and to attract resources from the international community in order to combat these calamities. Many Colombian administrations dedicated years to generate and export this guilt complex to the most important actors of the global arena.

For the Santos administration, this way to define "Colombianess" does not correspond to the country's situation. In the midst of economic stability, the eventual success of the peace talks, and the relatively successful containment of the security problems related to organized criminal groups, the government began to represent the country before its international audience in a different way. Today, we have witnessed a "New Colombia," a country that teaches and shares *know-how* about security problems even among the NATO members; a country "mature in the sphere of human rights"; an economy that easily enters the most exclusive international economic organizations; a diplomacy capable of contributing to the solution of the Arab-Israeli conflict, and a country that can exercise regional leadership (an unprecedented situation for Colombia). Colombia is, according to this recent attempt to define its international identity, a country without complexes and with great aspirations and international ambitions.

Thus, two fundamental projects have converged: to achieve peace and to reconstruct Colombia's international image. Both projects are intertwined and the success of one depends on the achievements of the other. This is the core of the current strategy of the peace process internationalization.

PARTICIPATION OF THE INTERNATIONAL COMMUNITY IN THE PEACE PROCESS

United States

During the current peace process, the United States has been publicly backing the negotiations but has not been participating directly. Notably, Washington has emphasized on several occasions that the United States neither takes part in the process nor collaborates with any of the participants; rather it has tended to stay away from the negotiation table, desiring not to have any public role in the process. At the same time, according to some reports, the United States has expressed its interest to be involved in a post-conflict settlement. In other words, the manifestations of support by the United States, although not accompanied by the direct involvement, are motivated by post-conflict aid and cooperation.

Although the participation of the United States has differed from its role in the peace talks in Caguán, it is important to note that two issues not directly related to bilateral relations between Colombia and the United States have been discussed and negotiated during the current talks: agrarian development and political participation. In contrast, the issue of drug trafficking may trigger partial and discrete participation of the United States in ongoing talks. Indeed, President Santos traveled to Washington to discuss this and other issues with President Barack Obama precisely the week when discussions about drug trafficking began between the Colombian government and the rebels.

By 2012, the Santos government was already receiving positive feedback from Washington as well as the media regarding its efforts to achieve peace.

Moreover, the appearance of the Colombian president on the front page of *Time Magazine* (the international edition) highlighted "his ability to bridge the U.S. and the rest of the hemisphere," and his objective to make Colombia "the new economic and diplomatic player in Latin America."[9] At the same time, in the context of the Summit of the Americas that occurred in Cartagena, President Obama highlighted Santos's determination to resolve the Colombian conflict. Obama confirmed his support for the Colombian president's efforts and assured that his government would be "a close ally" of Colombia.[10] The U.S. president and his officials would continue to use words, such as "ally," together with adjectives like "unconditional" or "strategic" during the peace process.

In August 2012, before publicly announcing the beginning of peace negotiations, Colombia's Ministry of Defense invited the U.S. general Stanley McChrystal, the NATO commander and former commander in Afghanistan, as a military consultant.[11] This invitation is an example of the already structural military internationalization of the armed conflict and of the historic cooperation between the United States and Colombia. The *Espada de Honor* program was launched in September 2013 as part of the strategy of continued military actions during the negotiations with the FARC.

When the decision to begin the negotiations with the FARC was made public, the United States announced: "[W]e welcome the efforts to put an end to this extensive conflict and achieve a lasting peace in Colombia. We have always been an unconditional ally to Colombia, its government and its people throughout the conflict."[12] Later, in September, Washington reiterated its defense and security positions, as well as its commitment to advance human rights and economic prosperity in Colombia.[13]

One of the first issues at the negotiation table that concerned bilateral relations with the United States was the request to set free Simón Trinidad and allow him to participate as a member of the FARC delegation.[14] Simón Trinidad was extradited in 2004 and has been charged with drug trafficking and terrorism. The U.S. government decided not to comment on the topic.[15] In October 2012, Roberta Jacobson, the Assistant Secretary of State for Western Hemisphere Affairs, declared: "[W]e will discuss anything, but we are still at a very preliminary stage of the negotiations."[16] Since then, the topic has not been addressed publicly.

The FARC insisted that the Simón Trinidad's pardon would be a "huge contribution" of the U.S. government to peace, as well as an "act of humanity."[17] Since then, Washington has limited itself to sporadic commentaries of support "for the consolidation of democracy, the rule of law, human rights and peace" by officials like the Vice-president and the Secretary of State without any specific reference to this topic.[18]

In 2013, there were several manifestations of the U.S. support of the peace process related to the post-conflict settlement. The best example is the proposal by a group of congressmen, headed by Jim McGovern and Jan Schakowsky, for an Assistance Package for Peace to reorient funds previously used for the war[19] in order to support the Victims and Land Restitution Law, The Ombudsman's Office of Colombia, and regional development programs.[20] The letter also made a request for U.S. Secretary of State John Kerry to review the fight against drugs because of "a predictable aftermath of the process is that Colombia will refocus from illicit crops fumigation toward development of rural territories."[21] The negotiations also addressed various issues such as human rights, land mines elimination, reintegration, and the creation of an independent truth commission.[22] However, Obama refused to comment on the congressional initiative arguing that he desired to respect the independence of the negotiating table.[23]

Cooperation with the United States has occurred in other ways. The United States, for instance, has sent an assistance package of 50 million dollars in support of the Victims and Land Restitution Law.[24] In April 2013, Washington committed to continue allocating resources to Colombia through the International Development Agency (USAID) during the peace process.[25]

The Fight Against Drugs[26]

Within the context of the current peace process in Havana, the Colombian government has attempted to follow a new approach to the illegal drugs issue, both at the negotiating table and away from it. Santos has changed the traditional position of the Colombian government, which followed a prohibitionist approach to the war on drugs, and replaced it with one characterized by greater openness to debating different strategies for addressing this problem. Even though Santos has not advocated a specific type of policy, he has insisted on the need to hold an open debate about the dominant global strategy and its clear shortcomings. This change in the government's position has been facilitated by the relatively marginal role played by the United States in the peace process, and Washington's diminished influence over Colombia as a result of the decreases in military and economic aid for the war on drugs and counterinsurgency programs.

Santos's presidential campaign began with a speech before the UN General Assembly in September 2010, where he spoke for the first time about the need to revise and redefine the war against drugs. He expressed concern about the contradictions of the war on drugs and called for a thorough review of the global strategy on the matter, stating:

> We note with concern the contradictions of some countries that, on the one hand, demand a frontal fight against drug trafficking and, on the other, legalize consumption or study the possibility of legalizing the production and trade of certain drugs . . . These contradictions make it a necessity . . . to come to

> an agreement and to review the global strategy against illicit drugs, in order to agree upon a unique global policy, more effective and within which all countries will contribute equally to this effort.[27]

In November 2011, Santos was interviewed by various media outlets in the UK and commented on his desire to lead a global discussion about the failed global strategies of the war on drugs. *The Guardian* reported that President Santos's voice was "becoming the key one in trying to set the terms for a new international discussion about the war." Santos stated, "[W]e are basically still thinking within the same framework as we have done for the last 40 years . . . A new approach should try and take away the violent profit that comes with drug trafficking . . . If that means legalising, and the world thinks that's the solution, I will welcome it. I'm not against it."[28]

Santos sought to be a leader in the discourse for the need to alter the drug war strategies, but he made clear that he was not willing to pay the high political cost of assuming and advancing a concrete position. On the contrary, the Colombian government would only change its position on drug policy in the event of an international consensus. Santos asserted: "What I won't do is to become the vanguard of that movement because then I will be crucified. But I would gladly participate in those discussions because we are the country that's still suffering most and have suffered most historically with the high consumption of the UK, the US, and Europe in general . . ."[29]

In April 2013, these declarations were followed by Santos's proposal at the Summit of the Americas to form an OAS special committee to analyze the hemispheric war against drugs and to propose new venues for action. The OAS Secretary General made public the content of this report very recently and it is expected to initiate a debate at least within the hemisphere.[30] Although this report was meant to be discussed at the 43rd Regular Session of the OAS General Assembly in Antigua, Guatemala, in June 2013, President Santos, the leading promoter of the drafting of the report, excused himself from attending the meeting. The discussion began but almost no significant changes to the hemisphere's approach to the war on drugs were agreed upon.

Also as part of this strategy, Colombia, Mexico, and Guatemala proposed a joint UN declaration requesting governments to start a discussion about drug policy. These governments did not mention legalization as an option but they insisted on the need to start a broad discussion that would eventually lead to deep reforms to the current anti-narcotics regime.

The change in the Colombian government's position has been made possible by the decline in Washington's influence over Colombia. In fact, there has been no public reaction on the part of the U.S. government following President Santos's various international statements, nor has there been any

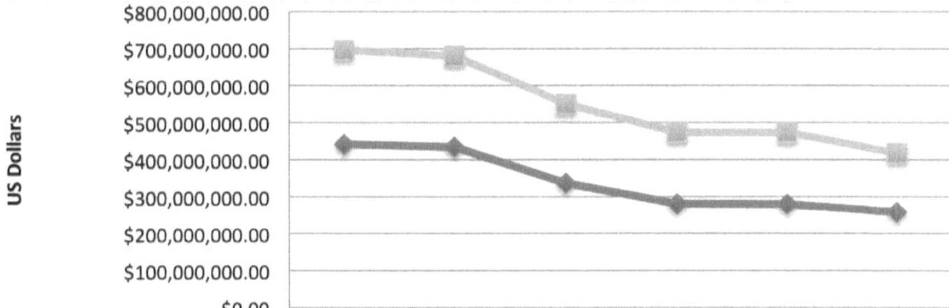

	2009	2010	2011	2012	2013	2014
Total Economic and Social Aid to Colombia	$254,699,183.00	$246,568,999.00	$213,176,000.00	$192,500,000.00	$193,488,732.00	$159,936,620.00
Total Military Assistance	$441,505,261.00	$434,177,248.00	$336,830,537.00	$280,454,537.00	$279,465,805.00	$257,678,917.00

Figure 8.2. US Assistance to Colombia
Some numbers for 2013 and 2014 are estimates. Source: http://justf.org

negative impact on the two countries' bilateral relations, at least publicly. This recent turn of events is explained by two different but complementary factors: first, as a result of the financial crisis, the United States cannot afford to continue supporting Colombia's military efforts. In fact, military support has been constantly decreasing since 2009, as Figure 8.2 shows. Consequently, Washington's ability to shape or influence Santos's position and activism on this topic has been severely undermined.

Second, as previously mentioned, Bogotá has not been able to keep framing Colombia's conflict in a way that would interest Washington and attract its military cooperation. However, this scenario has changed dramatically. The Obama administration's strategy with regard to the war on terror is more targeted than it was during the Bush administration, and Obama has no intention to expand or extend it to include the internal armed conflict in Colombia.[31] Such policies hinder Colombia's intention to frame its civil strife as part of the global war against terrorism and, consequently, make it more difficult to obtain military and economic resources from the United States. This strategy worked for Presidents Pastrana and Uribe but it will not work for President Santos, and his administration is aware of it.

These aspects of the bilateral relation, added to the fact that Colombia and Latin America are not high-priority items on Washington's foreign policy agenda, indicate that it is very unlikely that U.S. economic and military aid to Colombia will increase in the near future. As a result, it is to be expected that U.S. intervention, participation, and influence over the Colombian government and in the current peace process will remain minimal.

The current Colombian government has chosen to steer clear of pronouncements about the links between drug trafficking and subversive groups, and it has almost completely abandoned the use of terms such as "narco-terrorism" or "narco-guerrillas." Santos has not made any public remarks openly asserting the FARC's direct involvement with drug trafficking; and, at least in public, he maintains that he believes the FARC's claim that its members are not drug traffickers. Likewise, pronouncements about these links on the part of members of the military or the Minister of Defense have also become less frequent.

The "revisionist" discourse at the international level in connection to the current terms of the war on drugs, along with the abandonment of the strategy that linked the FARC directly with the illicit drug issue, allows the government to shape the conditions for conducting negotiations in a less polarizing manner, which is likely to facilitate speedier discussions. Furthermore, this shift allows the government to win over parts of the electorate and public opinion with more progressive views on this subject, preventing the FARC from attempting to win their support.

Latin America

The role of the region in the negotiations has been mostly focused on the legitimation of the peace process. From the beginning of the Santos administration, the region's support—especially from the leftist governments and neighboring states—has been seen as crucial for the negotiations.

As will be discussed further, the region approves and supports the negotiations. However, in contrast to previous administrations, the government has been efficient in its role as gatekeeper for regional participation in the dialogues: no international actor seems to have violated the expectations of the Colombian government and the FARC regarding their participation. Thus, the Santos government has assured international support with no interference. In addition, due to the possibility of an informal dialogue with the *Ejército de Liberación Nacional* (ELN), Brazil, Costa Rica, Uruguay, Venezuela, and Cuba recently demonstrated their interest in hosting the talks. However, no official confirmation of the future talks or the location on the part of the Colombian government has occurred.

Venezuela

The scope of Venezuela's participation in the peace process has been determined by the Colombian government and has adhered to the criteria established from the beginning. Hugo Chávez was one of the first to learn about Santos's intention to reach out to the FARC. He was considered a key figure that could convince the Colombian guerrillas and help achieve an agreement. At the beginning of the talks, the presence of the Chávez government was of high importance.

Santos's efforts to reestablish and normalize the deteriorated relations with Venezuela from the beginning of his mandate serve as evidence of the importance he attributed to the participation of Venezuela in the peace talks. However, once the negotiations began, Santos's government kept Chávez's influence under control. Thus, Venezuela has acted as an accompanying country in the process, but has not significantly affected the dynamics of the negotiation.

The presence of Venezuela at the negotiation table may have been a response to the need to involve international actors that are politically and ideologically similar to the rebels.[32] They are more likely to have leverage over the guerrillas and serve as a liaison with the government. Moreover, Venezuela is an example of an elected leftist government and a socialist state democratically elected, rather than a government who achieved power by using military means.[33] The Colombian government is interested in promoting this model at the negotiation table.

Two events have affected Venezuela's role in the peace process: the death of Hugo Chávez in March 2013 and Henrique Capriles's visit with Juan Manuel Santos in June of the same year. Both events showed that Venezuela is the most volatile country of the peace process participants, and the Colombian government's effort to contain this volatility has not been entirely successful.

After several crises damaged bilateral relations during the Álvaro Uribe administration, Santos began his presidency by demonstrating his desire to reestablish relations with Venezuela and Ecuador. Not long after assuming office, the Ministries of Exterior in Bogotá and Caracas agreed to create working groups,[34] while the Colombian ambassador was allowed to return to Venezuela.[35] Once relations were reestablished, Venezuela began to support the Colombian government in its effort to achieve peace. As evidence, Venezuela extradited the ELN rebel Nilson Teran in December 2010. Regarding this act, Chávez declared that he desired peace in Colombia and that he does not support war.[36]

Since 2012, Chávez began demanding "evidence of peace intentions" from the guerrillas in his discourse.[37] Given that the secret stage of the peace process started approximately at the same time, Chávez might have been asking the FARC to demonstrate its political will to be part of the process. He stated, "We are willing to support the search for peace in Colombia if we are asked to."[38] Since then, Venezuela has constantly called for "evidence of peace" from the FARC. The first meeting between Venezuelan and FARC envoys occurred in the beginning of 2012. Indeed, Chávez was informed about the arrangements and it was due to his support that important levels of trust were reached between the Colombian government and the rebels.[39] Later it was revealed that before his meeting with the Colombian government, the rebel leader Timochenko met with Chávez in Venezuela to discuss the process.[40] The first meeting between the government and the rebels took place in South Cesar, in a rural area of Rio de Oro. Alejandro Eder and a government official from Acción Social attended the event as government representatives, while Rodrigo Granda and Andrés Paris attended as guerrilla representatives.[41] The second meeting occurred with Chávez's assistance in Barinas, Venezuela, where the location of a formal dialogue was discussed.[42]

While there were rumors about a peace process in Colombia, Venezuela, Cuba, and Norway remained silent. However, the Venezuelan TV channel Telesur was first to inform about the agreements between the Colombian government and the FARC and several previous meetings that began in May 2012.[43] When the agreement about peace talks was announced, Cuba and Norway were declared "guarantors" and Venezuela and Chile would participate as "accompanying countries" during the process.[44] From the beginning, Venezuela was assigned the role of logistics coordinator, facilitator, and assistant in the Accord to End the Conflict.

After Chávez's reelection, he had a cancer relapse and was hospitalized in December 2012. After years of cancer treatment in Cuba, Venezuela's president died in March 2013. The loss of a key figure in the peace process generated controversy as Chávez was considered the regional leader who had the most political influence on the FARC. By March 2013, the acting president, Nicolás Maduro, argued that he would fulfill the promises Hugo Chávez made and he would continue to facilitate peace in Colombia. Maduro declared, "Our government remains determined to support as much as possible president Santos's government, the sides in conflict who are at the negotiation table in Havanna."[45] Although it had a slight impact on the peace talks, Chávez's death has unlikely drastically affected the dynamics of the dialogues. His presence was much more decisive at the moment of the rapprochement between the two countries.

However, the change of the government did provoke a diplomatic crisis between Colombia and Venezuela that eventually led Santos to request José Mujica, the president of Uruguay, to be an alternative at the negotiation table. In June 2013, President Maduro accused Santos of supporting the opposition after the ex-presidential candidate Henrique Capriles visited Colombia. The Colombian government decided to resolve the crisis through diplomatic means and not to provoke Venezuela.[46] The FARC were worried about the deteriorating relationship between the two countries, highlighting the role Venezuela played in the process, and contracting Roy Chaderton to obtain information about the situation.[47] Eventually, the stalemate ended when Maduro reassured publicly his support for peace talks.[48]

In June of 2013, Maduro announced that the ex-president of Brazil Lula had intended to mediate his meeting with Santos.[49] This meeting had occurred in July in order to fix the relationship between Colombia and Venezuela after the Capriles crisis. The foreign minister of Venezuela, Elias Jaua, confirmed Venezuela's will to collaborate to achieve "the necessary and just peace for Colombia," stating that his country will always accept invitations to participate in the peace process.[50]

Cuba

Cuba has been the host country for the dialogues. Its involvement during the process has included logistics assistance and premises arrangements for the negotiations. It was also responsible for collaborating with the Colombian government in maintaining the utmost confidentiality of the talks.

Despite its decrease in geopolitical significance since the end of the Cold War,[51] Cuba historically has been known as a highly influential guerrilla sponsor.[52] As a guarantor, Cuba has assumed the responsibilities related to providing credibility to the process, guaranteeing the mutual trust of the actors, monitoring the compliance, interpreting position proposals, and preventing misunderstandings.[53] From this perspective, its role is more proactive than that of an accompanying country but it still does not have mediating capacity, and its task is limited to maintain the atmosphere of negotiation.

Cuba, like Venezuela, contributed at the initial stage of the rapprochement of the parties. An envoy of Raúl Castro was responsible for organizing the first meeting in the department of Cesar.[54] Likewise, further meetings took place on Cuban territory, including the signing of the "General Accord to End the Conflict and Build a Stable, Enduring Peace," which marked the beginning of the public stage of the process. According to Telesur, the island was hosting meetings since May 2012.[55] Moreover, Cuba has offered its "good offices" in a possible dialogue with the ELN, when the latter informed about their intentions to negotiate.[56]

Chile

Chile also has been chosen as an accompanying country. This decision has been seen as a government's intention to increase regional presence by placing the then Community of Latin American and Caribbean States (CELAC) president at the negotiation table.[57] Moreover, Sebastián Piñera's administration was aligned with the Santos government in terms of political ideology.

For example, both countries participated in the preparation of the Pacific Alliance and agreed on military cooperation, training, and information sharing.[58] By August 2012, after the General Accord was announced, Chile confirmed its commitment to the success of the negotiation table and regional peace.[59] However, Chile has maintained a rather low profile, which may or may not change with the return of Michelle Bachelet to power.

Brazil

Although Brazil does not represent an "accompanying country," it has played—albeit indirectly—an important role in the dialogues. The Brazilian government has been consulting with Colombia on issues related to the negotiations, specifically agrarian development. Although the Colombian government has made efforts to limit Brazil's participation, it appreciated Brazil's contribution.

Brazil has played a crucial role since August 2010 when President Lula da Silva mediated the rapprochement between Juan Manuel Santos and Hugo Chávez[60] by organizing their meeting in Brasilia to normalize bilateral ties.[61] During the mediation, Santos mentioned the possibility of Brazil participating in the peace talks in some sort of capacity. The presidential candidate Dilma Rousseff suggested that Brazil would take part in the dialogue for peace if requested by Colombia.

In February 2011, the Brazilian government contributed in the rescue of five hostages held by the FARC by providing helicopters and planning the operation from San Gabriel to Cachoeira. Several months later, when new operations were announced, Colombia vetoed Brazil's participation.[62] As a result of the guerrilla's demands, the president of Colombia was compelled to request Brazil's assistance. Meanwhile, the rebels postponed the hostages' return date,[63] and the Brazilian foreign minister Antonio Patriota kept waiting for a formal request from the Colombian government to participate in the operation.[64] When the Colombian government issued an official request, Brazil accepted the request to participate and assisted in the hostage return in March 2012 by providing two helicopters and twenty officials and soldiers.[65] The Red Cross pointed out the high professionalism and dedication of Brazilian personnel during several days of the operation.[66]

In August 2012, when plans about the negotiations were made public, Brazil demonstrated its support for the process. Rousseff mentioned that President Santos had alerted her of such events.[67] In October, once the talks started, the Brazilian government showed again its support to Colombia by issuing a document, stating, "Brazil and South America support the rapid end of the armed conflict in Colombia."[68] The document exposes the arguments in favor of Santos's initiative of peace talks and states that Brazil has always been ready to support a negotiated solution to the conflict as long as the Colombian government requests so.[69] President Santos, in turn, stated Brazil's collaboration would always be welcomed.[70]

In November 2012, the Brazilian foreign minister, Antonio Patriota, revealed that he had met with Sergio Jaramillo, the High Commissioner for Peace in the Santos administration, to discuss the quest for peace, the Oslo meeting and the further development of the peace process. Since this period of Brazil's diplomatic activity until June 2013, there had been no relevant steps by the Brazilian government toward the peace process. However, the diplomatic crisis between Colombia and Venezuela made the former Brazilian President Lula da Silva a mediator between the presidents of Colombia and Venezuela.[71] After Henrique Capriles's visit, President Lula da Silva was required to fulfill his promise to guard the good relationship in the south of the continent.

Finally, the Colombian foreign minister María Ángela Holguín confirmed that Brazil had contributed to part of the agreements reached in Havana. Its contribution has been related mostly to the issues of agricultural co-ops and family agriculture, where Brazil's ideas helped obtain the first point of the agenda.[72] Similar to other countries, Brazil has showed interest in hosting the possible talks with ELN rebels.[73]

The European Union

The European continent has been rather distant from the arena of the process except for the participation of Norway, which assumed the role of a guarantor. The European Union's involvement has been similar to that of the United States in that it approves a coordinated settlement of the conflict and generates incentives to support the process but it does not intervene directly in the negotiations.

The EU's policies toward the peace process in Colombia were delineated in the end of 2011. During his visit to Colombia in October 2011, the EU Commissioner for Development, Andris Piebalgs, took stock of the results achieved in EU-funded cooperation programs and discussed the future of EU-Colombian cooperation with national authorities.[74] In November 2011, the European Commission approved the implementation of five financing agreements of fifty-five million euros (seventy million U.S. dollars) in support of Colombia's Victims and Land Restitution Law.[75] Besides multilateral aid, Sweden offered an annual financial assistance of 26 million dollars, depositing thirteen thousand directly for a humanitarian fund.[76]

Norway

Despite the fact that European countries have channeled their action through the EU, Norway's role should be highlighted to the extent it was selected as a guarantor of the negotiations. Norway had already taken part in the peace process in Caguán, and the government has experience in conflict resolution.[77] Therefore, its presence was viewed as the best option outside the continent to host the initial stages of the talks. Likewise, the election of Norway might have been a response to the need to involve the European community as well as to have an expert actor in conflict resolution.

Norway's role during the peace process can be divided into several stages. The first relates to the assistance while contacting the rebels in order to carry out first meetings. During this stage, Norway's officials assisted with logistical arrangements for the first secret contacts[78] and, later, escorted the FARC delegation from their camps to Cuba.[79] The second phase of Norway's assistance relates to its partial coverage of some costs endured by the parties. Finally, it has served as a consultant and contributed its knowledge to the negotiators and the government.

International Organizations

Notably, international organizations have been absent from the peace process.[80] Although some of them, such as the United Nations, have contributed to establishing the links between civil society and the negotiation table, they have not taken part in the talks in Havana. International organizations have acted as mediators between the Colombian government, the FARC, and civil society. In other words, they have contributed to the socialization of negotiations in Colombia and they have transmitted social demands and concerns to the negotiating table. This socialization also aims at obtaining international legitimation of the agreements in order to maintain a favorable image of dialogues both abroad and domestically.

The United Nations

The Colombian government used the General Assembly as an arena to share its achievements and difficulties, to ask the international community not to interfere in the peace process or to advocate for Colombia's right for peace.

In September 2010, President Santos stated that, in the case of a peace process, he would not accept international mediators. Once the preliminary talks were announced, the UN Secretary General demonstrated his approval of the rapprochement with the FARC[81] and, despite Santos's remarks, offered the UN good offices to mediate the talks if it was considered useful.[82] In September of 2010, Santos also appeared before the General Assembly to present the peace talks, his rules of the game as well as the role of the international community.[83]

Colombia also received support from the majority of the members of the Council on Human Rights for its peace process and the implementation of its Victims and Land Restitution Law but not for the military sector reform.[84] Moreover, the member countries supported Santos's human rights policies and Colombia would have been exempt from such commentaries if it were for the military reform and the high levels of impunity with regards to sexual violent crimes.[85]

With respect to the observations made by the International Criminal Court (ICC) about possible impunity derived from the Legal Framework for Peace and the nature of transitional justice in Colombia, the president has used the General Assembly to reveal his opinions on the topic. According to Santos, the world should "respect legal sovereignty of his country in defining its own investigative and legal mechanisms after more than fifty years of conflict."[86]

The last relevant episode occurred in 2013 when the UN High Commissioner for Human Rights visited Colombia on Santos's invitation. Once the Commissioner arrived to the country, the president declared publicly his intention to end the presence of the representative of the office in Colombia because "it was already a mature country in terms of human rights." The negotiation lasted two days, occurred mostly through the media, and resulted with an extension of the offices' presence for an additional year.

Based on the discussion, several conclusions can be made. On the one hand, the Colombian government does not feel comfortable with being monitored by a multilateral organization on such delicate issues such as human rights or its direct participation in the talks in Havana. On the other hand, NGOs point out that there is no evidence of a substantial improvement with regard to the human rights situation in Colombia and, therefore, Santos's argument about Colombia's maturity does not match reality.

The Interamerican System

The Interamerican system reform was another opportunity explored by the national government to de-internationalize, at least partially, the dynamics of the Colombian conflict. This intent to limit the involvement of international actors under the human rights agenda is recurrent in the peace process given that violations of these rights take place, mostly, in the context of the armed conflict.

After several decades of armed conflict and a serious humanitarian crisis as a result of such conflict, the Interamerican Commission on Human Rights (ICHR) has prioritized the Colombian case. At the beginning of the reform process, the ICHR visited Colombia in 1980 and 1997 and had several follow-up visits to monitor the demobilization and to gather evidence for specific cases. Moreover, since the mid-1990s, Colombia, as well as Cuba, has been included in Chapter IV of the ICHR Annual Report, commonly known as the "black list." For this reason, Colombia led the 2012 reform that addressed the criteria of inclusion in Chapter IV. Initially, Colombia criticized both the methodology and the effectiveness of the mechanism. Regarding the former, Colombia argued that the criteria used by the ICHR was too broad and the problems were common for the region in general and not only for countries of "special attention." From Colombia's point of view, this made the mechanism less effective, since it was an obstacle to the principles of universality, equal treatment, and objectivity.

This position was later shared by various states that also proposed to modify Chapter IV and substitute it with a mechanism similar to the Universal Periodic Review of the UN Commission of Human Rights. Colombia, in turn, saw an opportunity to benefit from the discussion and changed its initial intentions. It decided to appear as a Commission's collaborator by insisting that the Commission should pay more attention to states' efforts to improve their human rights situation, such as inviting the Commission to follow them in their own territory. Immediately after promoting this argument, Colombia announced its intention to invite the ICHR to its territory; the visit occurred in December 2012, which was one of the most critical moments of the reform process. Thus, Colombia positioned itself as an ally of ICHR by opening its doors to the Commission at the same time that the Commission was being criticized by several states. This strategy was effective because several months later, the ICHR incorporated in its regulations a provision that specified the ways states could avoid scrutiny under Chapter IV, which includes the invitation of the Commission to the state for inspections. Pursuant to the new provision, Colombia was excluded from the ICHR Annual Report 2012 Chapter IV for the first time in ten years. Thus, the launching of a new human rights public policy by the Santos administration has been accompanied by attempts to reduce international supervision in this realm.

FINAL CONSIDERATIONS

The review of international actors' participation in the current peace process in Colombia allows for a broader reflection on the topic. The Santos administration has skillfully built and maintained an international consensus that gives support and legitimacy to the peace process,[87] especially in the context of strong domestic criticism and public skepticism.

It is also clear that the design and implementation of Santos's internationalization strategy are based on past experiences. The roles assigned to the international actors have been clearly delineated and their interests taken into account, with no assumption that they will act exclusively in the interest of the peace process. The international actors have been primarily focused on generating trust between the parties, and the parties have been allowed to act only in the interest of the peace process without interfering. The Colombian government also has realized that the role of international actors can be more effective in the long run, in building local, regional and national initiatives.[88] Finally, the chaotic slogan of the Caguán peace process, "the more, the merrier," referring to international actors, was replaced by the principle of their selective, carefully designed and limited role.

However, some challenges remain. First, the internationalization process does not fit completely within the broader framework of Colombian foreign policy. Indeed, the Foreign Ministry rarely appears in relation to the peace process and there are occasionally strong tensions between the two. The most notable example is the disagreement between the negotiating parties with regard to the Colombian government's reaction to the ruling of the International Court of Justice that redefined the maritime border between Nicaragua and Colombia, depriving Colombia of its previously controlled waters in the Caribbean Sea.

In addition, the practice of compliance verification by an international actor can be a problem if this actor has not played a part at the negotiation table. It may happen if the parties are not aware as much as the international arbiter of the challenges and limitations in the implementation of the agreements.

Finally, there may be possible tensions between the Legal Framework for Peace and the Rome Statute of the ICC. These tensions have already compelled the Colombian government to promote the "right to peace" principle at the UN General Assembly and to demonstrate a better behavior and respect for human rights[89] as well as for the International Humanitarian Law in order to prevent the ICC interference by demonstrating cooperation and good will.[90]

NOTES

1. Thanks to Yulia Vorobyeva for translating parts of this document from Spanish to English. It should be noted that all the quotes have been translated from Spanish to English.

2. Sandra Borda, *La internacionalización de la paz y de la guerra en Colombia durante los Gobiernos de Andrés Pastrana y Álvaro Uribe. Búsqueda de legitimidad política y capacidad militar* (Bogotá: Ediciones Uniandes, 2012).

3. James Murdoch and Todd Sandler, "Economic growth, civil wars, and spacial spillovers," *Journal of Conflict Resolution* 46, no. 1 (2001): 91–110.

4. Sandra Borda, *La internacionalización de la paz y de la guerra en Colombia durante los Gobiernos de Andrés Pastrana y Álvaro Uribe. Búsqueda de legitimidad política y capacidad militar* (Bogotá: Ediciones Uniandes, 2012).

5. "Venezuela y Chile acompañarían el proceso de paz," *El Espectador*, Aug. 29, 2012, http://www.elespectador.com/noticias/paz/venezuela-y-chile-acompanarian-el-proceso-de-paz-farc-articulo-370909.

6. In July 2008, a debate on the role of international actors in the Colombian conflict began. This time the central figure was Jean Pierre Gotard, a Swiss citizen who had been acting as a mediator for the liberation of hostages with the authorization of the Colombian government. Gotard, an external adviser for the Swiss government, visited on numerous occasions the *Zona de Distension* during the peace process with the Pastrana administration, and he convinced the FARC to liberate two foreigners. The Colombian government found evidence of this transaction in Reyes's computer: Gotard appeared there as the bearer of US$500.000 that the government confiscated from the FARC in San José de Costa Rica. Apparently, this was the amount of money he paid to the FARC for the liberation of these two people. But the Colombian government found more evidence of Gotard's relationship with the FARC: he was a professor of many Colombian students in Switzerland, among them, the son of Alfonso Cano, FARC's main head commander after Tirofijo's death in 2008 (Apoyo Del Gobierno De Suiza Al Intercambio Humanitario Sigue Firme, Dice Embajada En Bogotá 37 Correos De Pc De Reyes, Sombra Sobre Gestión De Facilitador Suizo Gontard Fue Profesor Del Hijo De Cano 2008). The Colombian Attorney General decided to open a formal judicial process and to call Gotard to testify, but only hours after, the Swiss government asked the Colombian government "to cease its attacks against Gotard" (Suiza Pide No 'Atacar' Más A Gontard 2008). Colombian Minister of Defense Juan Manuel Santos accused Gotard, some Swiss nongovernmental organizations and the Swiss government itself, of supporting the FARC, or at least, of allowing them to enter and exit the country easily (Afp 2007).

7. A very well-known incident during Pastrana's peace process supports this point: Andrés Felipe, a twelve-year-old child whose father was a policeman kidnapped by the FARC for over three years, suffered from a terminal cancer and his wish was to see his father, for the last time, before dying. Pastrana met with Castro and told him about this case in an attempt to find collaboration to pressure the FARC. Castro immediately wrote a letter and he asked his ambassador in Colombia to hand it to Manuel Marulanda, FARC's head commander, directly. According to Pastrana's account of the meeting, Castro said that he had never asked a favor to the FARC—and they, on the other hand, have asked him plenty. "That is why I am going to write to them so they liberate the father of this kid before he dies" (Pastrana 2006, 445). The FARC's answer to Castro was almost a revolutionary cliché. They argued that the problem was not only Andrés Felipe but all the social inequities in the country and the thousands of kids that die in poverty while the oligarchy does nothing for them (Pastrana 2006, 445). Andrés Felipe died on December 18th and could not see his father who, desperate due to his son's disease, tried to escape and was killed by the FARC. Castro's lack of power to influence the FARC's behavior was now public and another proof of the FARC's historic international isolation.

8. The work of this committee has been funded mainly by the Colombian government and will be available to the public in April 2013.

9. "'Colombia, un modelo': Time," *El Tiempo,* Apr. 13, 2012, http://www.eltiempo.com/archivo/documento/CMS-11556067.

10. "'Es otro paso hacia el final del conflicto': Obama," *El Tiempo*, Apr. 16, 2012, http://www.eltiempo.com/archivo/documento/CMS-11577315.

11. "Excomandante de la OTAN en Afganistán nos asesora en Defensa," *El Tiempo*, Aug. 25, 2012, http://www.eltiempo.com/archivo/documento/CMS-12163991.

12. "EE. UU., OEA y Unión Europea respaldan contactos de Gobierno con FARC," *El Tiempo*, Aug. 28, 2012, http://www.eltiempo.com/archivo/documento/CMS-12172203.

13. "Venezuela, Chile y Noruega saludan las conversaciones con las FARC," *El Tiempo*, Sept. 4, 2012, http://www.eltiempo.com/politica/conversaciones-de-paz-venezuela-chile-y-noruega-saludan-las-conversaciones-con-las-farc_12193872-4; "EE.UU. apoya el proceso de paz," *Revista Semana*, September 4, 2012, http://www.semana.com/mundo/articulo/eeuu-apoya-proceso-paz/264177-3.

14. "Insistencia de FARC en 'Simón Trinidad' no afectaría el proceso," *El Tiempo*, September 7, 2012, http://www.eltiempo.com/archivo/documento/CMS-12201387.

15. Ibid.

16. "EE. UU. apoya la paz, pero se muestra prudente sobre 'Trinidad,'" *El Tiempo*, October 19, 2012, http://www.eltiempo.com/archivo/documento/CMS-12315988.

17. "Con petición de indulto para 'Trinidad,' FARC sorprenden al Gobierno," *El Tiempo*, November 23, 2012, http://www.eltiempo.com/archivo/documento/CMS-12397582.

18. "Fundación Carter se comprometió a apoyar proyectos para la paz," *El Tiempo*, January 15, 2013b, http://www.eltiempo.com/archivo/documento/CMS-12514350; "'Colombia es modelo para América Latina': John Kerry," *El Tiempo*, January 24, 2013, http://www.eltiempo.com/archivo/documento/CMS-12545282; "Gobiernos del mundo reaccionaron tras anuncio en La Habana," *El Tiempo*, May 26, 2013, http://www.eltiempo.com/archivo/documento/CMS-12825563; "Joe Biden inicia agenda sobre paz y comercio en Bogotá," *El Tiempo*, May 27, 2013, http://www.eltiempo.com/archivo/documento/CMS-12825769; "Joe Biden ratifica apoyo de EE. UU. a proceso de paz en Colombia," *El Tiempo*, May 27, 2013, http://www.eltiempo.com/archivo/documento/CMS-12827502; "Estados Unidos ratificó respaldo al proceso de paz," *El Tiempo*, August 12, 2013, http://www.eltiempo.com/archivo/documento/CMS-12987843; "'Estados Unidos no va a abandonar este proceso de paz': Kerry," *El Tiempo*, August 12, 2013, http://www.eltiempo.com/archivo/documento/CMS-12988083.

19. "Congresistas de EE. UU. firman respaldo al proceso en La Habana," *El Tiempo*, March 30, 2013, http://www.eltiempo.com/archivo/documento/CMS-12717155.

20. "Así debe ser el nuevo apoyo de EE.UU. a Colombia," *Revista Semana*, April 14, 2013, http://www.semana.com/nacion/articulo/asi-debe-nuevo-apoyo-eeuu-colombia/340398-3

21. "Congresistas de EE. UU. firman respaldo al proceso en La Habana," *El Tiempo*, March 30, 2013, http://www.eltiempo.com/archivo/documento/CMS-12717155.
22. "Así debe ser el nuevo apoyo de EE.UU. a Colombia," *Revista Semana*, April 14, 2013, http://www.semana.com/nacion/articulo/asi-debe-nuevo-apoyo-eeuu-colombia/340398-3.
23. "El Factor Pepe," *Revista Semana*, August 24, 2013, http://www.semana.com/enfoque/articulo/el-factor-pepe/355192-3.
24. "EE.UU. reitera apoyo a proceso de paz en Colombia," *Revista Semana*, April 26, 2013, http://www.semana.com/nacion/articulo/ee-uu-reitera-apoyo-proceso-paz-colombia/341292-3.
25. "EE. UU. ratificó apoyo a Colombia en proceso de paz con las FARC," *El Tiempo*, April 30, 2013, http://www.eltiempo.com/archivo/documento/CMS-12770033; "EE. UU. mantendrá recursos para lucha contra terrorismo en Colombia," *El Tiempo*, May 1, 2013, http://www.eltiempo.com/archivo/documento/CMS-12772865.
26. This section is partially based on Sandra Borda, *The Search for Negotiated Peace and the Fight Against Illegal Drugs* (NOREF Report, September 2013), http://www.peacebuilding.no/Regions/Latin-America-and-the-Caribbean/Colombia/Publications/The-search-for-a-negotiated-peace-in-Colombia-and-the-fight-against-illegal-drugs.
27. Organization of American States, *Scenarios for the Drug Problem in the Americas* (Washington, DC: OAS, 2012), http://oas.org/documents/eng/press/Scenarios_Report.PDF, accessed 2013.
28. Mulholland, John. Juan Mauel Santos: "It is time to think again about the war on drugs." *The Guardian,* November 12, 2011, http://www.theguardian.com/world/2011/nov/13/colombia-juan-santos-war-on-drugs.
29. Ibid.
30. Organization of American States, *Scenarios for the Drug Problem in the Americas* (Washington, DC: OAS, 2012), http://oas.org/documents/eng/press/Scenarios_Report.PDF, accessed 2013.
31. Bob Dreyfus, "Will Obama end the long war in terror?" *The Nation*, June 8, 2013, http://www.thenation.com/article/174682/will-obama-end-long-war-terror#; Peter Baker, "Obama recasts war in terrorism," *Boston Globe*, May 24, 2013, http://www.bostonglobe.com/news/nation/2013/05/23/obama-narrow-focus-war-terrorism/FUPYLPPUJZ9IR0bBHPqtRM/story.html.
32. Sandra Borda, *La internacionalización de la paz y de la guerra en Colombia durante los Gobiernos de Andrés Pastrana y Álvaro Uribe. Búsqueda de legitimidad política y capacidad militar* (Bogotá: Ediciones Uniandes, 2012), 60.
33. Miguel Barreto, "El rol de la comunidad internacional en el proceso de paz y en el post-conflicto en Colombia" (presentation, the VII Latin American Congress of Political Science, Bogotá, Colombia, September 25–27, 2013).
34. "Santos y Chávez refrendarán mejoría de las relaciones en Miraflores," *Revista Semana*, November 2, 2010, http://www.semana.com/politica/articulo/santos-chavez-refrendaran-mejoria-relaciones-miraflores/124007-3.
35. "Santos destaca los avances alcanzados con Venezuela," *El Tiempo*, August 21, 2010, http://www.eltiempo.com/archivo/documento/CMS-7873978.

36. "Chávez confirma la entrega del guerrillero del ELN," *Revista Semana*, December 29, 2010, http://www.semana.com/nacion/articulo/chavez-confirma-entrega-del-guerrillero-del-eln/126552-3.
37. "Chávez, dispuesto a apoyar búsqueda de un acuerdo de paz en Colombia," *El Tiempo*, January 14, 2012, http://www.eltiempo.com/archivo/documento/CMS-10945821.
38. Ibid.
39. "Así se llegó al acercamiento con las Farc," *El Tiempo*, September 2, 2012, http://www.eltiempo.com/archivo/documento/CMS-12186341.
40. "'Antes de Cuba, Chávez se reunió 8 horas con Timochenko': Vicenç Fisas," *El Tiempo*, September 30, 2012, http://www.eltiempo.com/archivo/documento/CMS-12266792.
41. "Así se llegó al acercamiento con las Farc," *El Tiempo*, September 2, 2012, http://www.eltiempo.com/archivo/documento/CMS-12186341.
42. Ibid.
43. "Silencio en Cuba en torno a presunto acuerdo entre Colombia y las FARC," *El Espectador*, August 27, 2012, http://www.elespectador.com/noticias/paz/silencio-cuba-torno-presunto-acuerdo-entre-colombia-y-f-articulo-370513.
44. "Venezuela y Chile acompañarían el proceso de paz," *El Espectador*, August 29, 2012, http://www.elespectador.com/noticias/paz/venezuela-y-chile-acompanarian-el-proceso-de-paz-farc-articulo-370909.
45. "Maduro se pondrá al servicio de la paz de Colombia," *Revista Semana*, March 11, 2013, http://www.semana.com/mundo/articulo/maduro-pondra-servicio-de-paz-colombia/336426-3.
46. "Crisis con Venezuela, hora de la cabeza fría," *El Tiempo*, June 2, 2013, http://www.eltiempo.com/archivo/documento/CMS-12840062.
47. Ibid.
48. "Venezuela bajó tono a ataques contra Colombia," *El Tiempo*, June 4, 2013, http://www.eltiempo.com/politica/ARTICULO-WEB-NEW_NOTA_INTERIOR-12845864.html.
49. "Lula, mediador para encuentro Santos-Maduro," *El Tiempo*, June 8, 2013, http://www.eltiempo.com/archivo/documento/CMS-12854364.
50. "Santos se reunirá con el presidente Maduro en la frontera," *El Tiempo*, July 16, 2013, http://www.eltiempo.com/archivo/documento/CMS-12932522.
51. Sandra Borda, *La internacionalización de la paz y de la guerra en Colombia durante los Gobiernos de Andrés Pastrana y Álvaro Uribe. Búsqueda de legitimidad política y capacidad militar* (Bogotá: Ediciones Uniandes, 2012), 80.
52. Miguel Barreto, "El rol de la comunidad internacional en el proceso de paz y en el post-conflicto en Colombia" (presentation, the VII Latin American Congress of Political Science, Bogotá, Colombia, September 25–27, 2013).
53. Vicenç Fisas, *Anuario de Procesos de Paz 2013* (Barcelona: Icaria Editorial, 2013).
54. "Así se llegó al acercamiento con las Farc," *El Tiempo*, September 2, 2012, http://www.eltiempo.com/archivo/documento/CMS-12186341.

55. "Silencio en Cuba en torno a presunto acuerdo entre Colombia y las FARC," *El Espectador*, August 27, 2012, http://www.elespectador.com/noticias/paz/silencio-cuba-torno-presunto-acuerdo-entre-colombia-y-f-articulo-370513.

56. "Cinco países se ofrecieron para ser sede de diálogos de paz con ELN," *El Espectador*, September 23, 2013, http://www.elespectador.com/noticias/paz/cinco-paises-se-ofrecieron-ser-sede-de-dialogos-de-paz-articulo-448131.

57. Miguel Barreto, "El rol de la comunidad internacional en el proceso de paz y en el post-conflicto en Colombia" (presentation, the VII Latin American Congress of Political Science, Bogotá, Colombia, September 25–27, 2013), 16.

58. "Chile y Colombia suscriben documento sobre cooperación en materia de defensa," *Revista Semana*, March 24, 2011, http://www.semana.com/nacion/articulo/chile-colombia-suscriben-documento-sobre-cooperacion-materia-defensa/237318-3.

59. "Venezuela, Chile y Noruega saludan las conversaciones con las FARC," *El Tiempo*, September 4, 2012, http://www.eltiempo.com/politica/conversaciones-de-paz-venezuela-chile-y-noruega-saludan-las-conversaciones-con-las-farc_12193872-4; Revista Semana, "Piñera dice que Chile hará todo lo que le pidan en proceso de paz FARC," September 7, 2012, http://www.semana.com/politica/articulo/pinera-dice-chile-hara-todo-pidan-proceso-paz/264342-3.

60. "Canciller Holguín dice que si hay acuerdo entre Santos y Chávez se restablecerán relaciones," *El Tiempo*, August 8, 2010, http://www.eltiempo.com/archivo/documento/CMS-7849700.

61. "Lula recibirá a Santos el 1 de September en Brasilia," *Revista Semana*, August 9, 2010, http://www.semana.com/mundo/america-latina/articulo/lula-recibira-santos-September-brasilia/120326-3.

62. "Reunión clave este domingo para examinar las próximas liberaciones," *El Tiempo*, January 28, 2012, http://www.eltiempo.com/archivo/documento/CMS-11016448.

63. "Se reactiva proceso para liberaciones," *El Tiempo*, February 13, 2012, http://www.eltiempo.com/archivo/documento/MAM-5192120.

64. "Brasil aún no ha recibido pedido para ayudar en liberaciones," *El Tiempo*, February 13, 2012, http://www.eltiempo.com/archivo/documento/CMS-11129261.

65. "Brasil colaborará en liberación de uniformados en poder de las FARC," *El Tiempo*, February 27, 2012, http://www.eltiempo.com/archivo/documento/CMS-11227601.

66. "Firman protocolos de seguridad para liberaciones de 10 secuestrados," *El Tiempo*, March 21, 2012, http://www.eltiempo.com/archivo/documento/CMS-11395383;, "Brasil inicia preparativos para liberaciones," *Revista Semana*, March 30, 2012, http://www.semana.com/nacion/articulo/brasil-inicia-preparativos-para-liberaciones/255670-3.

67. "Desde Obama hasta Dilma enviaron mensajes de apoyo al proceso de paz," *El Tiempo*, September 5, 2012, http://www.eltiempo.com/archivo/documento/CMS-12194479.

68. "Espaldarazo de Brasil a proceso con las FARC," *El Tiempo*, October 5, 2012, http://www.eltiempo.com/archivo/documento/CMS-12283324; "Gobierno de Brasil anuncia su apoyo al proceso de paz," *Revista Semana*, October 5, 2012,

http://www.semana.com/nacion/articulo/gobierno-brasil-anuncia-su-apoyo-proceso-paz/265878-3.

69. Ibid.

70. "Dilma Rousseff le ofrece a Santos la ayuda de Brasil en proceso de paz," *EL Tiempo*, October 10, 2012, http://www.eltiempo.com/archivo/documento/CMS-12293834; "Rousseff le ofrece ayuda a Santos en el proceso de paz," *Revista Semana*, October 9, 2012, http://www.semana.com/politica/articulo/rousseff-ofrece-ayuda-santos-proceso-paz/266119-3.

71. "Lula, mediador para encuentro Santos-Maduro," *El Tiempo*, June 8, 2013, http://www.eltiempo.com/archivo/documento/CMS-12854364.

72. "'Estamos frente a un proceso (de paz) inédito': Canciller," *El Tiempo*, September 3, 2013, http://www.eltiempo.com/archivo/documento/CMS-13044272.

73. "Cinco países se ofrecieron para ser sede de diálogos de paz con ELN," *El Espectador*, September 23, 2013, http://www.elespectador.com/noticias/paz/cinco-paises-se-ofrecieron-ser-sede-de-dialogos-de-paz-articulo-448131.

74. "Máximo responsable de cooperación europea visita Colombia," *Revista Semana*, October 31, 2011, http://www.semana.com/nacion/articulo/maximo-responsable-cooperacion-europea-visita-colombia/248746-3.

75. "Colombia firma convenios de cooperación con Unión Europea," *Revista Semana*, November 2, 2011, http://www.semana.com/nacion/articulo/colombia-firma-convenios-cooperacion-union-europea/248809-3.

76. "'La paz se construye desde abajo': Suecia," *El Tiempo*, September 15, 2013, http://www.eltiempo.com/politica/ARTICULO-WEB-NEW_NOTA_INTERIOR-13065324.html.

77. Miguel Barreto, "El rol de la comunidad internacional en el proceso de paz y en el post-conflicto en Colombia" (presentation, the VII Latin American Congress of Political Science, Bogotá, Colombia, September 25–27, 2013), 15.

78. "Así se llegó al acercamiento con las Farc," *El Tiempo*, September 2, 2012, http://www.eltiempo.com/archivo/documento/CMS-12186341; "Venezuela, Chile y Noruega saludan las conversaciones con las FARC," *El Tiempo*, September 4, 2012, http://www.eltiempo.com/politica/conversaciones-de-paz-venezuela-chile-y-noruega-saludan-las-conversaciones-con-las-farc_12193872-4.

79. "'Antes de Cuba, Chávez se reunió 8 horas con Timochenko': Vicenç Fisas," *El Tiempo*, September 30, 2012, http://www.eltiempo.com/archivo/documento/CMS-12266792.

80. Sandra Borda, 2013. *Escenarios posibles frente al proceso de paz colombiano. Efectos internos y regionales*. (Bogotá: Friedrich-Ebert Stiftung), 3, http://library.fes.de/pdf-files/bueros/la-seguridad/10153.pdf.

81. "Ban ofrece su mediación en acercamientos entre Gobierno y las FARC," *Revista Semana*, August 29, 2012, http://www.semana.com/mundo/articulo/ban-ofrece-su-mediacion-acercamientos-entre-gobierno-farc/263820-3; "ONU ofrece mediación en diálogos de paz entre el gobierno y las FARC," *El Espectador*, August 29, 2012, http://www.elespectador.com/noticias/paz/onu-ofrece-mediacion-dialogos-de-paz-entre-el-gobierno-articulo-371009.

82. "Presidente reitera voluntad de paz y ONU ofrece," *El Tiempo*, August 30, 2012, http://www.eltiempo.com/archivo/documento/CMS-12178223.

83. "Presidente Santos presentará los diálogos con las Farc ante la ONU," *El Tiempo*, September 24, 2012, http://www.eltiempo.com/archivo/documento/CMS-12247663.

84. "En la ONU, países respaldaron proceso de paz y hubo críticas a fuero," *El Tiempo*, April 23, 2013, http://www.eltiempo.com/archivo/documento/CMS-12757342.

85. "Los "pecados" de Colombia ante ONU," *Revista Semana*, April 23, 2013, http://www.semana.com/nacion/articulo/los-pecados-colombia-ante-onu/341043-3.

86. "Colombia busca blindar en la ONU el proceso con las FARC," *El Tiempo*, September 8, 2013, http://www.eltiempo.com/archivo/documento/CMS-13052532.

87. Sandra Borda and Fernando Cepeda, "Sobre la internacionalización de la paz en Colombia: aprendiendo las lecciones del pasado," in *Proceso de paz en Colombia. Participación de actores internacionales,* eds. Sandra Borda and Fernando Cepeda Ulloa (Bogotá: ECOE Ediciones, 2012), ix-x.

88. Virginia Bouvier, *Colombia, Building Peace in a Time of War* (Washington D.C.: USIP, 2009), 427.

89. Kathryn Sikkink, Barbara Frey and Lyons Amanda, "Reporte temático de política exterior colombiana: derechos humanos y derecho internacional humanitario," in *Misión de política exterior 2009-2010,* eds. Sandra Borda, et al. (Bogotá: Ediciones Uniandes, 2011), 459-520.

90. Eugenia Suárez, "El marco jurídico para la paz: lecciones aprendidas para Colombia desde otros procesos de paz en el mundo" (presentation, the VII Latin American Congress of Political Science, Bogotá, Colombia, September 25–27, 2013).

Chapter Nine

The Oscillating Relationship Between Colombia and Venezuela

Luz del Socorro Ramírez

The relationship between the Colombian and Venezuelan governments has always fluctuated between rapprochement and tension.[1] The governments have yet to reach a consensus on various agreements and struggle to reconcile their institutional and structural differences and border disputes—both on land and at sea—and, more recently, the differing political and economic models of both countries have contributed to this erratic relationship that vacillates between friendly alliance and strained tolerance. This chapter examines the relationship between the Colombian and Venezuelan governments, focusing on the relations during the Álvaro Uribe administration (2002–2010) and Colombian-Venezuelan relations during the first three years of the Juan Manuel Santos government (2010–2018). The first part of this chapter examines the various Colombian mandates, while the second portion focuses on the intensification of immigration problems, border security, and trade issues.

During the last three decades of official Colombo-Venezuelan relations four well-defined phases can be identified, and, it could be argued that we are witnessing a fifth phase. Over these various periods, it is possible to identify continuity as well as changes in the nature of the tensions between the two countries. Diplomatic relations during these periods resulted from border interactions and the political dynamics in both countries. Various events also have impacted the bilateral relationship.

NEUTRALITY AND REJECTION

The first phase, occurring between the years 1999 and 2002, corresponds to the period in which the terms of Presidents Hugo Chávez and Andrés

Pastrana (1998–2002) coincided. Both leaders inherited national issues that affected the relations between the two countries, and a mutual mistrust over various marine and submarine skirmishes also increased tensions. President Chávez distanced himself from President George W. Bush, launching a comprehensive strategy in order to balance against the U.S. and stimulate a multipolar world, prompting new international agencies. Chávez also cultivated alliances with governmental, political, and social actors in distinct countries, and supported left-wing movements in Latin America and the Caribbean. Conversely, the intensification of the internal armed conflict in Colombia, especially in border areas shared with Venezuela and Ecuador in conjunction with the failure of the Colombian state to respond led Pastrana to adopt a double strategy: to strengthen the military capacity of the state and to advance the negotiation process with the *Fuerzas Armadas Revolucionarias de Colombia* (FARC). Pastrana provided the guerrillas with a de-militarized zone where they would be free from government interference. The guerrillas' utilization of the de-militarized zone and their decision to continue the war, compounded by governmental mistakes, had various consequences for bilateral relations. Chávez responded by distancing himself from Washington and reacted against Plan Colombia, a counter-narcotics initiative financed by the U.S., even banning U.S. airplanes from flying over the territory for counter-narcotic purposes. In addition, Chávez requested admission to *Mercado Común del Sur* (Mercosur), withdrew from the Andean Community and the Group of Three, and questioned the Free Trade Area of the Americas (FTAA). At the same time, Pastrana supported Plan Colombia and requested Colombia's entry into the North American Free Trade Agreement (NAFTA), or at least an establishment of a bilateral free trade agreement with Colombia's neighbors to the north.

Eventually, mutual fears and ever-increasing distrust greatly impacted bilateral relations. Venezuela feared that the increasing relations between Bogotá and Washington could become problematic for the consolidation of the Bolivarian Alliance (ALBA alliance) and could help Colombia gain a military advantage in the maritime dispute over the Gulf of Venezuela.[2] Colombia also wanted to defeat the guerrillas and did not want the guerrillas to receive support from the ALBA countries, fearing that the ALBA alliance's proximity with the Marxist-guerrillas could greatly impact security in the region. Hence the mutual perception by both governments led to adverse positions and tensions between the countries.

The declaration of Chávez's neutrality on February 9, 1999, in the Colombian armed conflict and his willingness to talk with guerrilla leaders without the consent of the Colombian government[3] contributed to the conflict. On August 10, 1999, Colombia witnessed the signing of a memorandum of understanding between the Venezuelan government and the FARC regarding what is referred to as the "borders project." Another crucial event that increased tensions occurred on July 6, 2000, when a video was broadcast of representatives of the Venezuelan armed forces talking with the FARC.[4] The announcement of the emergence of "Venezuelan paramilitaries organized by Colombian paramilitaries"[5] resulted in frequent and mutual accusations and contributed to the souring of relations between the two presidents.

Internal events within Venezuela also impacted bilateral relations. On April 11, 2002, a failed coup d'état occurred, and Lucas Rincon, a general inspector of the armed forces and an individual with the highest military ranking announced the end of Chávez's tenure in office. This announcement in conjunction with the growing opposition that Chávez had created throughout the continent contributed to the unclear position of the Colombian government. The Colombian ministers of affairs and foreign trade and a high command of the armed forces made favorable statements about interim president Pedro Carmona. In sum, the Colombian government hoped to stabilize relations with Venezuela during this period and improve cooperation with regard to the internal armed conflict as this situation impacts the security of both countries as well as the region as a whole.

MUTUALLY ADVANTAGEOUS APPROACH

The second phase, from early 2003 to November 21, 2007, began immediately after Chávez was reelected for office. This period coincided with Álvaro Uribe's first term as well as part of his second term in office. In 2003, Chávez and Uribe declared various mandates and relations deteriorated drastically by the end of the year due to an incident referred to as "*case Granada*": Colombian security forces arrested the so-called FARC Chancellor, who received Venezuelan identification and protection.[6] However, the pressure from the Bolivarian and the FARC movements led experts to question the legality of the actions of the Venezuelan government only increasing tensions and causing deterioration in diplomatic relations. Both countries believed that they had evidence of blatant violations of international law. It was alleged that the Colombian government had led an undercover security operation in Venezuela without notifying authorities while the Venezuelan government had granted citizenship and special treatment to the Colombian guerrillas.[7]

Both the Colombian and Venezuelan governments launched bold initiatives to ease tensions. On the Colombian side, President Uribe offered his support to verify the alleged presence of Colombian paramilitaries in Venezuela who were arrested in Venezuelan territory. On July 14, a month before the

Venezuelan referendum convened for the revocation of Chávez's mandate, Uribe visited him in El Tablazo, Zulia, where he announced that he would not purchase military tanks or position them along the border. Furthermore, he supported Chávez's continuity in power and invited him to visit Colombia after the referendum. On the Venezuelan side, Chávez appeared in Cartagena, Colombia, on November 10, 2004, and affirmed that he would not support any subversive groups.[8]

In addition, both presidents revived critical border infrastructure projects and launched a bi-national gas pipeline.[9] They also discussed the possibility of an inter-oceanic connection, which, if materialized, would make the two countries strategic partners. Colombia received more benefits from the bilateral agreements, particularly as a result of the 2003 economic contraction in Venezuela. The commercial bilateral balance tripled since 2004 in favor of Colombian exports, which increased by 400 percent.

However, the relationship between the two countries continued to deteriorate as a result of Chávez's defense of the Bolivarian Alliance (ALBA),[10] and his assertions that he would protect his alliance from any external threats. Uribe, conversely, was more concerned about internal enemies, such as the guerrillas, than he was about the paramilitaries. The tensions increased over various border disputes, and Venezuela objected to the Colombian government allowing armed groups to leave the country. The Uribe administration, in turn, responded by chastising its neighbor for allowing various armed actors—specifically the FARC—to enter Venezuelan territory.

In 2005, the presidents met on several occasions in multilateral events and they also held three state visits. During this period, it appeared that a rapprochement had occurred between Uribe and Chávez as negotiating committees developed the possibility of a settlement with regards to disputed territory. Various humanitarian initiatives and exchanges also began in January 2006. During the presidential inauguration of the new Bolivian president, Evo Morales, in La Paz, Bolivia, Chávez stated that he accepted the petition made to the FARC proposing to send the victims, which included a congressman who was kidnapped, to Venezuela. In August 2007, Uribe caved to international and national pressure in favor of the humanitarian agreement and allowed Chávez to act as a facilitator of the hostages. However, in the process, Chávez and the guerrillas became deeply involved in the situation, creating new tensions. The Colombian government attempted to define the rules enabling them to control the scope of the negotiations and manage the information and deadlines related to the bargaining process. At the same time, Uribe affirmed that President Chávez was the only person whom the FARC should respect and surrender the hostages to. This was not an obstacle for

Uribe as on November 21 he ended Chávez's role in the hostage negotiations, informing the Venezuelan president via television.

RUPTURE AND THREATS

The abrupt and hostile disengagement of Chávez from the role of hostage facilitator increased tensions between the two countries. This third phase characterized by tensions lasted until 2010. As a result of such events, the relations between the two presidents evolved from a friendly relationship to a rivalry best characterized by fierce political competition. Chávez responded to Uribe's decisions with an escalation of personal insults and threats. He also continued developing his own strategy for the release of hostages. Chávez declared that the guerrillas were part of the Bolivarian project before a Legislative Assembly, even promising to grant them belligerent status.

After accusing Chávez of being an expansionist and a friend of terrorists, Uribe retaliated further and Colombian security forces seized evidence that the hostages were alive; this evidence was intended to be delivered to the Venezuelan president. The seized videos showed the world the terrible conditions of the hostages. Shortly after, Uribe silently attended an international staged media event prepared by Chávez to broadcast the return of some hostages, including the son of one of them whom was born in captivity, who ended up "stealing the show" because the FARC could not comply with the meeting since Uribe announced that the child was under Colombian state supervision.

Uribe launched an operation in 2008 against the guerrilla camp in Ecuadorian territory, which resulted in the deaths of FARC leaders, including Raúl Reyes.[11] Chávez then expelled the Colombian ambassador from Venezuela and closed the Venezuelan embassy in Bogotá as a result of such actions, which constituted a violation of Ecuadorian sovereignty. In essence, Chávez broke down all diplomatic and commercial relations with Colombia and deployed battalions and the air force to the border, threatening war if the Colombian government attempted similar operations in Venezuelan territory. Bogotá responded by arguing that the Colombian government had evidence from computers seized from the guerrillas, which clearly revealed that the guerrillas received support from not only Venezuela, but also Ecuador and Nicaragua.

The Rio Group presidential summit, held in Santo Domingo on March 7, 2008, served as a forum for improving relations between the Colombian and Venezuelan governments. Chávez reestablished relations with Colombia, implicitly recognizing that the Colombian conflict had become a serious security threat and urged the FARC to disarm. This petition, however, had no impact as the FARC continued to operate in Colombia. In 2008, the Colombian state began a series of military strikes against the FARC, which resulted in the deaths of several top leaders. In 2009, Chávez and Uribe met on two occasions, and tensions increased after the discovery of equipment in an FARC camp that had been sold to the Venezuelan army by Sweden. The distrust between Venezuela and Colombia only continued to increase.

U.S. officials visited Bogotá on several occasions and denounced the Venezuelan government and its cantankerous relationship with Uribe,[12] who was a true ally of the Bush administration and was not concerned about angering his Colombian neighbors as he had the support of Washington. Uribe began negotiating with the Pentagon about Colombian military bases. Uribe continued his offensive strategies and presented reports to the Organization of American States (OAS) that Venezuela continued to support the Colombian guerrillas. As a result, Chávez froze bilateral relations and decided to withdraw the Venezuelan ambassador once again. Chávez also mobilized troops to the borders, sought to end bilateral trade, expropriate Colombian companies, and canceled various projects such as the bi-national pipeline.

NICOLÁS MADURO: NEW TENSIONS OR A PROMISING FUTURE?

With Nicolás Maduro, the situation started to follow the same patterns as the previous cooperative phase. It happened when Maduro assumed the vice-presidency after Chávez's reelection on October 7, 2012. The first official visit that the Minister of Foreign Affairs, Elias Jaua, received was from Maria Angela Holguin, the Colombian Minister of Foreign Affairs. According to Maduro, Maria Angela Holguin stated, "The most important thing about my coming here is to convey all the solidarity to the Venezuelan government, the Venezuelan people and to pray for the health of President Chavez."[13] On this occasion, Maduro reiterated to the Minister of Foreign Affairs that Venezuela would continue its relations in Colombia.

In his farewell, on December 8, Chávez requested that in case he was not able to come back and retake power, new elections would be held. Nevertheless, the Executive, the National Assembly and the Superior Court of Justice demanded "administrative continuity." The Colombian government as well as its Latin American and Caribbean peers respected the unusual decision by the Venezuelan governmental powers with the aim to avoid a crisis during the transition.

At the CELAC Summit on January 13, Santos met with the Venezuelan vice-president and Foreign Relations Minister in Santiago, Chile to "inform each other about the peace process." Maduro emphasized that before Chávez's last surgery in Cuba, Chávez told him that "he yearned that the peace process was signed sooner than later that same year in 2013. He believed that it was time for peace." Shortly after, he added: "I will be . . . at President Santos' disposition and with the involved parties, in order to help Colombia achieve peace. This is an oath."[14] Chávez later died from cancer in March 2013, and Santos attended Chávez's funeral and the Colombian Ministry of Foreign Affairs maintained relations with Maduro while he was the interim president. Despite these events, bilateral relations did not improve even after the death of Chávez, primarily due to the complex and uncertain nature of the Venezuelan transition. In addition, it was not easy for the Colombian government to decide how to proceed after a close presidential election where Maduro won by a narrow margin of 1.5 percent.[15]

During a *Unión de Naciones Suramericana* (UNASUR) meeting organized for the purpose of analyzing the Venezuelan situation, the Colombian president defended the need to audit the electoral results against the proposal by the governments of Brazil, Argentina, and the ALBA alliance who argued that countries should accept and recognize the official results. The UNASUR meeting resulted in the recognition of demands of each of the parties, and Maduro assumed office, but the votes also were audited. In addition, the organization decided to investigate various incidents of violence after the elections. The Colombian president attended Maduro's inauguration ceremony in Caracas, Venezuela.

The UNASUR meeting helped decrease the unrest. In the middle of the post-electoral tension, the Electoral Council only verified the electronic ballots while the opposition requested a comparison of the paper ballots and the number of voters in the manual records as well as an audit of all the voting instruments, including the registration machines that document the fingerprints of the voters. A thorough examination of such records as well as the various voting irregularities would have helped with the processing of complaints about irregularities such as the inconsistencies in the number of voters and the number of votes. The opposition refused to recognize Maduro as the president and argued that coercion and intimidation occurred during the electoral process and electoral observers were expelled from various polling stations. The Colombian Foreign Ministry expressed concern regarding the treatment of the Venezuelan opposition.

The Colombian government, however, was not the only government critical of the election proceedings; the Peruvian Foreign Ministry argued that it was going to consult and call a meeting as a result of the election violence since Peru held the Pro-tempore presidency of UNASUR. Maduro responded to such actions with sharp criticism. UNASUR, however, was the only organization allowed to be present in the Venezuelan elections, and, indeed, some of the electoral members of the mission observed some irregularities. It was believed that UNASUR could help both parties reach agreements on serious common problems regarding voting fraud and develop a peaceful resolution to the problem.

In this context of extreme domestic polarization in Venezuela, President Santos agreed to have a meeting in his office with the leader of the Venezuelan opposition, Enrique Capriles, informing Maduro in advance.[16] The first who reacted was Diosdado Cabello, president of the Venezuelan Legislative Assembly, who believed that such a visit constituted an act of aggression on behalf of the Colombian government. The Foreign Minister argued that Venezuela would have to evaluate whether or not it could continue being part of the peace process. Later, in a meeting with the UN High Commissioner for Human Rights in Geneva, the Foreign Minister denounced that "in Bogotá there is a conspiracy against the economy of Venezuela, and armed paramilitary groups have been permitted to cross into our country. This created a platform where a dark character directs operations of psychological war and spreads rumors."[17]

In spite of having been informed in advance by Santos about the meeting with Capriles, Maduro retaliated against Santos, claiming that the Colombian government had developed a plan to overthrow him. He hypothesized that having received Capriles was indicative of betrayal. Immediately after, Maduro threatened to reconsider the Venezuelan accompaniment mission in the negotiation process with the Colombian guerrillas. Then, he denounced what he argued were Colombian assassination attempts, implying that President Santos knew about such conspiracies. In June 2013, Maduro declared, "We are neutralizing the plots against our country. It is well known that the principal conspiracies against our homeland have been hatched in Bogota. All of Venezuela knows this and we've given proof of it."[18] The Venezuelan Foreign Minister Elias Jaua criticized the Santos administration for meeting with Capriles, calling it "a knife in the back."[19] Jaua argued, "We have done everything we can to help find peace for the Colombian people. It's not right that in Colombia they are promoting and legitimizing someone who openly refuses to acknowledge the institutions of the Venezuelan state."[20]

From the Colombian side, many interpretations unfolded with the decision to receive Capriles. Santos responded to criticism, stating, "It is absurd to think . . . that the Colombian government is interested or, even worse, that it is supporting any kind of action to destabilize the government of Venezuela."[21] Some individuals argued that such actions constituted a presidential error that angered its neighbor who remained silent when Santos requested in UNASUR the recount of the election votes, and particularly when its Foreign Minister insisted in the necessity for dialogue among the parties. President Álvaro Uribe attempted to lead a regional reaction against the Bolivarian process (ALBA) and to intervene in the understanding between the governments of the two countries in order to encourage the Venezuelan opposition to protest against the rapprochement between Chávez and Santos. Others viewed the reception of Capriles as a response to former Colombian president Andrés Pastrana, who from an electoral perspective questioned the Colombian government's relationship with the Maduro government. Overall, the reactions about the reception of Capriles have been mixed as some people have criticized both Santos and the Foreign Minister for their actions. In fact, some individuals went as far as to argue that the foreign minister should resign as a result of this controversy. Ultimately, these gestures by Santos represented an attempt to improve his image for his future electoral campaign and the subsequent elections in 2014.

President Santos did not ease the tensions after the disagreement with the Venezuelan government. In June 2013 he announced he would sign an agreement with the North Atlantic Treaty Organization (NATO) intending for Colombia to become a member in order to involve the military forces in the post-conflict stage. Perhaps to calm his critics, the government flaunted the announcement of an agreement with NATO and the invitation by the OECD to become a member. NATO, however, corrected this annoucment as Colombia does not belong to the North Atlantic region. Roberta Jacobson of the U.S. State Department declared that "'our goal is certainly to support Colombia as being a capable and strong member of lots of different international organizations, and that might well include NATO.'"[22] The Colombian Defense Minister had to explain that the government did not attempt to become a member of NATO, but rather to become "a partner" such as Australia, New Zealand, and Japan. The Colombian ambassador, Alexander Vershbow, declared that the "Allies have agreed to pursue tailored cooperation with Colombia on a case-by-case basis, in areas of common interest and that by signing this accord, NATO and Colombia stress their shared interest in consultation and cooperation. The Security of Information Agreement does not formally recognize Colombia as a NATO partner but constitutes a first step for future cooperation in the security field."[23]

These two aforementioned initiatives by Santos could have indicated a change in his government in terms of international politics, and the decision to receive Capriles could have been part of this change. If that was the case, there are many speculations, and it could mean that the Colombian government does not believe that Latin America should be, or is capable of, overcoming difficulties and "thinking bigger"; thinking bigger refers rather to the country's entry to the "big leagues" of the OECD, NATO, and the Pacific Alliance. It is possible that the government concluded that close relations between Latin American and Caribbean countries is not feasible, much less capable of translating into stability, cooperation, improvement in the negotiation capabilities, and relevance in the world. Perhaps the Santos administration has not perceived an effective solidarity from the neighbors in its efforts to solve the armed conflict, or has assumed that other alliances are required to confront transnational crime and the internal armed conflict. Another possibility is that the Colombian government perceived that the geopolitical game in the Caribbean has taken greater proportions and that national interests take place outside the neighboring zone.

The pressures by Uribe, such as meetings between Santos and Capriles and the rapprochement with NATO, have enabled Maduro's government to speculate about a supposed Colombian conspiracy against the ALBA alliance and to denounce the alleged assassination attempts organized from Bogotá. Just as it had occurred during Chávez's tenure in office, such declarations show that there is an intention to portray the Colombian government as the enemy and an aggressor toward Venezuela in order to unify and to strengthen the Chávez supporters (*chavismo*) within the population and to confront increasing discontent. Such reactions do not match the limits the situation itself imposes on Venezuela, and, ultimately requires Venezuela to strengthen collaboration with Colombia.

The former Vice-President and Foreign Minister of Venezuela Jose Vicente Rangel could be the spokesperson of anti-colombianism. On June 9, 2013, he denounced Colombia arguing that the opposition bought airplanes to travel to the "military bases the U.S. has in Colombia." In his column in *Últimas Noticias*, he referred to an alleged Colombian idea of geopolitical annexation that would have led to the territorial loss of Venezuela in la Guajira and the border treaty of 1941, signed, according to his words, by the military weakness of Venezuela, which guaranteed Colombia the navigability through the Venezuelan rivers without any compensation. In addition, he argued that the meeting between Santos and Capriles was similar to the controversial incident of the Caldas sloops river's crisis. He concluded: "Colombia in NATO? It is a step that will destabilize the region. For Venezuela it is a serious warning . . . [and] requires redefining the relationship with Colombia. Later, with the adverse reaction, it seems that Santos got upset."[24] Maduro invited Rangel to become a member of the State Council in order to examine the relationship with Colombia.

BORDER AND BINATIONAL ISSUES

Four types of issues (population, border, security, and trade) have become increasingly important in the bilateral relations. However, not all of these issues appear on the agenda, while others are sometimes mentioned. On the contrary, other issues have achieved significant progress during the relations between Santos and Chávez. Other key topics, however, could suffer grave setbacks if tensions increase between the two governments.

The population dynamics that has impacted the relationship between both countries has changed over time. The periods of intense Colombian labor migration to Venezuela, such as the ones that occurred in the seventies during the rise in oil prices, now belong to the past. The economic situation, political polarization, and Venezuelan insecurity have drastically decreased Colombian migration to Venezuela. Border disputes also resulted in high levels of anti-Colombianism, which since the nineties had disappeared from the Venezuelan political and cultural spectrum. Since then, it was presumed that the migrations were part of a Colombian attempt to occupy Venezuelan territories and were viewed as national security matters. During Chávez's tenure, the treatment of migrants became a political rather than a socioeconomic topic.

In terms of migration, one of the major causes of tensions has been the displacement of Colombians to Venezuela as a result of the internal armed conflict. There have been massive migrations of people from Colombia fleeing after a massacre or confrontation between the Colombian state and the various internal armed actors. Some people have attempted to return to Colombia after such events and other smaller-scale displacements have occurred in Colombia often as a result of violence, but also for economic reasons. Some Colombians, for example, have migrated to Venezuela in search of steady income and basic social services. According to the UNHCR, between 2001 and 2010, 200,000 displaced Colombians arrived to Venezuela; of that number, 2,700 received the refugee category, while 118,290 still require international protection.[25]

Another major problem regarding migration has been the legalization of a significant portion of illegal Colombians in Venezuela who began migrating in the 1970s and never changed their legal statuses. For decades, this situation generated serious consequences because this group of migrants was, in essence, a population without a homeland or rights. The so-called Identity Mission of the Chávez government sought to combat the problem and provided Venezuelan legal documents and identifications to most of the Colombian immigrants. At the same time, Chávez also provided Colombians residing in Venezuela with legal documents and IDs. Such actions created a severe problem because identity cards were not always distributed properly, and did not follow the appropriate protocols for obtaining dual citizenship. In fact, many people have their date of birth registered in both countries and others obtained the IDs without completing the proper documentation. Nevertheless, the number of Colombians with Venezuelan documents substantially increased in the last decade, granting them the right to vote and participate in different programs, social services, and other state benefits. In moments of tension, these people face various challenges, particularly in terms of their ability to migrate, as their claims about their Venezuelan identity have not always been respected.

Colombia also has experienced increasing levels of Venezuelan professionals and investors who have sought to escape conflict in Venezuela and emigrated to Colombia. In particular, the rates of Venezuelans immigrating to Colombia have drastically increased during the 2000s. Venezuelans in various sectors, including academia, media, business, and energy, have continued to migrate to Colombia.

The increases in the population have not been part of the binational agenda. However, the Negotiating Commission has not invested significant time on this issue and has treated it as a Colombian labor-migrant matter. On various occasions, intergovernmental meetings have addressed the displaced people and Venezuelan institutions have assisted the refugees or the Colombian settlements from that side of the border. The new Venezuelan migration toward Colombia is perceived by the Bolivarian movement as a troubling factor and identifies them as a national security threat. Conspiracies exist that attempts to overthrow or assassinate the Venezuelan president will come from Colombia as the opposition and the Colombian government will align with other sectors in the United States to conduct such plots.

BORDERS WITHOUT INSTITUTIONALIZATION OR RATIONALIZATION

Colombia and Venezuela share a large border that has been a cause of controversies. In the northern border of Alta Guajira lives the largest binational indigenous community, the Wayuu. This region is home to the most intense disputes over land and sea delineation. The tropical forest in the Perija and the Catatumbo basin generate shared strategic ecosystems that lack a mutual strategy for the protection of these regions. There is also the Andean zone, which is the most populated and developed zone, and its transportation system connects the two countries with its national political center and with a part of the territory of each country. However, building, expanding, or even painting the two international bridges requires endless negotiations that, when moved forward, are slowed down as a result of various tensions. The hillside and the plains of this region create an extensive shared flatland that is inhabited by a closely organized population, to the point that the Araucanians have to pass through Venezuela to stock up on products, such as Cucuta. Finally, the southern region is home to the Orinoquia-Amazonia border. Its great biodiversity and its wide rivers could allow binational strategic projects and exchanges between Colombia, Venezuela, and Brazil, but tensions continue. Not even the management of the national parks, which are adjacent to each other, is coordinated.

The constant fluctuation between tensions and cooperation has caused both governments to view the interactions of the various populations as problematic. Colombian and Venezuelan governments view these border issues as major challenges as opposed to opportunities to cooperate. Adding to the complications is the fact that the populations living in the border regions have particular ideas that do not always coincide with the goals of the central governments in Bogotá and Caracas. It is also important to recognize that the Colombians on the border depend on not only the roads but also upon the fuel and subsidies of Venezuela. Conversely, the Venezuelans have depended on Colombian goods and services in the past. Yet the national tensions have often exacerbated the border problems.

Another key aspect that is important to mention when discussing the Venezuelan-Colombian border is the flow of illegal goods that traverse the border. Oil is one of the goods that is smuggled across the border for various reasons. Venezuela sells some of the cheapest oil in the world and its subsidy is fixed. However, Colombian oil is extremely expensive and its price increases throughout the year. As a result, large containers of oil are smuggled and subsequently distributed in the streets of the Colombian border cities. Various actors, including guerrillas, facilitate the process of smuggling. Both governments have been unable to stop the smuggling of oil as the leaders in Bogotá and Caracas are detached from the realities of the illicit trade.

The oil rates have been agreed upon so that the Venezuelan oil company PDVSA could sell to the Colombian Ecopetrol or to the authorized retailers on either side of the border are not enough to satisfy the local demand and are reduced even more due to the illegal internal smuggling in Colombia. The same happens with the oil subsidiaries that the Colombian government allocates to those areas, or with the cooperatives formed by the binational indigenous Wayuu community, who gather small retail distributors in an effort to legalize the oil that they consume, which is blocked by different kinds of illegal networks.

Another problem occurs because many of the businesses along the border benefit from the contraband, which, in turn helps complicate Colombo-

Venezuelan relations. The binational trade derived from free commerce and transportation between centers of production and commerce as a result of the Andean integration initiatives have led to increases in tensions between the two governments and were particularly problematic during the Uribe and Chávez administrations. These new tensions have not been resolved, and, as a result, many border businesses take advantage of the contraband, the disparity in the exchange rates and the measures by the Commission for the Administration of Currency Exchange (Cadivi) in Venezuela.

The border economies have been dynamic and, as a result, services and labor market have felt the negative impact of the tensions between the central governments. Sanctions and the paralysis of mechanisms to manage all the border issues as well as the end of the construction of the integration border zones (ZIF) have increased the costs for the local and legitimate businesses. After twenty years of discussing the ZIF proposal the authorities and local organizations suggested, the central governments accepted its implementation. In the cooperative phase between Uribe and Chávez, the local actors achieved its delimitation and started the operation of roundtables in order to identify economic forces and infrastructure projects required for modernization. However, the tension between the two presidents at the end of 2007 halted further development of the proposal.[26] This process did not occur during the period in which Chávez and Santos coincided, primarily due to the increase in the centralization and the predominance of the opposition groups in the border governments on the Venezuelan side until the end of 2012.

The foreign ministers of the Chávez and Santos administrations decided to advance various development projects to improve the border situation, yet little progress was obtained. The Colombian government created a border initiative through border consultations that sought to identify productive social and cultural binational projects that would help transform the border. The greatest progress was achieved with the comprehensive development strategy for eleven municipalities in Catatumbo which allocated 1.7 trillion Colombian pesos to help increase security for border inhabitants as well as promote economic development and job creation, among other goals. The government of Venezuela also promised in 2010–2011 to buy sugar cane in the north of Santander.

Santos and Chávez recovered urgent infrastructure projects, but they were subsequently delayed as a result of increasing tensions between the central governments. Government tensions occurred over various conventional crossing points at the border such as Paraguachon (in the Guajira area), Santander and Bolivar (in the Andean domain), and Tienditas. Efforts were made to improve the pedestrian crossings between Boca de Grita and Puerto Santander, Delicias and Herran and to authorize the Paez Bridge. Colombian and Venezuelan leaders also started negotiations in order to build electric interconnections and create a small thermoelectric grid between Puerto Inirida y San Fernando de Atabapo (in the Orinoco-Amazonas domain). If the tensions continue during the Maduro and Santos administrations, many of these essential projects will be paralyzed.

INSTITUTIONAL AND SECURITY PROBLEMS

In Colombia, the lack of state presence has fueled the armed conflict as well as other national problems along the borders. Due to the lack of state control, the guerrillas have colonized isolated territories, which has enabled them to resolve social issues, control the transfers of national resources, and monitor the flow of illegal goods. Also, other initiatives have been launched to collect oil and mine royalties. For the Colombian paramilitaries, the alliances with politicians, landlords, state security agents, and various mafia organizations have been crucial. Four of the six zones where armed conflict has occurred correspond to Colombo-Venezuelan border areas.[27] In these zones, guerrillas and paramilitaries have disputed business and strategic routes since the mid-1990s.

On the Venezuelan side, the Colombian guerrillas, taking advantage of the minimal state presence, penetrated the social, political, and institutional sectors of Venezuela. Before the Chávez administration, different Venezuelan governments agreed on diverse and multiple settlements with the Colombian guerrillas with the purpose of constraining them in order to "avoid problems on their territory."[28] However, Chávez and the various political actors have not always agreed on how to address the guerrillas and their activities. At times some groups have supported them, while others barely tolerated them as a result of ideological factors. Maximum support occurred when Chávez attempted to recognize the guerrillas and ally with them against Uribe after he cancelled Chávez's role in the negotiations and authorized the use of Colombian military bases for the United States.[29] On several occasions, Chávez insisted that Venezuela does not support drug traffickers or guerrilla organizations. Meanwhile, the Venezuelan Bolivarian Liberation Forces (FBL), in certain moments has been supported or has disputed spaces and businesses with various Colombian guerrilla organizations.

More than political support and military action in Venezuela, the guerrillas—as well as the paramilitaries—have taken advantage of the high levels of corruption on both sides of the border. In addition, the internal armed actors also profit from various illicit activities, such as drug trafficking and the smuggling of gasoline. Guerrillas and paramilitaries also benefit from the growing Venezuelan de-industrialization, which worsened as a result of the continuous change in public officials. After the 2001 and 2002 oil strike and the coup of 2003, political polarization resulted in the opposition tolerating official corruption. The various internal actors have also taken advantage of the fact that Chávez suspended the agreements with the U.S. Drug Enforcement Administration. In addition, the shifting routes have caused illicit drug trafficking through Venezuela and has always resulted in the arrival of various distinct Colombian "cartels" as well as criminal bands, which have been referred to as the BACRIM: The "*Rastrojos*," "*Urabeños*," and the "*Loco*" Barrera as well as "*Zetas*" and the Sinaloa cartel from Mexico. Venezuela also has witnessed the increase in Dominican organized criminal networks searching for new smuggling routes to the United States and the Caribbean or to Europe through Africa.

In this context, both Colombia and Venezuela have witnessed a consolidation of criminal structures on both sides of the border as well as the increasing power of mafias and guerrillas that influence local political elites that are associated with criminalities and play a role in the reconfiguration of territorial disputes. Neo-paramilitary groups also have emerged in Venezuela and the statistics regarding illegal armed activities on the border are quite informative.[30] It is estimated that one million barrels per year are smuggled across the border as well as nine million bottles of whiskey. In addition, many firearms traverse the border as well as cocaine headed toward the United States, Africa, and Europe. The different illegal groups continue to fight among each other for territorial control and trafficking routes. Extreme levels of violence have resulted from the competition for control. In addition, increases in delinquency have impacted transnational criminality throughout the 2000s. This factor, along with the beginning of Bolivarian militias, increased the number of civilians with legal and illegal weapons and has resulted in the proliferation of violence and civilian insecurity in Venezuela, exceeding the rates of violence in Colombia and Mexico.

However, an important development is a result of the reiteration from both governments concerning joint efforts to combat drug trafficking, organized crime, extortion, and kidnapping. In May 2012, a meeting was held among the military and police commanders from both countries and information sharing has allowed for coordinated joint operations between Colombian police forces and the National Anti-Drug Office (ONA) of Venezuela.

The Colombian government extradited Walid Makled to Caracas and such actions were solicited by the United States. The Venezuelan government also has made symbolic deliveries of guerrilla members, the most significant was the delivery of Joaquin Perez Becerra, an individual from Switzerland who was associated with the FARC, along with the delivery of four other people accused of being *Ejército de Liberación Nacional* (ELN) members. The extraditions of the guerrillas ceased due to pressure from the *chavista* movement who impeded the extradition of Julian Conrado, who was apprehended in May 2011. Information sharing and conjoint operations have resulted in the arrest of drug traffickers, paramilitaries, and leaders of the criminal groups, particularly Bacrim leaders. The most significant capture of leaders were of the arrests of "*Loco*" Barrera and "*Valenciano*" and "*Diego Restrojo*." Due to the proliferation of insecurity in Venezuela, Maduro announced *Plan Patria Segura,*[31] which sought to advance various border issues and launch a campaign against corruption. These two decisions were intended to combat organized criminal activities on both sides of the border.

UNEVEN ECONOMIES

During the overlap between the Chávez and Santos administrations, the Venezuelan government repaid part of its debt to Colombian investors and authorized the payments of 1,000 of the 1,200 dollar debt.[32] Some accounts, however, have remained unpaid. In addition, both governments revived the possibility of extending the binational gas pipeline to Central America and Ecuador, along with the oil pipeline between the Orinoco Strip and the Colombian Pacific, accompanied by railways that mobilize passengers, cargo, steel, iron, and nickel. Possibilities were opened up to Colombian companies to participate in the domestic and vehicular gasification in Venezuela and for Ecopetrol to play a role in oil exploration and production in Apure-Barinas and the Orinoco belt. In addition, the Chinese governments have expressed interest in such projects.

In late May 2012, the Venezuelan Assembly approved the partial agreement on balanced trade and preferential rates for compensation of goods and trade defense, which includes an immediate suspension clause with the mere filing of the complaint of the treaty before the Latin-American Integration Association (ALADI). The partial agreement enforced in October 2012 gave preference to 91 percent of the Colombian assets without applying any tariffs, while the remaining 9 percent will have a preferential tariff between 40 and 80 percent.

The governments also agreed on boosting productive and sectorial alliances for food, textiles, cattle, housing and construction materials, automotive and energy industries and projects in basic, intermediate and livestock sales equally, broadening defined frequencies and routes for bidirectional development of tourism. They have tried to create a monthly database for price references for each country to avoid surcharges, and to concretize payments through Cadivi and not the Central Bank. However, the diversified bilateral trade that had developed between production businesses and the consumption centers outside the border decreased after 2008, when exports from Colombia to Venezuela reached 400 million dollars while exports from Venezuela to Colombia were calculated at $100 million. With the Chávez-Santos trade agreements, commerce started to slowly grow again. In 2011, trade closed at 1.74 billion dollars; 1.216.5 of the $1.74 billion was Colombian exports to Venezuela. In addition, Venezuelan exports to Colombia totaled $533.6 million. In 2012, Colombian exports reached $2.5 billion and Venezuela barely exported $500 million to Colombia.[33] The reduced figures for Venezuelan exports can be explained by the country's deindustrialization and the scarcity of dollars. It also is important to note that the periodic devaluations distort the value of the bolivar, which impedes the flux of capital and makes imports more expensive.[34]

The agreements on the rules of the game and possible business of the Chávez-Santos period have been interfered by various measures such as the devaluation of the Venezuelan currency in February 2013, which will reduce Colombian exports already affected by the revaluation of the peso. In the midst of the controversies over the meeting between Santos and Capriles, the Colombian Finance Minister, stated:

> Currently Venezuela has great needs, it has serious problems with the supply of essential goods and commodities Colombia can offer. But, we have to be creative in the area of payments. What I told the three Venezuelan ministers who were here (Colombia) is that I was ready to travel to Caracas to find ways to pay the sales Colombian producers can make in Venezuela. We are being creative searching for options of payment. They are a rich country, they have oil reserves, which simply having access to those reserves or establishing future commitments on oil could be a form of payment. Also, a neutral exchange system can be framed: that is not the official rate of 6.30 bolivares, neither the parallel market rate. We are open. What we want is to propose to them what we want to sell. They have a problem with powder milk; Colombia has huge quantities of powder milk. There are talks about the existing needs. There are also talks about a major deficit in terms of food, and we know of course that we have the industry to produce what Venezuela needs.[35]

Such possibilities, however, were put on hold for the review of the binational relationship announced by Maduro's administration.

CONCLUSIONS

The oscillations between cooperation and conflict as well as the differences in political, economic, and international projects have defined the past fifteen years of Colombo-Venezuelan relationships. The relations between the two countries have previously been defined by border disagreements for almost two centuries. The encounter between the Santos and Chávez governments introduced significant changes in contrast with the previous presidential periods under Chávez, Pastrana, and Uribe. In contrast with the first period, the differing opinions of each side and their divergent international actions during the fourth period did not damage the relationship. On the other hand, the second and third periods were intense and can be characterized by rapprochement as well as mutual tension and political competition. Both governments believed a moderate relationship based on mutual respect was beneficial.

The placing of the Colombian guerrillas at the top of the agenda in terms of the bilateral relationship allowed Venezuela to be a decisive complement when dialogues the Colombian government and the guerrillas first started, partially as an expression of the need to end the armed confrontation to restore its own security. Both governments assumed that border conflict could not be solved just with domestic treatment and that the creation of binational and international organized criminal networks has to be confronted through a joint effort. Stable communication and the sharing of information between the governments have endorsed important achievements against the internal armed actors. Yet communication was not enough when compared with the magnitude of the accumulated problems and lost opportunities.

A solid reestablishment of these conflicts requires an improvement of the security forces by the police and the military as local governments demand institutions that guarantee the coexistence and encourage development, as well as more efficient, transparent, and democratic institutions. In addition, it is necessary to empower the border communities so that every area in a region might be improved. Finally, the current drug policies have failed in regards to its maintenance of peace at the borders, and, therefore, these policies should likely be reevaluated and revised as well.

Colombia has to overcome important border vulnerabilities derived from the internal armed conflict, the civil precariousness of the state, and the lack of development. Venezuela suffers from various economic, security, organizational, and institutional problems. A suitable answer to the border necessities requires a comprehensive effort on the part of both nations.

The Santos-Chávez period was plagued, nevertheless, by other worrisome and constant characteristics in the relationship. Much of the relationship has relied on the dialogue between the central governments. The international relationship therefore is subjected to a costly fluctuation between conflict and cooperation among the presidents, even more costly for the border communities of both countries.

The absence of authorities on the borders, as well as the paralysis of the negotiations have prevented a confrontation of the effects at the border in the periods of intergovernmental distance, that, along with the impacts of the economic realities from both sides, have worsen the precarious living conditions of the poor communities. Nonetheless, a joint and sustained effort is pending, which is essential if the accumulated problems at the borders are going to be resolved.

Confronting the complexity of the relationship between Venezuela and Colombia despite differences in political, economic, and geopolitical options requires not only the action of the two governments and the productive economic and trade centers from both sides, but also strong bonds and the interdependencies in the shared borders. Now, even if such connections have been decisive to help ease the tensions, its informality removes the capacity to conceive and construct themselves as a region and to influence the national political centers in order to create basic agreements with local participation. From the civil society of both countries, the efforts in favor of a better understanding of the complex circumstances that each country faces and the bilateral relationship itself, would have to emerge, as well as in favor of, at least a coexistence (if not alliance) between the two neighbors.

The fact that a complex relationship relies only on the dialogue between the central governments prevents the reactivation of military negotiation commissions that could guarantee a minimal base on the management of common issues even in times of the various differences between Bogotá and Caracas. This institutionalization of the relationship has become even more necessary in moments of uncertainty such as the one that has emerged with the political transition in Venezuela and the negotiations with the guerrillas in Colombia.

On the other hand, in these fifteen years of the Bolivarian process and three Colombian governments, trade has ceased to be the driving force of this relationship. In the 2000s, the relationship moved away from the governmental ups and downs before the tensions that began at the end of 2007. These critical years between Chávez and Uribe, which concluded in August 2010, helped to disconnect the two economies, which, as the political models became more different, had lost its mutual benefits and had paralyzed investments. Since then, the two countries stopped being the second trade partner of the other. Chávez nationalized various industries. Without intermediaries or participation of former businessmen that negotiated with their Colombian partners, he structured agreements around its projected "endogenous" economy. In addition, the exchange had become more difficult with the reliance on the availability of foreign currency and its allocation by political decisions.

The overvaluation of the peso as well as legal insecurity and the struggles of the Venezuelan economy, have caused Colombian investors to lose interest in the neighboring market. They maintain a great prudence in orders and deliveries, prefer cash sales, and most importantly, they seek new markets for their exports. Colombia has increased negotiations of free trade agreements with countries from South America, Central America, the Caribbean, Canada, the United States, the European Union, Korea, Japan, and China.

Ultimately, three elements that helped relations between Santos and Chávez could disappear in the future: the respect for the opinions of each country, the direct interaction (with no participation of a third country), and the insertion of the relationship in the general framework of the South American union. Such complex situations require mutual understanding between neighbors whose symbiotic relationship is essential to the well-being of the region.

NOTES

1. Thanks to Nilda Garcia for translating this document from Spanish to English.
2. Rongxing Guo, *Territorial and Conflict Management: The Art of Avoiding War* (New York: Routledge, 2012), 43.
3. Periorizarion proposed in Ramírez Socorro "Colombia y Venezuela: una intensa década de encuentros y tensiones," in *Hugo Chávez: Una década en el poder*, eds. Ramos Francesca, Romero Carlos and Ramírez Hugo Eduardo (Bogotá: Centro Editorial del Rosario, 2010). See Socorro Ramírez, "Colombia-Venezuela: ¿Un sólido reencuentro?," Universidad de los Andes, seccional Mérida, *Cuadernos sobre Relaciones Internacionales, Regionalismo y Desarrollo* 7, no. 13 (2012).
4. Video recorded on July 7, 2001, and released in Caracas on January 23, 2002, showing images of Venezuelan military negotiating with the FARC. "Chávez no descarta reunión con rebeldes colombianos sin autorización de Pastrana," *El Nacional*, Caracas, August 10, 1999. "Bogotá espera que Chávez respete parámetros fijados para hablar con la guerrilla," *El Nacional*, February 12, 1999. "Venezuela negociará con quien tiene el poder," *El Nacional*, Caracas, August 11, 1999. "Relaciones en el punto más bajo," *El Tiempo*, August 20, 1999. "Colombia y Venezuela: paz, paz en la frontera," *El Espectador*, August 22, 1999. "Vecino inamistoso," *El Espectador*, November 26, 2000.
5. "Crece la polémica por paramilitares," *El Tiempo*, Julio 3, 2002, 1–12
6. It refers to the capture in Caracas of Rodrigo Granada, also known as "the chancellor of the FARC," apparently through the payments of gratifications to Venezuelan military personnel by Colombian security organisms. Granada, as the guerrilla spokesman, participated in Caracas in an event that enjoyed official patronage and had Venezuelan identity documents without fulfilling the legal requirements. "FARC califican detención de Ricardo Granada como un precedente lamentable del gobierno venezolano," *El Tiempo*, January 4, 2005.

7. For more on the FARC in Venezuela, see "FARC in Venezuela," *InSight Crime,* http://www.insightcrime.org/groups-venezuela/farc-in-venezuela,; "Los tentaculos de las FARC en Venezuela," El Espectador, May 18, 2010.

8. "Las palabras de Chávez en Cartagena en noviembre del 2004," *Noticias 24*, January 14, 2008.

9. In August 2003, the head of state along with U.S. armed forces argued that Colombia was "a strong ally," and warned Chávez: "whichever neighbor that gives assistance and shelter to terrorists is on the wrong side of the war and we will have to develop intelligence and work with the neighboring governments so the latter does not occur," *El Nacional*, August 13, 2003, pp. B-5. "Alto militar de E.U. pide a Venezuela aclarar su posición frente al terrorismo," *El Tiempo*, August 12, 2003. Héctor Latorre, "Colombia: apoyo de EE.UU," *BBC Mundo*, August 12, 2003, http://news.bbc.co.uk/hi/spanish. "Críticas a Chávez y elogios a Uribe," *El Tiempo*, April 30, 2004, 1, 7. "Estados Unidos respalda al presidente Uribe y exige a Chávez definir postura frente a FARC," *El Tiempo*, January 17, 2005. "Venezuela, una fuerza negativa: E.U," *El Tiempo*, January 19, 2005, 1–2. "Estados Unidos pide a Caracas detener a terroristas," *El Tiempo*, January 25, 2005, 1–2.

10. For more on ALBA, see "ALBA-TCP," http://www.alba-tcp.org/en/contenido/alba-tcp-eng.

11. "Top FARC Leader Killed by Troops," *BBC News*, March 1, 2008.

12. *El Nacional*, August 13, 2003. "Alto militar de E.U. pide a Venezuela." Latorre, "Colombia: apoyo de EE.UU." "Críticas a Chávez y elogios a Uribe." "Estados Unidos respalda al presidente." "Venezuela, una fuerza negativa: E.U." "Estados Unidos pide a Caracas."

13. Rene Tamayo, "Latin America in Solidarity with Chavez and His Government," *Juventud Rebelde*, January 22, 2013.

14. "Maduro: Nos pondremos al servicio de la paz de Colombia," *Terra*, March 12, 2013.

15. Deisy Buitrago and Andrew Cawthorne,"Venezuela's Maduro Holds Rare Dialogue with Opponents," *Reuters*, December 18, 2013.

16. "Venezuela denuncia en ONU presunta conspiración desde Bogotá," *Terra*, June 13, 2013.

17. Ibid.

18. Correo del Orinoco, "Venezuela "Destabilization Plan": Colombian Government Meets Venezuelan Opposition," *Global Research*, June 7, 2013.

19. Ibid.

20. Ibid.

21. Johnny Crisp, "Claims Colombia wants to destabilize Venezuela 'ridiculous': Santos," *Colombia Reports*, May 31, 2013.

22. "NATO Rules Out Colombia Membership," *Defense News*, June 4, 2013.

23. "NATO and Colombia Open Channel for Future Cooperation," *North Atlantic Treaty Organization*, June 25, 2013.

24. José Vicente Rangel, "El vecino y las provocaciones," *Aporrea,* October 6, 2013, http://www.aporrea.org/internacionales/a167814.html.

25. For more, see UNHCR, "2014 UNHCR Country Operations Profile—Colombia," http://www.unhcr.org/cgi-bin/texis/vtx/page?page=49e492ad6.

26. This process is documented with the participation of local actors that developed it in *Venezuela Hoy: Miradas Binacionales*, coord. Socorro Ramírez (Bogotá: IEPRI de la Universidad Nacional de Colombia—Universidad del Rosario, 2008).

27. Perijá-Catatumbo, where the "Timochenko" have acted and the former paramilitaries now called criminal groups (Bacrim); the Andean foothills, where the ELN can be also found; Amazonia, where the FARC works; Orinoquia and Amazonia, where the FARC acts.

28. Hernando Gómez Buendía, "El impasse con Venezuela," *La Semana,* January 1, 2001. See also "Toques heterodoxos," *El Universal,* February 2, 2002.

29. For more on the military bases in Colombia, see Juan Forero,"South American Leaders Assail U.S. Access to Colombian Military Bases," *The Washington Post,* August 29, 2009.

30. For more on smuggling see, Tamara Pearson, "Fuel Smugglers Making Large Profits, Venezuelan Authorities Crack Down," *Venezuelaanalysis,com*, October 15, 2013.

31. "Maduro anuncia relanzamiento del Plan Patria Segura," *El Tiempo*, January 13, 2014.

32. For more on Venezuelan debts, see "Venezuela to Repay $336M of Debt to Colombia," *Colombia Reports*, November 18, 2010.

33. "Relación económica entre Colombia y Venezuela, de amores y odios," *El Espectador*, March 6, 2013.

34. "Frontera colombo-venezolana: ilegalidad sin límites," *Perspectiva,* June 18, 2013.

35. "Colombia está dispuesta a abastecer a Venezuela, ratifica MinHacienda," *MinHacienda*, May 29, 2013, http://www.minhacienda.gov.co/HomeMinhacienda/saladeprensa/Historico/Colombia-esta-dispuesta-a-abastecer-a-Venezuela-ratifica-MinHacienda.

Chapter Ten

Security Cooperation in Bolivia and Colombia in the Twenty-First Century

Marten W. Brienen

At the start of the twenty-first century, both Bolivia and Colombia—two of the three major producers of coca and cocaine—appeared to be on a somewhat similar trajectory in their efforts to combat the cultivation of coca for diversion into the manufacture of cocaine. Both countries had embraced the notion that the production of cocaine presented a security threat to the nation, and both countries had come to depend very heavily on the United States for material, economic, and structural support in their efforts to eradicate the (over-)production of coca.[1] Moreover, United States agencies operated directly in both countries, with their own boots on the ground. In Bolivia, the U.S. Drug Enforcement Administration (DEA) was directly involved in the eradication—through force—of coca from the Chapare region of Cochabamba department.[2] The U.S. Agency for International Development (USAID) was active in the creation of programs to incentivize farmers to switch from coca to other export-oriented crops—mainly coffee.[3] Bolivian forces were trained by U.S. personnel, and their operations were coordinated by U.S. specialists.[4] Bolivia's draconian anti-drug law, known as *ley 1008*,[5] is rumored to have been written primarily by United States personnel.[6] By any account, Bolivia found itself firmly aligned with the United States in its war on drugs.

The Colombian government had managed to convince the U.S. to enact Plan Colombia,[7] which created a wealth of resources to help the Colombian government combat the production of coca and its derivatives. In the aftermath of the terrorist attacks of September 11, 2001, Colombia managed furthermore to rephrase its struggle in terms of a fight against "narcoterrorists," therewith enabling the country to redirect a good portion of the funding from counternarcotics operations to counterrevolutionary operations targeting the two main armed opposition forces (The *Fuerzas*

Armadas Revolucionarias de Colombia-FARC) and the *Ejército Nacional de Liberación*-ELN).[8] As in Bolivia, Plan Colombia relied heavily not only on U.S. funding, but also on the direct involvement of U.S. personnel to help the country eradicate coca, destroy cocaine laboratories, and combat the organized criminal networks responsible both for the trafficking of cocaine to the United States and for shocking violence that had plagued the country during the 1980s and 1990s. Indeed, part of the rationale behind Plan Colombia was that it constituted in effect a last-ditch effort to bring the country back from the brink of becoming a failed state in the context of a decades-long struggle with revolutionary armed forces, drug trafficking organizations, and the exceptional levels of violence that had plagued Colombian society as a result of the activities of both.[9]

Indeed, when looking at these two countries at the outset of the century, one might be struck by the similarities in their approach to the problems associated with the production and trafficking of drugs. Not only were both countries very actively and enthusiastically engaged in the global war on drugs, but both were governed by political factions very sympathetic to U.S. concerns and sensibilities, ranging from their preference for neoliberal reforms and participation in U.S.-led efforts for economic integration under the umbrella of Free Trade initiatives, to their willingness to make the U.S. struggle against drug trafficking a domestic priority.

Between the early years of the twenty-first century and the political realities of 2014, quite a bit has changed. Indeed, Bolivia and Colombia have since embarked on profoundly different paths politically and economically, and this has resulted in a significant divergence in their respective efforts to combat the production of coca and the export of cocaine to regional and global markets. Colombia has remained aligned with the United States and continues to cooperate in the U.S.-led war on drugs. Furthermore, the country has made overtures toward other Western organizations, including the North Atlantic Treaty Organization (NATO).[10] Bolivia, on the other hand, has undergone a very significant shift in its economic and political orientation. Once a reliable U.S. ally, the country has become a part of the Pink Wave and has consequently aligned itself with the late Hugo Chávez's Venezuela, Rafael Correa's Ecuador, Dilma Roussef's Brazil, and other members of the Latin American left.[11] One of the consequences has been that Bolivian president Evo Morales has become an outspoken critic of a number of Colombian initiatives, especially those that he regards as evidence of collaboration with what he considers U.S. imperialism.

In this chapter, I will offer an analysis of that divergence in the context of the war on drugs and I will comment on the significance of that development in terms of regional security cooperation. In order to make sense of the rather drastic contrast that has developed between the Bolivian and Colombian governments, I will explore some of the fundamental differences between the Colombian and Bolivian cultivation of coca and the role of both countries in supplying the global market for cocaine, as well as some of the fundamental differences in the positions taken by both governments in terms of the place and role of coca and cocaine within the social context of domestic security. I also will analyze the difficulties inherent to the very notion of international cooperation on security between cocaine-producing countries as a result of the inherent conflict between national interests and regional security within the framework of the so-called balloon effect.

COCA CERO AND PLAN COLOMBIA

Given that Bolivia and Colombia started this century with a serious ongoing effort to combat the cultivation of coca, it is important to explain in some detail what these efforts consisted of. As I stated in my introductory remarks, both were—and continue to be—major producers of coca, responsible for more than half of the world's supply of coca.[12] Moreover, both countries were firmly within the U.S. sphere of influence, having opted to cooperate very closely with the United States in its war on drugs.

Bolivia became a party to the U.S.-led war on drugs in the 1980s, when severe economic crisis forced the administration of Paz Estenssorro to accept loans that came with significant conditions—the so-called Shock Therapy[13]—and that served furthermore to place the country in a position where it was vulnerable to the pressures exerted by the United States, which at the time was going through the moral panic of the "crack epidemic" and had, under President Ronald Reagan, relaunched the war on drugs in 1982 with a particular focus on supply-side measures.[14] During the 1970s, Bolivia had become a major producer of coca—a traditional Bolivian crop dating back several thousand years[15]—for the burgeoning cocaine market, the acreage dedicated to coca cultivation increasing from an estimated 34,000 acres in 1977 to some 143,000 acres by 1983, making it the second largest producer of coca in the world.[16] Under pressure from the United States to combat its increasingly well-developed coca industry, Bolivia became an active partner in the war on drugs, though not necessarily an enthusiastic one.[17]

U.S. pressure on Bolivia to implement the supply-side approach of the renewed war on drugs resulted first and foremost in the formulation of the 1988 *ley 1008*, which regulated coca and the trafficking of controlled substances, and which has been widely regarded as comparatively draconian by Bolivian standards—indeed so much so that under the law, which remains in effect in 2014, drug trafficking is considered to be a worse crime than murder as measured by the penalties imposed for each offense.[18] In addition to the draconian nature of the penalties imposed under this law, it also created a special tribunal for drug-related offenses, in which the usual constitutional protections do not apply to those accused of involvement in the production, use, and trafficking of illicit substances. Moreover, the law introduced the concept of *coca excedentaria*—"excess coca" cultivation—consisting of all coca grown beyond 30,000 permitted acres in the Yungas of La Paz and subject to eradication.[19]

In addition to *ley 1008*, which is rumored to have been drafted entirely within the walls of the U.S. embassy's compound in La Paz, the United States began offering material support for specialized policing in the areas where coca was cultivated—the Yungas of La Paz and the Chapare of Cochabamba—providing funding and training for the *Unidad Móbil de Patrullaje Rural* (Mobile Rural Patrol Unit or UMOPAR). Later on in that decade, the activities of UMOPAR were subsumed into those of another U.S. funded and trained agency, the *Fuerza Especial de Lucha contra el Narcotráfico* (FELCN). It is widely accepted that the activities of the FELCN were coordinated by the DEA from its offices within the embassy compound in La Paz.[20]

Notwithstanding the fact that the United States had been successful in persuading the country to adopt the measures described above, throughout the 1990s Bolivia remained a reluctant partner in the fight against the scourge of drugs.[21] Bolivia's participation in the effort was deeply unpopular, posing a particularly difficult problem for the political factions vying for control in the still nascent democratic system: too much enthusiasm for participation in the counternarcotics project spearheaded by the United States was not regarded as a recipe for electoral victory, while resistance to it came with economic risks, as the country remained heavily dependent on U.S. support for its economic health.[22] At the same time, it was widely understood that effective eradication of coca would have negative economic effects of its own, as the illicit trade did inject significant amounts of much needed foreign revenue into the national economy.[23] The result was a somewhat unenthusiastic participation which did not have an especially devastating impact on the *cocaleros* and their trade: the country fairly consistently hovered around a total acreage of 110,000 acres of coca for much of the decade, slightly below the 125,000 acres of coca estimated for 1990.[24]

This situation changed dramatically with the election of former dictator Hugo Bánzer Suárez in 1997. Bánzer had made no bones about his intent to take the war on drugs seriously, and he launched the *coca cero* (zero coca) initiative, by which was meant the eradication of all *coca excedentaria* from the country, as part of his *Plan Dignidad* (Dignity Plan).[25] Aided again by the United States, the initiative involved the creation of yet another specialized force to eradicate coca in the form of the *Fuerza de Tarea Expedicionaria* (FTE).[26] Unlike previous efforts, however, the *coca cero* initiative promised to eradicate *coca excedentaria* entirely by 2002 and involved the heavy militarization of the Chapare in order to do so. From 1998 onward, the FTE slashed and burned its way through the coca farms of the Chapare, meeting ever-increasing resistance from the shocked *cocaleros* whose farms were being burnt to the ground. In response, the *cocaleros* organized *comités de autodefensa* (self-defense committees) to protect their small farms and the livelihoods that depended on them.[27] The result was a cycle of ever-increasing violence that quickly became a national media event and helped launch the political career of at least one *cocalero* activist: Evo Morales. Notwithstanding the growing public outrage, the scores of deceased *cocaleros*, and the growing resistance, the effort resulted in significant success: by 2000, the acreage for *coca excedentaria* had been reduced to no more than about 5,000 acres—less than one-twentieth the acreage that had been planted just three years before.

As is generally the case with supply-side efforts in the war on drugs, the net effects of U.S.-sponsored efforts in the Bolivian arena are hotly debated. While President Banzer's public proclamation that *coca cero* had been achieved ahead of schedule turned out to have been in error—given that some 5,000 acres remained—the initiative did indeed drastically reduce Bolivian production of coca.[28] The price of this "victory," however, would turn out to be rather dramatic in its own right, as I shall discuss in the next section. Moreover, the reduction of Bolivian output would famously result in a shift of that production back to Peru, much as supply-side efforts in Peru in the 1990s had shifted coca cultivation to Colombia.[29]

Colombia's role in the business of cocaine trafficking has been much different from Bolivia's, in that Colombia, unlike Peru and Bolivia, is not a traditional producer of the crop. Colombia's importance in the trade has traditionally been in the manufacture of illicit cocaine for the North American market, originally using raw coca imported from Peru and Bolivia.[30] The tremendous profits that could be realized in the United States ultimately spurred the rise of the infamous Colombian cartels—the Cali and Medellín cartels that dominated the trade in the 1970s and 1980s—which added to the ongoing threat posed to the Colombian state by the armed revolutionaries of ELN and FARC, thus further destabilizing an already precarious political situation.[31] Its importance in the supply chain was primarily that of manufacturer and exporter, rather than producer of the raw material. This situation changed once efforts were made in Peru—and later Bolivia—to attack the cultivation of coca as well as the transport of coca to Colombia—the "air bridge"—

thereby starving the Colombian laboratories of the raw material needed for their highly profitable trade and spurring the development of a home-grown coca industry, which was positioned to very rapidly overtake both Peru and Bolivia in importance.[32] The pre-existing armed conflict made it especially difficult to control the emergence of this new branch of the cocaine trade. Moreover, the relative weakness of the Colombian state and the lack of control that the state exercised over significant portions of its national territory helped transform drug trafficking cartels into exceptionally daring organizations—extremely well-funded above all—that enabled it to effectively pose a direct threat to the stability and integrity of the state apparatus itself. The 1980s and 1990s were thus marked by a veritable explosion of violence, and Colombian society was quite rapidly transformed into one of the most violent on the planet, in which both cartels and revolutionaries engaged in kidnapping, bribery, extortion, assassination, and bombings.[33]

Seeking an answer to the violence that was crippling Colombian society and severely destabilizing the state—putting it at risk of becoming a failed state—President Andrés Pastrana Arango (1998–2002) proposed a solution modeled after the Marshal Plan that had helped Europe recover from the destruction of the Second World War. Plan Colombia, as it ultimately became known, was originally intended to enable the Colombian state to rebuild its institutions and to address the sources of the violence that had brought society to its knees, focusing on both the drug trafficking organizations and the armed revolutionaries of ELN and FARC.[34]

While Pastrana had hoped for significant contributions from a variety of countries and multilaterals, the United States would prove most willing to provide significant financial and material support, eventually approving an agreement that focused primarily on the counternarcotics effort with a significant emphasis on strengthening the capacity of the Colombian military and police.[35] It has been argued that the militarized nature of Plan Colombia as it emerged from negotiations with the administration of Bill Clinton significantly reduced the enthusiasm for support on the part of prospective European partners, thus resulting in a rather smaller total package than had originally been Pastrana's target.[36]

The resulting effort helped address Washington's concerns perhaps more than Colombian ones, but did constitute a very significant injection of foreign assistance into Colombian institutions. In addition, Plan Colombia included significant U.S. personnel—500 military and 300 civilian—to assist in military training, in counternarcotics efforts, and in efforts to replace coca cultivation with more acceptable crops for the international markets. Colombia proved more willing to engage in strategies it had not been able to implement in either Peru or Bolivia, including aerial spraying of coca (and poppy) fields.

The combined effort certainly did bear fruit—much as the *coca cero* initiative had in Bolivia—as Colombian coca acreage dropped significantly in the years following the implementation of Plan Colombia.[37]

While the United States had been somewhat singularly focused on the drug manufacturing and trafficking aspects of Plan Colombia, the terrorist attacks of September 11th, 2001, created an opportunity for the Colombian administration to refocus the effort. Santos's predecessor, President Álvaro Uribe Vélez, was able to convince his U.S. partners not only to increase funding for Plan Colombia, but also to redirect a significant portion of the funding to efforts to combat the FARC in part by convincing them to regard these armed rebels as "narco-terrorists" and thus to reframe the conflict within the context of the global war on terror.[38] Indeed, as efforts to combat the drug trafficking organizations that had emerged from the ruins of the dominant cartels of the 1980s and early 1990s bore fruit, it was the FARC that became increasingly engaged in the business of cocaine manufacturing and exports, the illicit industry becoming a steadily growing source of income for the organization.[39]

The two projects, then—*coca cero* and Plan Colombia—however much they were tied to the single issue of the trafficking of cocaine, were rooted in profoundly different circumstances. Plan Colombia had been envisioned as an effort to save the Colombian state from failing and in doing so avert the disaster of an emerging narco-state ready to supply the U.S. market with all the cocaine it could consume. Colombia was confronting shocking levels of violence from criminal organizations and armed resistance groups (now regarded as narco-terrorist organizations) that directly challenged the state apparatus itself and were eroding the ability of the state to function even in those areas where its control was the greatest. For the Pastrana administration, Plan Colombia represented an almost last-ditch effort to save Colombia from cartels and their violence. In this, the eradication of coca was instrumental, but as a means to an end.

In Bolivia, on the other hand, no such state collapse was under way nor was the state confronting armed resistance or particularly high levels of criminal activity and violence. Indeed, Bolivia was then as it remains today among the safest countries in the Western Hemisphere, with comparatively low levels of violent crime.[40] Efforts to combat the cultivation of coca were first and foremost the result of U.S. pressure rather than the result of internal processes. Popular support for these efforts was always thin, and the role of the Bolivian state in combating drug trafficking has long been understood as an unwelcome imposition by foreign interests, especially given the legitimate traditional uses of coca in Bolivian society. To almost any Bolivian, coca is a relatively harmless substance and one that is fundamentally different from cocaine. Moreover, the country itself had not experienced high levels of drug abuse—although there appears to be some unfavorable change in usage patterns. To put it bluntly, the war on drugs has been perceived by Bolivians as a foreign imposition that has brought the country no benefits, while costing hardworking Bolivians their livelihoods and sometimes even their lives.[41]

FROM COCA CERO TO COCALERO

It is in this context that we must understand the very significant divergence that took place in the early twenty-first century. While Colombia would continue on its path of eradication and ongoing efforts to bring the fight to drug traffickers and armed rebels alike, Bolivia was about to break free from its U.S. allies and embark on a different political path that included a bit of a love affair with leaders of the emerging Latin American left. In order to understand Bolivia's apparent change of heart, it is necessary to analyze in some detail the structure of Bolivian coca cultivation, given that the *cocalero* resistance to the *coca cero* initiative was at the very heart of this change. What was it about Bolivian society that would allow it to not only change allegiances so drastically—swinging from a U.S. ally in the war on drugs to joining the so-called Pink Wave—and ultimately to elect a *cocalero* (note the absence of the word "former") into the Palacio Quemado?

As I have noted above, coca is not a traditional Colombian crop, and large-scale cultivation did not occur in the country until the supply of Bolivian and Peruvian coca was interrupted in the early to mid-1990s. In effect, the cultivation of coca in Colombia exists exclusively in the service of the manufacture of cocaine and was overseen from the very beginning by cartels involved in the trafficking of drugs to North American markets. One cannot look at the cultivation of coca in Colombia as something that could exist separately from the violence that cartels wrought upon Colombian society.

The Bolivian reality is vastly different. Coca has been cultivated in the Bolivian and Peruvian highlands and valleys since time immemorial, and it remained an important crop both during the Inca conquest and the subsequent Spanish conquest.[42] While *criollo-mestizo* society has long frowned upon the use of coca by the indigenous farmers and miners, and long regarded its traditional consumption as a vice akin to licentiousness and alcoholism, it also was understood to be good for industrial and mineral output and therewith good for the national bottom-line.[43] The cultivation of coca was never suspect in and of itself and certainly was never regarded as an activity that could or should be criminalized. In that sense, it has historically been regarded as not much different from the cultivation of potatoes or quinoa—except that it could be taxed more aggressively. While Bolivians generally understand that the legitimate domestic market is limited in scope and that excess production of coca feeds into an international system that revolves around the consumption of cocaine,[44] the notion of coca cultivation as in and of itself a legitimate economic activity has remained firmly entrenched in Bolivian everyday society.

The long history of coca cultivation in the Bolivian highlands and valleys has meant that this activity is accompanied by a level of social control among the communities involved, including those that were not traditionally engaged in that activity—especially the Chapare province of Cochabamba department. Indeed, most of the coca that is diverted to the production of cocaine for export to regional markets—as Bolivia is not a major supplier to the North American market—is cultivated in the Cochabambino tropics of Chapare. The development of coca farming in that region began in the late 1960s and increased during the 1970s, after the region had been opened up for settlement with the help of a USAID financed infrastructural construction project—mainly consisting of the construction of a main road into the region, which until then had been difficult to reach.[45] During the 1970s and 1980s, the region became host to scores of unemployed miners from the tin mining camps of the high plains, where mining activity—the economic mainstay of Bolivia since the discovery of silver deposits in the early colonial era—was slowly grinding to a halt.[46] The attractiveness of coca cultivation to these former miners resides first and foremost in the fact that coca is an exceptionally easy plant to cultivate even for the novice farmer, yielding a product that these former miners were intimately familiar with, while in addition commanding a price that allowed these farmers to maintain a basic livelihood that would not otherwise be obtainable. The growing market for cocaine during that period guaranteed that a market existed for their produce, while the economic activity of coca farming itself was considered to be an entirely legitimate traditional endeavor.

The *cocalero* communities that appeared in this region generally retained the political cultures of the mining camps from where they hailed, as expressed by their tendency to name the communities for the mining camps of origin. Moreover, they often retained the syndical organization that had marked the tremendous political activity of the mining camps of old, which had been hotbeds of political activity since the 1940s.[47] The communities thus reproduced the *sindicatos* that had been instrumental in the political organization of the mining camps, also tending to reflect their mining-based predecessors in name. We are then looking at *cocalero* communities that have historically been steeped in the language of anti-imperialism and that retain very high levels of both social and political organization.[48] It should not have surprised anyone, then, that these communities would respond to the violence inflicted upon them—in the name of the Northern imperialist enemy, no less—much as they would have done, and indeed had done, when confronted with similar oppression in the mining camps themselves: with marches, blockades, and other forms of protest organized by the syndicalist *federaciones especiales* that served as the overarching political structure of the individual *sindicatos* in which the *cocaleros* were organized.[49]

It is important to note the non-subversive nature of the protests: the miners of old and their *cocalero* successors had since the 1952 National Revolution believed in the ability of the state to serve the people, and in the ability of the workers and farmers to force the state to meet their demands. They had consistently done so throughout Bolivian history, with the notable exception of the era of military rule of the 1970s. *Cocalero* political activism thus cannot be regarded as anti-state or revolutionary in nature, and was not intended to overthrow the state itself, but rather the political factions who had taken charge of it. The *cocalero* struggle was not against the Bolivian state—as the struggle of the FARC is against the Colombian state—but against Sánchez de Lozada's *Movimiento Nacionalista Revolucionaria* (MNR).

This matters in this context for two reasons: first, the high level of internal organization within the *cocalero* communities has meant that there is no space within them for the direct involvement of drug trafficking organizations, and especially not ones who would use violence as a means of persuasion. The *federaciones especiales* had the strength to stand up against the militarized forces of the state's anti-drug efforts, and certainly would not permit violent drug trafficking organizations to take over. Of course, it is understood that coca is delivered to such organizations in the end, but they have not been allowed to take over the *cocalero* communities themselves; what happens beyond them is another's concern.[50] This in turn has made it extremely difficult to accuse the communities of direct involvement in illegal activities beyond the cultivation of coca alone or to point to the social cost of drug trafficking in terms of the associated criminality and violence. The strength of the syndicates and federations has in part prevented such criminality from becoming a social problem that concerns Bolivians, while at the same time allowing the communities to retain their air of dignified labor and to avoid being associated directly with the dark underbelly of the rest of the cocaine supply chain.

Secondly, this high level of political organization and the ability of the communities to organize large-scale protests meant that the *cocaleros* were able to present their case to the Bolivian public in a spectacularly successful manner. Through their protests, they were able to make the case that Bolivian blood was being shed on behalf of an imperialist power to solve the western problem of addiction. Using their long tradition of political organization and leftist idealism, they were able to tie the plight of the Bolivian *cocalero* to the broader problem of nationalism in the face of exploitation and oppression by foreign interests.[51]

The latter was to become the most politically significant with the rise of *cocalero* activist Evo Morales, who as head of the united *federaciones especiales* became a fixture in Bolivian protest first against efforts at eradication of coca in the Chapare—a popular cause in and of itself—and subsequently in broader protests against perceived imperialist interests in the context of the wildly unpopular proposal put forth by the Sánchez de Lozada administration to export recently discovered deposits of natural gas via Chile to the United States.[52] Economically, this made good sense as, at the time, the price for natural gas in the state of California was peaking at roughly seven times the market rate in the Southern Cone.[53] However, in spite of the obvious economic incentive, the Bolivian population understood this proposal in light of the country's previous experiences with raw material exports, which had contributed relatively little to Bolivian economic development, while generating huge amounts of revenue for investors overseas.[54] Furthermore, both the United States and Chile were regarded by many Bolivians as "enemies" of the Bolivian people: Chile because of its occupation of the Bolivian coastal province since the 1878–1882 Pacific War, and the United States for various reasons, centered around its imperialism and exploitation of the poor.[55] It was Morales who managed to tie the two issues together under the single banner of Bolivian national pride: Bolivian protesters loudly proclaimed that Bolivian gas was not for sale, while also viewing the war on drugs as an unwelcome imposition that served no legitimate national interest: Bolivians, after all, did regard coca as a perfectly legitimate traditional crop with an important place in Bolivian culture and society, while the country had no significant problems with either addiction or violence.

The result of these protests was the removal of President Sánchez de Lozada from office in a moment somewhat reminiscent of the 1946 popular uprising against Gualberto Villarroel, the first Bolivian president from the MNR to which Sánchez de Lozada himself belonged. The similarities were likely not lost on Sánchez de Lozada, who fled the country for the United States, no doubt hoping to avoid the fate of his unfortunate predecessor, who had been lynched in front of the Palacio Quemado.[56] Sánchez de Lozada was succeeded—somewhat reluctantly—by his second-in-command, Carlos Mesa Gisbert, whose presidency was marked by an effort to appease the angry masses and thus to keep the country together long enough to make it to the next elections. This involved concessions ranging from allowing each *cocalero* to grow one *cato* (four-tenths of an acre)[57] of coca, to the shuttling of the plan that would have funneled Bolivian natural gas through Chile to the United States. In addition, he vowed never to use violence to suppress the protests—including the blockades that were crippling La Paz's economic activity and causing food shortages—and to enter into dialogue with the many claimants.[58] It proved too much for the deeply intellectual Mesa Gisbert, who resigned after proclaiming that the country was "ungovernable."[59] In both the fall of Sánchez de Lozada and Mesa Gisbert, it had been Evo Morales who had been the key figure on the barricades. Never before had a Bolivian of such humble origins brought down two legitimate presidents.

If Morales's electoral victory in 2005 had not been entirely preordained, it was quickly made so by the hapless U.S. ambassador, who stoked the country's ire by accusing Morales of involvement in drug trafficking and effectively threatening the Bolivian population with retaliation were it to elect Evo Morales president.[60] Thus began the rise of the first wholly indigenous, Aymara-speaking, Bolivian president.[61]

One should not make the mistake, as U.S. officials have done to their detriment, of mistaking Morales's support for the *cocalero* cause as support for cocaine. Although Morales quickly positioned himself as the voice of anti-American sentiment—arguably more effectively than like-minded leaders such as Rafael Correa and Hugo Chávez—and he was clearly unsympathetic to U.S. agents still active in the country, the election of Evo Morales—and his subsequent two reelections—did not lead to any dramatic shift in the Bolivian state's commitment to controlling the country's output of coca. The willingness to attack the problem using the formula pushed by the United States during previous administrations—and indeed in Colombia—which involved the militarization of the counternarcotics effort evaporated, and the DEA was expelled from the country in 2008—as was USAID from the Chapare, due to its involvement in the eradication effort there. Nevertheless, even in the aftermath of the expulsion of the DEA efforts toward the eradication of coca continued with some measurable success.[62] What had changed was the level of violence involved in those efforts—which was primarily the result of Carlos Mesa Gisbert's refusal to employ violence—switching to a system of voluntary eradication. This did not lead, as U.S. officials had argued, to an increase in production: indeed, Bolivian production has consistently fallen during Morales's tenure. It is probably not coincidental that this reduction coincided with the relatively good economic conditions the country has experienced as a result of its natural gas exports.

It should be noted that Morales has found himself in a bit of a quandary when it comes to the coca conundrum. While his alliance with the leaders of the Pink Wave and the economic windfall from natural gas exports have meant that the United States has little means through which to pressure the country to address the problem of coca cultivation and cocaine exports according to its wishes, the reality has long been that the United States is not the main consumer of Bolivian cocaine. Rather, Bolivia supplies the regional market, including Argentina and Brazil—the latter now the second largest consumer of cocaine in the world.[63] Although both countries have been supporters of the Morales administration, there is pressure on Bolivia from these allies to address the problem of Bolivian cocaine, which is associated with rising levels of addiction and violent crime especially in Brazilian society. Thus, even in the absence of viable U.S. pressure, Bolivian coca cultivation has remained a problem in terms of Bolivia's foreign relations.

Moreover, while Bolivians do not regard the cultivation of coca as a criminal activity that should be suppressed in and of itself, there is very little support in Bolivian society for those who deal in cocaine. When Bolivians argue that "*coca no es cocaína*," they effectively mean that to be taken quite literally. Drug abuse is regarded very negatively, and Bolivians are exceptionally weary of the criminal activity that is associated with drug use, drug manufacturing, and drug trafficking.[64] Indeed, although *ley 1008* has consistently been regarded as a U.S. imposition and resistance against it was a mainstay of Morales's protests, the criticism leveled against it are focused primarily on the place and role of coca as such within the legal framework created by the law. There is virtually no appetite in Bolivian society to reduce the draconian sentences for drug traffickers and abusers—indeed, there is broad support in Bolivian society for a judicial framework that is "tough on crime."[65] Consequently, in spite of Morales's frequent rhetoric against the law, in 2014 it has remained in effect practically unaltered.

In Bolivia, then, coca cultivation itself—and even the trafficking of cocaine—has not given rise to high levels of crime and violence. The organizational capacity and high levels of social control and cohesion among *cocalero* communities effectively warded off the emergence of criminal networks that employ violence as a means of persuasion. Rather, the relative instability—within the framework of a functional democratic system—that marked the early twenty-first century had been the direct result of U.S.-sponsored efforts to combat the cultivation of coca with force. Bolivians accept that it is necessary, even desirable, to combat criminal activity. It is, however, not widely accepted that coca cultivation should count as criminal behavior. As a result, the emphasis of U.S.-sponsored efforts at supply-side reduction of coca cultivation was widely regarded as wrongheaded, misguided, immoral, and allowed the *cocaleros* to present their case to the public as one pitting poor farmers engaged in a traditional activity against the violent might of the arch-imperialist and his Bolivian puppets. In the Bolivian public imagination, the perpetrators of violence against the innocent were DEA agents, not drug cartels.

BOLIVIAN-COLOMBIAN RELATIONS UNDER MORALES, URIBE, AND SANTOS

As I have noted, the circumstances in which the superficially similar efforts of *coca cero* and Plan Colombia developed were remarkably different. The cultivation of coca emerged in both countries at different times and for very different reasons. Moreover, coca production in Colombia was associated from the very beginning with criminal activity and high levels of violence, whereas in Bolivia the popular perception was that any violence associated with the cultivation of coca was perpetrated by U.S. counternarcotics agents and their Bolivian collaborators, rather than by drug cartels or guerrilla organizations. This explains to some extent why there was effectively very limited collaboration between the Bolivian and Colombian governments even while counternarcotics efforts in both countries were in full swing at the very start of the twenty-first century, and even though in both cases those efforts were supported both materially and financially by the United States. The Bolivian effort was sufficiently different in nature within the domestic context to make it very difficult to translate lessons learnt in either country to the reality on the ground in the other. Indeed, during the Pastrana and Banzer presidencies, we find very little evidence to translate their counternarcotics struggle into a shared security collaboration.

The one thing they did have in common during this time was, of course, the heavy reliance on the United States, and it was really only in U.S. offices where a real connection was made between the two cases. While Bolivians and Colombians were engaged internally in profoundly different endeavors in terms of the significance of the effort to eradicate coca, U.S. officials still regarded both as fronts in a single war on drugs. This found expression in the Andean Counternarcotics Initiative (ACI), which from the U.S. point of view constituted an overarching strategy to deal with coca and cocaine in the Andean region as a whole.[66] This meant to some extent that so long as Bolivia and Colombia—and Peru—remained active allies of the United States in the war on drugs, and allowed the DEA and other U.S. agencies to play a significant role in drug enforcement in these countries, it would have the ability to coordinate such activities from a central location. In that sense, the argument can be made that the involvement of the DEA and related agencies and their personnel in these countries represented some concerted and coordinated effort that spanned them together, even if there was little to no direct cooperation between the national governments themselves.

The election of Evo Morales threw a wrench in the limited level of cooperation, as he moved steadily toward the removal of U.S. interests from the Bolivian counternarcotics effort. Given that he had agitated very actively against the presence of U.S. personnel in the Chapare and had argued forcefully that the violence that had gripped that region was attributable entirely to U.S. interventionism in Bolivian domestic affairs, it was inevitable that he would have to address this U.S. presence, which he did by expelling the DEA from the country in 2008.[67] Moreover, steeped in the rhetoric of anti-imperialism as a member of the *cocalero* communities of the Chapare, he very quickly made it known that his sympathy lay with other members of the Pink Wave, becoming especially close to Hugo Chávez of Venezuela. Indeed, Morales rapidly positioned himself as an outspoken critic of imperialism, colonialism, and any undue outside influence on Latin American affairs, asserting his political independence by embracing Fidel Castro and sidling up to then president Mahmoud Ahmedinejad of Iran. In part, Morales had the freedom to shake off old ties to the United States due to the influx of foreign exchange as a result of dramatically increased natural gas production, which effectively eliminated the country's dependence on foreign benefactors.[68] Morales's Bolivia simply no longer needed the IMF, the World Bank, or the United States for its economic health.

Given that Colombia's struggle was rooted first and foremost in the problem of violence perpetrated by armed rebels and drug cartels, it is not surprising that Colombia remained very invested in its ties to the United States and the financial and material support that continued to flow from Plan Colombia—and the ACI. The election of Álvaro Uribe in 2002 added to this dependence, especially as Uribe was particularly focused on the elimination of the FARC, which had murdered his father some decades earlier. Uribe was more of a hardliner than his predecessor, and sought successfully to convince the United States that the struggle against the FARC was as important to internal security as the elimination of the cartels.[69] Of course, Uribe's hardline stance against the rebels served to further isolate Colombia amid the wave of leftist electoral victories that swept much of the continent, leaving Colombia surrounded by neighbors with a leftist bent—with the exception of Panama—and some expressed sympathy for the ideology espoused by the revolutionary armed forces the Colombian government was attempting to squash with the assistance of its "imperialist" ally from the north. That isolation increased as accusations were made that Venezuela was providing assistance to the FARC, prompting a series of angry exchanges between Uribe and Chávez. As a staunch—though consistently independently minded—ally of Chavez's regime, Morales repeatedly spoke out against his Colombian peer, denouncing his reliance on the United States and the presence of U.S. troops in South American soil.[70]

Regional tensions flared further in 2008, when the Uribe administration sent troops into Ecuadorian territory to engage FARC rebels hiding out near the Colombian border. The response from Rafael Correa and his Venezuelan ally was swift, as both countries ordered thousands of troops to their respective borders with Colombia and Chávez angrily announced that any such incursion into Venezuelan territory—suspected to host yet more FARC rebels—would result in war.[71]

Morales, deeply suspicious of anyone who would willingly cooperate with the United States, consistently railed against Uribe and his militarism. Indeed, in his mind, Colombia's struggle against armed rebels was little more than a shallow pretext for a U.S. military presence in the region: speaking of the U.S. involvement in the counterrevolutionary effort in Colombia, Morales argued that "[the United States] fosters terrorism in order to justify North American bases [in Latin America]."[72] Moreover, the counternarcotics effort served the same dark purpose, as he stated that "I am convinced that the United States works to grow drug trafficking in Colombia in order to justify a military base" and thus, the November 2009 agreement to allow the United States the use of seven Colombian airbases constituted an "invasion" of South America.[73] Morales's distaste for Uribe was probably best expressed in the aftermath of the 2010 Cancún summit of the Rio Group—during which Uribe had engaged in a bit of a shouting match with Chávez—when he described Uribe as the "*chapulín colombiano*," who had been sent as "an agent of the empire" to derail the summit.[74]

The inauguration of President Juan Manuel Santos in 2010 appeared to create an opening for the improvement of Colombia's rather sour relationship with its neighbors. The deep rift with neighboring Colombia was addressed on a state visit to Caracas in November of 2010, which allowed both countries to reestablish diplomatic relationships—broken off in the aftermath of the Ecuadorian crisis.[75] The Santos presidency also resulted, in 2012, in the first state visit Evo Morales had undertaken to Colombia as well as the creation of a framework for security collaboration with regard to counternarcotics operations, in which Colombian personnel would offer training to their counterparts.[76] Santos's willingness to engage in peace talks with the FARC—which angered his predecessor to no end—was also helpful in mending some of the troubled relationships in the region.

The thaw did not last particularly long. The relationship between Santos and Nicolás Maduro—Hugo Chávez's successor—soured within two years. Moreover, to the annoyance of Morales, Santos did not back away from Colombia's close relationship with the United States in its counternarcotics and counterrevolutionary activities, which continued even as peace talks with the FARC were under way. In no way did the Santos administration loosen the country's ties to the United States, and indeed there were efforts in 2013 to build new relationships with the North Atlantic Treaty Organization (NATO), prompting an outcry among the members of the Pink Wave, including Morales who, jumping to conclusions with regard to Colombia's intentions, exclaimed: "Colombia's request to become a member of NATO is a threat to our continent, a conspiracy against the anti-imperialist governments [of the region]. It is a provocation to Venezuela, Nicaragua, Ecuador, and Bolivia. We will not allow it."[77] He further remarked, "How is it possible that Colombia asks to be part of NATO? Why? To hurt Latin America by letting NATO invade us like they have invaded Europe and Africa? [. . .] When they can't stop the democratic revolutions and the recuperation of our natural resources, the empires use their force in an attempt to invade us once again."[78]

CONCLUSION: THE BALLOON EFFECT AND COUNTERNARCOTICS COOPERATION

It would be fair to state that the relationship between Colombia and Bolivia took a nosedive after the election of Evo Morales. Morales tends to view the world through the lens of anti-imperialism and has consequently proven himself to be profoundly suspicious of those who would collaborate with what he likes to refer to as "the empire" (i.e., the United States). Such collaborative efforts, especially when they involve military assistance, are quickly regarded as an attempt to invade Latin America and plunder its natural resources. His distaste for Uribe was particularly notable. Under these circumstances, it is hardly surprising that even though Morales's ascent by no means meant the end of counternarcotics efforts in Bolivia—which continued under his watch, resulting in relatively good results overall—there was little chance that his administration would collaborate actively with the Uribe administration on this front. The notion of military or police training would be especially unpalatable, given his tendency to view Colombia as somewhat of an imperial advance base, a U.S. foothold on South American soil. While the electoral victory that propelled Santos to the Colombian presidency appeared to create an opening, in the context of Colombia's continued dependence on the United States, the relationship quickly soured again.

However, the significance of the rather bad relationship between Bolivia and Colombia since 2005 should be regarded in the light of the much better relationship during the previous period. The relationship itself may have been friendly, but this did not translate into any substantive collaborative efforts. In terms of true security cooperation between the two countries, then, the rather dismal rapport between Morales and his Colombian colleagues has not had much of an effect. While there is very little cooperation in 2014, this does not in effect constitute a worsening of the situation. Bolivia, then, has evolved from not being a factor in Colombian foreign policy at all to becoming an irritant. How are we to interpret the lack of cooperation between these two major producers of coca and cocaine?

In the first place, as I have attempted to show above, the cause for the lack of cooperation can be found in part in the fact that the fight against illegal drugs has very different connotations in both countries. In Colombia, the fight against cocaine was first and foremost a fight against drug trafficking organizations that wrought tremendous violence in Colombian society. As the state managed to suppress the cartels and reduce the levels of violent crime, the business of cocaine manufacture and export fell increasingly to the armed rebel groups—primarily the FARC—which were able to translate the U.S. demand for cocaine into a reliable and rather large revenue stream to support their efforts. In Colombia, then, counternarcotics efforts remain a question of internal security. The same cannot be said for Bolivia, where the fight against coca and cocaine was never born of internal pressures. Bolivians in general have little sympathy for criminals, but they fundamentally do not regard the *cocaleros* themselves as engaged in immoral or criminal behavior. The strong internal structure of the *cocalero* communities has contributed to a situation in which those communities have managed to retain control over their product and have thus prevented criminal networks from becoming too visible. In Bolivia, it could be argued that the counternarcotics strategies pursued by the United States posed a far greater threat to internal security and national cohesion than drug trafficking organizations and *cocaleros* ever did. As a result, the approach taken by Colombia could not be translated to the Bolivian reality, at least not without dire consequences with regard to the political and social stability of Bolivian society.

Secondly, the electoral victory of Evo Morales firmly placed Bolivia in the anti-imperialist camp, whereas Colombia remained an active U.S. ally in the drug war. This realignment led to significant tension between the countries, especially as Venezuela—Bolivia's most fervent supporter—provided support for the armed resistance (or narco-terrorism, depending on whom we ask) against the Colombian state. Colombia's enthusiasm for western support and its efforts to seek direct assistance from the west—including its conversations with NATO, its willingness to host U.S. airbases, and so on—were regarded as deeply offensive by the avowedly anti-American Morales, who viewed each of these moves as evidence of imperial encroachment into South America and Colombia as the enabler of colonial and imperialist powers seeking to expand their nefarious influence over the continent. There was, as a result, little love lost, especially between Uribe and Morales. This notwithstanding the fact that even after the expulsion of the DEA from Bolivia, the country certainly did not become a safe haven for drug traffickers.

The third and perhaps most important reason is one that goes beyond the clash of personalities and ideological convictions that has characterized Bolivian relations with Colombia during Morales's tenure. In effect, basic economics make coordination of the suppression of cocaine between the Andean producer countries an effectively unattractive proposition. This is the result of the relative inelasticity of demand for cocaine among heavy users: the success of one producer country in reducing the output of cocaine, will not result—in the short-term—in a reduction in demand for the product. This translates into an increased price, which in turn results in an added incentive for producers and potential producers to cultivate coca. That is to say that successful counternarcotics efforts in Peru necessarily meant that it became more attractive to Colombian and Bolivian peasant farmers to either increase their production of coca or even to switch from other produce to the now more lucrative coca. As a result, the cost of suppression will rise in both of those countries. In the literature, this effect has been described as the "balloon effect," which describes the movement of production from those areas where significant efforts are undertaken to eradicate coca to other areas where this is not (yet) the case. In essence, were we to assume that each of the major producer countries—Colombia, Peru, and Bolivia—has a legitimate interest in the eradication of coca—or *coca excedentaria*—then we must arrive at the conclusion that these countries are in effect engaged in an arms race in which the goal is to shift production from the homeland into one of the other producer countries. To put it more simply: none of these countries have a particularly good incentive to aid their fellow producer countries in their fight against the production of coca, since the predictable result is that they themselves will then have to confront a larger problem at home as a direct result is driving up the cost of suppressive measures at home. The best one producer country can hope for, if it wishes to avoid the complications that arise from all too active a cocaine industry, is that one of the other producer countries fails in its efforts to suppress that trade.

NOTES

1. The notion of overproduction refers to the Bolivian situation, in which the production of a certain amount of coca remains legal to meet domestic demand for traditional usage of the leaf. As a result, Bolivian efforts are aimed at the eradication of so-called *coca excedentaria*, or coca overproduction, as the goal is not to reduce total production to zero. Will Reisinger, "The Unintended Revolution: U.S Anti-Drug Policy and the Socialist Movement in Bolivia," *California Western International Law Journal* 39, no. 2 (2009): 259–262; Bettina Schorr, "Von nützlichen Feinden und verfehlter Politik: Der Drogenkrieg der USA in Bolivien," in *Bolivien: Staatszerfall*

als Kollateralschaden, ed. Thomas Jäger (Wiesbaden: VS verlag für Sozialwissenschaften, 2009): 184–185; Kathryn Ledebur, "Bolivia: Clear Consequences," in *Drugs and Democracy in Latin America: The Impact of US Policy*, ed. Coletta Youngers and Eileen Rosin (Boulder: Lynne Rienner Publishers, 2005): 154–157.

2. Ledebur, "Bolivia: Clear Consequences," 151–155.

3. Kenneth D. Lehman, *Bolivia and the United States: A Limited Partnership* (Athens: University of Georgia Press, 1999): 202. Reisinger, "The Unintended Revolution," 257–259.

4. Linda Farthing and Benjamin Kohl, "Social Control: Bolivia's New Approach to Coca Reduction," Latin American Perspectives 37, no. 4 (2010).

5. The law included provisions that made involvement in the production and trafficking of controlled substances the worst crime one could commit under Bolivian criminal law, with sentencing guidelines that far exceeded the maxima for violent crime, including rape and murder. See: Diego Giacoman, "Drug Policy and the Prison Situation in Bolivia." In Pien Metaal and Coletta Youngers, *Systems Overload: Drug Laws and Prisons in Latin America* (Washington, DC: WOLA, 2011): 22–23.

6. Solimar Santos, "Unintended Consequences of United States' Foreign Drug Policy in Bolivia," *The University of Miami Inter-American Law Review* 33, no. 1 (2002): 138.

7. Jonathan D. Rosen, "Plan Colombia and Beyond: Pastrana to Santos (2000 to 2012)" (2012). Open Access Dissertations. Paper 880.

8. Nazih Richani, *Systems of Violence: The Political Economy of War and Peace in Colombia* (Albany: State University of New York Press, 2002).

9. See Chapter 13 in this volume.

10. Which I will address later in this chapter.

11. On the notion of the "Pink Wave," see: G. Lievesley and S. Ludlam, *Reclaiming Latin America: Experiments in Radical Social Democracy* (London, UK: Zed, 2009).

12. UNODC, World Drug Report 2006 (New York: United Nations Publications, 2006), 81.

13. Benjamin H. Kohl and Linda C. Farthing, *Impasse in Bolivia: Neoliberal Hegemony and Popular Resistance* (London, UK: Zed Books, 2006): 65–73.

14. It should be noted first that the relaunch of the war on drugs in 1982, which had originally been President Richard Nixon's project, preceded the appearance of crack-cocaine in the U.S. marketplace in 1984. With regard to the moral panic of the so-called crack epidemic, see: Michelle Alexander, *The New Jim Crow: Mass Incarceration in the Age of Colorblindness* (New York: The New Press, 2010).

15. Steven B. Karch, *A Brief History of Cocaine* (Boca Raton: CRC Press, 2006), 11; Paul Gootenberg, *Andean Cocaine: The Making of a Global Drug* (Chapel Hill: University of North Carolina Press, 2008), 16.

16. Kevin Healy, "The Boom within the Crisis: Some Recent Effects of Foreign Cocaine Markets on Bolivian Rural Society and Economy," *in Coca and Cocaine: Effects on People and Policy in Latin America*, ed. Deborah Pacini and Christine Franquemont (Cambridge, UK: Cultural Survival, Inc. and LASP, 1986): 112.

17. Lehman, *Bolivia and the United States*, 210–212.

18. The constitutionality of the law has been called into question. See: Giacoman, "Drug Policy and the Prison Situation in Bolivia," 22–23.
19. Reisinger, "Unintended Revolution," 259–262.
20. Schorr, "Von nützlichen Feinden," 183.
21. Lehman, *Bolivia and the United States*, 210–212.
22. This was a lesson learnt by President Gonzalo Sánchez de Lozada, whose campaign had included the slogan "coca no es cocaina" in order to garner support and to present himself as a political force capable of resisting U.S. demands and pressures.
23. Lehman, *Bolivia and the United States*, 210–211; Washington Estellano, "From Populism to Coca Economy," Latin American Perspectives 21, no. 4 (1994): 39–40.
24. UNODC, (New York: United Nations Publications, 2006), 81.
25. Ledebur, "Bolivia," 154–157.
26. Reisinger, "Unintended Revolution," 267–268.
27. Reisinger, "Unintended Revolution," 267–268.
28. Schorr, "Von nützlichen Feinden," 85.
29. In what is the classic example of the "Balloon Effect." Paul Gootenberg, "Between Coca and Cocaine: A Century or More of U.S.-Peruvian Drug Paradoxes, 1860–1980," *Hispanic American Historical Review* 83/3 (2003): 119–150.
30. Daniel Mejía and Carlos Esteban Posada, "Cocaine Production and Trafficking: What Do We Know?" *World Bank Policy Research Working Paper No. 4618* (Washington, D.C.: World Bank, 2008): 8–10.
31. Francisco E. Thoumi, *Illegal Drugs, Economy, and Society in the Andes* (Baltimore: The Johns Hopkins University Press, 2003): 93–108.
32. Thoumi, *Illegal Drugs*, 84–91.
33. Thoumi, *Illegal Drugs*, 103–108.
34. Eduardo Pizzaro and Pilar Gaitán, "Plan Colombia and the Andean Regional Initiative: Lights and Shadows," *Addicted to Failure: U.S. Security Policy in Latin America and the Andean Region*, ed. Brian Loveman, (Lanham, MD: Rowman & Littlefield, 2006), 69.
35. Thoumi, *Illegal Drugs*, 227–231.
36. Thoumi, *Illegal Drugs*, 230.
37. UNODC
38. Thoumi, *Illegal Drugs*, 230; Pizzaro and Gaitán, *Plan Colombia and the Andean Regional Initiative*, 69.
39. Thoumi, *Illegal Drugs*, 105–107.
40. UNODC, *Global Study on Homicide 2013: Trends, Context, Data* (New York, N.Y.: United Nations Publications, 2013).
41. Santos, "Unintended Consequences" 138.
42. Steven B. Karch, *A Brief History of Cocaine* (Boca Raton, FL: CRC Press, 2006), 11.
43. D. Carrasco Michel and G. Cámara Virreira, "El alcohol y la hoja de coca ¿vicios indígenas?: La prensa estigmatizando a las revueltas indígenas" *Punto Cero* 15/20 (2010): 35–42.
44. Daniel Kurtz-Phelan, "'Coca Is Everything Here': Hard Truths about Bolivia's Drug War," *World Policy Journal* 22, no. 3 (2005): 105.

45. James Painter, *Bolivia and Coca: A Study in Dependency* (Boulder, CO: Lynn Riener Publishers, 1994), 110; Healy, "The Boom," 102.

46. Jeffrey R. Webber, *From Rebellion to Reform in Bolivia: Class Struggle, Indigenous Liberation, and the Politics of Evo Morales* (Chicago: Haymarket Books, 2011), 57–59.

47. Miners had been a significant political force since the 1940s, and especially so in the aftermath of the 1952 National Revolution, in which they played a decisive role.

48. Robert Lessmann, Das neue Bolivien: Evo Morales und seine demokratische Revolution (Zürich: Rotpunkt Verlag, 2010), 129–130.

49. Lessmann, *Das neue Bolivien*, 129–131.

50. Kurtz-Phelan, "Coca Is Everything Here," 105.

51. Reisinger, "Unintended Revolution," 276–278. Ledebur, "Bolivia: Clear Consequences": 151–155.

52. Pilar Domingo, "Evo Morales, the MAS, and a Revolution in the Making." In Jean Grugel and Pía Riggirozzi, *Governance after Neoliberalism in Latin America* (New York: Palgrave MacMillan, 2009): 118–123

53. Manuel Dussan, "Bolivia: Enormous Reserves, Political Restrictions." In *Gas Market Integration in the Southern Cone*, ed. Paulina Beato et al., (Washington, DC: Inter-American Development Bank, 2004): 60–62; Willem Assies, "Bolivia: A Gasified Democracy," *European Review of Latin American and Caribbean Studies* 76 (2000): 29–30.

54. Marten Brienen, "Interminable Revolution: Populism and Frustration in 20th Century Bolivia," SAIS Review 27, no. 1 (2007): 21–23.

55. Herbert S. Klein, *A Concise History of Bolivia* (Cambridge: Cambridge University Press, 2003): 141–143.

56. Herbert Sanford Klein, *Bolivia: the Evolution of a Multi-Ethnic Society* (Oxford, UK: Oxford University Press, 1992): 219–221.

57. 0.16 hectares.

58. One of the immediate causes for Sánchez de Lozada's fall had been the use of violence to break the blockade of La Paz by protesters. See: Domingo, "Evo Morales," 122.

59. Barr, "Another Uncompleted Revolution," 73.

60. Even Morales himself has acknowledged the role the ambassador played in ensuring his victory. See James Surowiecki, "Morales's Mistake." *The New Yorker*, 23 January 2006.

61. Santos, "Unintended Consequences," 129.

62. UNODC, *World Drug Report* 2012, 35.

63. Luna D'Alama, "Brasil é o segundo consumidor mundial de cocaína e derivados, diz estudo" *O Globo*, 5 September 2012, Section G1.

64. Or indeed for criminals in general: Mitchell Seligson, Amy Erica Smith, and Elizabeth E. Zechmeister, *The Political Culture of Democracy in the Americas, 2012: Towards Equality of Opportunity* (Nashville, TN: LAPOP, 2012): 197.

65. Bolivia. Defensoría del Pueblo. *XV informe a la asamblea legislativa plurinacional* (La Paz, Bolivia: Canasta de Fondos, 2013): 77–78.

66. Eduardo Pizzaro and Pilar Gaitán, "Plan Colombia and the Andean Regional Initiative: Lights and Shadows," in *Addicted to Failure: U.S. Security Policy in Latin America and the Andean Region*, ed. Brian Loveman, (Lanham, MD: Rowman & Littlefield, 2006).

67. Reisinger, "Unintended Consequences," 280.

68. Mark Weisbrot, Rebecca Ray, and Jake Johnston, *Bolivia: The Economy During the Morales Administration* (Washington, D.C.: CEPR, 2009).

69. See: Chapter 13 in this volume.

70. Jeb Blount and Katia Cortes, "Bolivia, Colombia Cross Swords on Benefits of U.S." 19 January 2007. Retrieved, 17 November 2014, from http://www.bloomberg.com/apps/news?pid=20601086&sid=ak7Abl_0hrgg

71. Paul Vallely, "The Big Question: Why has Colombia invaded Ecuador, and why is Venezuela joining the fight?" *The Independent*, 5 March 2008.

72. Agencia EFE, "EE.UU. fomentó narcotráfico en Colombia para justificar bases: Evo Morales," *El Espectador*, 1 December 2009, section: El Mundo.

73. EFE, "EE.UU. fomentó narcotráfico en Colombia."

74. Agencia EFE, "Evo dice que Uribe es el 'chapulín colombiano." 27 February 2010. *Noticias 24*. Section América Latina, retrieved, 17 November 2014, from http://www.noticias24.com/actualidad/noticia/145435/evo-dice-que-uribe-es-el-chapulin-colombiano/comment-page-8/

75. Leo Palmer, "Ecuador to continue investigation into DAS wiretaps," *Colombia Reports*, 5 July, 2010.

76. ABI, "Colombia y Bolivia acuerdan cooperación en lucha contra el narcotráfico y seguridad," *El País*, 16 March 2012.

77. Anonymous, "Evo Morales: '¿Para qué quiere entrar Colombia a la OTAN?'" *DW*, 3 June 2013.

78. Anonymous, "Evo Morales attacks Colombia's attempt to seek NATO membership" *Buenos Aires Herald*, 4 June 2013.

Chapter Eleven

Narrating Success

Colombian Security Expertise and Foreign Policy

Arlene B. Tickner and Mateo Morales Callejas

In 2007, a report of the Center for Strategic and International Studies (CSIS)[1] hailed what was for all practical purposes no less than a miracle. Colombia had come "back from the brink," overcoming apocalyptic predictions of state collapse and domestic anarchy only a few years earlier when a series of unrelated factors converged to create the "perfect storm." In the mid-1990s, political violence worsened as violent nonstate actors, both guerillas and paramilitaries, grew in size, territorial presence and military strength, largely due to a reshuffling of the drug trade and a growing intersection between it and the armed conflict. While the Revolutionary Armed Forces of Colombia (FARC) achieved control over key coca-producing areas and delivered a series of humiliating blows to the armed forces, the paramilitary umbrella group, the United Self-Defense Forces of Colombia (AUC), conducted a brutal campaign against the guerrillas in which presumed civilian sympathizers were also terrorized. The resulting humanitarian crisis, as measured in homicides, massacres and forced displacement, became one of the worst in the world. At the same time, the crisis of governance that ensued from allegations that Ernesto Samper (1994–1998) received campaign contributions from the Cali drug cartel, along with severe U.S. isolation of the Colombian president, weakened the Colombian state beyond its already chronic anemia.[2]

In combination, these developments confirmed the thesis that the Colombian state had undergone severe decay. So much so that it was believed in some U.S. and Colombian circles that if measures were not taken immediately, the FARC could conceivably take over power. Given the potential implications of both state collapse and a guerrilla victory for United States security and trade interests in Colombia and the Andean region, a multi-billion, multiyear aid package, Plan Colombia, was devised to assist the country in enhancing its capacity to combat the dual threats of drugs and insurgency. An increased U.S. role in the Colombian crisis was also actively sought out by the government of Andrés Pastrana (1998–2002).

Both Pastrana and his hard-line successor, Álvaro Uribe (2002–2010), made use of a "weak state" discourse in order to justify the need for greater American involvement and ultimately, intervention in the country's internal crisis.[3] As late as 2003, around the time of the U.S. invasion in Iraq, Uribe reinforced this portrayal of Colombia by claiming that the conflict in his country was much worse than anything in Iraq. However, by 2004, both policy makers in Bogotá and Washington, think tanks, international and regional financial institutions, and the media slowly began to refer to Colombia as a country that, with the help of the United States, had been able to avert disaster.[4] Colombia's security situation improved considerably during the second Uribe government (2006–2010) and has continued to do so during that of Juan Manuel Santos (2010–2018). The state has achieved greater control over the countryside, thousands of paramilitary fighters have demobilized, punishing defeats have been delivered to the guerrillas, and large numbers of rebels have voluntarily surrendered. Key indicators of violence have also declined. Arguably, the "war on drugs" too has resulted in relative gains as measured by illicit crop acreage and total cocaine production in Colombia, although these are largely offset by the public health and environmental consequences of aerial fumigation, and by the migration of drug cultivation, production, trafficking routes and violence elsewhere in the region, most notably Peru and Bolivia, and Mexico, Central America, and the Caribbean.

Trends such as these have underwritten a "success story" which is at the root of the Santos government foreign policy strategy. According to this dominant narrative, Colombia's main asset, security know-how gained through its battle against narcotics and nonstate violent actors, can and should be exported to other countries in Latin America and elsewhere plagued by drug-related crime and violence. Since the mid-2000s, Colombia has fielded increasing numbers of requests for security cooperation from many different governments. According to the Colombian Ministry of Defense,[5] between 2005 and May 2013, police and military training was provided to 17,352 individuals from forty-seven different countries in areas ranging from ground, air, maritime and river interdiction, police testimony, explosives, intelligence operations, psychological operations, and Commando JUNGLA, the United States' designed signature elite counternarcotics program.

Colombia's metamorphosis from "failing state" to "success story" and even a "model" for others to emulate is difficult to understand without resorting to discourse.[6] Although Plan Colombia was successful in terms of improving certain aspects of the country's security landscape, others remained relatively unchanged. Moreover, during the Uribe presidency "success" arguably came at the price of further erosion of democracy, as embodied in the triple para-politics, wire-tapping and false positives scandals that erupted between 2006 and 2009 during his second government.[7] What this suggests is that the correspondence between empirical facts and the stories told about Colombia has been imperfect at best.

In this chapter, we argue that the framing of the Colombian "success story" has allowed the Santos government to deploy a narrative about the recent past that has been crucial to buttressing the country's regional and international recognition and influence. No less important, the United States' active role in recounting this "stunning" transformation has been functional to Washington's own interests by justifying its considerable U.S. $8 billion investment in Colombia between 2000 and 2012, for setting it up as a model for export to other countries, and for subcontracting know-how from the Colombian armed forces, thus deflecting concerns about its political meddling in Mexico, Central America, and the Caribbean. The chapter begins by discussing post-positivist approaches to foreign policy that highlight the importance of discourse in the construction of specific subjectivities and realities. Based upon a simple analytical framework that we derive from this literature, we examine the ways in which the "success story" has been articulated by officials from the Colombian and the U.S. governments, and reproduced by the media and academic and policy think-tanks. In all these cases we identify a common story line that highlights Colombia's transition from a security basket-case to an example to be admired and emulated. Subsequently, we explore the ways in which changes in U.S. security policy and the decline in its power in the Western Hemisphere, in combination with the "insecurity epidemic" currently plaguing much of Latin America and the Caribbean has provided a fitting stage for Colombian expertise to be exported. The chapter concludes with a brief reflection on the potential shortcomings of Colombia's current role as a security-maker.

THE "HOW" OF FOREIGN POLICY

Most foreign policy analysis is positivist in nature and, thus, concerned with explaining "why" specific decisions, courses of action and strategies are adopted, and with identifying those variables that account for given outcomes. In contrast, post-positivism is largely responsible for introducing "how" questions into the study of world politics by pointing to the constructed and social nature of (international) reality.

According to Nicholas Onuf, "[S]aying is doing; talking is undoubtedly the most important way we go about making the world what it is."[8] Discourse not only constitutes reality but also makes it intelligible. In particular, discursive practices create subjects, objects and relations between them. By focusing on the social construction of reality, post-positivism thus asks "how" the conditions of possibility of specific foreign policy outcomes came about, something that is essentially taken for granted by positivist approaches.[9] Therefore, it provides insights into the construction of subjects, identities and problems that make specific courses of action seem reasonable, necessary or conversely, unadvisable.

The types of explanation derived from "why" and "how" are quite different. While "why" based analysis, in keeping with the idea of problem-solving theory, works within the limits of a pre-given reality, "how" focuses more on the ways in which this reality came about and to what effect, thus expanding prevalent understandings of the foreign policy process. For example, David Campbell argues that state identities are secured by the representation of danger and threats, under the assumption that the state's ontological status is not static and must be continuously reenacted.[10] In this reading, foreign policy is crucial to the production of identity as it is the main site in which the state interacts with its most threatening "others," namely other states.

Roxanne Lynn Doty, in turn, provides a provocative "blueprint" for examining how the surrounding contexts for foreign policy, such as those constituted through the identification of existential threats to the state, become thinkable.[11] According to this author, "[T]he possibility of practices presupposes the ability of an agent to imagine certain courses of action. Certain background meanings, kinds of social actors and relationships must already be in place."[12] The "blueprint" offered by Doty for tracing this process entails three interrelated concepts: presupposition, predication, and subject positioning. Presupposition refers to background knowledge that constructs a specific kind of reality in which given courses of action become thinkable and others unthinkable, and predication to the descriptive characteristics attached to given subjects through the use of specific adjectives and adverbs. By linking particular subjects to objects (or backgrounds), a reality is created in which distinct subjects adopt specific roles (or positions).[13] When discourses pronounced by diverse state actors are coherent and stable in terms of the characteristics and positions attributed to certain subjects, it can be argued that a "dominant discourse" exists.[14]

In the specific case of Colombia, as we will see, discourses that portray the country as a "net security exporter" after it "returned from the brink" constitute it as a specific type of subject with certain attributes and capacities. By linking Colombia to the wave of drug-related insecurity that plagues Latin America and the Caribbean, and to the changing U.S. role in the region, a reality is created in which exporting Colombian security expertise becomes not only thinkable but almost imperative.

COLOMBIA: FROM "FAILING STATE" TO "SUCCESS STORY"

Since the mid-2000s, "Colombia" has been constructed through public discourses that underscore this country's transition from a "failing state" to a "success story" in terms of state strengthening and improvement in key security indicators. In this process both Colombian and U.S. authorities have played a central role.

Diverse studies suggest that indeed, the country has experienced an important transformation in terms of institution-building, which has in turn translated into a greater state presence in the national territory.[15] State strengthening has been largely limited to the coercive and extractive aspects of statehood essential for state consolidation. Diverse sources point to the advantages of this strategy, adopted consistently throughout the Uribe (2002–2010) and Santos (2010–2014) administrations, in no small measure due to U.S. support through Plan Colombia.[16] In addition to significant reductions in homicides, kidnappings, and terrorist attacks, foreign investment has risen dramatically while citizen perceptions of security in most parts of the country have improved considerably.

Nevertheless, Colombia continues to be a troublesome case in terms of other objective and subjective dimensions of stateness, defined in terms of the fiscal health and social spending required to provide effective public services.[17] Additionally, although state presence has increased geographically, in many areas in which it has asserted itself coercively speaking, the Colombian state continues to exhibit severe institutional weaknesses related to its administrative duties, the enforcement of the law and justice, the protection of private property, and accountability.[18] Corruption and impunity too have remained stubbornly elevated, impairing the strengthening of many state capacities and responsibilities. The 2013 Transparency International Corruption Perceptions Index ranks public sector corruption in Colombia at a high 94 out of a total of 175 countries. The country also boasts a critical human rights record, even when taking into account relative recent improvements. According to the Center for Historical Memory, for example, 5.7 million Colombians, amounting to 15 percent of the total population, are victims of forced internal displacement, while most extrajudicial killings committed by the military during the Uribe government have gone unpunished.[19]

Notwithstanding the ambiguities that surround Colombia's "success," as suggested by our brief discussion, both the Colombian and the U.S. government have made strategic use of this narrative in order to represent the country as a model state-builder. Although the limited space of the chapter makes a systematic analysis of official discourse during the Santos administration implausible, several examples suffice to illustrate how Colombia's representation has shifted. In addition to overcoming state weakness and improving internal security, the dominant story line points more widely to achievements in other areas, such as drugs, democracy, human rights, and the economy. Repeated reference to Colombia's near "rebirth" and to widespread international recognition of its achievements, make the "success story" all the more powerful and seductive.

The following passages from speeches delivered by President Juan Manuel Santos and former U.S. Secretary of State, Hillary Clinton, create a "before" and an "after" in Colombia's recent history that coincides largely with the implementation of Plan Colombia and with the Uribe and Santos governments, both of which purportedly brought the country back from the threshold of disaster. According to Santos:

> . . . ten years ago we were on the verge of being considered a failed state . . . You have seen all that has been done on the security side by president Uribe with his Democratic Security Policy, after which the country started changing and began implementing longer-term policies, not just in the security realm but also in the economy. The country continued to evolve and in ten years it is completely different from what it was ten years ago.[20]

He continues:

"The problem that we had was that of a democracy crippled by the drug cartels. That is no longer the case."[21]

Clinton, in turn, states:

> I remember vividly when my daughter and husband visited in 2000, when Plan Colombia was just beginning. It was a country terrorized by drug traffickers and guerrillas who controlled vast parts of territory and who could strike in any major city. Foreign policy experts, in this city and so many other places, were calling it a failed state. Ten years later, I traveled to Colombia as Secretary of State. And this time, I walked through the streets of downtown Bogotá. I visited a bakery run by former FARC and paramilitary members—and let me tell you, it's not every day that you get to sample the baked goods of former guerrillas . . . Where citizens once lived in fear to exercise their right to vote, now we have peaceful democratic elections that are really the envy of so many other countries that have not been able to make that transition.[22]

Santos and Clinton both underscore the idea that "before" Plan Colombia and Uribe's Democratic Security Policy, the state was on the verge of collapse, violent non-state actors controlled large swaths of the national territory and the population was terrorized, while "after," the state has become strong, security has improved, democracy is vibrant, drug trafficking is no longer a vital threat, armed actors have demobilized and been reintegrated into society, and the economy has started to flourish. One of the main effects of discourses such as these is that recent Colombian history is reduced to a neat and linear process through which the country has overcome its most serious challenges.

However, according to this narrative, success is not limited to the security realm or even to democracy. In myriad other statements made by distinct government authorities, a strong bond is created between improvements in domestic security and other areas that comprise Colombian stateness, including social policy, corruption, and human rights. Take, for instance, President Santos's hailing of a "New Colombia":

> . . . where we are not still chained to poverty, inequality, corruption and violence. A New Colombia where we free ourselves of the fear that clips our wings . . . A New Colombia that shines today at home and abroad, converting itself into an example for the rest of the world. It is amazing how people now say: look at Colombia, observe Colombia, do what Colombia does.[23]

Ironically, a special report published in June 2013 by the *Financial Times*[24] and titled identically, recounts triumphs similar to those highlighted above. As in the case of the previous example, here Colombia is represented as a country reborn, not only due to the elimination of violence, but perhaps more importantly, to its supposed victory in the fight against poverty, inequality, and corruption.

Notwithstanding the persistence of negative empirical trends in human rights, distinct government speeches also highlight positive trends within the armed forces. In addition to creating a nexus between security and human rights, the armed forces are poised as superior and thus worthy of international respect in both realms. According to Santos:

> I feel very proud when I hear international analysts and many of the people that have joined me say that the evolution of our armed forces in terms of human rights is superior to that of all other armed forces in the world. The speed with which we changed a culture, the speed with which we explained to the armed forces that their legitimacy depended upon the respect for fundamental rights of the citizenry. . . .[25]

He also declared that "the Air Force has become an international model of respect for International Humanitarian Law."[26]

Colombian accomplishments in the "war on drugs," in particular, are considered a key source of moral authority, although they too easily slip into other achievements in completely unrelated areas such as poverty. For the Colombian president:

> . . . if there is a country that has paid a high price in the fight against drug trafficking, it is Colombia. If there is a country that can say that it has learned to fight against all of the stages of the drug chain, it is Colombia . . . With that moral authority we are saying to the world that the problem continues, that it is transforming, mutating, and that we need to discuss it . . . It is a source of pride that today presidents come to Colombia to congratulate our armed forces, and that our other force, the social force . . . is producing marvelous results . . . And we are becoming, now hear this, a model country in the fight against poverty.[27]

Both Colombia's security know-how and its position of moral authority derived from the costs of the war on drugs help legitimize the exportation of the country's experience. However, by posing the "success story" in wider terms, other foreign policy objectives also become thinkable. For example, Colombian membership in the Organization for Economic Cooperation and Development (OECD) has been pitched not only as a well-deserved acknowledgment of recent economic and social progress but also the key to greater international attention, and with it, increased prosperity and well-being. Santos states:

> What does it mean for Colombia and for Colombians to be admitted to the OECD? It means that we are going to improve the quality of our public policies and that we are going to measure ourselves with the highest standards. It means that investor confidence in our country is going to grow even more, which translates into more employment, more competitiveness and better standards of living for all Colombians. It means that Colombia continues to insert itself in the world's most important economic and *political venues.* Everyone will be looking at Colombia![28]

United States officials, as mentioned previously, have played a fundamental role in narrating Colombia's "amazing transformation" (a term coined by current U.S. Secretary of State, John Kerry in his August 2013 visit to Bogotá),[29] which in no small measure is attributed to sustained U.S. assistance. Clearly, it is the very uniqueness of this experience as constituted in foreign policy statements that makes it a potential model for other countries to follow. Equally important, as highlighted in the following statement by Hillary Clinton, Plan Colombia has been tremendously cost effective in comparison to other recent U.S. ventures such as Afghanistan or Iraq:

> So Colombia, in short, had gone from a source of danger to itself and others to a source of inspiration to all of us and to becoming a vital partner in the great debates of our time. Now, the real credit goes to the Colombian people and to the leaders who had to make very hard choices, not just once or twice, but over and over again. But the United States played an important, some would say an

> essential role. The money we invested in Plan Colombia over that decade, while significant, is less than we spend in Afghanistan in a single week.[30]

If indeed, as the statements included here suggest, Colombia has achieved monumental positive change that contrasts with failures elsewhere, such as the Middle East,[31] and if, for this very reason, the country has become a "model for hope," the next "logical" step would be for Colombia's success to be replicated in other parts of the world.[32] This is precisely the idea that the U.S. and Colombian governments began pushing as early as 2011. For example, former Deputy Secretary of State, James B. Steinberg claims that: ". . . what has been especially rewarding for me is to see the growing role that Colombia is playing on the regional and international stage. As we like to say in our business, Colombia has gone from being a consumer of security to a provider of security and support for others who face even greater challenges."[33]

Parallel to Colombia's own efforts to become a security exporter, with U.S. support, in February 2012 a Strategic High Level Security Dialogue (HLSSD) began between the two countries. Several months later, at the Summit of the Americas meeting in Cartagena, Presidents Santos and Obama announced plans to develop an Action Plan on Regional Security Cooperation in order to support capacity-building in Central America, the Caribbean and eventually, West Africa. As we will discuss in the next section, acting hand-in-hand with Colombia has allowed the United States to "lead from behind," thus avoiding many of the pitfalls associated with direct security involvement in Latin America.

THE UNITED STATES: FROM HEGEMON TO REGIONAL PARTNER?

In the past decade U.S. foreign and security policy has undergone significant change. On the one hand, Latin America and the Caribbean have become less important for the country's key strategic concerns, which gravitate largely around the Middle East and Asia. On the other, its economic and fiscal crisis has led to reductions and a reshuffling of military, social and economic assistance to the region.[34]

Discursively speaking, such shifts have translated into U.S. calls for greater shared responsibility with Latin American countries and with the use of new adjectives to refer to this distinct kind of relationship, including "partners," "mutual respect," "shared interests," "common values," and "non-intervention." The following reflection by Hillary Clinton about U.S.-Latin American relations reflects this change: "The President will build on the pledge he made at the Summit of the Americas early in his presidency to work as 'equal partners' in a 'new chapter of engagement' based on 'mutual respect and common interests and shared values.'"[35]

Secretary of State John Kerry's November 2013 announcement before the OAS that the Monroe Doctrine was dead may have produced chuckles among Latin American audiences who already knew this to be the case years before. However, what is telling about his statement is the way in which the end of U.S. interventionism is presented as an act of good-will and a decision, not the result of shifts in hemispheric power:

> Today, however, we have made a different choice. The era of the Monroe Doctrine is over . . .
>
> As U.S. President Barack Obama noted in his visit to Mexico and Costa Rica last May, there are no "senior partners," rather equal partners focused on areas of common interest, including enhancing economic prosperity and cooperating on regional security . . .
>
> It will require courage and a willingness to change, but above all, it will require a higher and deeper level of cooperation between us, all of us together as equal partners in this hemisphere . . .[36]

In addition to portraying the United States as a benevolent partner who has chosen to shift the way in which foreign relations are conducted with its Latin American neighbors, by representing regional countries as a potential source of prosperity on equal footing with the United States, the burden of responsibility for diverse hemispheric problems is also effectively transferred to them.

Reflecting this view, Wendy Sherman, Undersecretary for Political Affairs of the State Department, sustains:

> . . . we are committed to working with partners, all over the hemisphere, to advance and defend common interests and values, and we won't be shy about speaking up, clearly, and acting, to that end. We are convinced that the capabilities and experience of people throughout the Americas will be a vital ingredient in a stable, prosperous and secure world.[37]

Given lessened resources, power and interest in Latin America, Washington has promoted a more active role for its Colombian counterpart, as discussed in the previous section, and at the same time encouraged regional countries to seek out new ways of dealing with their security problems via cooperation and partnership. Colombian security expertise and the search for "new" solutions to regional insecurity are mutually reinforcing. Roberta Jackson, Assistant Secretary of the Bureau of Western Hemisphere Affairs, echoes this quite clearly when she states:

> I think one of the striking things about the Colombian security forces and their capability is the way in which they are now providing that expertise, that capability to other countries around the world. I think, at last count, Colombia's training of other countries' police and military forces was close to 40 different countries, many of them in Central America or in the Caribbean as well as Africa. And so there are a lot of people around the world looking to those very capable security forces.[38]

In short, by painting the United States as a respectful and equal partner eager to work with Latin America in search for common solutions to shared problems, official discourse acts to neutralize the interventionist past. This non-intrusive mind-set is reaffirmed by the promotion of Colombia as a security provider, which reflects Washington's willingness to allow Colombia to take the lead in providing training, even though the United States continues to be the main contributor of military assistance in Latin America.[39] Lastly, Colombia's direct and extensive experience with drug trafficking and armed insurgency, and its alleged prowess in solving "violent puzzles" present themselves as one, if not the most innovative security fix for many parts of the region.

LATIN AMERICAN SECURITY EPIDEMIC

In addition to considering the construction of subjects, namely, Colombia and the United States, and their relative positioning, our analysis of the discursive processes by which Colombian security expertise has become acknowledged and embraced would be incomplete without a discussion of the specific (social) context within which the "success story" narrative has taken place. Namely, the so-called security "epidemic" currently plaguing many countries of Latin America has provided a fitting setting for the exportation of Colombian know-how.

According to the UNDP Human Development Report for Latin America 2013–2014, the region has undergone two large waves, one economic and social, and the other criminal.[40] At the same time that the region has improved consistently in areas such as health, education, and poverty and inequality reduction, violence has risen to "epidemic levels." 11 out of 18 countries included in the report experience more than ten homicides per 100,000 inhabitants annually, while over one million killings were reported region-wide between 2000 and 2010. In addition to these objective indicators citizen perceptions of insecurity and victimization have increased considerably. On average, only 43 percent of Latin Americans feel safe, 33 percent feel unsafe and 50 percent consider the security situation to have worsened.[41] This generalized context of insecurity is particularly severe in the countries of the Northern Triangle (El Salvador, Guatemala, and Honduras), where organized criminal activities have grown exponentially.

Admittedly, Latin America's and especially, Central America's security predicament is highly worrisome. However, discourse (or speech acts)[42] such as "endemic situation," "exponential growth in violence," "levels similar to an armed conflict" or "an individual has a four times higher risk of being killed in this region than anywhere else in the world,"[43] lend themselves to the securitization of problems ranging from poverty, social protest, youth crime and petty crime to drug-related organized crime, and to the application of "exceptional," usually militarized solutions. Media coverage too has contributed negatively to citizen perceptions of insecurity by overstating and hyping the occurrence of violent crimes.[44]

In addition, in many statements made by governmental officials and representatives of international organizations such as the World Bank and the Inter-American Development Bank, security and economic stability are presented as inextricably linked, reinforcing the idea that a worsening security situation will have catastrophic consequences for the economy and for foreign investment.[45] Although insecurity and violence may undoubtedly affect economic development and investor confidence, discourses that represent the relation between the two so in such unproblematic and automatic terms make the adoption of "effective" and "successful" policies capable of guaranteeing a secure environment imperative.

In this sense, we would argue that a general setting has been created in sub-regions such as Central America that makes possible, if not absolutely necessary, the adoption of new strategies to combat insecurity. Colombian security expertise is one of the main practices that have been embraced precisely due to this country's "success" in combating similar problems at home, and its discursive positioning as an authoritative voice with moral authority on the subject, as discussed previously. The fact that the region has grown increasingly skeptical of traditional mechanisms of security cooperation,[46] especially bilateral assistance provided by the United States, makes South-South cooperation such as that provided by Colombia all the more appealing, as suggested by the following passage: "The time of unilateral, apocalyptic wars against distinct threats is over, thanks to the leadership of heads of state such as President Santos . . . The winds of reform are blowing in the realm of security . . . There was a clear regional pronouncement on the need to find a new, integral strategy to combat illegal drug trafficking."[47]

Of course, one of the main ironies of Colombian South-South cooperation is that the know-how being exported is largely rooted in the very same security policies imparted to Colombia by the United States!

CONCLUSION

As we have argued in this chapter, "how" (or post-positivist) based foreign policy analyses highlight the ways in which discursive practices create different international subjects as well as the relations that exist between them. In the specific case of Colombia, what we have described as a "success story" construed mainly through Colombian and U.S. official discourse, and widely embraced by the media and academic think-tanks, has been fundamental in shifting this country's image from that of a failing state and security-taker to that of a strong state and security-maker. Changes in U.S. security policy and in its relations with Latin America, along with a security problematic in the region that screams for help, have worked together to create the contextual conditions of possibility for the exportation of Colombian security expertise.

Table 11.1 summarizes the different predicates and practices attached to Colombia, the United States and Latin America. The table was compiled by extracting descriptive characteristics and capacities attributed to all three actors from speeches delivered by Colombian and U.S. officials between 2011 and 2014.[48] Notwithstanding the specific terms and expressions used, the coherence that exists between distinct adjectives and adverbs is striking. First, Colombia's present traits and capacities are consistently and positively contrasted with its tragic recent past. Second, the relation between the United States and Colombia is portrayed as a strategic partnership in which Colombia's successes, most importantly, its security expertise, are a source of inspiration for others and thus at the forefront of joint efforts to provide security to other countries in need. And third, U.S.-Latin American relations are described as one of equality, mutual respect, and harmony of interests.

Surely, if Colombia's "success" is so widely recognized and its security expertise sought out by growing numbers of countries, the dominant discourse that we have identified must be at least partially "true." However, ascertaining the "truth" or "falsity" of the Colombian "success story" and the strengths or weaknesses of its security cooperation is not the objective of this chapter. Rather, our point is that stories such as those that have been told about Colombia through foreign policy discourse create specific realities that condition public debate and political decision, thus precluding discussion and courses of action located outside of reality so constituted.

Generally speaking, Colombian security know-how packaged so neatly as "success" should set off at least a few alarms. First, it minimizes the fact that the armed forces and the country's intelligence agencies have been involved in severe human rights violations and other illegal acts, even in recent times. To wit, the so-called false positives scandal, involving nearly 5,000 extrajudicial executions of young men presented falsely as guerrillas killed in combat, and the illegal wiretappings conducted by the Administra-

Table 11.1. Predicates and Practices

Colombia	*United States-Colombia*	*United States-Latin America*
• *Ten years ago we were on the verge of becoming a failed state* • *The country is completely different from what it was ten years ago* • *New Colombia* • *Shines inward and outward* • *Not just in the security realm but also in the economy* • *Our armed forces in terms of human rights is superior to that of all other armed forces in the world* • *Democracy crippled (. . .) that is no longer the case* • *Model country in terms of combating poverty* • *A country that can document positive results* • *Moral authority* • *Expertise* • *Model* • *An example to follow in the rest of the world* • *Do what Colombia does* • *We definitely have something to offer* • We can reach other regions	• *It was a country terrorized by drug traffickers and guerrillas* • *The only success story so far is Colombia* • *We see a level of security and economic growth not enjoyed in decades* • *Colombia provides a model for hope* • *Source of inspiration to all* • *Amazing transformation* • *Vital partner in the great debates of our time* • *Has experience* • *From a consumer of security to a provider of security* • *Support for others* • *Willingness to help* • *The United States of America is proud* • *The United States played an important (. . .) an essential role* • *Colombia an ever-more vital strategic partner*	• *The era of the Monroe Doctrine is over* • *There are no senior partners* • *Equal partners* • *Fellow leaders* • *As nations, as neighbors, we rise and fall together* • *Areas of common interest* • *A story of a once troubled region that has seen its largest nations emerge as respected players on the global stage* • *Working together* • *Shared platform for global success* • *Shared responsibility* • *Partnership and equality* • *Common interests and values* • *Work of the United States, as your partner and friend*

Source: created by authors

tive Security Department (DAS), subsequently dissolved, both exploded during the second Uribe administration.

Second, although on paper Colombia offers a multidimensional approach to international security cooperation, with emphasis on diverse aspects of citizen security,[49] the fact that the Colombian police and military personnel that train foreign forces have been enveloped in a fifty-year armed conflict and a thirty-year "war on drugs" may make this strategy difficult to apply in practice and may instead reinforce the militarization of security and the reproduction of existing policies.

Third, positioning Colombia as a security exporter offers multiple benefits from a U.S. standpoint that need to be examined further. In addition to reducing the fiscal burden of large sums of military and socioeconomic aid, many U.S. officials concede that Colombian know-how is "just as good" as that of the United States[50] and it offers the added benefit of reproducing U.S. inspired counternarcotics strategies without this country's direct involvement. In keeping with its current "light footprint doctrine," security partnerships such as the one that Washington has built with Bogotá also lend themselves to greater invisibility and thus, lessened accountability, neither of which seems especially advisable from a public interest perspective.

Finally, in the case of those countries in Latin America and especially, Central America, that receive Colombian security expertise, insufficient scrutiny has been paid to the appropriateness and effectiveness of training provided by that country. Increasing portrayal of countries such as Guatemala and Honduras as having states verging on collapse creates a reality, similar to the one experienced by Colombia before its "metamorphosis," that demands urgent and decisive action such as that which only a "success story" admired throughout the world may be capable of providing.

NOTES

1. Peter DeShazo, Tanya Primiani and Phillip McLean, *Back from the Brink: Evaluating Progress in Colombia, 1999–2007* (Washington, D.C.: CSIS Press, 2007).

2. Cynthia J. Arnson and Arlene B. Tickner, "Colombia and the United States. Strategic Partners or Uncertain Allies?" in *Contemporary U.S.-Latin American Relations. Cooperation or Conflict in the 21st Century?,* eds. Jorge I. Domínguez and Rafael Fernández de Castro (New York: Routledge, 2010) 164–196.

3. Arlene B. Tickner, "Intervención por invitación: claves de la política exterior colombiana y de sus debilidades principales," *Colombia Internacional*, Vol. 65 (2007): 90–111.

4. Juan Gabriel Tokatlian, "La construcción de un 'Estado fallido' en la política mundial: el caso de las relaciones entre Estados Unidos y Colombia," *Análisis Político*, Vol. 64 (2008) 97.

5. Ministerio de Defensa de Colombia, Memorias al Congreso (Bogotá: Ministerio de Defensa) 124–125.

6. For an interesting critique, see Adam Isacson, "Colombia: Don't Call it a Model" (Washington, D.C.:Washington Office on Latin America, 2010).

7. These scandals, which erupted between 2006 and 2008, entailed revelations of links between members of the political elite and paramilitaries (*parapolítica*), illegal surveillance by state authorities (*chuzadas*) and extrajudicial killings of male civil-

ians committed by the Colombian army and presented as guerrillas killed in combat (*falsos positivos*).

8. Nicholas Onuf, "Constuctivism: A User's Manual." *International Relations in a Constructed World*, eds., Vendulka Kubálková, Nicholas Onuf and Paul Kowert (Armonk, New York: M.E. Sharpe, 1998) 59.

9. Roxanne Lynn Doty, "Foreign Policy as a Social Construction: A Post-Positivist Analysis of U.S. Counterinsurgency Policy in the Philippines," *International Studies Quarterly*, Vol. 37, No. 3 (1993) 298.

10. David Campbell, *Writing Security. United States Foreign Policy and the Politics of Identity* (Minneapolis: University of Minnesota Press, 1998) 8–10.

11. Roxanne Lynn Doty, "Foreign Policy as a Social Construction."

12. Roxanne Lynn Doty, "Foreign Policy as a Social Construction," 298.

13. Roxanne Lynn Doty, "Foreign Policy as a Social Construction," 306.

14. Roxanne Lynn Doty, "Foreign Policy as a Social Construction," 312.

15. See, for example, Andreas E. Feldmann, "Measuring the Colombian 'Success Story,'" *Revista de Ciencia Política*, Vol. 32, No. 3 (2012) 739–752; Mónica Pachón, "Colombia 2008: Éxitos, peligros y desaciertos de la política de Seguridad Democrática de la Administración Uribe," *Revista de Ciencia Política*, Vol. 29, No. 2 (2009) 327–353; Francis Fukuyama and Seth Colby, "Half a Miracle," *Foreign Policy*, (April 25, 2011) http://www.foreignpolicy.com/articles/2011/04/25/half_a_miracle; Alfredo Rangel, "*La sostenibilidad de la Seguridad Democrática*," (Fundación Seguridad y Democracia: Bogotá, 2005); García Villegas, Mauricio and José Rafael Espinosa (2012), *La debilidad institucional de los municipios en Colombia*, Bogotá: Friedrich Ebert Stiftung (FESCOL), http://library.fes.de/pdf-files/bueros/kolumbien/09888.pdf.

16. Ministerio de Defensa de Colombia, "*Logros de la Política Integral de Seguridad y Defensa para la Prosperidad, PISDP*," Dirección de Estudios Estratégicos (Bogotá, Ministerio de Defensa Nacional, 2013); Barómetro de las Américas, "*Cultura Política de la Democracia en Colombia y las Américas, 2012: Hacia la igualdad de oportunidades*," eds. Juan Carlos Rodriguez Raga and Mitchell A. Seligson, http://www.vanderbilt.edu/lapop/colombia.php.

17. CEPAL, "El *Estado bajo escrutinio: opinión pública, estatalidad y desempeño gubernamental en América Latina*," eds. Carlos Sojo, Juan Carlos Feres and Pablo Villatoro (Santiago: Naciones Unidas, 2011) http://www.eclac.cl/publicaciones/xml/2/45472/LCR2174e.pdf.

18. FESCOL, "Proyecto instituciones ad hoc para municipios en Colombia: la debilidad institucional de los municipios en Colombia."

19. Centro Nacional de Memoria Histórica, ¡*BASTA YA*! Colombia: Memorias de guerra y dignidad (2013) http://www.centrodememoriahistorica.gov.co/micrositios/informeGeneral/descargas.html; Annual report of the United Nations High Commissioner for Human Rights, "Report of the United Nations High Commissioner for Human Rights on the Situation of Human Rights in Colombia" (2012) http://www.hchr.org.co/documentoseinformes/informes/altocomisionado/informe2012en.pdf.

20. "Palabras del Presidente Juan Manuel Santos en el foro Invertir en Colombia," en *El País*, (Presidencia de la República, abril 18, 2012).

21. Colombia es el país más exitoso en la lucha contra el narcotráfico, (Presidencia de la República December 6, 2012), http://wsp.presidencia.gov.co/Prensa/2012/Diciembre/Paginas/20121206_01.aspx.

22. Hillary Clinton, "U.S., Colombia Hold High-Level Partnership Dialogue," second U.S.-Colombian High-Level Partnership Dialogue, (Washington, D.C. May 31, 2011) http://www.state.gov/s/d/former/steinberg/remarks/2010/169313.htm, accessed 2013.

23. "Palabras del Presidente Juan Manuel Santos en la presentación de la segunda edición del libro 100 colombianos," (Presidencia de la República January 31, 2014), http://wsp.presidencia.gov.co/Prensa/2014/Enero/Paginas/20140131_03-Palabras-del-Presidente-Juan-Manuel-Santos-en-la-presentacion-de-la-segunda-edicion-del-libro-100Colombianos.aspx, accessed 2013.

24. Financial Times, "*The New Colombia 2013*" (June 3, 2013), http://www.ft.com/intl/reports/new-colombia-2013.

25. "Palabras del Presidente Juan Manuel Santos en la Conferencia Nacional de Derechos Humanos y Derecho Internacional Humanitario," (Presidencia de la República December 13, 2012), http://wsp.presidencia.gov.co/Prensa/2012/Diciembre/Paginas/20121213_03.aspx.

26. "Palabras del Presidente Juan Manuel Santos en el aniversario número 91 de la Fuerza Aérea Colombiana," (Presidencia de la República November 8, 2010), http://wsp.presidencia.gov.co/Mensajes/Paginas/DerechosHumanos.aspx, accessed 2013.

27. "Palabras del Presidente Juan Manuel Santos durante el lanzamiento del Plan Integral de Seguridad para el departamento de Bolívar," (Presidencia de la República January 31, 2013), http://wsp.presidencia.gov.co/Prensa/2013/Enero/Paginas/20130131_07.aspx, accessed 2013.

28. "Palabras del Presidente Juan Manuel Santos sobre el ingreso de Colombia a la OCDE," (Presidencia de la República May 30, 2013), http://wsp.presidencia.gov.co/Prensa/2013/Mayo/Paginas/20130530_03.aspx.

29. John Kerry, "Remarks with Colombian Foreign Minister Maria Angela Holguin," (Bogotá, Colombia August 12, 2013), http://www.state.gov/secretary/remarks/2013/08/213076.htm.

30. Hillary Clinton, "U.S., Colombia Hold High-Level Partnership Dialogue."

31. David Petraeus and Michael O'Hanlon, "The Success Story Next Door," *Político* (September 24, 2013), http://www.politico.com/story/2013/09/general-david-petraeus-michael-ohanlon-the-success-story-next-door-97316.html.

32. See, for example, Douglas Bellet, "*Saving Afghanistan from Insurgency and a Narco-Economy: Can Lessons Learned in Colombia Chart a Course for a Fledgling State?*" (Newport: Naval War College, 2008); Alan Bourque, "*Changing U.S. Strategy in South America: Adjusting and Exporting Plan Colombia*" (Pennsylvania: U.S Army War College, 2004); Michael Kenney, "From Pablo to Osama: Counter-Terrorism Lessons from the War on Drugs," *Survival,* 45, No 3. (2003) http://faculty.maxwell.syr.edu/rdenever/PPA-730-27/Kenney.pdf, accessed 2013.

33. James B. Steinberg, "Remarks to the Center for Strategic and International Studies Colombia Conference" (Washington, DC, June 13, 2011), http://www.state.gov/s/d/former/steinberg/remarks/2011/169295.htm, accessed 2013.

34. Adam Isacson, Abigail Poe, Lisa Haugaard and George Withers, *Time to Listen: Trends in U.S. Security Assistance to Latin America and the Caribbean*, (WOLA: Washington, D.C., 2013) http://www.wola.org/sites/default/files/downloadable/Regional%20Security/Time%20to%20Listen/Time%20to%20Listen.pdf, accessed 2013.

35. Hillary Clinton, "Secretary Clinton's remarks at the Center for Strategic and International Studies (CSIS) on Latin America Policy," (Washington, D.C. May 18, 2011), http://iipdigital.usembassy.gov/st/english/texttrans/2011/03/20110318175407su0.0452038.html#axzz2svttLnXb.

36. John Kerry, "US Secretary of State Kerry Ends Controversial Latin American Foreign Policy," speech given at the OAS (November 19, 2013), http://www.ticotimes.net/2013/11/19/us-secretary-of-state-kerry-ends-controversial-latin-american-foreign-policy.

37. Wendy Sherman, "U.S. Policy and Engagement in the Americas," speech given at the Council of the Americas and the Center for Strategic and International Studies (CSIS), (Washington, D.C. February 28, 2012), http://www.state.gov/p/us/rm/2012/184853.htm, accessed 2013.

38. Roberta Jacobson, "Review of Vice President Biden's travel to Latin America and preview of Secretary Kerry's participation in the General Assembly of the Organization of American States," (Washington Foreign Press Center, Washington, D.C. June 3, 2013), http://fpc.state.gov/210194.htm, accessed 2013.

39. Adam Isacson, Abigail Poe, Lisa Haugaard and George Withers, *Time to Listen: Trends in U.S. Security Assistance to Latin America and the Caribbean*, (WOLA: Washington, D.C.: 2013), http://www.wola.org/sites/default/files/downloadable/Regional%20Security/Time%20to%20Listen/Time%20to%20Listen.pdf, accessed 2013.

40. PNUD, "*Seguridad Ciudadana con Rostro Humano: Diagnósticos y Propuestas para América Latina,*" Informe Regional de Desarrollo Humano 2013–2014, (New York: United Nations Development Programme, 2013).

41. PNUD, "*Seguridad Ciudadana con Rostro Humano: Diagnósticos y Propuestas para América Latina,*"

42. Security "speech acts" consist of the identification in public discourse of specific problems as "security" issues that constitute existential threats requiring emergency action; and acceptance by widespread audiences. See Barry Buzan, Ole Wæver and Jaap de Wilde, *Security. A New Framework for Analysis* (Boulder: Lynne Rienner Publishers, 1998).

43. Hasan Tuluy, Vice-president for Latin America and the Caribbean, World Bank, "En busca de soluciones para la seguridad ciudadana en América Latina y el Caribe," speech delivered at the International Conference-Workshop Soluciones Integrales para la Prevención del Delito y la Violencia, (Cali, Colombia June 26, 2013), http://www.bancomundial.org/es/news/speech/2013/06/26/hasan-tuluy-cali-inseguridad.

44. PNUD, "*Seguridad Ciudadana con Rostro Humano: Diagnósticos y Propuestas para América Latina.*"

45. Hasan Tuluy, "En busca de soluciones para la seguridad ciudadana en América Latina y el Caribe"; Discurso del Presidente Mauricio Funes en el Foro: Inseguridad

ciudadana en América Latina, Inter-American Development Bank, (Washington, D.C. April 19, 2013), http://www.presidencia.gob.sv/index.php/novedades/discursos/discursos/item/3515-foro-inseguridad-ciudadana-en-américa-latina.html.

46. Mauricio Funes, "Foro: Inseguridad Ciudadana en América Latina; Palabras del Secretario General de la OEA," Jose Miguel Insulza, en la Conmemoración del X Aniversario de la Declaración de Seguridad en las Américas, Organización de Estados Americanos, (Washington, D.C. October 28, 2013), http://www.oas.org/es/acerca/discurso_secretario_general.asp?sCodigo=13-0067, accessed 2013.

47. Hasan Tuluy, "En busca de soluciones para la seguridad ciudadana en América Latina y el Caribe."

48. The passages were obtained primarily on the following websites: Presidencia de la República de Colombia (http://wsp.presidencia.gov.co/Discursos/2014/Paginas/Febrero.aspx), Ministerio de Relaciones Exteriores de Colombia (http://www.cancilleria.gov.co/newsroom/speeches) and U.S. Department of State (http://www.state.gov/r/pa/ei/speeches/index.htm). Additionally, several direct quotes derive from: Andrés Schipiani, "Colombian Security Industry Exports its Expertise," (The Financial Times, June 3, 2013), http://im.ft-static.com/content/images/d2ec5854-cd1e-11e2-9efe-00144feab7de.pdf, accessed 2013; Tom Ricks,"Colombia´s Neglected Success Story," (Foreign Policy, July 29, 2010), http://ricks.foreignpolicy.com/posts/2010/07/29/colombias_neglected_success_story; and Michael E. O'Hanlon and David Petraeus, "The Success Story in Colombia," Research Brookings Institution (September 24, 2013), http://www.brookings.edu/research/opinions/2013/09/24-colombia-success-ohanlon-petraeus.

49. Ministerio de Defensa de Colombia, Memorias al Congreso 2012–2013 (Bogotá: Ministerio de Defensa, 2013).

50. Michael E. O'Hanlon and David Petraeus, "The Success Story in Colombia."

Section Five

CRITICAL ISSUES

Chapter Twelve

Human Rights Abuses in Colombia

From Uribe to Santos

Lisa Haugaard

As President Álvaro Uribe took power, he pledged to carry out a doctrine he called "democratic security." In his inaugural speech, it sounded promising: "Our concept of Democratic Security requires us to seek the effective protection of all citizens independent of their political creed or level of wealth."[1] He was motivated by "the sorrow of our nation's mothers, of orphans and the displaced people, in their name I will search my soul each morning so that the actions of authority that are taken have the purest intentions and the noblest implementation. I will enthusiastically support the nation's Armed Forces, and encourage millions of citizens to assist them. This increases our obligation to human rights, the respect of which is the only way to achieve security."[2] He cast the government's war against the guerrillas squarely as a war against terrorism; "[i]f a democratic state is effective in the guarantees it offers . . . the violence against it is terrorism. We don't accept violence to fight the government, nor to defend it."[3] However, as President Uribe's two terms in office unfolded, it became clear that he was less sympathetic to the victims of paramilitary and military violence than to the victims of the guerrillas, and that his concept of "democratic security" stressed security at the expense of democracy and human rights.

President Uribe immediately expanded and intensified the war against the guerrillas. Shortly after taking office, he issued a series of decrees granting special powers to the military and designating areas of the country as special consolidation zones. In these zones, security forces could restrict circulation, establish curfews and carry out warrantless searches, although some of these powers were subsequently limited by Colombia's Constitutional Court. Uribe called for citizens to become involved in the war effort, including as paid informants and as "peasant soldiers," local farmers who received training and worked part-time for the army. During this period, mass detentions were carried out in some areas of the country.[4] Uribe's escalated war against the guerrillas was popular with many Colombian citizens, who were fed up with the brutal actions of the guerrillas, especially their cruel practice of kidnapping for profit, holding victims hostage for years in inhumane conditions, as well as their use of land mines, reliance on child soldiers and other severe violations of international humanitarian law.

But Colombia's human rights groups and some journalists documented abuses by government forces and the close relationship between paramilitary forces and members of the army. They also criticized some of the Uribe administration's actions as authoritarian.[5] President Uribe responded by accusing, both in a general way and by name, human rights organizations, human rights defenders and journalists, calling them terrorists. The human rights defenders, and journalists he named claimed that these public, often televised accusations by the president of the country led to threats and attacks against them. Human rights groups also claimed that some human rights defenders were falsely accused, investigated and prosecuted on terrorism and other charges. Human Rights First documented thirty-two cases of "unfounded prosecutions" of human rights defenders during the Uribe administration.[6]

Despite the tense relationship between President Uribe and the nation's major human rights groups, the Uribe administration continued a program, started under President Andrés Pastrana (1998–2002) with U.S. funding, of providing protection to trade unionists, human rights defenders and journalists. This program offered bodyguards, bulletproof vests, metal detectors for offices, and other "hard" measures to protect those at risk. Human rights defenders appreciated this program, but stressed that government rhetoric in support of the legitimacy of their work and effective investigations of the attacks against them were even more essential.

PARAMILITARY VIOLENCE AND PARAMILITARY DEMOBILIZATION

During Uribe's first several years in office, collusion between members of the security forces and paramilitary forces was perhaps the most serious and widespread human rights violation, though this certainly continued a practice that had begun years before and had escalated during the term of his predecessor, President Andrés Pastrana. From 2002 to 2004, paramilitary groups carried out attacks against the civilian population, including massacres and targeted killings. The UN High Commissioner for Human Rights' office in Colombia in its 2004 report noted that it had received reports of

> paramilitary operations with inexcusable knowledge of the security forces, undue contacts between civil authorities and paramilitary commanders, statements made by members of the military forces concerning the imminent arrival of paramilitary groups, inaction on the part of the security forces in spite of the existence of fixed paramilitary bases close to military installations, and even the alleged provision of information to paramilitary groups by members of the police regarding possible targets. The office in Colombia was able to observe and continued to receive complaints concerning the positioning and consolidation of paramilitary groups in areas where the security forces had previously carried out counter-rebel operations, such as, for example, the area of Comuna 13 in Medellín or municipalities in eastern Antioquia.[7]

Uribe's efforts to demobilize paramilitary forces in 2005 had an important positive human rights impact, as the removal of some of the paramilitary leaders and troops from the battlefield diminished the number of grave abuses attributed to paramilitary forces, particularly massacres. This action also reinforced the idea that the military, rather than the illegal paramilitary forces, had responsibility to establish security.

However, a more thorough dismantlement would have been possible and preferable. Human rights groups harshly critiqued the paramilitary demobilization as a sweetheart deal between two forces that were never enemies. Noted human rights groups such as the Colombian Commission of Jurists and Human Rights Watch pointed out that the failure to vigorously interrogate and investigate demobilizing paramilitaries left paramilitary structures intact, notably those who financed and profited from paramilitary violence.[8] They observed that the worst abusers who confessed their crimes faced short prison terms of five to eight years, and that almost no land and fortunes were turned over by those who confessed.[9] The Justice and Peace unit of the Attorney General's office set up to prosecute the most serious paramilitary abusers has produced only fourteen convictions after eight years of operation.[10] The decision of Uribe in 2008 to extradite fourteen top paramilitary leaders to the United States after they had begun to reveal information about their allies in their *versiones libres* or public confessions put a sudden and near total stop to the limited truth telling that this unusual peace process provided. It also virtually ended access to remedies for some Colombian victims.[11] Mid-range paramilitary leadership are now beginning to leave jail cells from which some of them are believed to have continued to conduct operations; it remains to be seen if this will have an impact on levels of organized crime and human rights abuses in the areas to which they return.

A persistent problem has been that the Uribe administration and, to a degree, the subsequent Santos administration have insisted upon perceiving and treating the undemobilized and regrouped paramilitary bands that remained active as mere criminal bands, or "Bacrim." Human rights organizations have pointed out how these groups continued to use some of the same modus operandi, targeting human rights defenders, community leaders, unionists, and land rights activists. Over large sections of the countryside and some urban areas, paramilitary successor groups such as the Aguilas Negras, Urabeños and Rastrojos impose their will on communities, establishing curfews, controlling the drug trade, and threatening and murdering residents.

THE FALSE POSITIVES

The most serious human rights abuses committed under President Uribe's watch were the systematic, widespread extrajudicial executions of civilians by the armed forces known as "false positives." In 2004 and 2005, Colombian human rights groups began to report that civilians were being killed by soldiers, dressed in fatigues and presented as guerrillas killed in combat. Observing these cases appearing in diverse parts of the country, they began to carefully document them and pool their information. In 2007, they invited a group of international legal and human rights experts to participate in an international verification mission on extrajudicial executions. This mission[12] listened to witnesses, family members, and lawyers for 130 cases of extrajudicial executions in seven regions of the country. The mission heard remarkable similarities about how these abuses were taking place. In 2008, a group of determined mothers from the poor neighborhood of Soacha, outside Bogotá, came together to search for their disappeared sons. That same year, their efforts, along with a visit by the UN Special Rapporteur on Extrajudicial Executions and journalistic exposés by Colombian press, further revealed the extent of the problem. Not only were soldiers killing young men and dressing them up as guerrillas, they were actually purchasing young men, lured by promises of day jobs, from criminal recruiters, taking them to other parts of the country, and killing them in simulated battles. A national system of incentives for a body count, in which soldiers and officials received bounties and days off, was driving these horrific abuses.

The scope of these crimes is immense, and the Attorney General's office has been cited as investigating more than 3,000 civilians allegedly murdered by soldiers, most between 2004 and 2008. The 2012 report by the United Nations High Commissioner for Human Rights sets the number higher, asserting that the Attorney General's office has received complaints involving 4,716 victims of homicide presumably perpetrated by members of the security forces. The coalition of human rights groups in Colombia known as the *Coordinación Colombia Europa Estados Unidos* (CCEEUU) has documented 3,512 extrajudicial executions between 2002 and 2010 committed in 31 out of 32 provinces. Of the 80 percent of these cases for which a presumed perpetrator could be identified, 89.2 percent involved members of the armed forces, 8.6 percent the police, and the remainder were from the air force, navy and the prison system. At least 21 territorial brigades and 19 mobile brigades were identified as perpetrators. More than 44 percent of extrajudicial executions were in the zones where the First and Seventh divisions of the army operated.[13]

Although President Uribe publicly denied the scope of the abuses, his administration began in 2007 and 2008 to respond to pressure by the United Nations, Colombian human rights organizations, the International Verification Mission and the U.S. Embassy. While not establishing criminal or disciplinary responsibilities, the government dismissed twenty-seven high-ranking officials over the widening scandal. Defense Minister Juan Manuel Santos issued directives to the armed forces that forbade "homicides of protected persons," and, importantly, signed an agreement with the Attorney General's office that established that in cases of suspected extrajudicial executions, the civilian Attorney General's office, rather than the military justice system, would conduct the first examination of the crime scene. Hundreds of cases of alleged extrajudicial executions were shifted from the military to civilian justice system. These reforms, and no doubt the extensive media exposure that made replicating these specific abuses more risky, had an impact. By 2009, the number of extrajudicial executions reported began to decrease dramatically. However, justice for these enormous, institutionalized abuses remained slow and partial.

THE DAS SCANDAL

In February 2009, Colombia's leading news magazine, *Semana,* uncovered another serious scandal. The Department of Administrative Security (DAS), the intelligence agency directly under the presidency, was conducting widespread illegal surveillance of national and international human rights organizations and activists, journalists, judges, and members of opposition parties.[14] Not only was this intelligence agency conducting illegal surveillance, it was seeking to undermine opposition activists and even carrying out grave human rights crimes. Files released by the Attorney General's office included cover pages for a variety of DAS operations describing their goals as "generating controversy regarding NGOs," "generating division within opposition movements," "promoting actions to benefit the government in the 2006 elections," and "neutralizing influence in the Inter-American Commission on Human Rights."[15]

One of the most shocking elements involved sustained surveillance of the Supreme Court, which appeared linked both to the Supreme Court's deliberations regarding a proposed third term for President Uribe and to the "parapolitics" investigations by the Supreme Court into links between politicians and paramilitary forces.[16] One-quarter of the Colombian Congress as of November 2009 was under investigation, on trial or sentenced for collusion with paramilitary forces; of those, the vast majority were from the government's coalition.[17] Routine spying on human rights groups included sensitive information on preparation of court cases that involved government agents as defendants. Without noting the irony, DAS agents conducted obsessive surveillance of the book launches of *The Authoritarian Spell,* a critique by Colombian human rights groups of the Uribe administration's authoritarian tendencies. Protestant and Catholic church leaders involved in peacebuilding activities were followed. The DAS files revealed that DAS agents were also responsible for death threats against human rights activists and their children. And it went even farther, as the top DAS official Jorge Noguera was convicted in 2011 for handing over names of trade unionists and activists to paramilitary forces; some of these, including educator Alfredo Correa de Andreis, were subsequently killed. In July 2012, DAS official José Miguel Narvaez was indicted for his alleged role in planning the murder of journalist and humorist Jaime Garzón.[18] The Attorney General's investigation, according to Semana's coverage, indicated that high-ranking officials in the Presidential Palace were involved in ordering illegal wiretaps, although those investigations have never been concluded.[19]

Out of power, ex-President Uribe's star power has dimmed at least temporarily. Colombian media coverage of the former president has focused on his efforts to pick a fight via Twitter with his former defense minister, in adamant opposition to an advancing peace process. However, he retains important support and could return to political office. In addition, his human rights record is now being examined by the International Criminal Court (ICC) prosecutor's office, which has expressed interest in examining the pattern of extrajudicial executions in Colombia, as "there is sufficient reason to believe that [these acts] were committed due to a policy adopted at least at the level of certain brigades of the armed forces which constitutes a policy by a state or organization to commit such crimes." The ICC continues to analyze information "to clarify if this policy was created at higher levels of the state apparatus."[20] While Colombia's adherence to the Rome Treaty establishing the ICC only takes effect in January 2009, after the vast majority of the extrajudicial executions took place, the government's action or inaction to address and punish these abuses can be examined by the ICC.

JUAN MANUEL SANTOS COMES TO OFFICE: MORE RESPECT FOR HUMAN RIGHTS, BUT *IMPUNITY PERSISTS*

President Juan Manuel Santos explicitly sought to improve relations with Colombia's human rights community and repair Colombia's human rights image abroad as he assumed power. He pledged to "*desarmar la palabra,*" "unarm words," or deescalate the war of words between the Colombian government and human rights groups. His administration's top officials have not only generally refrained from attacking human rights groups, but have often spoken affirmatively about the role of human rights organizations in a democratic society. As President Uribe's denunciations of human rights activists and journalists had placed those individuals and groups at greater danger, this change in treatment was seen as significant both by activists and journalists themselves and by members of the international community.

It, however, was not a complete shift; for example, in 2011–12, government officials publicly lashed out at a community of displaced persons and a major human rights group with the accusation that they were profiting by creating "false victims," but after these organizations effectively defended themselves, the government appeared to retreat from this line of attack.

The Santos administration opened national and regional "Guarantee Roundtables" with human rights defenders throughout the country. These roundtables were intended to discuss the measures needed to create a climate in which human rights defenders—in the broad UN definition, ranging from human rights lawyers to national and local Afro-Colombian, indigenous, and women's leaders; IDP leaders, unionists, and community leaders—could carry out their jobs. Human rights organizations welcomed the discussion.

The Santos administration put in place some legislative or administrative changes intended to improve the framework for addressing the risks defenders face. The Attorney General issued a directive aimed at preventing specious cases from being filed against human rights defenders, and another one aimed at ensuring that attacks against defenders were adequately investigated. President Santos also disbanded the disgraced DAS intelligence agency, although disturbingly, many DAS agents were reassigned to other sensitive jobs, including in the Attorney General's office and the protection agency.[21] In the National Guarantee Roundtables, agreements were reached regarding the restructuring of the protection program. However, human rights groups asserted that not all their concerns were addressed and remained dissatisfied with the results.

HUMAN RIGHTS DEFENDERS STILL IN PERIL

This dissatisfaction stemmed primarily from the threats and attacks that human rights defenders continued to face. As *Somos Defensores*, an organization set up to collect data on attacks against defenders and conduct advocacy for their protection, noted, "While in Bogotá laws and regulations were discussed and put in place, the regions bleed because of assassinations, threats, arbitrary detentions, attacks and disappearances against defenders."[22] In both 2011 and 2012, attacks and threats against human rights defenders actually increased, according to the *Somos Defensores* database. In 2011, attacks against human rights defenders increased 36 percent compared to 2010, with a total of 239 defenders were attacked in 2011, compared to 174 in 2010. Fifty-nine percent of the attacks were threats, 20 percent assassinations, 10 percent arbitrary detentions, 7 percent physical attacks, 3 percent forced disappearances, and 1 percent other kinds of attacks, including arbitrary use of the legal system to harass defenders. There were 49 assassinations of defenders in 2011, compared to 32 in 2010. According to the campaign, "the threat of paramilitary groups for human rights defenders and social leaders increased significantly in 2011."[23] Paramilitary groups were the assumed perpetrators in 50 percent of the cases (all cases of attacks, including murders, threats, arbitrary detentions, etc.). State agents (police, army, SIJIN, prosecutors, etc.) were believed to be responsible for 17 percent of the cases; guerrillas were the assumed perpetrators in 4 percent of the cases; and 29 percent remained unknown.

In 2012, 357 men and women in Colombia were attacked for their work as human rights defenders, according to *Somos Defensores*, the highest number of aggressions against defenders registered by the database in the last ten years, and a 49 percent increase since 2011.[24] Sixty-nine defenders were assassinated, a jump from 49 assassinations in 2011. The sixty-nine defenders who lost their lives included indigenous leaders, people involved in organizing over mining companies, hip-hop musicians who organized against violence, youth leaders, community organizers, heads of victims' associations, land rights crusaders, union organizers, Afro-Colombian leaders, the organizer of a women's handicraft cooperative, and an LGBT defender. Of the sixty-nine murders, 9 were believed to have been committed by paramilitaries, 11 by the FARC guerrillas (a large increase over the previous year), 1 by the armed forces, and the vast majority remained unknown.

To a degree, these increased numbers may reflect the human rights community's greater ability to collect data as groups consolidated a centralized data collection system for abuses against defenders, as well as human rights defenders' greater willingness to report abuses. But there is no question but that human rights defenders remained in danger.

Somos Defensores placed the blame for this continued violence on the justice system's failure to investigate, prosecute and punish crimes against defenders. Even killings of defenders routinely went unpunished, and threats against defenders were almost never successfully investigated. For example, the State Department notes that the Attorney General's office was investigating forty-two cases of threats against human rights defenders during 2012, not one of which had yet resulted in a conviction by the year's end.

An International Verification Mission on Human Rights Defenders in November-December 2011 noted that the "vast majority of attacks against human rights defenders, including such serious crimes as murders and forced disappearances, remain unpunished.[25] The mission was informed of cases where the complainants even identified those who were threatening them by name, but investigations were not pursued. The mission asserted, "We have only learned of a few cases where the parties responsible for the attacks have been brought to justice." In particular, the mission noted that threats were almost never investigated, and break-ins into the offices of human rights defenders, which occur on a regular basis, are often assumed to be common crime. The verification mission "found that in many cases the attacks against human rights defenders are treated as isolated cases and classified as common crimes unrelated to their work in defense of human rights or their membership in a threatened community or group."[26]

Moreover, the revamped protection system continued to face bureaucratic problems, including delays in providing protection to people deemed at risk; budget cuts to some items, including fuel allocations for cars, which left some defenders exposed. A number of defenders were cut from the program, as their status was reevaluated at low-risk. In particular, the protection program has not yet grappled successfully with the challenges of providing protection to rural land rights' leaders and communities. A set of protection measures that might work well for an urban human rights lawyer does not translate into effective protection for a community of internally displaced persons returning to their lands in an area where those who caused the displacement still exercise considerable control.[27]

THE VICTIMS' LAW: A THING OF BEAUTY, MANY QUESTIONS ON IMPLEMENTATION

The Santos administration championed and shepherded through the Colombian Congress landmark legislation, the Victims and Land Restitution Law, which was signed into law on June 10, 2011. This remarkable legislation establishes the right of potentially hundreds of thousands of victims to financial reparations as well as land restitution or compensation. Notably, the law recognizes that victims not only of paramilitary and guerrilla forces, but also of the government's own armed forces, are entitled to reparations. The law, by marking a real departure from the previous administration and addressing the thorny subject of land rights, may have helped pave the way to negotiations with the guerrillas.

One contentious issue is that the law does not cover, or is not being interpreted to cover, victims of violence by paramilitary successor groups or Bacrim. This is compounded by the fact that many internally displaced persons (IDPs) also have been denied the government assistance provided to IDPs if they reported that they were displaced by the Bacrim. The Colombia representative for the International Committee of the Red Cross, Jordi Raich, in April 2012 decried the lack of attention to victims of the Bacrim. "We believe that victims of the armed conflict and of other situations of violence alike should receive support and reparation without discrimination. . . . The suffering of people affected by displacement, murder and disappearance is the same, regardless of the underlying cause. That's why it makes no sense to draw a distinction between the victims."[28]

Yet the major concern over the law is not its provisions—it is widely praised—but the difficulty in implementing it. At least fifty-six land rights leaders have been killed since 2002, several since the passage of the Victims' Law.[29] The killing of Manuel Ruiz and his fifteen-year-old son on March 23, 2012, and of Afro-Colombian leader Miller Angulo on December 1, 2012, for example, bring into question the government's willingness and capacity to protect returned and returning communities and land rights activists.[30] Moreover, the Victims' Law was barely beginning to be implemented as of mid-2013, with just several dozen judgments issued by special land tribunals. A field mission by the author and Lutheran World Relief to investigate application of the law in June 2012 on the northern Caribbean Coast showed that even municipal authorities enthusiastic about applying the law were at that time poorly prepared and lacked resources to implement it.[31] Our subsequent visit in June 2013 showed that a small number of individuals and communities were beginning to receive titles, but that the government lacked realistic plans to protect communities and families returning to areas where they remained at great risk. Nonetheless, if the government can greatly increase its attention to protection of land rights activists and communities, there is hope that even partial implementation of this ambitious law can have positive results.

The Santos administration's inability to protect activists and communities also has to be seen within the context of the central government's historical weakness in exercising power in many areas of the countryside. This is not just a question of controlling illegal armed groups but also curbing the power of rural elites that use such groups to expand access to land and resources.

BACKSLIDING ON IMPUNITY

In great contrast to President Santos's embrace of victims' reparations and outreach to human rights defenders were his efforts to limit civilian jurisdiction of military abuses. In 2012, President Santos championed a constitutional reform that, in its initial version, would have shifted many human rights crimes committed by members of the military from civilian to military courts. Under pressure from the United Nations and the U.S. Embassy, the reform was modified to exclude a list of seven crimes: crimes against humanity, genocide, forced disappearances, extrajudicial executions, sexual violence, torture, and forced displacement. However, human rights organizations remain concerned that cases involving two of these crimes, "extrajudicial executions" and "sexual violence," if committed prior to the law's implementing legislation, could be sent to military courts, as these specific terms were not previously codified as crimes in Colombian law. Moreover, other serious human rights violations such as arbitrary detentions and cruel, inhuman, or degrading treatment would be tried in military courts. Human rights organizations continue to express concern that many of the "false positive" cases, extrajudicial killings of civilians presented as combat kills, could be transferred from civilian to military courts. This is particularly concerning given that as of November 2012, the Attorney General's office reported that it had obtained convictions in only 192 cases of extrajudicial executions involving 589 military personnel and 13 members of the police since 2000, out of 1,726 cases of extrajudicial executions that it was pursuing.[32] Few high-ranking officials have yet been convicted.

The law establishes that the military justice system, rather than the civilian Attorney General's office, will now carry out preliminary investigations of alleged violations committed during military operations, reversing the important advance instituted by then-Defense Minister Santos. When doubts about jurisdiction arise, a mixed commission with military and civilian participation will determine jurisdiction, rather than a civilian judicial body. Finally, the law ensures that military members, including those convicted of serious crimes, serve their time in special "reclusion centers" rather than regular jails. Some analysts suggest that Santos may have struck a bargain with members of the military to limit judicial action against them in exchange for their support for the peace process with the FARC guerrillas that Santos launched in August 2012.[33] However, at the time of writing this reform is before Colombia's constitutional court, and the final decision is still pending on expansion of military jurisdiction.

The Santos administration is engaged in negotiations with the FARC guerrillas that could help bring an end to a fifty-year guerrilla war. The outcome regarding mechanisms for truth and justice has yet to be determined. Certainly, one drawback is that victims of violence and civil society sectors affected by the war have little space officially to participate in these negotiations. Moreover, as negotiations proceed the Colombian military is intensely waging war, including via aerial bombardments and other harsh tactics that are affecting the civilian population, particularly indigenous communities.

But if an agreement is reached and the FARC successfully demobilizes, the potential impact should improve respect for human rights in Colombia. It will do so by at least partially removing another brutal armed actor from the battlefield, and perhaps with time, by reducing the rationales available for government forces and members of Colombian society to tolerate and excuse human rights abuses committed by or in the name of the government.

THE UNITED STATES AND HUMAN RIGHTS UNDER URIBE AND SANTOS

The U.S. and Colombian governments maintain that Plan Colombia, launched in 2000, has led to an improvement in human rights and a reduction in violence. They point to the official homicide rate, which diminished from a rate of 70.2 per 100,000 inhabitants in 2002 to a rate of 31.4 per 100,000 in 2011.[34] This figure mixes common crime with conflict-related violence. The demobilization of some of the paramilitary forces and military successes in limiting guerrilla action contributed, but other factors that may contribute are specific anti-crime policies in large cities such as Medellín and Bogotá and domination of trafficking by one criminal band, temporarily reducing violence. Certainly, it is positive that the paramilitary forces' umbrella organization disbanded, and peace with at least the FARC guerrillas appears possible.

However, these security gains are still at risk, and respect for human rights remains tenuous. Conflict-related violence is still displacing over two hundred thousand people per year, and international humanitarian law violations by regrouped paramilitaries, guerrillas and members of the armed forces continue to affect communities, with indigenous and Afro-Colombian communities disproportionately experiencing the war's impact.[35]

Moreover, a before-and-after comparison does not begin to reveal the full human rights story. It ignores the horrific scope of the violence that occurred *during* the height of U.S. involvement.[36] From 2000–2004, paramilitary violence, often aided and abetted by members of the official security forces, spiraled upward. Some of the most vicious paramilitary massacres—Chengue, El Salado, Macayepo, and the Naya River massacre—occurred shortly after the United States launched its first billion-dollar aid package. The worst of the false positive scandal occurred at the high-water mark of U.S. assistance and training, from 2004 through 2008, after four and more years of extensive training of all levels of the Colombian armed forces by the U.S. military. The illegal surveillance and criminal activity committed by the DAS occurred after years of U.S. training, aid and equipment to Colombian intelligence operations. Between 2000 and 2011, over 3.3 million people were driven from their homes by violence.[37] Afro-Colombian and indigenous people were particularly affected by displacement and human rights abuses.

U.S. responsibility for abuses can be more directly traced. Military units receiving U.S. aid and training committed numerous extrajudicial executions, although so too did units not receiving aid. A detailed study by Fellowship of Reconciliation and U.S. Office on Colombia reveals that geographic areas where brigades received substantial U.S. aid and training coincided with areas that saw high levels of extrajudicial executions.[38] The United States provided wiretapping equipment to the DAS; while U.S. Ambassador William Brownfield claimed that U.S. equipment was not used in illegal surveillance, it is difficult to see how that could be determined.[39] Top agency officials were indicted for being involved in the illegal activities and the Attorney General's investigation showed that units conducting illegal surveillance relied on common interception rooms shared by DAS agents. Further information about the U.S. role in the DAS scandal is classified and thus difficult to evaluate.

The extradition of the top paramilitary leadership to the United States had a negative impact on revelations by paramilitary leadership about the politicians, military officials, and businesses that financed, supported, and collaborated with them. Once in jail in the United States, they had no incentive to name names; U.S. prosecutors struck deals with them based on cooperation in drug trafficking cases, ignoring their roles in massacres, targeted assassinations, torture and other gross human rights violations. Whether this silencing was intended by the U.S. government is another question; the extradition warrants were outstanding, and it appears to have been the Colombian government's decision to suddenly honor them.

U.S. policy toward Colombia is contradictory. U.S. security assistance is accompanied by human rights conditions in the foreign operations appropriations law, at the insistence of members of Congress and human rights organizations concerned since the start of Plan Colombia with the human rights record of the Colombian armed forces. These conditions require the State Department to certify that Colombia is "taking effective measures to investigate and prosecute gross human rights violations in civilian courts."

While the State Department has never certified that Colombia had not met the conditions, even during the height of the false positive scandal, the conditions have forced the State Department to justify to Congress that improvements are taking place in order for military aid to be released. The Senate Foreign Operations Subcommittee of the Appropriations Committee has temporarily frozen up to $110 million in military assistance over issues related to the conditions, particularly regarding extrajudicial executions. The State Department has also been obliged to meet with U.S. and Colombian human rights groups on a regular basis to assess progress on meeting the conditions. A separate law, the Leahy Law, requires the U.S. government to suspend assistance to specific units of a foreign security force that has committed grave human rights abuses without such abuses being investigated and prosecuted. A number of units have been barred from receiving assistance on that basis.

The net impact of the conditions has been that the State Department and U.S. Embassy has at times strongly raised human rights issues with the Colombian government. This has had concrete results; perhaps most importantly, it helped result in measures to reduce extrajudicial executions and begin to bring some cases to justice. In 2012, the U.S. government consistently raised objections to the Colombian government's efforts to expand military jurisdiction, and this pressure contributed to the Santos administration's modifications to the law to exclude more human rights crimes from military jurisdiction. None of these advances would have been possible without persistent efforts by Colombian and U.S. human rights groups to utilize the conditions and the particular commitment of Senator Patrick Leahy, chair of the foreign operations subcommittee.

The decision by then-House Speaker Nancy Pelosi to hold up consideration of the U.S.-Colombia free trade agreement in 2008—largely over concerns about the murder of trade unionists and lack of respect for international labor rights—also had a beneficial impact. Forced to address these issues, Colombian and U.S. government officials worked with trade union input to design a Labor Action Plan that committed the Colombian government to specific steps to protect trade unionists, investigate and prosecute attacks against them, establish a Labor Ministry, expand labor inspectors, end indirect employment practices in port, palm, sugar and other sectors, and carry out other important reforms to protect labor rights.[40] Once the trade agreement was approved by the U.S. Congress, however, the incentives to actually carry out the reforms were lessened. The Colombian government has expanded protection, devoted greater resources to investigations, and stood up to a Labor Ministry. However, trade unionists still face death threats, many unionists, although fewer, are still being assassinated, and many port, palm and sugar workers remain under indirect labor contracts.[41]

Substantial U.S. assistance to judicial institutions, protection programs and USAID's human rights aid program, have also at times had a beneficial impact. These programs also deserve scrutiny, in particular the abundant funding via the Department of Justice for the Attorney General's office. But the protection program saved lives, and the justice strengthening programs provided valuable training to numerous prosecutors. After concerns in 2005 that USAID's human rights program was applying a political litmus test to potential human rights partners, USAID's human rights program established a regular consultation process with Colombian and U.S. human rights groups that increased confidence in the program, one of the most extensive U.S.-funded human rights programs in the world.

However, the United States bears tremendous responsibilities for abuses committed by a military it financed and trained and by an intelligence agency which it supported. This lesson does not appear to have hit home. In his hearing to be confirmed as secretary of state, then-Senator John Kerry, whose Senate Foreign Relations Committee staffers had been fully briefed over several years on the false positive and DAS scandals, offered a glowing assessment of Uribe's tenure, declaring, "One of the great stories of Latin America is Colombia . . . President Uribe stepped up in a critical moment and began the process of rescuing that nation."[42] In 2011, the United States signed a security agreement with Colombia which establishes that Colombia will, with U.S. support, assist other nations with training programs.[43] While some of this assistance, such as exchanges regarding Colombia's innovative human rights defender protection program, may be quite positive, promoting members of the Colombian armed forces as shining examples to train Central American and other forces suggests that U.S. policy makers have not learned the human rights lessons of the recent past.

NOTES

1. Álvaro Uribe, "Retomemos el lazo unificador de la ley, la autoridad democrática, la libertad y la justicia social, Posesión como Presidente de la República," *Presidencia de la Republica,* August 7, 2002, http://www.presidencia.gov.co/prensa_new/discursos/discursos2002/agosto/discurso.htm, accessed 2013.
2. Ibid.
3. Ibid.
4. Winifred Tate, "The Wrong Road: Colombia's National Security Policy," *Latin America Working Group*, July 2003, http://www.lawg.org/storage/documents/the%20wrong%20road.pdf.
5. Plataforma Colombiana de Derechos Humanos, Democracia y Desarrollo, "El Embrujo Autoritario: Primer año de gobierno de Álvaro Uribe Vélez," *Georgetown*

University, September 2003, http://pdba.georgetown.edu/Security/citizensecurity/Colombia/evaluaciones/primeranoUribe.pdf

6. Andrew Hudson, "Baseless Prosecutions of Human Rights Defenders in Colombia: In the Dock and Under the Gun," *Human Rights First*, February 2009, http://www.humanrightsfirst.org/wp-content/uploads/pdf/090211-HRD-colombia-eng.pdf, accessed 2013.

7. *Report of the United Nations High Commissioner for Human Rights on the situation of human rights in Colombia* (New York: United Nations Human Rights, 2013), 13, http://www.ohchr.org/Documents/HRBodies/HRCouncil/RegularSession/Session22/A-HRC-22-17-Add3_English.pdf, accessed 2013.

8. "Smoke and Mirrors: Colombia's Demobilization of Paramilitary Groups," *Human Rights Watch,* August 1, 2005, http://www.hrw.org/reports/2005/07/31/smoke-and-mirrors, accessed 2013. See also numerous publications by the Colombian Commission of Jurists at www.coljuristas.org, accessed 2013.

9. The 2012 State Department report confirms that "there was little land or money confiscated from former paramilitary leaders" despite the fact that this was mandated by the Justice and Peace law governing the paramilitary demobilization.

Country Reports on Human Rights Practices for 2012, Colombia (Washington, D.C.: U.S. Department of State, April 2013), 14, http://www.state.gov/j/drl/rls/hrrpt/humanrightsreport/index.htm?year=2012&dlid=204438., accssed 2013.

10. Ibid

11. International Human Rights Law Clinic, University of California, Berkeley Law School, "Truth Behind Bars: Colombian Paramilitary Leaders in U.S. Custody," *Berkeley Law,* February 2010, http://www.law.berkeley.edu/files/IHRLC/Truthbehindbars.pdf. Accessed 2013.

12. The chapter author participated in this verification mission along with twelve other human rights experts from Europe and the United States.

13. Observatorio de Derechos Humanos y Derecho Humanitario, "Ejecuciones extrajudiciales en Colombia 2002–2010: Crímenes de lesa humanidad bajo el mandato de la política de defensa y seguridad democrática," *Coordinación Colombia Europa Estados Unidos,* September 2012, http://coeuropa.org.co/files/Ejecuciones%20extrajudiciales%202002-2010%20CCEEUU(1).pdf, accsessed 2013.

14. "Pierna Arriba," *Semana,* April 17, 2010.

15. Lisa Haugaard, Kelly Nichols, Abigail Poe and Gimena Sánchez-Garzoli, "Far Worse than Watergate: Widening Scandal regarding Colombia's Intelligence Agency," *Latin America Working Group*, June 2010, http://www.lawg.org/storage/colombia/farworsethanwatergatefinalfinal.pdf, accessed 2012.

16. "La declaración que revivió las chuzadas del DAS," *Semana,* April 10, 2013,

17. Adam Isacson, *Colombia: Don't Call it a Model*, (Washington, D.C.: Washington Office on Latin America, 2010).

18. *Country Reports on Human Rights Practices for 2012, Colombia*, (Washington, D.C.: U.S. Department of State, 2013), 9, http://www.state.gov/j/drl/rls/hrrpt/humanrightsreport/index.htm?year=2012&dlid=204438., accessed 2013.

19. "Pierna Arriba," *Semana,* April 17, 2010.

20. Office of the Prosecutor, "Situación en Colombia: Reporte Intermedio," (Den Haag, The Netherlands: International Criminal Court, 2012), 3, http://www.icc-cpi.int/NR/rdonlyres/3D3055BD-16E2-4C83-BA85-35BCFD2A7922/285202/OTP2012035032COLResumenEjecutivodelReporteIntermed.PDF, accessed 2013.

21. See the governmental decree establishing that DAS agents will be transferred to protection unit: "Decreto Número-406'7 de 2011," *Presidencia de la Republica,* October 31, 2011, http://wsp.presidencia.gov.co/Normativa/Decretos/2011/Documents/Octubre/31/dec406731102011.pdf, accessed 2013; see also "Se Crea Unidad de Protección a Cargo del Ministerio del Interior," *El Universal,* November 2, 2011.

22. "2011: Cada 8 dias fue asesinado un defensor de derechos humanos en Colombia," *Somos Defensores*, March 4, 2012, http://www.somosdefensores.org/index.php?option=com_content&view=article&id=105:2011-cada-8-dias-fue-asesinado-un-defensor-de-derechos-humanos-en-colombia-&catid=20:informe-siaddhh-2011&Itemid=11, accessed 2013.

23. Somos Defensores, "El Efecto Placebo: Informe Anual 2012: Sistema de Informacion de Agresiones sobre Defensores y Defensoras de Derechos Humanos en Colombia (SIADDHH)," *Issuu,* 30, http://issuu.com/gulcuec/docs/informe-siaddhh-somos-defensores-2012-espanol/1, accessed 2013.

24. Ibid.

25. The author participated in this verification mission on human rights defenders.

26. *Country Reports on Human Rights Practices for 2012, Colombia* (Washington, D.C.: U.S. Department of State, 2013), 14, http://www.state.gov/j/drl/rls/hrrpt/humanrightsreport/index.htm?year=2012&dlid=204438, accessed 2013.

27. "Letter to Secretary of State Hillary Clinton," *Latin America Working Group,* November 2011, http://www.lawg.org/storage/documents/Annual%20Reports/Clinton_Land_Rights_Letter_Nov_2011_english.pdf, accessed 2013.

28. Hannah Mead, "Victims of Armed Groups Not Receiving Equal Treatment: Red Cross," *Colombia Reports,* April 24, 2013, http://colombiareports.com/victims-of-armed-groups-not-receiving-equal-treatment-red-cross/, accessed 2013.

29. *Country Reports on Human Rights Practices for 2012, Colombia*, U.S. Department of State, 2013, 11, http://www.state.gov/j/drl/rls/hrrpt/humanrightsreport/index.htm?year=2012&dlid=204438.

30. Adam Isacson, *Colombia: Don't Call It a Model.*

31. Lisa Haugaard, Zoraida Castillo and Annalise Romoser, "Still a Dream: Land Restitution on Colombia's Caribbean Coast," *Latin America Working Group*, September 2012, http://www.lawg.org/storage/documents/Still_a_Dream.pdf, accessed 2013.

32. *Country Reports on Human Rights Practices for 2012, Colombia*, U.S. Department of State, April 2013, 7, http://www.state.gov/j/drl/rls/hrrpt/humanrightsreport/index.htm?year=2012&dlid=204438.

33. Maria Teresa Ronderos, "Diálogo de Paz en Bogotá," *El Espectador,* April 11, 2013.

34. Edward Fox, "Colombia Yearly Homicide Rate Shows 9% Drop," *Insight Crime*, December 7, 2012, http://www.insightcrime.org/news-briefs/colombia-yearly-homicide-rate-sees-7-drop, accessed 2013.

35. Gimena Sánchez-Garzoli, "Stopping Irreparable Harm: Acting on Colombia's Afro-Colombian and Indigenous Communities Protection Crisis," *Norwegian Peacebuilding Resource Center*, June 19, 2012, http://www.peacebuilding.no/Themes/Protection-of-civilians/Publications/Stopping-irreparable-harm-acting-on-Colombia-s-Afro-Colombian-and-indigenous-communities-protection-crisis, accessed 2013.

36. Lisa Haugaard, Adam Isacson and Jennifer Johnson, "A Cautionary Tale: Plan Colombia's Lessons for U.S. Policy Toward Mexico and Beyond," *Latin America Working Group*, November 2011, http://www.lawg.org/storage/documents/Mexico/lawgef%20cautionary%20tale%20f.pdf.

37. Figures provided by Consultoria para los Derechos Humanos y el Desplazamiento (CODHES), Numero de personas desplazadas por departamento de llegada, 2000–2010; 2011 figure in CODHES, "Incremento en vulneraciones a los derechos humanos: El desplazamiento masivo y la situación indigena," December 2012.

38. Fellowship of Reconciliation and U.S. Office on Colombia, *Military Assistance and Human Rights: Colombia, U.S. Accountability, and Global Implications*, (Nyack, N.Y.: Fellowship of Reconciliation, 2010), http://forusa.org/content/report-military-assistance-human-rights-colombia-us-accountability-global-implications, accessed 2013.

39. "No hubo equipo americano involucrado: Brownfield," *Noticias Uno,* March 15, 2009, http://noticiasunolaredindependiente.com/2009/03/15/noticias/embajador-eeuu/, accessed 2013.

40. Office of the U.S. Trade Representative, "Colombia Action Plan Related to Labor Rights," April 7, 2011, http://www.ustr.gov/webfm_send/2787.

41. AFL-CIO, "The Colombia Action Plan related to Labor Rights: The View through Workers' Eyes," *AFL-CIO*, July 2012, http://www.aflcio.org/content/download/38251/594971/version/1/file/report+version+2+no+bug.pdf, accessed 2013.

42. Adam Isacson, "Latin America Mentions in John Kerry's Confirmation Hearing," *Just the Facts,* January 25, 2013, http://justf.org/blog/2013/01/25/latin-america-mentions-john-kerrys-confirmation-hearing, accessed 2013.

43. "Joint Press Release on the United States—Colombia Action Plan on Regional Security Cooperation," *U.S. Department of State,* April 15, 2012, http://www.state.gov/r/pa/prs/ps/2012/04/187928.htm, accessed 2013.

Chapter Thirteen

The Role of the United States and the Military in Colombia

Adam Isacson

Assistance from the United States has made an indelible impact on Colombia's armed forces, and on their relationship with their country's democracy and society. The massive aid packages of the twenty-first century, combined with a militaristic turn in Colombian politics, have brought the capabilities of Colombia's army, navy and air force to levels that would have been difficult to imagine as recently as the 1990s. Colombia now has Latin America's largest army, and second-largest armed forces, and likely leads the region in intelligence, mobility, and special operation readiness.

Along with those greatly increased capabilities have come notable increases in the uniformed services' political clout, and in their influence over U.S. officials' perceptions of Colombia's challenges. U.S. assistance, which came with conditions, has also contributed to an increase in the military's accountability for human rights violations, though these gains are facing a growing backlash.

If Colombia enters into a post-conflict transition during the second half of the 2010s, its military may find the experience to be wrenching. On the other hand, the armed forces' newfound power and prestige might allow them to avoid some of the hardest adjustments in accountability, in capabilities, and in their role in society. The danger is that post-conflict Colombia's civil-military relations could end up being unbalanced in favor of the armed forces, to an extent without precedent in the country's history. While the U.S. government would share the blame for such an outcome, it can also do much to help avert it.

CIVIL-MILITARY RELATIONS IN 20TH-CENTURY COLOMBIA

Unlike most of its Latin American neighbors, modern Colombia has seen only one military government, which started and ended bloodlessly, through negotiation with civilian political elites, during a time of civil conflict between 1953 and 1958. The country has held elections every four years since then.

In general, those elites—organized for most of the twentieth century in two unified parties—held the armed forces at arm's length. Though a military career offered social mobility to poor Colombians, it did not offer entry into the circle of old, landed families who form its major cities' aristocracy. Military officers remained a separate, lower caste. "In Colombia, they are not socially important," a diplomat told anthropologist Winifred Tate. "People are embarrassed if their daughters marry a military officer."[1]

Colombia's civilian political class kept the armed forces' budgets low—2 percent of GDP as late as the early 1990s—and excluded them from legislating or governing where security was not concerned.[2] This arrangement was formalized during the 1958 restoration of civilian rule. Just before his inauguration, incoming President Alberto Lleras set the parameters of what analysts have referred to as a "pact": civilians would refrain from interfering in questions of defense and security, as long as the military stayed out of politics.[3]

During the second half of the twentieth century, then, civilians and soldiers remained in very separate spheres. Political leaders offered little guidance to the military's campaigns against a succession of leftist guerrilla insurgencies. The military had nothing to say about the country's social or economic management.

As a result, Colombia for decades lacked a consistent, unified security strategy. Soldiers and civilians in separate silos proved to be a poor means of ending an internal armed conflict, as the armed forces on their own, with no oversight or guidance, proved unable to defeat even the smallest insurgencies. Meanwhile many civilian leaders—especially regional political bosses, landowners, and the narcotraffickers who began to emerge in the early 1980s—confronted political opposition not through military institutions, but through a more sinister, brutal means: the proliferation of murderous paramilitary "self-defense groups." Many military officers willingly went along with this strategy, participating in the paramilitaries' creation and training, and aiding and abetting their many attacks on the civilian population.

Though unhelpful to the country's security situation, which steadily worsened during the 1980s and 1990s, the "pact" helped make Colombia's civil-military relations far calmer than those of its South and Central American neighbors. However, civil-military harmony was never perfect. "Politics" and "security" overlapped at times. The pact was shaken on the several occasions when elected leaders sought to negotiate peace with the military's archenemies in leftist guerrilla groups, when officers perceived civilian oversight of budgets or human rights to be too zealous, or when civilians sought to bring military human rights violators to justice.

During these episodes, the military often got its way. In the late 1990s and early 2000s, for instance, the high command scuttled the Samper government's proposed peace talks with the FARC and the Pastrana government's talks with the ELN, both of which were to occur in zones from which the military first had to pull out. The Uribe government's first defense minister was unable to overcome resistance to her attempt to improve oversight of military discretionary funds.[4]

While fears of military coups have been exceedingly rare, officers usually expressed dissent through "saber-rattling"—aggressive statements, often by retired but sometimes by active personnel—and through alliances with hard-right politicians.[5] While this tactic often worked, civilians usually came out ahead in the long term. Colombia's civilian leaders frequently fire generals and make leadership changes in the high command. (On the other hand, in the twenty-three years since Colombia began naming civilian defense ministers, it has had sixteen of them; they tend not to last long.[6])

U.S. RELATIONS WITH COLOMBIA'S MILITARY BEFORE PLAN COLOMBIA

To varying degrees throughout this period, the United States sought close relations with Colombia's armed forces, which in turn have been one of the more pro-U.S. militaries in the region. Colombia has been the largest supplier of students to the U.S. Army's School of the Americas and its successor, the Western Hemisphere Institute for Security Cooperation. Colombia is the only Latin American country to have sent troops to the Korean War. During the Cold War, especially after the 1959 Cuban revolution, U.S. national security planners—fearing that Colombia's structural inequality and vast ungoverned areas made it fertile ground for Communist uprisings—lavished Colombia's military with equipment and training.

By the 1980s, though, Washington's anti-Communist focus was on Central America. Colombia's leftist guerrillas were far from taking power, but the country faced a more immediate vulnerability: organized crime in the form of powerful, violent drug trafficking cartels. Nearly all U.S. security assistance to Colombia in the 1980s and the 1990s flowed within the framework of the war on drugs.

This, however, was not a mission that Colombia's armed forces viewed as a priority. Focusing on the guerrillas, they left combating cartels mainly to Colombia's National Police which, though located within the Defense Ministry, are outside the military chain of command. There were exceptions, like military support to the police-led effort to track down and kill Medellín cartel leader Pablo Escobar. But before 2000, the high command shunned the drug war as a law-enforcement mission, a distraction from counterinsurgency, and a major corruption risk.

As a result, the National Police, not the armed forces, received the bulk of U.S. security assistance during the 1980s and 1990s, including most of the hundreds of millions that flowed through the George H.W. Bush administration's 1990–1992 "Andean Initiative" anti-drug aid package, from which the military actually turned down some assistance that was restricted to the drug mission.[7] By the end of the 1990s, especially after a massive mid-decade purge of police agents believed to be corrupt, Colombia's National Police had developed a host of new capabilities, from intelligence and criminal investigations to commando operations, and had a strong cadre of backers, most of them Republican, in the U.S. Congress.

Colombia's armed forces had fewer backers in late-1990s Washington. Assistance had dropped to minimal levels for a force viewed as on the sidelines of the drug war, riven by corruption, facing serious allegations of human rights abuses, and suffering humiliating defeats at the hands of a FARC guerrilla group that had grown wealthy with drug profits. U.S. defense officials viewed the Colombian armed forces, a garrison-bound force heavily reliant on forcibly recruited young men, as poorly equipped, trained, and led.

In a 1997 cable to Washington, then-U.S. Ambassador Myles Frechette recorded that he warned Samper's newest defense minister, "[T]he U.S. is nervous about working with the military on counternarcotics issues, primarily because of pervasive corruption within the military. This includes not only corruption in procurement contracts, but military personnel themselves being corrupted by narcos."[8] At that time, Robin Kirk records a more colorful depiction of the U.S. government's assessment, stating:

> One U.S. embassy official had dubbed General [Manuel] Bonett [the armed forces chief from 1997 to 1998] and his advisers the 'Apple Dumpling Gang,' referring to the Disney movie featuring Don Knotts, whom Bonett closely resembled. The moniker conveyed the Americans' low opinion of the Colombian military's fighting skill, which the official had described to me as 'pathetic.'[9]

U.S. RELATIONS WITH COLOMBIA'S MILITARY DURING AND AFTER PLAN COLOMBIA

That began to change, dramatically, by the end of the 1990s. After the demise of the Medellín and Cali cartels, the FARC and the AUC paramilitaries had deepened their involvement in the drug trade, allowing them to multiply in size. The paramilitaries were carrying out near-daily massacres, and the FARC were overrunning military bases, defeating elite army units, and kidnapping thousands for ransom each year. Colombia became not just a center for cocaine production and transshipment, but also the main producer of coca.

The Clinton administration, and conservatives in the U.S. Congress, grew alarmed. White House Drug Czar Barry McCaffrey, a retired general who had headed the U.S. Southern Command, joined other officials in the Pentagon, and some in the State Department, in advocating an ambitious change in U.S. policy: a return to large-scale aid for Colombia's armed forces. Aid to the National Police alone, they argued, was not enough. These officials assured skeptics that this turn to the armed forces would be an anti-narcotics effort only, that—in this pre-September 11 climate of trepidation about foreign "quagmires"—they had no intention of involving the United States in a large new Central America-style counterinsurgency commitment. "I know that many are concerned that this aid package represents a step 'over the line,' an encroachment into the realm of counterinsurgency in the name of counternarcotics. It is not," Brian Sheridan, the Assistant Secretary of Defense for Special Operations and Low Intensity Conflict, told a congressional committee. "The Department has not, and will not, cross that line."[10] They further assured Congress and nongovernmental organizations that, as mandated by law, aid would not reach military units believed to be most responsible for human rights abuse and fostering of paramilitaries.

Washington's turn to Colombia's military began decisively at the end of 1998, when the Defense Department agreed to help Colombia's army form a new Counter-Narcotics Battalion, whose members would be subject to U.S. vetting for past involvement in corruption or human rights abuses. With this single initiative, Colombia's army overcame its discomfort with the counter-drug mission, and the United States—by helping to create a new unit from scratch—overcame the legal prohibition on aid to abusive units.

In 2000, the Clinton administration proposed, and the U.S. Congress passed, a large new aid package, three-quarters of it for Colombia's security forces, and most of that for Colombia's armed forces. Using counter-drug accounts in the foreign aid and defense budgets, this first contribution to "Plan Colombia"[11] helped expand the Army Counter-Narcotics Battalion into a full brigade, create a new counter-drug riverine brigade in Colombia's Navy, and equip these and other military units with helicopters, patrol boats, and other items. One of the Counter-Narcotics Brigade's principal missions was to improve security conditions on the ground in areas where U.S.-backed police aircraft were to spray herbicides over coca fields. The act of "creating security conditions" meant that, for the first time in many years, Colombian military units would use direct U.S. support to confront guerrillas.

After this initial offering of assistance, the floodgates of U.S. aid to Colombia's military opened up. The Bush administration took power in 2001, and defense officials immediately began exploring the possibility of moving beyond the counter-drug mission to include support for the military's larger war against guerrillas. As Colombia's guerrillas and paramilitaries were on the State Department's list of international terrorist organizations, the September 11, 2001, attacks undid any remaining reluctance to support counterinsurgency. A mid-2002 change in U.S. aid law allowed assistance funded through counter-drug budget accounts to be employed against Colombia's illegal armed groups.

At the same time, as an effort to negotiate peace with the FARC collapsed, Colombians elected Álvaro Uribe, a president who promised to intensify the military's anti-guerrilla offensive. While his predecessor, Andrés Pastrana, had dramatically increased military spending, Uribe did the most to undo the "pact" that reigned over Colombian civil-military relations during the second half of the twentieth century.

The hard-line president involved himself intimately in military affairs. His defense planners developed a set of initiatives, called the "Democratic Security" strategy, that required the armed forces to spend far more time away from their barracks, developing relations with the larger population and responding far more quickly to outbreaks of violence. With the new strategy came a series of sharp budget increases for the armed forces, funded by a new property tax levied on the wealthiest. Uribe aggressively defended the military from criticism, especially by human rights groups whom he characterized as "spokespeople for terrorism."[12]

While he blasted the armed forces' outside critics, Uribe micro-managed the officer corps' security strategy, routinely calling brigade and battalion commanders on their mobile phones at odd hours, demanding results. During his eight years in office, Uribe fired more generals and colonels than any of his predecessors. President Lleras's 1950s pledge to stay out of military affairs had been abandoned—but the military, pleased to have a president who defended and funded them while keeping them on the offensive, did not complain.

Uribe persistently called on the Bush administration to provide more military support, and got much of what he asked for, well beyond the old drug-war parameters. By 2004, U.S. military advisors and contractors were supporting a program to protect an oil pipeline from guerrilla attack. They were providing advice, intelligence, and logistical support—even including U.S. deliveries of food and fuel to the front—for a lengthy, 18,000-soldier offensive against the FARC in its longtime southern Colombian jungle strongholds. After the guerrillas' February 2003 capture of three U.S. citizen Defense Department contractors whose plane crash-landed in FARC territory, U.S. intelligence agencies and elite Special Operations units greatly intensified their super-secret collaboration with Colombia's armed forces: first for the years-long search-and-rescue effort, and then for a host of other missions, including raids that killed top guerrilla leaders. A late-2013 *Washington Post* investigation revealed the existence of a CIA and Joint Special Operations Command program that supplied Colombian forces both with intelligence about guerrilla leaders' locations and with the precision-guided munitions with which to kill them.[13]

Military aid also included initiatives to improve the doctrine, procedures, planning, and capabilities that U.S. officials had derided as weak in the 1990s. Advisors encouraged services to work much more closely on joint operations. Training, imagery, and equipment improved intelligence capabilities. Training and contractor support guaranteed maintenance of the aircraft that enabled the Colombian military to enjoy both mobility and air superiority. (This maintenance also carried a high price tag, with aviation service contracts exceeding US$200 million—about a third of military and police aid—by 2006.[14])

U.S. military aid came with human rights conditions. Though their strength varied over the years, they generally held up a portion of military assistance until the State Department could certify in writing that members of the Colombian armed forces accused of human rights abuses were being investigated and tried by the civilian justice system. Though this level of accountability for abuse remains hard to attain, the conditions gave important leverage to human rights defenders and prosecutors. As a result, by the end of the 2000s, the Colombian judicial system made dozens of landmark convictions, a handful involving generals and colonels.

Still, it was during the period of greatest U.S. assistance that Colombia's military, principally its army, perpetrated the so-called False Positives scandal. All over the country, soldiers and officers—under heavy prodding to achieve "results" in the conflict, often measured in body counts—began killing civilian non-combatants and counting them as members of guerrilla or paramilitary groups killed in combat. By 2012, Colombia's Prosecutor-General's Office was investigating, trying, or has won convictions for over 1,700 "false positive" cases, involving as many as 4,716 victims. The vast majority were perpetrated between 2004 and 2008.[15]

Human rights groups' reports, including the annual document from the UN High Commissioner for Human Rights, had been denouncing this phenomenon for at least three years, with little response, when the scandal broke in

2008. Colombians were shocked by revelations that a group of paramilitaries the army claimed to have killed near the Venezuelan border was, in fact, several young men they had lured from a poor Bogotá suburb with a promise of employment.

These revelations' aftermath worsened civil-military friction. Officers were angered by Defense Minister Juan Manuel Santos's summary firing of twenty-seven army personnel, including three generals.[16] Press coverage of the scandal's extent increased pressure on the military to allow personnel to face civilian justice for non-combat killings. Some of that pressure came from the U.S. legislative branch, where congressional appropriators like Sen. Patrick Leahy (D-Vermont), by 2007 the chairman of the subcommittee in charge of foreign aid, demanded accountability. Because "false positives" sought to make all killings look like combat killings, they worsened civil-military friction by making all episodes of combat suspect. Officers chafed at civilian prosecutors' subsequent efforts, including visits to sites of recent confrontations with armed groups, to verify that what occured was truly combat.

For their part, U.S. officials said they were unaware that their Colombian army counterparts were carrying out a wave of extrajudicial killings. While Wikileaks cables indicate that diplomats were aware of the allegations before 2008, their messages were muted, and the State Department duly produced its annual certifications. The desire to keep aid flowing without interruption, along with Colombian military officers' and Uribe government officials' repeated assurances that the allegations were false, clearly slowed the U.S. response.

The 2000 Plan Colombia aid package had provided Colombia's military and police with US$642 million in assistance. By 2010, the cumulative military and police aid total was US$5.7 billion, far more than any country outside the Middle East during those years.[17] The emphasis of this aid evolved over the decade. The initial Plan Colombia buildup provided dozens of helicopters and other equipment, along with light-infantry and similar training, to support new military units and expand counter-drug operations. This shifted to advice, intelligence, and maintenance support for Colombia's anti-guerrilla offensives.

In 2006, though, the U.S. Congress changed hands. Voters, in part due to frustration with the Iraq war, gave the Democratic Party a clear majority of both houses for the first time since 1994. According to U.S. legislative rules, the majority party has overwhelming control of the congressional agenda, including the right to draft budget legislation. In 2007, as the new Congress got to work on the 2008 foreign aid budget bill, it made some significant changes to U.S. aid to Colombia, cutting military aid by about a quarter, and shifting much of the savings to development and judicial aid. While counter-drug programs like herbicide fumigation continued, the U.S. contribution declined.

The main focus of post-2007 military assistance became support for a program that Defense Minister Santos called "Consolidation." This more sophisticated approach to guerrilla-controlled areas, which bore some resemblance to what Gen. David Petraeus and other U.S. military leaders would attempt in the Iraq and Afghanistan "surges," foresaw the military as the first phase of a larger attempt to get a functioning civilian government established in long-abandoned areas.

The Consolidation program—which persists today, though at a reduced intensity—enjoyed some successes, particularly in the historically conflictive La Macarena region in south-central Colombia. But it also had unintended but troubling consequences for civil-military relations. In practice, the first phase of operations, the introduction of military personnel into the area, often ended up being the last. Civilian agencies failed to show up, and soldiers found themselves filling the gap by carrying out a host of traditionally civilian roles, from road-building to leading community development planning meetings.

By the end of the 2000–2010 decade, the Colombian military was a force transformed from its "Apple Dumpling Gang" days. They had turned the tide against the FARC and ELN guerrillas: both had been reduced in numbers and pushed to marginal areas, and the FARC in particular had seen several top commanders killed, its secret communications exposed, and its leadership humiliated by a 2008 ruse that bloodlessly rescued fifteen prominent hostages, including the three Americans.

The armed forces enjoyed sky-high approval ratings in polls, which portrayed them as the most, or second-most, popular institution in the country. Even as the justice system grew more aggressive in pursuing military human rights violators, public opinion evidenced no similar desire for accountability. The Colombian military of 2010 had capabilities that would have been unimaginable to the military of 2000, with 275,000 members (plus 170,000 police, combining for a more than two-thirds increase), a tripled annual budget of US$14.7 billion by 2014, the world's fourth-largest fleet of sophisticated Black Hawk helicopters, vastly improved communications and intelligence capabilities, and—despite glaring human rights and corruption shortcomings that persist today—an evident increase in professionalism.[18]

It is hard, of course, to distinguish how much of this improvement owed to a decade of U.S. assistance, and how much owed to Colombia's own buildup and "Democratic Security" policy. Colombian civilian leaders like Uribe and Santos deeply involved themselves in security policy making and poured far more of the country's own resources into it. Compared to Colombia's defense budget, U.S. security assistance fell from the equivalent of one-sixth in 2000 to perhaps one-thirtieth in 2010. Still, even as diminished U.S. aid came to focus more on hard-to-attain capabilities, like technology and Special Operations, U.S. security planners and intelligence officials' role in guiding the overall strategy—though a well-kept secret—was most likely pivotal.

CIVIL-MILITARY RELATIONS IN TWENTY-FIRST-CENTURY COLOMBIA

This larger, more capable, more popular military has more political clout than at any other time in Colombia's recent history, with the possible (but not even certain) exception of the 1953–58 military government. To be certain, the old "pact" has not been totally undone. The military almost never weighs in publicly on social issues or the country's economic management. Though a determined defense minister can strongly influence the shape of the military's campaign plan, civilian leaders leave most strategy and doctrine to the armed forces.

Still, there has been significant erosion. The government of Juan Manuel Santos (2010–2018) has not had a smooth relationship with the officer corps. It named three different high commands during its first thirty-seven months.

Some of this is due to politicization. Though active-duty officers avoid making political statements in the press, they tend to be more politically conservative than the centrist Santos administration. This is evident in the many public statements of ACORE, the association of retired officers, which has been far more vocal and visible during the Santos years than before. It is also evident in the public statements of conservative ex-President Uribe, who has become Santos's most prominent political opponent. Uribe's statements walk a dangerous line by appealing directly to the officer corps with his complaints about Santos's security policies.

As was the case throughout the "pact" years, though, where the military has pushed back most strongly on Santos have been issues that touch on security policy. These included Santos's initial choice of a high command, led by a Navy officer, which generated strong resistance within the Army, which has more than six times more personnel. Adm. Edgar Cely was dismissed after one year. Subsequent armed-forces chiefs have been Army generals, and Defense Minister Juan Carlos Pinzón, who entered when Cely exited, is the son of an Army colonel. Pinzón's public statements are routinely more bellicose, and presumably more reflective of the officers' view, than the president's.

Two other issues of civil-military friction have been more central to President Santos's agenda: human rights, and the president's decision to negotiate peace with the FARC guerrillas.

The Colombian military's defiance on human rights is complex and paradoxical. It increased just as allegations of military involvement in abuses began to decline: after the "false positives" scandal broke in 2008, allegations of both extrajudicial executions and collaboration with paramilitaries decreased to levels not seen since documentation began in earnest in the 1980s. Despite the close relationship between the U.S. government and Colombia's armed forces, defiance increased just as U.S. support was increasing judicial authorities' capacity to prosecute human rights cases, and as U.S. pressure was encouraging the armed forces to cooperate with civilian investigators. And this defiance expressed itself in a mostly indirect way, through actions and intermediaries rather than open confrontation or threatening messages.

By the end of the 2000s, Colombia's military, especially the Army, was bristling at the civilian justice system's increasing oversight of its affairs. This oversight had been increasing since the Constitutional Court ruled in 1997 that human rights violations could not be considered "acts of service," and thus had to be tried by the civilian criminal justice system, and not a military system that had systematically failed to punish abuse in the past.[19] Subsequent years saw steady movement from military to civilian jurisdiction in human rights cases, some of it encouraged by U.S. and other international pressure. Though impunity remains the norm, Colombia has jailed more senior officers for human rights crimes than any Latin American country, except Argentina.

Especially after the "false positives" scandal, with prosecutors given access to combat scenes to verify that no crimes occurred, officers grew steadily angrier at the justice system. Interviews with officers at the time revealed either frustration with prosecutors and judges who simply "did not understand what combat is like," or a belief that a "judicial warfare" strategy was advancing, with wily guerrillas and their backers taking advantage of the justice system's intricacies in order to tie the most effective commanders' hands.[20]

By 2010, officers were frequently citing an internal poll of 5,000 soldiers, which found that the greatest concern of military personnel was "judicial insecurity": the likelihood of being caught up in legal red tape every time they went on an operation.[21] Retired officers and defenders on the right, including ACORE and a conservative think-tank, the Democracy and Security Foundation, said that morale was low as a result of increased civilian prosecutions, and that many military units were effectively engaged in a "sit-down strike," allowing guerrillas to advance as they abstained from going on the offensive for fear of being accused of rights abuse.[22] Military anger grew further in 2010 and 2011, after the justice system sentenced two senior retired officers for abuses committed during that most sensitive of cases, the 1985 guerrilla takeover of, and subsequent military onslaught on, the Palace of Justice in central Bogotá.

In October 2011, Minister Pinzón, the Santos government's strongest advocate of military interests, introduced legislation that sought to reform the constitution to move human rights cases first to the military justice system. The legislation would essentially undo a series of hard-won human rights reforms dating back to 1997, making future "false positives" and similar cases far harder to prosecute. The officer corps conspicuously attended debates and votes as the provision went through the Congress, where it enjoyed overwhelming support from mainstream parties.

The Obama administration pushed back hard against this *fuero militar* (military jurisdiction) provision, viewing its possible passage as a setback for its own rhetoric about how U.S. assistance had improved human rights in Colombia, as well as a clear violation of the human rights conditions that, according to foreign aid law, would force it to freeze a portion of military aid. Pressure from Washington, as well as from Colombian and international human rights groups, was instrumental in making the language of this reform less drastic. Still, it ultimately passed, only to be struck down in October 2013, on procedural grounds, by the Constitutional Court. Still, President Santos has vowed to reintroduce the measure in the Congress that takes power after March 2014 elections. As of late 2013, military discontent with the civilian justice system, current interviews with officers make clear, remains alight.

Many Colombian analysts speculate that the Santos government's abdication of civilian authority on human rights may have been a quid pro quo. President Santos needed military support for another initiative that the officer corps may have found hard to swallow: its negotiations with the FARC, which began their formal phase in October 2012. This is the fourth time that a Colombian government has sought to negotiate with the FARC, but the first time in which the Colombian military has been in such a position of battlefield strength and political clout. "There is no lack of people who might insinuate—in a low voice—that the reform to military jurisdiction was the '*contentillo*' [in Colombian Spanish, sort of like "throwing a bone"] for the security forces to maintain their support for the negotiations," an analysis in Colombia's *El Espectador* newspaper put it.[23]

From the beginning, Santos knew that the military had to be kept "in the tent" on the peace negotiations, which could easily be scuttled by discontent within the officer corps. From the start, his five-person negotiating team included both Army and Police representation. Retired Gen. Jorge Mora, who led the Army, then the armed forces, between 1998 and 2003, and Retired Gen. Oscar Naranjo, who led the police for five years ending in 2012, have since been in Havana, sitting across the table from guerrilla leaders.

Santos has also muted military objections to the negotiations by refusing to agree to the FARC's requests for a cease-fire, so as not to tie the armed forces' hands. While negotiators talk in Havana, they continue to fight every day in Colombia. This contrasts sharply with the failed 1998–2002 FARC talks, when a militarily stronger guerrilla movement refused President Andrés Pastrana's repeated calls for a bilateral truce. With an eye to military sentiments, President Santos also successfully insisted that defense, security, and the armed forces' structure not be included on the negotiating agenda.

Despite these appeasement efforts, military discontent with the talks has been a factor. "There is no consensus about the peace policy among the troops, even if the high command says otherwise," much-cited conservative defense analyst Alfredo Rangel said in March 2013. "I don't believe that things will come to 'saber-rattling,' but there is a noticeable reduction in effort in the fight against terrorism and narcotrafficking."[24]

In August 2013, President Santos abruptly changed the high command several months before the customary time for a handover of power. The government billed the new leadership as "a high command for peace and the post-conflict."[25] Press reports indicated that, in fact, the forced retirements may have happened in order to keep the Army chief, Gen. Sergio Mantilla, from ascending to the top of the armed forces. Mantilla was known within the Defense Ministry to be a vocal opponent of the FARC negotiations. In July 2013, Gen. Mantilla and Minister Pinzón reportedly had a sharp, shouted exchange of words about the peace process.[26] The general was forced out the next month.

In several statements, meanwhile, former President Uribe, a fierce opponent of the talks, has appealed directly to the military.[27] He has, for instance, proposed (in a letter to an imprisoned colonel's wife) that jailed military personnel be granted conditional liberty, a solution "that does not offend their honor, like the Santos government offends them by treating them the same as it treats guerrilla terrorism."[28] The former president clearly has military allies on this and other subjects; as María Isabel Rueda, a veteran columnist for Colombia's most circulated newspaper, *El Tiempo*, put it in 2014, "Soldiers have hearts too, and some of them still beat more with Uribe than with Santos."[29] In April 2013, when the government and the Red Cross were to transport new FARC negotiators from Colombia's jungles to Havana, Uribe posted the secret coordinates of the helicopters' pickup site on his Twitter account. Uribe received this information from a still-unnamed military officer with access to very privileged secrets. The episode forced the commander of the armed forces to insist publicly that the troops were not divided about the peace process and were not "saber-rattling," but investigations to find the leaker have gone nowhere.[30]

Amid this complicated relationship between the military and the Santos government's civilian leadership, the United States—as the Colombian military's main foreign benefactor and partner—has at times been a key player. In the debate over military courts' jurisdiction over human rights cases, U.S.

diplomats "burned through a lot of our capital," as one U.S. embassy official put it in an interview, to prevent the initial, sweeping version of the constitutional reform from becoming law.

At the same time, frequent interviews with both U.S. diplomatic and military personnel make evident some sympathy for the Colombian military's position. In off-the-record contexts, some (though certainly not all) officials echo the armed forces' arguments about judicial insecurity and the Colombian judicial system's poor understanding of military operations. In no interview, however, has a U.S. official echoed the Colombian military's accusation that prosecutions are part of a guerrilla plot. Still, that so many in the U.S. bureaucracy take the "judicial insecurity" position may be the result of U.S. officials' constant interactions with Colombian military personnel, which make the military point of view one of those they hear the most. This is especially the case for U.S. defense officials. To this must be added a likely desire to minimize allegations that, more than a decade into a very large military aid program, the recipient military still fiercely resists efforts to hold it accountable for large-scale abuses.

On the peace process, the Obama administration—from the president on down—issues periodic statements of support for the FARC talks. However, as of late 2013 many officials privately express skepticism that the negotiations will succeed, or that if they do, that they will bring peace. Numerous interviews and conversations reveal this skepticism most strongly in quarters of the U.S. government—the Defense Department, the State Department's narcotics bureau—that are in most frequent contact with Colombia's security forces. Meanwhile, perceptions in Colombia that the United States is close to ex-President Uribe—the arch-critic of the talks who is Colombia's only recipient of the Presidential Medal of Freedom—contribute to doubt the true depth of U.S. backing for the process.

UPCOMING CIVIL-MILITARY CHALLENGES

The issue of peace lies at the center of likely near-term civil-military friction in Colombia. As of this writing, the FARC negotiations have been moving slowly, but appear likely to reach an eventual accord. If this happens, even though the accords will not include changes to defense and security, the post-conflict phase could have a wrenching effect on Colombia's military. Officers will be expecting public gratitude for their role in weakening the FARC. Civilian leaders will praise them lavishly, but will then try to compel them to undergo two difficult sets of adjustments.

The first is on human rights. With the military jurisdiction law thrown out, as of late 2013, military personnel accused of human rights abuses have one more near-term opportunity to avoid accountability in the civilian justice system. That is the transitional justice scheme that would emerge from a successful peace process with the FARC.

A "Framework for Peace" constitutional amendment, passed in mid-2012 and upheld by the Constitutional Court in mid-2013, already offers the outlines of what that scheme might look like. The worst guerrilla human rights violators would have to undergo some sort of trials or confessions, followed by an undetermined number of years of incarceration, or some other form of deprivation of liberty.

While as of late 2013 this has yet to be negotiated, the Framework Law makes clear that a formula for reduced sentences could apply to military personnel as well as guerrillas. An eventual law cementing in place a transitional justice agreement with the FARC will also be likely, then, to include additional provisions for soldiers accused of serious human rights crimes. The military will want this: "There will not be peace here if our soldiers remain imprisoned or persecuted while [FARC leaders] Timochenko and Iván Márquez go to the Congress," an unnamed officer told the Colombian daily *El Espectador*.[31]

This presents the military with a quandary. The abusers within its ranks—currently there are over 4,000 military personnel being processed in the civilian justice system for non-combatant homicides—have a real possibility of avoiding long prison sentences (some convicted officers are currently serving maximum terms of forty years).[32] But achieving reduced sentences will require the armed forces, at their moment of victory, to endure the spectacle of officers forced to make humiliating confessions to civilian judicial authorities of the human rights crimes they committed, ordered, or witnessed.

The second challenge that peace poses is perhaps more painful for the military institution: reductions to its size, and perhaps to its day-to-day role. A post-conflict Colombia is unlikely to need 275,000 soldiers, sailors, marines, and airmen.[33] A fleet of Blackhawks, Super Tucanos, and Kfir fighter jets is expensive to maintain. It is possible that the most vocal proponent of a post-conflict defense cutback will be not leftist politicians, but a Colombian business class looking to reduce its tax burden.

With organized crime still strong, and a looming threat of Mexico or Central America-style violence, post-conflict Colombia may, in fact, need more than 170,000 police. Politicians and academics are already quietly floating proposals to move Colombia's National Police out of the Defense Ministry, where it has been since 1951, and into a new public security ministry. Military and police roles, hopelessly blurred by the conflict, may be redefined in a way that leaves the armed forces not only smaller, but with less to do.

The armed forces' concern about its post-conflict future is growing. Defense Minister Pinzón is endeavoring to assure the officers that their institution will not be reduced. "It would be a big mistake, because even if the terrorist organization disappears, it doesn't mean many of its crimes disappear," he said in October 2013, and has made similar statements on numerous occasions. "I personally think Colombia has a security budget that's very limited. We have to keep strengthening."[34] In an April 2013 speech to a military audience, President Santos listed several roles that the armed forces might play if the armed conflict ends, including foreign peacekeeping, disaster relief, combating narcotrafficking, and training personnel from other countries.[35] In October 2013, the Minister traveled throughout Central America, remarking often that Guatemala and El Salvador committed grave errors by reducing their armed forces after civil wars ended, only to see violent crime increase.[36]

CONCLUSION

The big unknown in postwar Colombia, then, is whether its military—with its far larger size, its political influence, its popularity, and its conspicuous U.S. backing—will easily accede to increased human rights accountability and a reduced size and role. The next few years could be a bumpy ride for a country accustomed to what, by Latin American standards, have been relatively smooth civil-military relations.

In the worst-case scenario, a combination of saber-rattling and political maneuver forces a new "pact" that heavily favors Colombia's armed forces. The military resists any attempt to hold its members judicially accountable, and manages to remain at its present size (or even larger) while taking on a host of internal roles—backup policing, infrastructure projects, and environmental protection—that, in most democracies, fall to civilians. Colombia's elected leaders, like those of its neighbor Venezuela, may find themselves in an uneasy co-government with an untouchable, unelected, untransparent military establishment.

If that scenario becomes reality, the United States would share some responsibility. A civil-military blowup during the second half of the 2010s would be deeply embarrassing to the U.S. government. Since Washington's turn toward Colombia's armed forces with Plan Colombia in 2000, U.S. advice, equipment, and technology have been instrumental to their transformation. This transformation brought significant security gains, especially the weakening—though not the defeat—of guerrilla movements. But this transformation has also created an institution to which Colombia's civilian leaders have difficulty saying "no."

Though U.S. aid is reduced from mid-2000s levels, Colombia's military continues to derive much of its advanced capacities, and some of its prestige, from its relationship with the United States. As Colombia approaches an ever more probable post-conflict period, the U.S. government can play a vital role in helping Colombia to avoid the worst-case scenario discussed above, and to forge a new "pact" in which civilians clearly guide security policy.

The question is whether the U.S. government is prepared to take on this challenge. To do so will require diplomats to resist the tide of disengagement from Colombia, and from Latin America, that began after the September 11 attacks and intensified after the 2008 financial crisis and winding down of Plan Colombia and the Mérida Initiative in Mexico.[37] Diplomatic and USAID resources devoted to Colombia will have to increase in post-conflict Colombia—but in the mid-2010s budget climate, this is not guaranteed to occur.

If U.S. diplomatic engagement on Colombia's transition withers, the military-to-military channel—which has been robust since Plan Colombia began, and is likely to remain so—would grow further in relative importance, frequency, and volume. As a consequence, the Colombian armed forces' own post-conflict perceptions and priorities may have still greater resonance in Washington than those of Colombia's elected civilian leaders. The military's view of Colombian politics may predominate in cables to Washington, and in mid-level officials' policy discussions.

If this happens, the U.S. government will end up doing nothing to help Colombia re-balance its civil-military relations, in effect failing to undo one of the most serious unintended consequences of the buildup that began with Plan Colombia.

Thankfully, this outcome is not guaranteed. The U.S. government's post-conflict policy toward Colombia may still prioritize healthy civil-military relations, going beyond past "pacts" to a structure that guarantees accountability and cements in place the primacy of the country's elected leaders. But doing so will require a strong political and financial contribution to Colombia's post-conflict transition, commensurate with the large investment that past U.S. administrations made in Colombia's war effort.

NOTES

1. Winifred Tate, *Counting the Dead: The Culture and Politics of Human Rights Activism in Colombia* (California: University of California Press, 2007), 259.

2. Government of Colombia, Departamento Nacional de Planeación, cited in Tomás E. Concha Sanz, "Fiscalización y Transparencia del Presupuesto Asignado a

la Defensa," in Comisión Andina de Juristas, *El Control Democrático de la Defensa en la Región Andina Série: Democracia No. 9* (Lima: CAJ, April 2004): 192.

3. Some examples: Alfredo Rangel Suárez, *Guerreros y Políticos: Diálogo y Conflicto en Colombia, 1998–2002* (Bogotá: Intermedio, 2003): 210–1.

Fabio Zambrano Pantoja, "Presentación," in Elsa Blair Trujillo, *Las Fuerzas Armadas: una mirada civil* (Bogotá: CINEP, 1993), 12; Francisco Gutiérrez, "El Escenario Colombiano," in Comisión Andina de Juristas, *El Control Democrático de la Defensa en la Región Andina Série: Democracia No. 9* (Lima: CAJ, April 2004): 82; Col. (R) Carlos Alfonso Velásquez, "La Dirección Política de lo Militar: Una Necesidad Estratégica," *Análisis Político* 38 (Bogotá: IEPRI, Universidad Nacional de Colombia, September-December 1999): 39.

4. Norbey Quevedo H., "La guerra interna en Mindefensa," *El Espectador,* November 17, 2003.

5. Nazih Richani, *Systems of Violence: The Political Economy of War and Peace in Colombia* (Albany: State University of New York Press, 2002), 38.

Andrés Dávila Ladrón de Guevara, "Dime Con Quién Andas: Las Relaciones Entre Civiles y Militares en la Colombia de los Años '90," in Rut Diamint (ed.), *Control Civil y Fuerzas Armadas en las Nuevas Democracias Latinoamericanas* (Buenos Aires: Universidad Torcuato di Tella, 1999), 372.

6. Government of Colombia, Ministry of National Defense, "Ministros de Guerra y Defensa," visited January 13, 2014 (Bogotá, Colombia: Defense Ministry), http://www.gsed.gov.co/irj/servlet/prt/portal/prtroot/pcd!3aportal_content!2fcom.pcc.pcc!2fPORTALMDN!2froles!2fcom.pcc.PortalMinisterio!2fMinistro!2fcom.pcc.historico!2fcom.pcc.historico_ministros, accessed 2013.

7. For more on this initiative, see Connie Veillette, *Andean Counterdrug Initiative (ACI) and RelatedFunding Programs: FY2006 Assistance* (Washington, D.C.: Congressional Research Service, 2006).

8. U.S. Embassy Bogotá cable, "Ambassador's January 12 Meeting with New MOD [Minister of Defense] Designate," January 13, 1997, obtained by National Security Archive http://www.gwu.edu/~nsarchiv/NSAEBB/NSAEBB69/col51.pdf, accessed 2013.

9. Robin Kirk, *More Terrible Than Death: Massacres, Drugs and America's War in Colombia* (New York: Public Affairs, 2003), 188.

10. Testimony of Brian E. Sheridan, Assistant Secretary of Defense for Special Operations and Low Intensity Conflict, before the House Armed Services Committee (Washington: Library of Congress, March 23, 2000) http://ciponline.org/old/colombia/032303.htm, accessed 2013.

11. For more on Plan Colombia, see; Connie Veillette, *Plan Colombia: A Progress Report* (Washington, D.C.: Congressional Research Service, 2005).

12. Presidency of Colombia, "Palabras del Presidente Álvaro Uribe Vélez en la Posesión del Nuevo Comandante de la FAC" (Bogotá: Government of Colombia, September 8, 2003) http://web.presidencia.gov.co/discursos/discursos2003/septiembre/fac.htm, accessed 2013.

13. Dana Priest, "Covert action in Colombia," *The Washington Post*, December 21, 2013. http://www.washingtonpost.com/sf/investigative/2013/12/21/covert-action-in-colombia/.

14. Numerous U.S. government sources cited at Just the Facts, "Grant aid to Colombia through International Narcotics Control and Law Enforcement," visited January 13, 2014 (Washington: CIP, LAWG, WOLA), http://justf.org/Program_Detail?program=International_Narcotics_Control_and_Law_Enforcement&country=Colombia.

15. United Nations High Commissioner for Human Rights, "Intervención del Señor Todd Howland, Representante en Colombia de la Alta Comisionada de las Naciones Unidas para los Derechos Humanos en la Universidad Sergio Arboleda de Bogotá" (Bogotá: UNHCHR, August 30, 2012) http://www.hchr.org.co/publico/pronunciamientos/ponencias/ponencias.php3?cod=144&cat=24, accessed 2013.

16. Juan Forero, "Colombia Fires 27 From Army Over Killings,"*The Washington Post,* October 30, 2008) http://www.washingtonpost.com/wp-dyn/content/article/2008/10/29/AR2008102901304.html.

17. According to numerous government sources cited at Just the Facts, "U.S. Aid to Colombia, All Programs, 2000–2010" (Washington: CIP, LAWG, WOLA, 2014) http://justf.org/country?country=Colombia&year1=2000&year2=2010, accessed 2013.

18. Government of Colombia, Ministry of National Defense, *Logros de la Política Integral de Seguridad y Defensa para la Prosperidad* (Bogotá: Defense Ministry, October 2013): 71 http://www.mindefensa.gov.co/irj/go/km/docs/Mindefensa/Documentos/descargas/estudios%20sectoriales/info_estadistica/Logros_Sector_Defensa.pdf, accessed 2013.

Frank López Ballesteros, "Colombia eleva la capacidad de sus fuerzas militares,"*El Universal*, January 7, 2014) http://www.eluniversal.com/internacional/140107/colombia-eleva-la-capacidad-de-sus-fuerzas-militares.

Sikorsky Aerospace Services, "Sikorsky Aerospace Services Launches State-of-the-Art BLACK HAWK Training Center in Colombia" (Rio de Janeiro: Sikorsky, April 9, 2013) http://www.sikorsky.com/About+Sikorsky/News/Press+Details?pressvcmid=fabdda3aaaeed310VgnVCM1000004f62529fRCRD, accessed 2013.

19. Government of Colombia, Corte Constitucional, Sentencia C-358/97 (Bogotá: Corte Constitucional, 1997) http://www.corteconstitucional.gov.co/relatoria/1997/c-358-97.htm.

20. Off the record interviews held by the author, or off-the-record question-and-answer sessions following presentations by the author, with generals or colonels of the Colombian armed forces, most recently in May 2010, December 2010, May 2011, November 2011, May 2012, June 2012, November 2012, May 2013, and September 2013.

21. Rafael Nieto Loaiza, "Fuero Militar,"*El Colombiano*, March 18, 2012) http://www.elcolombiano.com/BancoConocimiento/F/fuero_militar_1/fuero_militar_1.asp.

22. *La seguridad en Colombia continúa deteriorándose* (Bogotá: Universidad Sergio Arboleda, 2012) http://www.usergioarboleda.edu.co/Notisergio/estudio-seguridad-nacional.htm, accessed 2013.

23. "El fuero y el proceso de paz,"*El Espectador*, October 25, 2013) http://www.elespectador.com/noticias/politica/el-fuero-y-el-proceso-de-paz-articulo-454428.

24. Maria Del Rosario Arrazola, "Las tensiones de la tropa," *El Espectador,* April 15, 2013) http://www.elespectador.com/noticias/politica/articulo-415943-tensiones-de-tropa.

25. "La nueva cúpula de seguridad para el remate del gobierno Santos," *El Tiempo*, August 12, 2013 http://www.eltiempo.com/justicia/ARTICULO-WEB -NEW_NOTA_INTERIOR-12988554.html.

26. "¿Que significa la nueva cupula militar que nombro Santos?" *Semana,* August 14, 2013) http://www.semana.com/nacion/articulo/que-significa-nueva-cupula-mili tar-nombro-santos/353995-3.

27. Cecilia Orozco Tascon, "¿Incentivando un alzamiento militar?" *El Espectador*, April 10, 2013) http://www.elespectador.com/opinion/columna-415032-incenti vando-un-alzamiento-militar.28. "Uribe propone conceder libertad condicionada a miembros de Fuerzas Armadas," *El Espectador*, October 15, 2013) http://www. elespectador.com/noticias/politica/uribe-propone-conceder-libertad-condicionada-miembros-d-articulo-452257.

28. "Uribe propone conceder libertad condicionada a miembros de Fuerzas Armadas," *El Espectador*, October 15, 2013) http://www.elespectador.com/noticias/ politica/uribe-propone-conceder-libertad-condicionada-miembros-d-articulor-452257.

29. María Isabel Rueda, "'Soy un instrumento para la paz': general (r.) Freddy Padilla de Leon," *El Tiempo*, January 7, 2014) http://www.eltiempo.com/politica/ como-fue-el-llamado-de-santos-a-su-corazon_13339398-4.

30. "El fuero y el proceso de paz,"*El Espectador*, October 25, 2013) http://www .elespectador.com/noticias/politica/el-fuero-y-el-proceso-de-paz-articulo-454428.

31. "El fuero y el proceso de paz,"*El Espectador*, October 25, 2013) http://www .elespectador.com/noticias/politica/el-fuero-y-el-proceso-de-paz-articulo-454428.

32. UN High Commissioner for Human Rights, August 2012.

33. Ministry of National Defense, *Logros de la Política Integral de Seguridad y Defensa para la Prosperidad*: 71.

34. "Colombia Defense Minister Says Troop Cuts After Peace 'Big Mistake,'" *Reuters*, November 1, 2013. http://www.nytimes.com/reuters/2013/10/31/world/ americas/31reuters-colombia-security.html.

35. Presidency of Colombia, "Palabras del Presidente Juan Manuel Santos en el relevo número 100 del Batallón Colombia" (Bogotá: Government of Colombia, April 3, 2013) http://wsp.presidencia.gov.co/Prensa/2013/Abril/Paginas/20130403_04 .aspx, accessed 2013.

36. Juan Guillermo Mercado, "El Salvador aconseja a Colombia no reducir Fuerzas Militares," *El Tiempo*, October 2, 2013) http://www.eltiempo.com/politica/el-salvador -le-aconseja-a-colombia-no-reducir-fuerzas-militares-en-el-postconflicto_13094918-4.

37. For more on the Mérida Initiative, see Clare Ribando Seelke and Kristin M. Finklea, *U.S.-Mexican Security Cooperation: The Mérida Initiative and Beyond* (Washington, D.C.: Congressional Research Service, 2013), http://fas.org/sgp/crs/ row/R41349.pdf, accessed 2013.

Chapter Fourteen

Paradigm Shift?

Drug Policies and Strategies from Uribe to Santos

Coletta A. Youngers and Jonathan D. Rosen

The goal of this chapter is to examine the transition from Álvaro Uribe to Juan Manuel Santos and drug policy in Colombia. President Santos, the former Defense Minister during the Uribe administration, assumed power in Colombia and asserted that the "war on drugs" in Colombia has been a failure. Colombia has been at the epicenter of the U.S.-led war on drugs for decades and millions of Colombians have suffered from such failed policies. This chapter seeks to question whether Colombia is experiencing a paradigm shift in drug policy or whether Santos's comments are empty promises and are merely rhetoric.

URIBE AND PLAN COLOMBIA

President Uribe came to power vowing to combat the Revolutionary Armed Forces of Colombia (FARC). A great deal of his resources came from Plan Colombia, which was signed into law in July of 2000 by President Clinton. Plan Colombia sought to decrease the cultivation, production, and trafficking of drugs by 50 percent. However, the goals of Plan Colombia shifted drastically after the events of September 11, 2001, which allowed Uribe to reorient Plan Colombia from a counter-drug to counter-terrorism initiative. September 11 fundamentally altered U.S. foreign policy as the Bush administration implemented its global war on terror, which later was changed to the global war on terrorism. Uribe recognized that he could not fulfill his plans for combatting the FARC without the assistance of the United States. In turn, he "sold" President Bush the idea that Colombia did not have an internal armed conflict but rather a terrorist problem. He argued that the FARC are narco-terrorists or narco-guerrillas and that drug trafficking helped fuel the guerrillas, convincing Bush that Colombia needed U.S. help to combat the narco-terrorists. Uribe and Bush were a "match made in heaven" because they both had the same vision of the global war on terrorism. Uribe's Colombia also provided the Bush administration with another key element: non-Muslim terrorists. Colombia enabled Bush to silence critics who said that he was at war with the Muslim world. He could easily respond that his administration supported countries in the fight against terrorists anywhere in the world and could point to Colombia as an example.[1]

Uribe proved to be a loyal ally of the Bush administration. In return for his loyalty, President Bush went further than any other president, providing the Colombians with military aid and the resources necessary to combat the "terrorists." Piazarro and Gaitán assert that "the most significant change in U.S. military assistance to Colombia was removal of the condition, for the first time since the end of the Cold War, that military aid to Colombia be subject to its exclusive use in the war on drugs."[2] Piazarro and Gaitán argue, "George W. Bush crossed the 'invisible line' that, formally if not always in practice, separated the counter-narcotics fight from counterinsurgency programs. All Plan Colombia and the Andean Initiative funding may be used for both."[3] The blurring of the lines became apparent when President Bush submitted legislation designed to aid the Colombians against the "narco-guerrillas."

A major part of Plan Colombia under the Uribe administration was the aerial eradication programs designed to reduce and eventually eliminate the cultivation of coca. Determining whether or not aerial spraying initiatives have been successful can be measured empirically by analyzing the statistical results. It is important to recognize, however, that one has to be careful when examining the statistics because governments and international organizations have different methodologies and methods for arriving at the results. Moreover, measuring the eradication of coca is difficult because it is a clandestine business, and coca cultivators adapt in order to avoid detection. The important thing is that statistics provide a range—as opposed to an exact number—for authorities to determine the results of aerial spraying. An examination of the balance sheet reveals that aerial spraying has not only been ineffective but counterproductive because of the environmental damages and health problems that have resulted from such initiatives.

Despite spending billions of dollars, the area of cultivation increased in certain regions and drug trafficking continued unabated. Plan Colombia failed to achieve its goals of decreasing coca cultivation by 50 percent even though the United States sprayed hundreds of thousands of hectares of coca under cultivation. In 2002, for instance, the United States sprayed 130,364 hectares of coca fields according to the annual coca monitoring report on

Colombia by the UNODC. The number of hectares sprayed increased dramatically over the years.[4] In 2006, the United States recorded spraying a total of 172,025 hectares of coca. However, in 2007, a shift toward manual eradication occurred. In 2009, the total number of hectares sprayed was 101,940.[5]

Aerial spraying does not work for several fundamental reasons. Farmers have learned how to adapt in order to continue earning an income from coca cultivation. They have made it very difficult for an airplane to detect via satellite because they intermix coca with legal plants and can also grow coca in smaller plots to avoid detection.[6] Even after plants are sprayed, growers can put products—such as molasses—on the plants to ensure that the coca does not die. Profits from coca cultivation are often the only source of cash income for small farmers, and, therefore, they will migrate to new areas to grow coca or replant. As a result, short-term "successes" in coca eradication are quickly reversed. Ramírez Lemus, Stanton, and Walsh assert, "[t]hough large-scale producers are known to fragment their coca field in order to avoid detection, most small coca plots are cultivated by individual farmers for their own subsistence."[7]

While Uribe can be credited with improving security in Colombia, Uribe (and Plan Colombia) failed to decrease coca cultivation and drug trafficking.[8] In fact, the drug war in Colombia was counterproductive because it eroded support for the state in rural areas and, according to some experts, caused significant environmental degradation and resulted in health consequences for many people impacted by spray-drift.[9] It also pushed some of the country's poorest people deeper into poverty by depriving them of their primary source of income.

FAILURE OF MANUAL ERADICATION

In addition to aerial spraying, Plan Colombia allocated money for manual eradication and other programs such as crop substitution. Manual eradication presents several challenges. Farmers want to maximize their profits and, therefore, will produce crops that provide them with the greatest return. In addition to economic incentives, one of the major challenges revolves around the threats from guerrilla and right-wing paramilitary organizations that earn large profits from cocaine and can use violence and intimidation against peasants refusing to cultivate coca. A peasant living in rural Colombia may want to grow other legal crops but may not have a choice for that reason. Many of the areas where coca is cultivated are located in contested areas that are inundated with operatives from illegal armed groups and are among the most dangerous areas of the country. This also poses a threat to those who do the eradicating. Despite various initiatives designed to protect participants in manual eradication programs, reports indicate that violence still occurred against manual eradicators by various means, including fire from snipers as well as the use of improvised explosive devices and minefields. Reports indicate that the total number of individuals that died from participating in the manual eradication program reached 118 over a three year period (2005 to 2008).[10] Colombians must provide the participants in the manual eradication program with security in order to prevent them from being killed.

QUESTIONABLE VICTORIES AGAINST THE AUC

While the empirical evidence clearly demonstrates that President Uribe did not achieve the goals of Plan Colombia in terms of reducing drug production, one of his major accomplishments was the demobilization of the AUC, which was the major right-wing paramilitary organization operating in Colombia. Uribe's negotiations began in 2003 and obtained significant results. Over a period of three years (2003 to 2006), an estimated 32,000 AUC soldiers began to demobilize. Why did many of the leaders of the paramilitaries support the demobilization process? Adam Isacson explains, "While the negotiations with paramilitaries look like a giant leap toward peace, the reason it could fail is also the main reason why most paramilitary leaders support it: the agreement will most likely include a mechanism to grant the leaders amnesty in both Colombia and the United States for their crimes."[11] In addition, it is important to note that many of the leaders of the paramilitaries supported Uribe as a presidential candidate.[12]

Before praising Uribe, it is important to understand the reality of the demobilization process. Many of the officers and soldiers of the AUC demobilized into organized criminal networks.[13] The new criminal networks that have resulted from the demobilization of the AUC into criminal bands are referred to as *Bandas Criminales* (BACRIM).[14] The various groups that have emerged from the paramilitaries have continued to attack civilians and have been responsible for a plethora of human rights violations. BACRIM are different from the former paramilitary groups in several important ways. They are smaller and more decentralized and hence can be harder to detect. Bruce Bagley notes, "They tend to be politically much more deft and subtle in seeking political alliances inside the Colombian economic and political establishment, often hiding their political linkages through indirect and 'clean' candidates without records of paramilitary affiliations."[15] In addition, the BACRIM have expanded their activities beyond drug trafficking and into areas such as illegal gold mining in order to diversify their portfolios and different avenues for earning revenue necessary to finance their operations.[16]

It is important to note that different estimates exist regarding the number of individuals involved in the various groups that succeeded the paramilitaries. For instance, the Colombian National Police estimated that the groups have 3,749 members operating within Colombia as of 2010.[17] Other approximations are much higher, placing the numbers at 6,000 members. Others estimate that 6,000 groups operate within Colombia and stress that the members of such organizations are not concentrated in certain departments. Rather, they are located throughout Colombia, operating in 29 of the 32 departments that exist within Colombia. The Colombian state, however, remains weak and does not have a strong presence throughout many regions of the country.[18]

ELECTION OF JUAN MANUEL SANTOS

In 2010, Uribe left office in Colombia after he was denied the opportunity to run for a third term by the Colombian courts. Juan Manuel Santos, Uribe's Defense Minister, received 69 percent of the vote in a presidential-runoff that occurred on June 20, 2010.[19] Upon taking office, Santos quickly distinguished himself from Uribe in several important ways. One of the most important moments occurred when Santos recognized that Colombia did in fact have an internal armed conflict as opposed to a terrorist problem. Uribe responded to the statements made by Santos by publicly rebuking his former right-hand man. Hannah Stone writes:

> This was met with a furious response by his predecessor and one-time mentor, Alvaro Uribe, who insists that the country faces not an internal conflict, but a terrorist threat. The former president fired off a volley of Tweets via Twitter, complaining that the country's armed groups are terrorists fighting against a legitimate state, and do not deserve the status of belligerents, and should not be given political recognition.[20]

President Santos eventually initiated peace talks with the FARC and later the ELN.

ADDRESSING INTERNAL DISPLACEMENT

Upon assuming the presidency, Santos sought to address the internal displacement problem of millions of Colombians who have been forced to flee their homes as a result of the internal armed conflict and drug war. Colombia remains the world's leader with the largest number of individuals internally displaced, surpassing other war-torn countries, such as Iraq, Sudan, and Afghanistan.[21] Research indicates that approximately 117,000 Colombians are documented refugees (living in other countries) and have obtained official refugee status. This number, however, does not include the number of people who are located in other countries illegally and have not officially received refugee status.[22] Santos's Victims' Law is an effort to address the internal displacement as a result of the internal conflict.[23] The refugees, however, remain susceptible to attacks by illegal armed actors. In particular, "the refugee population that resides in the areas along the border with Colombia continues to be victimized by attacks perpetrated by Colombian illegal armed groups. Women and girls are particularly vulnerable to sexual violence and recruitment into trafficking networks."[24] The National Development Plan for 2010–2014 (PND) is the official program designed to assist displaced persons. However, the PND "does not include any concrete measures of prevention of displacement nor protection of this population during its displacement, return, or reintegration."[25]

SANTOS AND THE "WAR ON DRUGS"

Juan Manuel Santos sought to distinguish himself from his former boss and change directions on numerous other key policy issues. He sought to reposition Colombia internationally, seeking to improve relations with neighboring Venezuela, which hit an all-time low before he took office, and to reengage with Latin America as a whole. During Uribe's presidency, Colombia became isolated from the more progressive governments being voted into office across the region and was increasingly seen as a key ally of the U.S. government, precisely at a time when Latin American governments were seeking out independence from Washington on a range of policy issues. In reality, Uribe's Colombia remained the primary ally of the U.S. in Latin America during Bush's presidency as the administration's policies had negative consequences for the reputation, or "soft power,"[26] of the U.S. President Santos immediately sought a leadership role for Colombia within regional bodies and debates and to reframe relations with the United States, deemphasizing drug policy and security issues, while prioritizing economic and trade issues. Yet few expected that he would also stake out new ground in calling for a reconsideration of the prevailing international drug control paradigm.

Prior to joining the Uribe administration, Santos had shown a willingness to question the drug policies that the Colombian government was implementing. In June 1998, he signed a letter to then-United Nations Secretary General, Kofi Anan, on the opening of the 1998 UN General Assembly Special Session on Drugs calling for "a frank and honest evaluation of global drug control efforts . . ." as "we believe that the global war on drugs is now causing more harm than drug abuse itself." The letter was signed by hundreds of prominent individuals from around the world, including former UN Secretary General Javier Perez de Cuellar. Santos signed the letter in the name of the *Fundación Buen Gobierno*, which he founded in 1994. The letter concludes:

> Persisting in our current policies will only result in more drug abuse, more empowerment of drug markets and criminals, and more disease and suffering. Too often those who call for open debate, rigorous analysis of current policies, and serious consideration of alternatives are accused of 'surrendering.' But the true surrender is when fear and inertia combine to shut off debate, suppress critical analysis, and dismiss all alternatives to current policies. Mr. Secretary General, we appeal to you to initiate a truly open and honest dialogue regarding the future of global drug control policies—one in which fear, prejudice and punitive prohibitions yield to common sense, science, public health and human rights.[27]

President Santos appears to have taken those words to heart once he became the country's highest elected official. His calls for an international debate on drug policy came at a propitious moment. The ground-breaking 2009 report of the Latin American Commission on Drugs and Democracy[28] in many ways marked a turning point in the drug policy debate, as press coverage flourished and more and more influential individuals joined the Commission's call for drug policy reform. Former President Cesar Gaviria was one of the three ex-presidents that presided over that commission, ensuring significant coverage of its work—and that of the subsequent Global Commission—in the Colombian press. In short, Santos entered into a debate that had already begun about the high cost being paid by the Colombian people in waging a war against an illicit industry that nonetheless continued to flourish. But his contribution was particularly significant, as he was one of the first sitting presidents to not only call for debate, but to put the idea of legalization—long considered taboo—at the center of that debate.

PRESIDENT SANTOS SPEAKS OUT ON LEGALIZATION

In an interview with *Semana* magazine in February 2011, six months after taking office, Santos, when asked about the possibility of decriminalizing drugs, said: "It is an alternative we can discuss. I am not against any formula that is effective. And if the world decides to legalize and believes that will reduce violence and criminality, I can accompany that."[29] Over the coming year he reiterated both themes: the value of considering drug legalization and the necessity of forging a new international consensus before taking action at the national level.

At the same time, he reversed course and supported Bolivia's effort to gain international recognition for the coca leaf. The 1961 Single Convention on Narcotic Drugs mistakenly classifies the coca leaf—used in its natural form by indigenous Andean groups for centuries—as a narcotic drug. It also includes a provision, Article 49, that "coca leaf chewing must be abolished" within twenty-five years, a period that ended in 1989. In 2011, the Morales administration sought to amend the convention by deleting Article 49 and thereby acknowledging the traditional uses of the coca leaf.[30] In response, the U.S. government organized a "friends of the convention" group to oppose Bolivia's actions. The Colombian government initially filed a formal objection to the deletion of Article 49 of the 1961 Convention. However, reportedly following a phone call from President Morales, it reversed course and withdrew the objection. In the *Semana* interview, Santos said, "We adopted the position to accompany Bolivia because that is what is established in the Constitution: to respect ethnic indigenous groups with regards to this tradition."[31] The United States was successful in rallying enough support to block the proposed change, but the support received from Colombia showed that President Santos was not blindly wedded to U.S. dictates on drug policy, as had been the case with his predecessor.

The interviews that put Santos on the international map were published in two British newspapers, *The Financial Times* and *The Observer*. In February 2011, he responded to a question about legalization asked by *Financial Times* reporters by saying, "On that issue I am not a fundamentalist. If the world considers that legalization is a solution I would gladly go along with that. I can understand the benefits, and I can understand the arguments."[32] Later that year, in November 2011, President Santos told *The Observer*:

> I would talk about legalising marijuana and more than just marijuana. If the world thinks that this is the correct approach, because for example in our case we used to be exporters, but we were replaced by producers in California. And there even was a referendum in California to legalise it and they lost it but they could have won it. I ask myself how would you explain marijuana being legalised in California and cocaine consumption being penalised in Idaho? It's a contradiction. So it's a difficult problem where you set the limits. It's a difficult decision. For example, I would never legalise very hard drugs like morphine or heroin because in fact they are suicidal drugs. I might consider legalising cocaine if there is a world consensus because this drug has affected us most here in Colombia. I don't know what is more harmful, cocaine or marijuana. That's a health discussion. But again, only if there is a consensus.[33]

In that interview, he also pointed to the moral authority that he, as president of Colombia, brought to the debate: "I'm conscious of what this means. I've told President Calderón [of Mexico], 'You and I have a lot more authority to talk about this because our countries have spilled a lot of blood fighting drug traffickers and we should promote this discussion.'"[34] As explained in more detail below, Santos was successful in bringing Calderón, at the end of his presidency, into the debate.

In Colombia, Santos tended to have a more cautious tone regarding the "war on drugs." The Colombian military and police and a range of other institutions are for the most part deeply embedded in a "drug war" mentality. Many Colombians have lost their lives waging that war and public opinion at the time continued to be skeptical of reforms. And drug trafficking profits are a major source of income for all actors responsible for the country's high levels of violence. Yet in January 2012, Santos again spoke out, this time at an event in Cartagena. He referred to decriminalization as an "acceptable option" for Colombia, again with the caveat on the need for an international consensus to move in that direction. And this time, he went further and critiqued the prohibitionist approach, which, he argued "stimulates the business." He asserted, "Take away the profits from organized crime" and use those for public education campaigns to reduce consumption. These are "practical solutions," which adopted globally would be more effective. He referred to the "war on drugs" as like being on a "stationary bike. One looks around and it is the same. The panorama changes, but the problem continues. Now we have the criminal gangs at the service of drug traffickers."[35]

SPARKING A REGIONAL DEBATE

Santos was not the only sitting president at the time speaking out on the need to promote a discussion of alternative drug policies. He was joined by Guatemalan president Otto Pérez Molina, who spoke out forcefully on the need to consider drug legalization, and eventually by Uruguayan president José Mujica, who crafted a proposal to create legal, regulated cannabis markets in that country.[36] (When the proposed law was first announced in June 2012, Santos spoke out strongly against it, reiterating his call that no country should go it alone but rather wait for a new international consensus to emerge.) However, it was Santos who played the most crucial role in ensuring a regional debate on the topic. Colombia was host to the April 2012 Summit of the Americas, and Santos ensured that in the private, closed-door meeting of the hemisphere's presidents, the only issue discussed was drug policy. Following that meeting, Santos announced that the presidents were calling upon the Organization of American States (OAS) to produce a report analyzing the results of present policy and exploring alternative approaches. While a range of viewpoints was represented in the Cartagena summit, a consensus was forged on the need to debate alternative approaches.

The significance of this development cannot be underestimated. For years, Washington has used its diplomatic and economic muscle to squash any dissent on drug control policies. Colombia felt that acutely when in 1997 the U.S. government "decertified" the Colombian government after it claimed to have obtained evidence that drug traffickers had contributed to then-President Samper's electoral campaign. (Colombia was also "decertified" in 1998 and 1999.) Years later, former U.S. president, Bill Clinton, apologized, saying that in hindsight it was clear that the U.S. response had weakened the hands of the government vis-à-vis the FARC. The tables were turned at the Cartagena summit, with Latin American countries for the first time taking on a leadership role in recognizing that present policies have, in many cases, failed to meet the desired objectives. Latin American leaders argued that many people have suffered as a result of the war on drugs and promoted a debate on alternative approaches.

It is important to note, however, that the role of the OAS in the process—according to informal reports, the U.S. condition for supporting the report—was met with some skepticism. Many countries in the region were increasingly looking to the Union of South American Nations (UNASUR) and the Community of Latin American and Caribbean States (CELAC) for leadership on regional issues. On drug policy in particular, the OAS's Inter-American Drug Abuse Control Commission (CICAD) is perceived by many as very strongly influenced by the U.S. government, which appoints its director and provides much of its funding. In the end, however, through this process the OAS emerged at the forefront of the regional drug policy debate, as explained in greater detail below.

Perhaps given the skepticism around the OAS role, President Santos insisted that an analytical report in and of itself was not enough. With significant financial support from the Colombian government, a scenarios planning process was also launched. Santos had been involved in a similar effort related to the Colombian conflict in 1996, led by Reos Partners and the *Centro de Liderazgo y Gestión* (CLG), based in Bogotá—a process that likely influenced his decision to seek to bring the FARC to the negotiating table. He wanted to use the same methodology and apply it to drug trafficking. According to Reos Partners:

> To initiate the scenarios process, Reos, CLG, and the OAS put together a staff team from across the Americas . . .; conducted dialogue interviews with

> 75 leaders from throughout the hemisphere, including current and former heads of state; and invited 46 exceptional individuals—from security, business, health, education, indigenous cultures, international organizations, the justice system, civil society, and politics—to form a scenario team. The scenario team's task was to construct relevant, challenging, plausible, and clear scenarios of what could happen in the future regarding drug policy, based on current trends and including relevant political, economic, social, cultural, and international dynamics. These scenarios would not be forecasts of what will happen or recommendations of what should happen over the coming years. The goal was to create radically different ways of understanding—and responding to—'the drug problem.'[37]

The four scenarios are *Together, Pathways, Reliance* and *Disruption.* Of these, *Pathways* is the most ground-breaking. It posits that present prohibitionist policies cause too much harm; the alternative is to explore and learn from regulatory frameworks, beginning with cannabis.[38]

In a parallel process, OAS Secretary General José Miguel Insulza, with the support of OAS staff from the Secretariat for Multidimensional Security and CICAD, undertook a comprehensive study with input of a working group composed of multilateral officials, government representatives, academics and civil society experts. The result was six detailed studies (annexes to the final report) that were condensed into one analytical report. That and the scenarios report were formally presented to the presidents of Colombia and Panama (where the next Summit of the Americas took place in 2015) on May 17, 2013.[39]

In the reports, the OAS clearly states that its intention is not to provide policy recommendations; however, some of the policy alternatives it suggests are groundbreaking for a multilateral institution. According to the International Drug Policy Consortium (IDPC):

> . . . the last chapter of the analytical report, 'Contributions to the Debate' suggests some useful policy alternatives. The report calls for drug use to be treated from a public health perspective, for people who use drugs not to be criminalized and hence for the decriminalization of drug consumption . . . In debunking the 'one size fits all' approach to drug policy, the final chapter underscores that drug issues need to be addressed in different ways in different countries depending on the challenges they face. Hence, countries should be given the flexibility to adopt approaches tailored to individual needs. Finally, two far-reaching policy alternatives are included at the very end of the last chapter. First, the report underscores the value of assessing 'existing signals and trends that lead toward the decriminalization or legalization of the production, sale and use of marijuana,' noting that, 'Sooner or later decisions in this area will need to be taken.'[40] Second, the report opens the door to convention reform: 'Greater flexibility could lead to the possibility of amending domestic legisla-

tion or promoting changes to international law.'[41] For the first time, a regional multilateral organization has raised the issue of reform of the international drug control conventions.[42]

At the May 2013 presentation of the reports, President Santos declared: "I am committed to continuing to promote a deep, serious, and responsible debate with regional and global leaders, experts, universities, and think tanks to start—the sooner the better—generating new responses to addressing this serious problem that continues to plague humanity."[43] The next opportunity for debate came just weeks later, at the OAS General Assembly meeting which took place in Antigua, Guatemala, from June 4 to 6, 2013, where—for the first time—drug policy was the focus of debate. As with the April 2012 Summit, no consensus was reached in Antigua on a new path forward; however, consensus was again reached on continuing the debate. The hemisphere's Foreign Ministers adopted a declaration[44] that calls for a multilayered process of consultation on drug policy issues in a variety of national and regional forums, taking into account the OAS studies just described, and concludes by entrusting the OAS Permanent Council to convene a Special Session of the OAS General Assembly in 2014 to focus on drug policy issues.[45] The OAS reports and the process laid out in Antigua ensure that drug policy will remain at the top of the hemispheric agenda for the foreseeable future.

REPERCUSSIONS IN THE UNITED NATIONS

President Santos—joined by Guatemalan president Perez Molina and then-Mexican president Calderón—also took the call for an international debate to the United Nations. At the September 2012 UN General Assembly meeting, they issued a formal statement highlighting the need to "review the approach" of present drug policies and calling on the United Nations to "exercise its leadership . . . and conduct a profound reflection to analyze all available options, including regulatory or market measures, in order to establish a new paradigm that prevents the flow of resources to groups involved in organized crime." The statement concludes by asking the UN to host "an international conference to allow the necessary decisions to be made in order to achieve more effective strategies and tools with which the global community faces the challenges of drugs and their consequences."[46] These sentiments were echoed in the declaration of the Ibero-American Summit—including all countries of Latin America, Spain and Portugal—which took place in November 2012.

In December 2012, it was announced that a special session of the UN General Assembly would be convened in early 2016 on the "world drug problem."[47] The *Report of the Third Committee on International drug control* to the General Assembly states that the UNGASS review will include "an assessment of the achievements and challenges in countering the world drug problem, *within the framework of the three international drug control conventions and other relevant United Nations instruments* (emphasis added)."[48] Yet meaningful drug policy reform ultimately necessitates convention reform and a key question remains as to whether or not the issue of convention reform will finally appear at the negotiating table. The OAS analytical report just described may give impetus to such efforts. As of August 2013, it is not yet clear how active the Colombian government will be in attempting to shape the UNGASS process.

DRUG POLICY CONTINUITY AT HOME

As explained above, President Santos has moved cautiously on the domestic front. He is careful not to criticize ongoing counterdrug efforts in his own country. For the most part, when talking of the failures of current international drug control policies he points out that Colombia's "success" has moved the problem elsewhere, primarily Central America. Both the U.S. and Colombian governments put forward Plan Colombia as not only successful, but as a model for other countries in the region to emulate. In June 2012, the U.S. Defense Department claimed that "Colombia now serves as a regional training base to help other nations in their counterdrug efforts."[49] Colombia's security forces train, advise, and provide other assistance to their counterparts in other countries, including Central America.[50] According to *Just the Facts*, "Between 2010 and 2012, Colombia trained 9,983 military and police personnel from 45 countries—the top recipients being Mexico, Panama, Honduras, Ecuador and Peru."[51]

During President Santos's first two years in office, little change was noted in the drug policies implemented on the ground in Colombia. With regard to coca cultivation, the trend of declining use of aerial fumigation that began in 2009 continued through 2012, though according to U.S. government figures 98,185 hectares were sprayed that year. Manual eradication also continued to decline; in fact, the budget for manual eradication decreased by over half between 2010 and 2012. This coincided, interestingly, with steady decreases in the overall level of coca cultivation, which by 2012 had declined to 78,000 hectares. Historically, the U.S. government and the UN have reported widely divergent statistics on coca cultivation in the country. For that same year, 2012, UNODC reported that the Colombian coca crop had declined to 48,000 hectares. Both the United States and the UN, however, show a downward trend in coca cultivation. This is attributed—at least in part—to a return to marijuana cultivation, "creating what's been called Colombia's second marijuana bonanza," and a shift toward illegal mining, now more lucrative than coca.[52] In short, the trend toward declining coca cultivation in Colombia that has continued under the Santos government appears to have more to do with changes in the nature of the cocaine and other illicit industries than with either aerial or manual eradication.

INITIATION OF A DIALOGUE ON NATIONAL-LEVEL REFORMS?

By the very end of 2012, however, President Santos took the first step toward initiating a dialogue on domestic level reforms. On December 26, the Minister of Justice announced the creation of a Drug Policy Commission (*Comisión Asesora para la Política de Drogas en Colombia*) tasked with evaluating present drug policies and presenting the Colombian government with a series of recommendations for future drug policies. Operating under the Ministry of Justice, the Commission is composed of ten members and two "special invitees," former President César Gaviria and former director of the National Police, retired General Óscar Naranjo. Though the Commission members are presented as having a variety of viewpoints, its composition tilts toward the reform-oriented. In addition to former President César Gaviria (member of the Global Commission on Drug Policy), it includes former Constitutional Court member Rodrigo Uprimny (a leading reform advocate) and Universidad de los Andes economics professor Daniel Mejía Londono (a leading economist working on drug policy issues), who chairs the commission. As noted by *La Silla Vacia*, which refers to it as "*una commission de rupture*" (or a commission designed to make a break from the past), President Santos is finally sending a "clear signal that he intends to align internal policy with his international discourse."[53]

On May 21, 2013, the Drug Policy Commission released its first document, focused on drug consumption, which recommends numerous far-reaching reforms.[54] It calls for consumption to be treated as a public health issue and explicitly states that dependent drug users should not be criminalized; in other words, the possession of small amounts of drugs for personal use should not be a criminal offense. It calls for evidence-based treatment and harm reduction policies for such users. The Commission also points out the need to recognize that most drug consumption is recreational—and therefore causes no harm to individuals, their families or communities—and that this needs to be taken into account in developing adequate policies.

Table 14.1 Coca Cultivation in Colombia

	2001	*2002*	*2003*	*2004*	*2005*	*2006*	*2007*	*2008*	*2009*	*2010*	*2011*	*2012*
Cultivation (Hectares)	169,800	144,450	113,850	114,100	144,000	157,000	167,000	119,000	116,000	100,000	83,000	78,000
ProductionPote-ntial (Metric Tons)	700	585	445	410	500	510	470	280	280	255	190	175
Eradication (Air)	84,251	122,695	127,112	131,824	134,474	164,119	148,435	129,876	101,573	97,836	103,302	98,185
Eradication (Manual, Hectares)	1,745	2,762	4,220	6,232	37,540	42,110	64,979	95,731	60,954	43,957	34,592	30,486

Source: ONDCP http://www.whitehouse.gov/ondcp/targeting-cocaine-at-the-source (accessed 20 August 2013)

The call for decriminalizing drug use marks a dramatic reversal of the approach adopted by the Uribe administration. Between 1994 and 2009, possession of small amounts of drugs for personal use was not prosecuted in Colombia, due to a Constitutional Court ruling that states that the possession of a "minimum dose" of drugs cannot be penalized when it occurs "in the exercise of their personal rights . . . and the defendant did not affect others."[55] Upon taking office, former Colombian president Álvaro Uribe immediately began to amend the country's constitution in order to allow for the criminalization of possession for personal use. After repeated efforts, Uribe was finally successful. In a subsequent citizen security law, an article was included to eliminate the provision in the previously existing law allowing for possession for personal use, thereby codifying the results of the constitutional change into law. However, in June 2012, the Constitutional Court ruled on the article in the citizen security law referred to above, stating that the constitution does not allow penalizing consumers. The Colombian Supreme Court issued similar rulings in cases of individuals prosecuted for carrying drugs for personal use.

This issue will now have to be resolved through a reform of Colombia's National Drug Law, which has been in the works since President Santos took office. The first draft of the new drug law included a provision which would also have enacted into law Uribe's amendment to criminalize consumption. However, after the Constitutional Court ruling referred to above and input from civil society and other experts, a revised draft law was circulated which would maintain Colombia's long-standing policy on drug consumption. In January 2013, Colombia's Justice Minister, Ruth Stella Correa, announced that the revised drug law to be presented to Congress will also decriminalize possession for personal use of small amounts of synthetic drugs, such as ecstasy and methamphetamines, and would maintain such practice for cocaine and marijuana, which is still allowed under current law.[56] The final presentation of the draft drug law to the Colombian Congress is now pending the input provided by the final report of the Drug Policy Commission, which, as of April 2014, had yet to be released.

The Drug Policy Commission has already had an impact at the international level. In July 2013, the Guatemalan government sent a delegation to Bogotá to learn about the model adopted in Colombia for setting up a similar commission in that country. Civil society groups in Mexico and other countries are calling on their governments to create similar commissions to evaluate and recommend alternative drug policies. It may be some time, however, before the impact of the Colombian Drug Policy Commission can be seen at the national level. President Santos has, to a large degree, staked the success of his presidency on reaching a negotiated settlement with the FARC and thereby putting an end to the country's decades-long civil conflict. Those talks are progressing slowly. Santos has already staked out solid ground internationally in pushing for a meaningful drug policy debate and is well-positioned to consolidate his international role (in time for the 2016 UNGASS) and vigorously pursue a national drug policy reform agenda.

CONCLUSION

Former Colombian president Uribe placed all of his faith in the Bush administration for support for his war on "narco-terrorism." The Bush administration rewarded Uribe for his loyalty and provided his administration with increasing levels of aid. By the end of Uribe's presidency, he hardly had an ally in the region, as he had alienated many neighboring countries with his desire to combat the internal "terrorists" operating within Colombia. The border crossing to capture Raúl Reyes in Ecuador resulted in substantial tension between the two countries. Uribe also accused both Ecuador and Venezuela of assisting the ELN and the FARC. In sum, Uribe's presidency did not improve the "soft power"[57] of Colombia in the region, nor did it help promote cooperation between Colombia and its neighbors.[58]

In sharp contrast, President Juan Manual Santos sought to restore the country's regional standing and to reshape relations with the United States, downplaying drug policy and security issues while emphasizing trade and economic ties. Of particular significance, he recognized the existence of an internal armed conflict in Colombia and initiated peace negotiations with the FARC and later the ELN. Drug policy is one of the agenda items in the negotiations with the FARC. On that agenda are alternative and economic development, prevention and public health, and addressing the problem of drug trafficking. In the negotiations on rural development policy, the FARC called for an end to the criminalization of coca farmers, economic development in coca growing regions, and an end to aerial and forced manual eradication. Ultimately, improving the livelihoods and economic opportunities for rural farmers combined with gradual and cooperative coca eradication is the most promising alternative for ensuring long-term and sustained coca reduction. While at the time of writing this chapter, it is too hard to predict what will happen in the negotiations, agreement on certain basic principles for ending forced eradication and promoting economic development in coca growing regions could be a significant step towards developing and implanting drug policies that are more humane and more effective. Indeed, that would represent a paradigm shift in Colombian drug policy.

NOTES

1. For more on Uribe and Plan Colombia, see Jonathan D. Rosen, "Plan Colombia And Beyond: Pastrana to Santos (2000 to 2012)" (2012). Open Access Dissertations. Paper 880.

2. Eduardo Pizzaro and Pilar Gaitán, "Plan Colombia and the Andean Regional Initiative: Lights and Shadows," in *Addicted to Failure: U.S. Security Policy in Latin America and the Andean Region*, ed. Brian Loveman (Lanham, Maryland: Rowman & Littlefield, 2006), 69.

3. Pizzaro and Gaitán, *Plan Colombia and the Andean Regional Initiative*, 69.

4. *Colombia: Coca Cultivation Survey 2011* (Bogotá, Colombia: UNODC, 2012),80. Adam Isacson, *Colombia: Don't Call it a Model: On Plan Colombia 10th Anniverary, Alaims of "Success" Don't Stand Up to Scrutin* (Washington, D.C.: WOLA, 2010), 1–13.

5. *Colombia: Coca Cultivation Survey 2011*, 8–107, 80.

6. Interview approved by Institutional Review Board of the Univeristy of Miami with Daniel Mejín; see also Jonathan D. Rosen, *Plan Colombia And Beyond: Pastrana to Santos* (2000 to 2012)" (2012). Open Access Dissertations. Paper 880.

7. María Clemencia Ramírez Lemus, Kimberly Stanton, and John Walsh, "Colombia: A Vicious Cricle of Drugs and War," in *Drugs and Democracy in Latin America: The Impact of U.S. Policy,* eds Coletta A. Youngers and Elieen Rosin (Boulder, CO: Lynne Rienner Publishers, 2005), 61–98, 117.

8. See Bruce Bagley, "Seminario De Seguridad" (El Colegio de La Frontera Norte, http://www.youtube.com/watch?v=sMeqNJzWXCo), accessed 2014.

9. "Plan Colombia: The harmful impacts of aerial spraying of coca and poppy crops," *AIDA*, http://www.aida-americas.org/en/project/plancolombia, accessed October 2014.

10. *Drug Reduction Goals were Not Fully Met, but Security has Improved; U.S. Agencies Need More Detailed Plans for Reducing Assistance* (Washington, D.C.: GAO Report, 2008), 1–25, 115.

11. Adam Isacson, *Optimisim, Pessimism, and Terrorism: The United States and Colombia in 2003* (Washington, D.C.: Center for International Policy, 2004), 245–255, 251–2.

12. "Uribe: Yo no Me Reuní Con Paramilitares, Articulo OnLine Archivado " *Semana,* April 23, 2008; Juan Forero, "Cousin of Colombian President Arrested in Death Squad Probe" *The Washington Post*, April 23, 2008.

13. *Drug Reduction Goals were Not Fully Met, but Security has Improved; U.S. Agencies Need More Detailed Plans for Reducing Assistance*, 26.

14. Bagley, *Drug Trafficking and Organized Crime in the Americas: Major Trends in the Twenty First Century* (Washington, D.C.: Woodrow Wilson International Center for Scholars, 2012),17; Elvira Maria Restrepo and Bruce Bagley, eds., *La Desmovilizacion De Los Paramilitaries En Colombia: Entre La Esperanza y El Escepticismo* (Bogotá: Colombia: Uniandes, 2011).

15. Bagley, *Drug Trafficking and Organized Crime in the Americas: Major Trends in the Twenty First Century* 17; Elvira María Restrepo and Bruce Bagley, eds., *La Desmovilizacion De Los Paramilitaries En Colombia: Entre La Esperanza y El Escepticismo* (Bogotá: Uniandes, 2011); Miriam Wells, "BACRIM The Greatest Threat to Colombia Land Restitution: HRW," *InSight Crime*, September 19, 2013, http://www.insightcrime.org/news-briefs/bacrim-are-the-greatest-threat-to-colombia-land-restitution-hrw (accessed October 2014).

16. Mariel Perez-Santiago, "Colombia's BACRIM: Common Criminals or Actors in Armed Conflict?" *InSight Crime,* July 23, 2012, http://www.insightcrime.org/news-analysis/colombias-bacrim-common-criminals-or-actors-in-armed-conflict, accessed September 23, 2014.

17. "World Report 2011: Colombia | Human Rights Watch " http://www.hrw.org/world-report-2011/world-report-2011-colombia (accessed 8/28/2012, 2012).

18. "World Report 2011: Colombia | Human Rights Watch " http://www.hrw.org/world-report-2011/world-report-2011-colombia (accessed 8/28/2012, 2012). For more on the results and consequences of Plan Colombia, see Jonathan D. Rosen, "Plan Colombia And Beyond: Pastrana to Santos (2000 to 2012)" Open Access Dissertations. Paper 880, chapter 3, part 2.

19. Eduadro Posada-Carbo, "Colombia After Uribe," *Journal of Democracy* 22, no. 1 (2011), 137–151.137.

20. Hannah Stone, "The War of Words Over Colombia's Conflict" *InSight Crime*, May 9, 2011, http://www.insightcrime.org/insight-latest-news/item/884-the-war-of-words-over-colombias-conflict (accessed 8/26/2012, 2012).

21. 2014 UNHR country operations profile- Colombia, UNHCR: The UN Refugee Agency, http://www.unhcr.org/pages/49e492ad6.html, accessed October 2014.; Michael Solis, "Colombia's Internally Displaced People," *Huffington Post*, September 13, 2010.

22. *Human Rights During the Juan Manuel Santos Administration's First Year in Office* (Washington, D.C.: WOLA, 2011), 14.

23. *Human Rights During the Juan Manuel Santos Administration's First Year in Office*, 1–25, 13.

24. Ibid., 14.

25. Ibid., 14. In the report, the authors put this in bold for emphasis.

26. For more on the concept of soft power, see Joseph S. Nye, Jr. *Soft Power: The Means to Success in World Politics* (New York, N.Y.: Public Affairs, 2004).

27. Coletta Youngers, "Colombia's new president should call for a dialogue on drugs," *Transnational Institute Drug Law Reform Project*, August 18, 2010, http://druglawreform.info/en/weblog/item/556-colombias-new-president-should-call-for-a-dialogue-on-drugs, accessed 2013.

28. Drugs and Democracy: Toward a Paradigm Shift (Commission on drugs and democracy, 2009).

29. "Preferiría no reelegirme," *Semana.com,* February 15, 2011. Author's translation.

30. For additional information see, Tom Blickman, "Coca leaf: Myths and Reality," *Transnational Institute Drug Law Reform Project*, http://www.tni.org/primer/coca-leaf-myths-and-reality, accessed 2013.

31. Ibid. Author's translation.

32. John Paul Rathbone and Naomi Mapstone, "FT Interview Transcript: Juan Manuel Santos," *The Financial Times*, February 13, 2011.

33. John Mulholland, "Juan Manuel Santos: 'It is time to think again about the war on drugs,'" *The Guardian,* November 12, 2011; Jamie Doward, "Colombia president calls for global rethink on drugs, *The Guardian*, November 12, 2011, 3.

34. Ibid.

"Santos: Despenalizar la droga sería aceptable para el país, si el mundo lo hace," *S*35. *emana.com*, January 28, 2012.

36. For additional information, see "Uruguay Steps Forward with Marijuana Legalization Vote," *WOLA*, August 2, 2013. http://www.wola.org/news/uruguay_steps_forward, accessed 2013.

37. Adam Kahane, "Reos Partners Supports 'Game-Changing' Scenario Project on Drugs in the Americas," *Reos Partners Quarterly Newsletter*, Issue No. 15, August 2013.

38. For additional information on the OAS reports see, *Launching the Debate: The OAS Reports on Hemispheric Drug Policy,* (London, UK: Internatioanl Drug Policy Consortium, 2013), http://idpc.net/publications/2013/07/idpc-advocacy-note-launching-the-debate-the-oas-reports-on-hemispheric-drug-policy, accessed 2013.

39. The analytical and scenarios reports can both be found at: http://www.oas.org/en/media_center/press_release.asp?sCodigo=E-261/13.

40. OAS, *The Drug Problem in the Americas,* 104.

41. Ibid.

42. *IDCP Briefing Paper- The drug policy reform agenda in the Americas (Version 2),* August, 16, 2013, http://idpc.net/publications/2013/08/idpc-briefing-paper-the-drug-policy-reform-agenda-in-the-americas-version-2, accessed 2013.

43. Quoted in Adam Kahane, "Reos Partners Supports 'Game-Changing' Scenario Project on Drugs in the Americas."

44. Declaration of Antigua Guatemala "For a Comprehensive Policy against the World Drug Problem in the Americas": http://www.oas.org/consejo/GENERAL%20ASSEMBLY/AG43regular.asp.

45. For more analysis on the Antigua meeting and final declaration, see http://idpc.net/blog/2013/06/latin-american-leaders-chart-course-for-drug-policy-debate

46. *Declaración conjunta de los Gobiernos de Colombia, Guatemala y México,* October 1, 2012.

47. The first such meeting was the one in 1998 referred to previously.

48. United Nations General Assembly (4 December 2012), *International Drug Control, Report of the Third Committee*, Sixty-seventh session, Agenda item 104, A/67/459.

49. Donna Miles, "Commander: 'Beyond the Horizons' to Have Far-reaching Impact," *U.S. Department of Defense,* June 29, 2012, http://www.defense.gov/news/newsarticle.aspx?id=116966, accessed 2013.

50. For additional information see: http://justf.org/blog/2013/02/12/and-without-us-aid-colombias-training-other-security-forces-increases?utm_content=coletta.youngers%40gmail.com&utm_source=VerticalResponse&utm_medium=Email&utm_term=here&utm_campaign=[Blog]%20Secretary%20of%20State%20Kerry%27s%20trip%20to%20Colombia%20and%20Brazilcontent

51. "Secretary of State Kerry's trip to Colombia and Brazil," *Security Assistance Monitor,* August, 15, 2013, http://justf.org/blog/2013/08/15/secretary-state-kerrys-trip-colombia-and-brazil, accessed 2013.

52. "Is Colombia Winning the Drug War?," *The Global Post,* June 21, 2013. For more on the statistics, see *Colombia: Coca Cultivation Survey 2012* (Bogotá, Colombia: UNODC, 2013).

53. André Bermúdez Liévano, 'Santos comienza a aterrizar su discurso internacional sobre drogas,' January, 1, 2013, *La Silla Vacía,* http://www.lasillavacia.com/historia/santos-comienza-aterrizar-su-discurso-internacional-sobre-las-drogas-41218, accessed 2013.

54. Comisión Asesora para la Política de Drogas en Colombia, *Lineamientos para una política pública frente al consumo de drogas,* May 2013.

55. Corte Constitucional, *Sentencia C-221/94, Despenalización del Consumo de la Dosis Personal, Bogotá, 5 de mayo de 1994.*

56. 'Se podrían cargar tres pastillas de droga sintética,' *El Tiempo*, January 29, 2013.

57. Joseph S. Nye, Jr., *Soft Power.*

58. Sibylla Brodzinksy, "Uribe, A Bush Ally, Treads on Shaky Ground," *Time*, February 20, 2007; "US to expel Venezuelan diplomats in retaliation," *BBC*, October 2, 2013; Leo Palmer, "Ecuador to continue investigation into DAS wiretaps," *Colombia Reports,* July 5, 2010.

Analytical Conclusions

Colombia's Balance Sheet in the Second Decade of Twenty First Century

Bruce M. Bagley and Jonathan D. Rosen

This volume has analyzed the major challenges and opportunities that Colombia faces in the twenty-first century. The goal of the analytical conclusions is to provide some lessons and key points from the volume and examine the major obstacles that Colombia faces in the future. The conclusion is divided into several sections. The first part analyzes the progress that Colombia has made over the last decades, focusing on the economic growth and socioeconomic improvements. The next sections examine the major challenges such as the lack of social inclusion of many Colombians. Colombia also faces many obstacles with the peace process, particularly in the implementation of an agreement. After analyzing the peace process, this concluding section highlights the security challenges with the emergence of new criminal bands, known as the BACRIM. The chapter ends with an examination of many of the political obstacles that Colombia faces, such as high levels of corruption, impunity, and weak institutions.

TREMENDOUS PROGRESS

Colombia has made remarkable progress over the last several decades of the twentieth century and the first decade of the twenty-first century. The Colombian economy, for example, has expanded rapidly. The Gross Domestic Product (GDP) of Colombia was $117 billion in 2004. In 2009, the GDP of Colombia was $233.82 billion,[1] and in 2013, Colombia's GDP increased to $378.1 billion.[2] The GDP percentage growth rate was 4.1 percent in 2012, and the 2014 forecasts are 4.6 percent.[3] In March 2014, Colombia became the third largest economy in Latin America, surpassing Argentina. Colombia witnessed a relatively stable peso over the previous year with an exchange rate of 1,990 pesos per $1, demonstrating that the Colombian economy is a stable economy.[4] In addition, Colombia's exports of goods and services as a percentage of GDP have increased overtime from 26.6 in 2004 to 30.3 in 2012.[5]

Colombia also has experienced increases in oil production. In 1980, Colombia produced a total of 134,000 barrels per day. In 2005, Colombia produced 548,352 barrels per day; in 2013, Colombia's production increased to 1,028,473 barrels per day.[6] Colombia's proved reserves also have increased significantly overtime. As of January 2014, research indicates that Colombia had an estimated 2.4 billion barrels of proven crude oil reserves.[7] Chris Kraul argues, "Over the first half of this year, Colombia's average production was 983,000 b/d." He continues, "The year-to-date average is also 100,000 b/d under the target set by the government to balance its 2014 books."[8] Thus, Colombia has experienced significant improvements and become a key energy producer.

In part due to its economic success, Colombia has lifted large numbers of the population out of poverty. The percentage of the population living below the national poverty line has decreased drastically from 47.4 in 2004 to 37.2 percent in 2012.[9] Unemployment also has decreased from 13.2 percent of the total labor force to 10.8 percent in 2011.[10] In May 2014, Colombia's unemployment decreased to 8.8 percent, which represented the lowest rate seen in years. Nina Damsgaard states, "Between March and May 2014, the number of private employees grew 4.9% while self-employed workers grew 1.8% compared to the same period in 2013, according to the DANE figures. At the same time the number of employees in government jobs saw a decrease of 3.7% from 2013 and the number of people employed as day labors fell as much as 7.5%."[11]

The Colombian government also has extended health care coverage to most Colombians and life expectancy in Colombia has increased from 72 in 2004 to 73.8 years-old in 2012.[12] A 2010 Doctors Without Borders[13] report discusses many of the challenges. An astounding 78.6 percent of the individuals surveyed in the report revealed that they had difficulty accessing healthcare services because the closest treatment center was located too far away. The report indicates that 41 percent of the individuals interviewed responded that they did not have the necessary access to healthcare because they lived in poor areas that have been particularly hard hit as a result of the internal armed conflict.[14]

POVERTY AND INEQUALITY

Colombia has experienced decreases in the percentages of people living in poverty. The percentage of Colombians living on less than $1.25 per day was 21.1 in 2005 and 16.3 percent in 2010. In 2011, the percentage of Colombians who earned less than $1.25 per day decreased to 14.5, representing significant progress. However, there are significant challenges that exist as 15 million Colombians live in poverty as of 2012.[15] Colombia has one of the worst income wealth distributions in the entire Western Hemisphere and more must be done to decrease inequality and increase opportunities for Colombians seeking to improve their economic situations. In 2004, the top 10 percent of Colombians accounted for 46.5 percent of all income. The percentage of the income held by the top 10 percent of Colombians decreased slightly to 44.4 in 2010. On the other hand, in 2010, the lowest 10 percent accounted for .9 percent of income in Colombia.[16] Lars Christian Moller, a Senior Country Economist for Colombia at the World Bank, states:

> While it is on the decline in Colombia, progress could have been much faster with a less unequal income distribution. Income poverty fell from 47.7 percent in 2003 to 34.1 percent in 2011. Poverty fell exclusively as a result of income growth as income inequality remained largely unchanged: the Gini coefficient was 0.55 in 2011—the same as in 2003. Our calculations show that if Colombia had the same income distribution as Peru, poverty would have been ten percentage points lower than it is today, i.e., around 25 percent.[17]

One of the ways to reduce inequality is to raise income taxes and use the revenue generated to invest money toward decreasing poverty.

EDUCATION

Public expenditures on education have increased over time from 13.8 percent of the total percentage of government expenditures in 2006 to 15.8 in 2012.[18] However, access to quality education for the poor and middle class sectors of society remains rather limited. In 2010, only 37.2 percent of young Colombians continued their education after high school.[19] Education remains a crucial factor in order for Colombians to obtain jobs with steady incomes, enabling them to compete in the globalized world. While slight improvements have been made, the Colombian government must do more to increase access to affordable, high quality education. Access to education also is essential for decreasing inequality and fostering social inclusion. This, however, requires significant investment on behalf of the government. Investing in education is worthwhile as such investments will help improve the competitiveness of the country.

COMPETITIVENESS, INFRASTRUCTURE, AND SOCIAL INCLUSION

Colombia's competitiveness in the globalized world is severely hamstrung by the failure to invest in improving infrastructure that enables goods to reach the markets. The Inter-American Development Bank (IDB) approved a $25 million loan in December 2013[20] to help Colombia increase its private investments to improve infrastructure in the country, which has been quite problematic, particularly for individuals residing in rural parts of Colombia. Colombia has become reliant on mineral exports and petroleum, and the result is that the manufacturing sector has declined. Colombia will continue to face extreme competition with the rise of other powers such as Brazil, India, and China.

Despite the aforementioned improvements, the way forward is quite difficult. Major decisions must be made regarding how to carry out social inclusion policies more effectively. The 15 million inhabitants[21] living in the rural countryside of Colombia face many challenges as Colombia opens its economy to agricultural imports. The challenges in the countryside represents some of the most difficult hurdles that Colombia must overcome. The Colombian government must develop policies to alleviate poverty and incorporate peasants into the legal economy, which will be quite difficult as many peasants rely on coca cultivation because they can cultivate coca anywhere and other products do not grow as easily in the countryside. In addition, peasants often lack the infrastructure to bring goods to the market.

THE PEACE PROCESS

As hard as overcoming the major socioeconomic challenges are, even more difficult are the political issues that Colombia must face such as the peace process, institutional consolidation, and reforms to lower the high levels of violence and conflict that have characterized Colombian society for the last half century. President Juan Manuel Santos has built on the military advancements of the Uribe administration. As discussed in Marc Chernick's chapter in this volume, the Santos administration is currently negotiating with the FARC. The negotiations include five substantial items as well as one operational item. The list of items on the agenda are as follows: end of the conflict, political participation, victims, solution to the illicit drugs issue, integral agricultural development policy, and the implementation, verification, and ratification of the peace agreement.[22] While major progress has been made on three of the five tenants of the peace agreement, skepticism exists about the commitment of the FARC on the sixth issue. Adam Isacson argues:

> FARC negotiators have voiced some reluctance to turn in their weapons after signing a peace accord. Still, disarmament—or some form of putting weapons "beyond use," as was done in Northern Ireland—plus some form of demobilization, will undoubtedly be immovable Colombian government conditions for

> ending the war. Once collective demobilizations take place, Colombia must contend with a wave of former fighters, most of whom have almost no education or marketable skills and severe cases of post-traumatic stress.[23]

President Santos likely will confront a referendum and it will be opposed by Uribe. This could represent a major derailing of the peace process and could force Colombia into war.

Many experts have questioned the role of Washington in the Colombian conflict. Lisa Haugaard argues:

> The United States government, which has done so much to fuel the war, can do much to support the peace. The United States should continue vocal support for the peace process and advocate for the inclusion of victims in the discussion of the next chapter of the accord. The United States government should embrace the voluntary, community-based vision for drug policy, without aerial spraying, laid out in the drug policy chapter, and should fully transform its assistance from war to peace.[24]

What is clear is that there is not going to be more support from the United States in the form of a Plan Colombia, which provided the Colombians with $8 billion over its twelve year life-span (2000 to 2012).[25] Regarding the role of the U.S. and assistance, Isacson argues:

> Still, U.S. assistance programs often move slowly, and the time to start planning for post-conflict support is fast approaching. Above all, budget planners must prepare to provide support at the same, or greater, levels of assistance that Colombia has been receiving since the mid-2000s. The past several years' steady 10–15 percent annual reductions in assistance to Colombia would have to end, and reverse, upon the signing of a peace accord.[26]

Therefore, it appears that the Colombian government will have to go it alone and finance the implementation of a post-conflict agreement. The estimated cost of such a plan is $44 billion (90 trillion pesos)[27] over the next ten years. Roy Barreras, a Colombian Senator, stated, "'There will need to be adjustments, modifications, and we need budget reform, a structural tax reform for peace.'"[28] President Santos traveled to Europe in November and asked the Europeans for assistance.[29] The Colombian government, however, cannot depend on the United States and the European Union does not have the money to pay. Beyond negotiating, implementing, and paying for the peace process, Colombia must address institutional weaknesses such as strengthening the judiciary and improving governance at the municipal and departmental levels, which often have been plagued by corruption and inefficiency.

THE BACRIM

One of the biggest threats to security and prosperity in Colombia are the criminal bands or BACRIM, who have become the successors to the paramilitaries, and, in essence, are neo-paramilitaries. An estimated 30 percent of all human rights violations that occur in Colombia can be attributed to the BACRIM, which represent a grave threat to security in the country.[30] These organizations have infiltrated local and departmental governments and continue to have a political presence in Colombia. Jeremy McDermott argues:

> There is a perception in certain regions that the BACRIM are a political force, since their violence often targets unionists, land restitution activists, and social movements that threaten business interests. The most likely reason for focusing their violence on these groups, however, is that the BACRIM operate as guns for hire. They are utilized by business and criminal interests to terrorize or eliminate opponents, but this does not mean these 'political' actions are an inherent function of their existence.[31]

The BACRIM, therefore, are more than just criminal bands because they have many of the same institutional structures of the paramilitaries.

CLIENTALISM, CORRUPTION, AND IMPUNITY

Colombia must deal with clientalism and grave problems in the political system. Colombia continues to be plagued by high levels of corruption at all levels of society. According to the Corruption Perception Index, in 2013, Colombia scored a 36 on a scale from 0 to 100 with zero being the most corrupt and 100 being the most clean. As a result of its problems with corruption, Colombia ranked 94th out of 177 countries in 2013.[32] According to the 2011 *Global Integrity Report,* on a scale from 1 to 100 with 1 being very weak and 100 being very strong, Colombia scored a 54 on anti-corruption Non-Governmental Organizations. In addition, Colombia received a 61 for judicial independence, fairness, and citizen access to justice.[33]

In addition to corruption, Colombia is afflicted by extremely high levels of impunity as many perpetrators of crimes simply go unpunished. María Victoria Llorente and Jeremy McDermott argue:

> Impunity continues as a chronic problem in Colombia, notwithstanding a series of reforms over the last decade—including the 2008 formalization of a national shift to an oral, accusatorial system of justice and the budgetary efforts to put such reform into motion. Unfortunately, not only has the attempt to overhaul the system and to expedite the process of justice shown little progress, but the

> estimated rate of impunity has not decreased and remains over 90 percent, even for homicides.[34]

More must be done to strengthen institutions and decrease such high levels of impunity.

GLOBAL INTEGRATION AND SOCIAL INCLUSION

Colombia is a large territory with a population of nearly 50 million people. The country is rich in a variety of resources from minerals to petroleum. Colombia has substantial industrial bases and a capable entrepreneurial class. Colombia must look toward the twenty-first century and integrate into the global economy. This requires addressing economic bottlenecks, institutional weaknesses, and implementing reforms. Political reforms that lead to greater social inclusions are crucial. The Washington Office on Latin America released a report arguing:

> The peace talks offer an opening to reunite a society torn apart by conflict. Decades of violence have created marginalized populations. From rural ethnic communities to the urban poor, and from persecuted political movements to demobilized combatants, Colombian society still suffers deep rifts. Integrated programs that promote broad social inclusion are key to establishing a lasting peace and to addressing the harms of the drug, production, trafficking and problematic use.[35]

In sum, social inclusion remains a major challenge in Colombia, and the government must address this problem.

Colombia also must address systematic violations of human rights. In 2012, for instance, Colombia was ranked as the most dangerous country for union members.[36] At least forty community leaders and human rights defenders were killed in 2012 alone. In the same year, twenty trade union members were murdered, demonstrating that human rights violations are rampant in Colombia. Indigenous groups also have suffered grave human rights abuses, particularly as a result of the internal armed conflict. In July 2013, for example, 1,500 indigenous individuals were forced to flee their lands in the Cohcó Department. Unfortunately, this is an all too common event and demonstrates the grave human rights abuses that continue to occur in Colombia.[37] Human Rights Watch has continued to monitor abuses and has

> . . . documented abuses in Tumaco against more than 70 victims since 2013 in which there is strong indication the FARC was responsible, including 12 killings, 3 disappearances, 6 cases of attempted forced recruitment, and 5 cases of

> torture, among other types of abuse. Human Rights Watch documented abuses against 16 victims in recent years in which evidence points to the perpetrators being paramilitary successor groups, including the disappearance of three teenage girls and attempted forced recruitment of two teenage boys.[38]

As of March 2013, Colombia had more than 4.7 million individuals who had been internally displaced.[39]

In essence, Colombia needs to make effective the guarantees of the 1991 constitution. The failure to implement the civil rights protections could lead to increases in social discontent, which, in turn, could result in social explosions. The failure to incorporate many parts of Colombian society also could create urban unrest and social movements.

If Colombia does not realize its potential, it will move backward and conflict could increase with the guerrillas, and drug trafficking and organized crime could worsen. The key challenge, therefore, becomes how Colombia converts is potential into a reality. In order to do this, Colombia must address its underlying problems.

Ultimately, Colombia has great promise, but the government must resolve many issues. If not, Colombia will continued to be plagued by violence, drug trafficking, human rights abuses, and inequality, among other challenges.

NOTES

1. For more, see The World Bank, http://data.worldbank.org/indicator/NY.GDP.MKTP.CD/countries/CO?display=graph, accessed October 2014.
2. The World Bank, http://data.worldbank.org/country/colombia, accessed October 2014.
3. The World Bank, http://www.worldbank.org/en/publication/global-economic-prospects/data?variable=NYGDPMKTPKDZ&region=LAC, accessed October 2014.
4. Patricia Rey Mallén, "Colombia Surpasses Argentina As Latin America's Third- Largest Economy Due to Inflation, Currency Changes, GDP Growth," *International Business Times*, March 25, 2014.
5. The World Bank, http://data.worldbank.org/indicator/NE.EXP.GNFS.ZS/countries/1W?display=graph, accessed October 2014.
6. U.S. Energy Information Administration, http://www.eia.gov/countries/country-data.cfm?fips=co#pet, accessed October 2014.
7. U.S. Energy Information Administration, http://www.eia.gov/countries/country-data.cfm?fips=co#pet, accessed October 2014.
8. Chris Kraul, "At the Wellhead: Colombia takes a sobering look at its oil industry," *Platts*, http://blogs.platts.com/2014/08/25/colombia-oil-exploration/, accessed October 2014.
9. The World Bank, http://data.worldbank.org/indicator/SI.POV.NAHC/countries/CO?display=graph, accessed 2014.

10. The World Bank, http://data.worldbank.org/indicator/SL.UEM.TOTL.ZS/countries/CO-XJ-XT?display=graph, accessed October 2014.

11. Nina Damsgaard, "Colombia's unemployment rate lowest in 14 years: govt," *Colombia Reports,* Jun 27, 2014.

12. The World Bank, http://data.worldbank.org/indicator/SP.DYN.LE00.IN/countries/CO-XJ-XT?display=graph, accessed October 2014.

13. Doctors Without Borders, http://www.doctorswithoutborders.org/country-region/colombia, accessed October 2014.

14. Scott Kobewka, "Many Colombians face limited access to healthcare: Survey," http://colombiareports.co/many-colombians-face-limited-access-to-healthcare-survey/, accessed October 2014.

15. Christian Leonard, "15 million Colombians live in poverty," *Colombia Reports*, May 17, 2012.

16. The World Bank, http://data.worldbank.org/indicator/SI.DST.FRST.10/countries/CO?display=graph, accessed October 2014.

17. Lars Christian Moller, "Breaking with history: Why Colombia needs a more progressive tax system," *The World Bank*, December 17, 2012 http://www.worldbank.org/en/news/opinion/2012/12/17/why-colombia-needs-a-more-progressive-tax-system, accessed October 2014.

18. The World Bank, http://data.worldbank.org/indicator/SE.XPD.TOTL.GB.ZS/countries/CO-XJ-XT?display=graph, accessed October 2014.

19. "Colombia's Goal: More Success in Higher Education, More Opportunities for Youth," *The World Bank*, January 24, 2013. http://www.worldbank.org/en/news/feature/2013/01/24/colombia-more-success-in-higher-education-more-opportunities-for-youth, accessed 2014.

20. "Colombia to increase private investment in infrastructure with IDB support," Inter-American Development Bank, December 5, 2013. http://www.iadb.org/en/news/news-releases/2013-12-05/private-investment-in-infrastructure-in-colombia,10681.html, accessed 2014.

21. According to the World Bank, 11,653,673 people lived in rural Colombia between 2009 and 2013. Banco Mundial, http://datos.bancomundial.org/indicador/SP.RUR.TOTL, accessed 2014.

22. Adam Isacson, *Ending 50 Years of Conflict: The Challenges Ahead and the U.S. Role in Colombia* (Washington, D.C.: WOLA, 2014),

23. Ibid, 13–14

24. Lisa Haugaard, "Colombia: Peace and Drugs," *The Huffington Post*, May 19, 2014.

25. For more on Plan Colombia, see: Jonathan D. Rosen, *The Losing War: Plan Colombia and Beyond* (Albany, N.Y.: SUNY Press, 2014).

26. Adam Isacson, *Ending 50 Years of Conflict,* 16.

27. "Posconflicto costaría al país 90 billones de pesos," Octubre 8 de 2014. *Portafolio.co*

28. "Peace will cost Colombia $44 billion over 10 years, senator says," *Reuters*, Oct 8, 2014, sec: world.

29. Ibid.

30. Marguerite Cawley, "BACRIM Responsible for 30% of Human Rights Violations in Colombia," *InSight Crime*, April 16, 2013, http://www.insightcrime.org/news-briefs/bacrim-perpetrators-of-30-crimes-reported-in-colombia-govt, accessed 2014.

31. Jeremy McDermott, "The BACRIM and Their Position in Colombia's Underworld, *InSight Crime*, May 2, 2014, http://www.insightcrime.org/investigations/bacrim-and-their-position-in-colombia-underworld, accessed October 2014.

32. Corruption Perception Index 2013, Transparency International, http://www.transparency.org/cpi2013/results

33. *Global Integrity Report: 2011. Executive Summary* (Washington, D.C.: Global Integrity, 2011), 18.

34. María Victoria Llorente and Jeremy McDermott, "Colombia's Lessons for Mexico, in *One Goal, Two Struggles: Confronting Crime and Violence in Mexico and Colombia,* eds Cynthia J. Arnson, Eric L. Olson with Christine Zaino (Washington, D.C.: Woodrow Wilson International Center for Scholars), 19.

35. *Peace, Drug Policy, and an Inclusive Society: Eleven Ways Colombian and FARC Negotiators can Reform Drug Policy and Build a Lasting Peace* (Washington, D.C.: WOLA, 2013), 4.

36. "A Dismal Anniversary: U.S.-Colombia Labor Action Plan Still Lacking Implementation Two Years Later," *WOLA,* April 10, 2013, http://www.wola.org/commentary/a_dismal_anniversary, accessed October 2014; Survey of violations of Trade Union Rights: Freedom of Association—Collective Bargaining-Strike, http://survey.ituc-csi.org/Colombia.html?lang=en, accessed October 2014.

37. Annual Report: Colombia 2013, *Amnesty International*, May 23, 2013, http://www.amnestyusa.org/research/reports/annual-report-colombia-2013?page=show, accessed October 2014.

38. "Colombia: FARC Bettering Afro-Colombian Areas," *Human Rights Watch*, July 30, 2014, http://www.hrw.org/news/2014/07/30/colombia-farc-battering-afro-colombian-areas, accessed October 2014.

39. "2014 UNHCR country operation profile-Colombia," UNHCR: The UN Refugee Agency, http://www.unhcr.org/pages/49e492ad6.html, accessed October 2014.

Selected Bibliography

Aprile-Gniset, Jacques. *La crónica de Villarica*. Bogotá: Ediciones Antropos, 1991.

Arenas, Jaime. *La guerrilla por dentro:Análisis del ELN colombiano*. Bogotá: Tercer Mundo, 1971.

Bagley, Bruce. *Drug Trafficking and Organized Crime in the Americas: Major Trends in the Twenty-First Century*. Washington, D.C.: Woodrow Wilson International Center for Scholars, 2012.

Bagley, Bruce Michael. *Political Power, Public Policy and the State in Colombia: Case Studies of the Urban and Agrarian Reforms During the National Front, 1958–1974*. Unpublished Ph.D. Thesis, Department of Political Science, University of California at Los Angeles, 1979.

Berry, Albert. "Has Colombia Finally Found an Agrarian Reform that Works" in James K. Boyce, Stephen Cullenberg, Prasanta K. Pattanaik and Robert Pollin, eds., *Human Development in the Era of Globalization: Essays in Honor of Keith B. Griffin*. Cheltenham, U.K. and Northhampton, MA, USA: Edward Elgar, 2006.

Beittel, June S. *Peace Talks in Colombia*. Washington, D.C., Congressional Research Service, 2013.

Bonet, Jaime and Meisel Roca, Adolfo. "Polarización del ingreso per cápita departamental en Colombia," *Ensayos sobre Política Económica* 25, no. 54 (2007).

Marguerite Cawley. "BACRIM Responsible for 30% of Human Rights Violations in Colombia," *InSight Crime*, April 16, 2013, http://www.insightcrime.org/news-briefs/bacrim-perpetrators-of-30-crimes-reported-in-colombia-govt, accessed 2014.

Centro de Memoria Histórica (CMH). *Justicia y paz ¿Verdad judicial o verdad histórica?* Bogotá: Centro de Memoria Histórica, 2012.

Cabrera, Mauricio. *10 años de revaluación*, Bogotá: Oveja Negra, 2013.

Gómez, Juan Carlos and Jiménez, Juan Pablo. T*ax Structure and Tax Evasion in Latin America*, Serie Macroeconomía del Desarrollo, no. 118 (Santiago: CEPAL, 2012).

Cepeda Ulloa, Fernando, *La mesa de Unidad Nacional*. Bogotá: ECOE, 2011.

Cepeda Ulloa, Fernando Cepeda. *Narcotráfico, financiación política y corrupción.* Bogotá: ECOE, 2011.

Cepeda Ulloa, Fernando. *Pérdida de investidura 1991–2011: una herramienta eficaz contra la corrupción de los congresistas, diputados y concejales*. Bogotá: ECOE, 2011.

Chernick, Marc. "Colombia. Does Injustice Cause Violence?" in *What Justice? Whose Justice? Fighting for Fairness in Latin America*, ed. Susan E. Eckstein and Timothy Wickham-Crowley. Berkeley: University of California Press, 2003, 185–214.

Lynn Coleman, Bradley. *Colombia and the United States. The Making of an Inter-American Alliance, 1939–1960*. Kent, Ohio: Kent State University Press, 2008.

Crandall, Russell. *Driven by Drug: US Policy Toward Colombia*. Boulder, Colo.: Lynne Rienner Publishers, 2002.

de Janvry, Alain and Sadoulet, Elisabeth. "Path-Dependent Policy Reforms: From Land Reform to Rural Development in Colombia," in Karla Hoff, Avishay Braverman and Joseph E. Stiglitz, *The Economics of Rural Organization: Theory, Practice and Policy*. New York, N.Y.: Oxford University Press, 1993.

Departamento Nacional de Planeación (DNP). *Plan de financiación* para la sostenibilidad de la *Ley 1448 de 2011,* Documento Conpes No. 3712. Bogotá: Departamento Nacional de Planeación, 2011.

DeShazo, Peter, Primiani, Tanya and McLean, Phillip. *Back from the Brink: Evaluating Progress in Colombia, 1999–2007*. Washington, D.C.: CSIS Press, 2007. *Drug Reduction Goals were Not Fully Met, but Security has Improved; U.S. Agencies Need More Detailed Plans for Reducing Assistance*. Washington, D.C.: GAO Report, 2008.

ECLAC. *La inversión extranjera directa en América Latina y el Caribe 2002*. Santiago, Chile: Naciones Unidas, 2003.

Elster, Jon. *Closing the Books*. Cambridge: Cambridge University Press, 2004.

Erten, Bilgre and Ocampo, José Antonio. "Super Cycles of Commodity Prices since the Mid-Nineteenth Century," *World Development* 44, pp. 14–30, 2013.

Fajardo M., Darío. *Haciendas, Campesinos y Politicas Agrarias en Colombia, 1920–1980.* Bogotá: Universidad Nacional de Colombia, Centro de Investigaciones Para el Desarrollo, 1986.

Fedesarrollo. *Infraestructura de transporte en Colombia*, Report to Cámara de Comercio de Infraestructura. Bogotá: Fedesarrollo, 2012.

Green, John. *Gaitanismo, Left Liberalism and Popular Mobilization in Colombia.* Gainesville: University Press of Florida, 2003.

Haugaard, Lisa. "Colombia: Peace and Drugs," *The Huffington Post*, May 19, 2014.

Haugaard, Lisa. Nichols, Kelly, Poe, Abigail, and Sánchez-Garzoli, Gimena, "Far Worse than Watergate: Widening Scandal regarding Colombia's Intelligence Agency," Latin America Working Group, June 2010, http://www.lawg.org/storage/colombia/farworsethanwatergatefinalfinal.pdf.

Henderson, James D. *Modernization in Colombia. The Laureano Gómez Years, 1889–1965*. Gainsville: University Press of Florida, 2001.

Holmes, Jennifer S., Gutiéreez de Piñeres, Sheila Amin and Curtin, Kevin M. *Guns, Drugs & Development in Colombia.* Austin, TX: University of Texas Press, 2008.

Human Rights During the Juan Manuel Santos Administration's First Year in Office Washington, D.C.: WOLA, 2011.

Isacson, Adam. *Don't Call Colombia a Model: On Plan Colombia 10th Anniversary, Claims of "Success" Don't Stand Up to Scrutiny*, Washington, DC: WOLA, 2010.

Isacson, Adam. *Ending 50 years of Conflict: The Challenges Ahead and the U.S. Role in Colombia*. Washington, D.C., WOLA, 2014.

Isacson, Adam. *Optimisim, Pessimism, and Terrorism: The United States and Colombia in 2003* Washington, D.C.: Center for International Policy, 2004.

Jaramillo, Carlo Felipe. *Liberalization, Crisis and Change in Colombian Agriculture.* Boulder, Colorado: Westview Press, 1998.

Kahane, Adam. "Reos Partners Supports 'Game-Changing' Scenario Project on Drugs in the Americas," *Reos Partners Quarterly Newsletter*, Issue No. 15, August 2013.

Kirk, Robin. *More Terrible Than Death: Massacres, Drugs and America's War in Colombia*. New York: Public Affairs, 2003.

Lipton, Michael. *Land Reform in Developing Countries; property rights and property wrongs.* London: Routledge, 2009.

López, Hugo and Núñez, Jairo Pobreza y desigualdad en Colombia: diagnóstico y estrategias. Bogotá: DNP, 2007.

Llorente, María Victoria and McDermott, Jeremy. "Colombia's Lessons for Mexico," in *One Goal, Two Struggles: Confronting Crime and Violence in Mexico and Colombia*, eds Cynthia J. Arnson, Eric L. Olson with Christine Zaino. Washington, D.C.: Woodrow Wilson International Center for Scholars, 1–45.

Loveman, Brian. "U.S. Security Policies in Latin America and the Andean Region," in *Addicted to Failure: U.S. Security Policy in Latin America and the Andean Region*, ed Brian Loveman, Lanham, Maryland: Rowman & Littlefield Publishers, 2006, xi–xxiii.

Lars, Christian Moller. "Breaking with history: Why Colombia needs a more progressive tax system," *The World Bank*, December 17, 2012 http://www.worldbank.org/en/news/opinion/2012/12/17/why-colombia-needs-a-more progressive-tax-system, accessed October 2014.

McDermott, Jeremy. "The BACRIM and Their Position in Colombia's Underworld, *InSight Crime*, May 2, 2014, http://www.insightcrime.org/investigations/bacrim-and-their-position-in-colombia-underworld, accessed October 2014.

Nye, Jr, Joseph S. *Soft Power: The Means to Success in World Politics.* New York, N.Y.: Public Affairs, 2004.

Ocampo, José Antonio. "Un siglo de desarrollo pausado e inequitativo: La economía colombiana, 1910–2010," in *Colombia 1919–2010*, eds. María Teresa Calderón and Isabela Restrepo. Bogotá: Taurus, 2010, 119–196.

Pasquino, Gianfranco e Pelizzo, Riccardo. *Parlamenti democratici*. Bologna: Il Mulino, 2006. *Peace, Drug Policy, and an Inclusive Society: Eleven Ways Colombian and FARC Negotiators can Reform Drug Policy and Build a Lasting Peace*, Washington, D.C.: WOLA, 2013.

Presidencia de la República. *La revolución pacífica: Plan de desarrollo económico social 1990–1994*. Bogotá: Departamento Nacional de Planeación, 1991.

Programa de las Naciones Unidas para el Desarrollo. *Informe Nacional de Desarrollo Colombia.* Bogotá: PNUD, 2011.

Ramírez Lemus, María Celmencia Stanton, Kimberly and Walsh, John. "Colombia: A Vicious Circle of Drugs and War," in *Drugs and Democracy in Latin America: The Impact of U.S.* Policy, Coletta Youngers and Eileen Rosin, eds, Boulder, CO: Lynne Rienner Publishers, 2005, 99–142.

Restrepo, Elvira María and Bagley, Bruce eds. *La Desmovilizacion De Los Paramilitaries En Colombia: Entre La Esperanza y El Escepticismo*. Bogotá: Uniandes, 2011.

Reyes, Alejandro. *Guerreros y campesinos: El despojo de la tierra en Colombia*. Bogotá: FESCL, Grupo Editorial Norma, 2008.

Ribando Seelke, Clare and Finklea, Kristin M. *U.S.-Mexican Security Cooperation: The Mérida Initiative and Beyond*. Washington, D.C.: Congressional Research Service, 2013.

"Report of the United Nations High Commissioner for Human Rights on the situation of human rights in Colombia," United Nations Human Rights, January 7, 2013, 13, http://www.ohchr.org/Documents/HRBodies/HRCouncil/RegularSession/Session22/A-HRC-22-17-Add3_English.pdf.

Rosen, Jonathan D. *The Losing War: Plan Colombia and Beyond.* Albany, N.Y.: SUNY Press, 2014.

Samuels, David and Shugart, Matthew. *Presidents, Parties, and Prime Ministers How the Separation of Powers Affects Party Organization and Behavior*. Boston, Cambridge University Press, 2010.

Sanchez, Gonzalo and Meertens, Donny. *Bandoleros, gamonales y campesinos: El caso de la Violencia en Colombia*. Bogotá: El Ancora, 1983.

Soberg Shugart, Matthew and Mainwaring, Scott. "Presidentialism and Democracy in Latin America: Rethinking the Terms of the Debate," in *Presidentialism and Democracy in Latin America*, eds. Scott Mainwaring and Matthew Soberg Shugart. New York: Cambridge University Press, 1997.

Sartori, Giovanni. *Parties and Party Systems: A Framework for Analysis.* Cambridge, U.K.: University Press, 1976.

Serrano, Mónica and Toro, María Celia. "From Drug Trafficking to Transnational Organized Crime in Latin America," in Mats Berdal and Mónica Serrano, eds., *Transnational Organized Crime and International Security*. Boulder, Lynne Rienner Publishers, 2002.

Stone, Hannah. "The War of Words Over Colombia's Conflict" *InSight Crime*, May 9, 2011, http://www.insightcrime.org/insight-latest-news/item/884-the-war-of-words-overcolombias-conflict, accessed 8/26/2012, 2012.

Tate, Winifred. *Counting the Dead: The Culture and Politics of Human Rights Activism in Colombia.* California: University of California Press, 2007.

Tickner, Arlene B. "Intervención por invitación: claves de la política exterior colombiana y de sus debilidades principales," *Colombia Internacional*, Vol. 65 (2007): 90–111.

Velez, María Alejandra. *FARC-ELN evolución y expansión territroial. Documente 2000–2008.* B Veillette, Connie, Plan Colombia: A Progress Report. Washington, D.C.: Congressional Research Service, 2005.

Villarraga, Álvaro. *El proceso de paz en Colombia, 1982–2002*, Vol. 5. Bogotá: Fundación Cultura Democrática, 2013.

Index

About the Editors and Contributors

ABOUT THE EDITORS

Bruce M. Bagley holds a Ph.D. in Political Science from the University of California, Los Angeles. His research interests are in U.S.-Latin American relations, with an emphasis on drug trafficking and security issues. From 1991 to 1995 he served as the Associate Dean of the Graduate School of International Studies at the University of Miami. Prior to his appointment at UM, he was an Assistant Professor of Comparative Politics and Latin American Studies at the School of Advanced International Studies (SAIS) of the Johns Hopkins University. His lists of recent publications include but are not limited to: *The International Relations of Latin America* (New York: Routledge, Forthcoming. Coauthored with Betty Horwitz); *La desmovilización paramilitar en Colombia: Entre la esperanza y el escepticismo* (Bogotá: Editorial Universidad de los Andes, 2011. Coedited with Elvira Maria Restrepo).

Jonathan D. Rosen is research professor at the Institute of International Studies at the Universidad del Mar in Mexico. In 2009, Dr. Rosen earned his Bachelors from the University of Miami, where he studied Political Science and Business Administration. He graduated magna cum laude and received the departmental award in Political Science. Dr. Rosen earned his Master's in Political Science from Columbia University. He received his Ph.D. in International Studies from the University of Miami in 2012. Dr. Rosen was awarded the Distinguished Fellowship at the Center for Latin American Studies at UM. His publications include: *The Losing War: Plan Colombia and Beyond* (Albany, N.Y.: SUNY Press, 2014); Jonathan D. Rosen and Marten

W. Brienen, eds. *Prisons in the Americas in the Twenty-First Century: A Human Dumping Ground* (Lanham, Maryland, Lexington Books, 2015).

ABOUT THE CONTRIBUTORS

José Antonio Ocampo is professor and director of the Economic and Political Development Concentration in the School of International and Public Affairs, Member of the Committee on Global Thought and co-President of the Initiative for Policy Dialogue at Columbia University. He also heads the Rural Development Commision convened by the President of Colombia and is the Chair of the Committees for Development Policy, an expert committee of the United Nations Economic and Social Council (ECOSOC). He was previously United Nations Under-Secretary-General of for Economic and Social Affairs, Executive Secretary of the UN Economic Commission for Latin America and the Caribbean, and Minister of Finance, Agriculture and Director of the National Planning Department of Colombia. He also served as Professor of Economics at the Universidad de los Andes and of Economic History at the National University of Colombia, and Visiting Fellow at Universities of Cambridge, Oxford and Yale. Dr. Ocampo received his Ph.D. in economics from Yale University in 1976.

Albert Berry is professor emeritus of Economics at the University of Toronto. He holds a Ph.D. from Princeton University. His main research fields are Economic development, International economics. His publications include: Albert Berry and Frances Stewart, "Globalization, Liberalization, and Inequality: Real Causes," Challenge: *The Magazine of Economic Affairs* 43, No. 1 (2000), 42–92; Albert Berry, "Small-Scale Non-Agricultural Exports as a Route to Employment Creation and Poverty Alleviation," *Konjunturpolitik* 43, No.3 (1997), 275–298; Albert Berry, "Poverty Policy in Latin America During the 1980's," Review of Income and Wealth 43, No. 1 (1997), 119–129.

Sandra Borda is associate professor of political science and international relations at los Andes University, in Bogotá, Colombia. She holds a Ph.D. in Political Science from the University of Minnesota as well as an M.A. in International Relations from the University of Chicago, and an M.A. in Political Science from the University of Wisconsin. Her research seeks to explain why and how domestic parties to civil wars decide to invite international actors to participate in their struggles. Her recent publications include: Borda, Sandra, 2013, *La Internacionalización de la paz y de la guerra en Colombia durante los gobiernos de Andrés Pastrana y Álvaro Uribe. Búsqueda de legitimidad* *política y capacidad militar*, Ediciones Uniandes, Enero de 2013. Borda, Sandra (Co-ed). 2011. *Misión de Política Exterior: Informe Final y Documentos*. (Foreign Policy Commission: Final Report and Documents). Borda, Sandra, and Tickner, Arlene (Eds). 2011. Relaciones internacionales y política exterior de Colombia (Foreign Policy and International Relations in Colombia), *Colección Ciencia Política 40 años*. Bogotá: Ediciones Uniandes

Marten W. Brienen currently teaches in the Political Science department at Oklahoma State University. Previously, he served as the director of Academic Programs in Latin American Studies at the University of Miami. In that capacity, he was responsible for advising students in the undergraduate, graduate, and dual degree programs, as well as tending to the day-to-day business of the programs. He received his Bachelor's and Master's degrees in Latin American History from the University of Leiden in the Netherlands, studied at the Université de Paris-Sorbonne, and received his Ph.D. in Social Sciences from the University of Amsterdam. His publications include "Warisata y la renovación de la educación rural indigenal boliviana, 1932–1948." In Alicia Civera, Juan Alfonseca, and Carlos Escalante (eds), *Campesinos y escolares: la construcción de la escuela en el campo latinoamericano (siglos XIX y XX)*. Mexico City: El Colegio Mexiquense, 2011; "Interminable Revolution: Populism And Frustration In 20th-Century Bolivia." In *The SAIS Review XXVII/1* (2007): 21–34.

Fernando Cepeda Ulloa graduated as Doctor in Derecho y Ciencia Politicas at the National University, in Bogota, Colombia (1962). He did graduate work at The New School for Social Research, New York (1961–1962). Dr. Cepeda Ulloa promoted the Political Science Department, the School of Law, The Center for regional inter-disciplinary studies, and the Center for International Studies at the Universidad de los Andes, in Bogotá, where he was Secretary General, Vice Rector, Acting Rector, Dean of the School of Law etc. Visiting Fellow at Saint Antony¨s College, Oxford University. He was a member of the Permanent International Court of Arbitration. Dr. Cepeda Ulloa was Minister of the Interior (1986), Minister of Communications (1987–88), Presidential Advisor (1978). Ambassador in the United Kingdom (1988–90), United Nations (New York-1991) Canada (1992–1994), Organization of American States (1997–98), France (2006–2011). In addition, he has published several books and academic papers. He was a Columnist in the daily newspaper El Tiempo for several decades.

Marc Chernick is director of the Center for Latin American Studies and is a professor of political science and conflict resolution in the School of

Foreign Service of Georgetown University. He also serves as director of the Georgetown-Los Andes program on conflict resolution and human rights at the University of Los Andes in Bogotá, Colombia. He previously taught and served as director of the Latin American studies program at the Johns Hopkins School of Advanced International Studies, and earlier as the assistant director of the Institute of Latin American and Iberian studies at Columbia University, and worked for several years as a professor at the National University of Colombia in Bogotá and as a visiting professor/ researcher at FLACSO-Ecuador in Quito and the Institute of Peruvian Studies in Lima.

He has written widely on issues of violence, guerrilla insurgencies and peacemaking in Colombia and in Latin America, and has served as a consultant for the World Bank, UNDP, USAID, the governments of Norway, Sweden and Switzerland, and for other international organizations and NGOs on issues of human rights, democracy, early warning and conflict resolution in Colombia and elsewhere in Latin America and Africa. Chernick has a Ph.D. in Political Science from Columbia University.

Malcolm Deas graduated from New College in 1962, and was a Fellow of All Souls College from 1962–1966. He was one of the original staff of the Latin American Centre, founded at that time by Sir Raymond Carr with support from the Ford Foundation, and was a Fellow of St Antony's College, Oxford University and University Lecturer in the Government and Politics of Latin America from 1966 until his retirement in 2008. He served for a decade as Managing Editor of the Cambridge University Press monographs on Latin America, during which time the majority of the titles in that series appeared. From 1990 to 1994 he was an advisor in Colombia to President César Gaviria's Consejería de Seguridad y Defensa, which worked to design policies to reduce Colombia's high levels of violence. He has an Honorary Doctorate from the Universidad de los Andes, Bogotá. He was the University's Senior Proctor, 1986–1987, and is an Emeritus Fellow of St Antony's College.

Santiago Gómez is a political scientist from the Universidad de Los Andes and a Psychology student at the same institution.

Lisa Haugaard is executive director of the Latin America Working Group. As director and previously as senior associate, she has spearheaded advocacy on human rights and peace issues in Latin America for two decades. She directs advocacy on Colombia, Central America, development and military aid and policy and coordinates coalition campaigns with U.S. and Latin American partners. Haugaard has testified multiple times before the U.S. Congress and produced reports, memos, and blogs on human rights topics. She has participated in international human rights verification missions in Colombia, Mexico and Central America, including on extrajudicial executions, human rights defenders, migrant rights, and electoral observation.

Prior to her work at the LAWG, she was executive director of the Central America Historical Institute in Washington, DC and writer, editor and translator for the Jesuit Instituto Historico Centroamericano in Managua, Nicaragua. She has a BA from Swarthmore College, a Master's degree in Latin American studies from New York University, and was a Fulbright scholar in Central America.

Adam Isacson joined the Washington Office on Latin America in 2010, after fourteen years working on Latin American and Caribbean security issues with the Center for International Policy. At WOLA, his Regional Security Policy program monitors security trends and U.S. military assistance to the Western Hemisphere. Adam Isacson has published and cowritten dozens of reports and articles, testified before Congress several times, and led several congressional delegations. Before WOLA and CIP, he worked for the Arias Foundation for Peace and Human Progress in San José, Costa Rica.

Mateo Morales Callejas is a Master's student in the Political Science Department at the Universidad de los Andes, Bogotá, Colombia.

Juan Pablo Milanese is an associate professor and researcher in the Department of Political Studies at the Universidad Icesi in Cali, Colombia. He holds a Ph.D. in Political Sciences from the Università degli Studi di Bologna and a Master's, in International Relations from the same University. His research interests are comparative politics, political institutions, international and Latin American politics.

Luz del Socorro Ramírez is a political scientist and coordinates the Colombia-Venezuela Group, which is a project of the Universidad Nacional de Colombia and Universidad Central de Venezuela. She was professor at the Institute for Political Studies and International Relations at the Universidad Nacional in Colombia and now is an independent consultant. She holds a Ph.D. from the University of Paris 1 (Sorbonne). She is a prolific scholar and has an extensive publication record on border conflicts

Angelika Rettberg is associate professor in the department of Political Science at los Andes University in Bogotá, Colombia. She holds a Ph.D. from Boston University. Her research interests are linked to the political economy of armed conflicts and peacebuilding. Some of her recent publications include: Rettberg A. (2014). "Encuentro con los otros: Perspectivas para la reconciliación en Colombia" (Meeting the Others: Perspectives on Reconciliation in Colombia), in Arias, M.A., Camacho, A., Ibañez A.M., Mejía, D. and Rodríguez C. (eds.), *Costos económicos y sociales del conflicto en Colombia: ¿Cómo construir un posconflicto sostenible?*, Bogotá: Ediciones Uniandes; Nussio, E., Rettberg A., and Ugarriza J. E. (2014), "Victims, Non-Victims, and Their Opinions on Transitional Justice: Evidence from the Colombian Case," Social Science Research Network Working Paper Series; Rettberg A. (ed.) (2012) *Construcción de paz en Colombia*. Ediciones Uniandes, (ISBN 978-958-695-747-2); and Rettberg A. (ed.) (2010) Conflicto armado, seguridad y construcción de paz. Ediciones Uniandes. (ISBN 978-958-695-548-5).

Arlene B. Tickner earned her Ph.D. from the University of Miami and holds a M.A. degree in Latin American Studies from Georgetown University. She is a professor of International Relations in the Department of Political Science at the Universidad de los Andes in Bogotá, Colombia. Her research deals with relations between the U.S. and Colombia, Latin American security, Colombian foreign policy and sociology of knowledge. Some of her most recent works include: Co-editor (with David Blaney), *Claiming the International* (Routledge) and *Thinking International Relations Differently* (Routledge).

Coletta A. Youngers is a leading expert on international drug control policy and drug policy related developments in Latin America. She has over twenty years of experience working on human rights and political developments in the Andean Region and U.S. foreign policy toward the Andes. Youngers is a consultant with WOLA's drug policy reform project, which promotes more effective and humane drug policies through dialogue and up-to-date analysis of developments in the region. She has helped coordinate a series of informal drug policy dialogues bringing together officials, academics legal experts and others to discuss ways to effectively move beyond the failed "war on drugs." Youngers is co-editor of *Drugs and Democracy in Latin America: The Impact of U.S. Policy* (2004). She joined the staff of WOLA in 1987, specializing in human rights, democracy and U.S. policy toward Peru, Bolivia, and Colombia. Prior to joining WOLA, Ms. Youngers was a project manager at Catholic Relief Services and on the editorial staff of Latinamerica Press/Noticias Aliadas, both in Lima, Peru.